PLAYFUL PERFORMERS

AFRICAN CHILDREN'S MASQUERADES

PLAYFUL PERFORMERS

SIMON OTTENBERG
DAVID A. BINKLEY
EDITORS

LONDON AND NEW YORK

First published 2006 by Transaction Publishers

2 Park Square, Milton Park, Abingdon, Oxfordshire OX14 4RN
711 Third Avenue, New York, NY 10017

Routledge is an imprint of the Taylor & Francis Group, an informa business

First issued in paperback 2017

Copyright © 2006 Taylor & Francis

All rights reserved. No part of this book may be reprinted or reproduced or utilised in any form or by any electronic, mechanical, or other means, now known or hereafter invented, including photocopying and recording, or in any information storage or retrieval system, without permission in writing from the publishers.

Notice:
Product or corporate names may be trademarks or registered trademarks, and are used only for identification and explanation without intent to infringe.

Library of Congress Catalog Number: 2005043972

Library of Congress Cataloging-in-Publication Data

Playful performers : African children's masquerades / Simon Ottenberg and David A. Binkley, editors.
   p. cm.
  Includes bibliographical references and index.
  ISBN 0-7658-0286-4 (cloth : alk. paper)
   1. Masks—Social aspects—Africa. 2. Masquerades—Africa.
3. Children—Africa—Social life and customs. 4. Rites and ceremonies—Africa. 5. Folklore—Performance—Africa. 6. Folklore and children—Africa. 7. Africa—Social life and customs. I. Ottenberg, Simon.
II. Binkley, David Aaron. III. Title.

GT1748.A35P53 2005
391.4'34—dc22

2005043972

ISBN 13: 978-0-7658-0286-6 (hbk)
ISBN 13: 978-1-138-51310-5 (pbk)

Contents

Acknowledgments   vii

Introduction: An Overview   1
    Simon Ottenberg and *David A. Binkley*

Part 1: Integrated Masquerades

1. *Ndòmò* Ritual and *Sogo bò* Play: Boy's Masquerading among the Bamana of Mali   49
    Mary Jo Arnoldi
2. Boys and Masks among the Dogon   67
    Walter E. A. van Beek
3. Gender Differences and Performance Styles in *Öjija* among Children in Two Ekeiti Towns   89
    John R. O. Ojo

Part 2: Emulating Masquerades

4. From Grasshopper to Babende: The Socialization of Southern Kuba Boys to Masquerade   105
    David A. Binkley
5. Emulation in Boys' Masquerades: The Afikpo Case   117
    Simon Ottenberg
6. *Omepa* and *Onyeweh* Children's Masquerades   129
    Robert W. Nicholls
7. Three Points of View of Masquerades among the Ijo of the Niger River Delta   151
    Anna A. Hlavácová
8. At the Threshold: Childhood Masking in Umuoji and Umahia   159
    Chika O. Okeke

Part 3: Independent Masquerades

9. The *Alikali* Devils of Sierra Leone: Play, Performance, and Social Commentary   167
    Jeanne Cannizzo

10. Masked Children in an Urban Scene: The Bissau Carnival   181
   Based on the writings of *Manuel Rambout Barçelos,*
   Nicolau Fara Gomes, Felix Siga, and *Harriet C. McGuire;*
   edited with additional comments by *Simon Ottenberg*
11. The Dodo Masquerade of Ouagadougou   207
   Priscilla Baird Hinckley

Part 4: Girls' Masquerading

12. Kalumbu and Chisudzo: Boys' and Girls' Masquerades   221
   among the Chewa
   Kenji Yoshida
13. Playing with the Future: Children and Rituals in   237
   North-Western Province, Zambia
   Elisabeth L. Cameron and *Manuel A. Jordán*

Contributors   247

Index   251

Illustrations follow page   164

Acknowledgments

The editors wish to thank the authors of the essays in this volume for their contributions, and for their patience, over a number of years, in awaiting its completion. Their interest and ideas have greatly assisted us in the quest for a broad and diversified view of African children's masquerades. We are all pioneers in the study of this subject.

We also wish to thank the many individuals cited in the footnotes of this introduction by name, who have provided us with numerous helpful suggestions and ideas, substantive data, and video tapes. Their scholarly comradeship has very greatly improved the quality of this book.

Simon Ottenberg, who originated this project, has been responsible for gathering the materials on West Africa, and David A. Binkley for those from Central and Southern Africa.

Introduction: An Overview

Simon Ottenberg and *David A. Binkley*

There is an extensive and sophisticated scholarly literature on adult masquerading in Africa, as well as on children's masquerading during adolescent initiation. However, there has been little understanding of masquerading by young children before initiation, generally between the ages of four and twelve. Publications on initiation masquerades and on adult masking occasionally mention children's pre-initiation masquerading, though often in an anecdotal manner, without serious analysis. Yet children's pre-initiation masquerades in Africa are widespread and more varied than has been realized, ranging from brief performances to those sophisticated in style. Detailed analyses of children's pre-initiation masquerades–how they are learned, experienced, performed, and passed on to other children–contribute to our knowledge of African childhood play. They also add to our understanding of the roots of the skill that adult masqueraders display in their performances.[1]

African children's masquerades are often simpler than adult ones, in the quality of the masks and dress, the dance and music, and the length of their performances. Except for a few significant instances, they lack serious religious qualities. But their apparent simplicity belies their significance for the children involved, and for studies of all African masquerade forms.

The contributors to this volume consider children's masquerade performances in a broad manner. This includes not only taking into account the children who wear masks, but those who accompany them in song, in dance, in playing music, and as observers. Background cultural features are also important. We look at performance as a whole, as the masqueraders often do themselves.

History and Change in Children's Masquerades

We know little of the origins of children's pre-initiation masquerades in Africa. The editors might speculate that in earlier centuries children were so under the control of tradition, and of parents and other adults, that they rarely masked. The existence of children's masquerades in modern urban centers, and in a number of indigenous cultures, where these did not exist in the past, hints at its recency. On the other hand, there are cases where these masquerades appear to be deeply entwined in their cultures, suggesting that they have had a long life. There are also several African myths, discussed in this volume, of masking having originated with children. It is likely that children's masquerades existed in selected areas of Africa in pre-colonial times. The actual histories of children's pre-initiation masking that we possess, presented in several chapters in this volume, are of urban masquerade, which do not extend back in time more than several hundred years. We know little of the history of rural children's masking.

The cases of children's pre-initiation masquerades discussed in this introduction and in the individual essays range in time from the 1940s into the 1990s. It is a work not only on the most recent developments. The essays indicate that there has been a considerable variety of children's pre-initiation masquerading in Africa, the forms that they take, and how these are changing. They are found in traditional and modern settings, in rural and urban sites. They mainly occur in West Africa, though there are instances from the continent's central and southern regions. Most of the chapters contain previously unpublished data and analyses; only a few are of reprinted material. They are written in the context of years of major cultural, political, and economic change in Africa; the end of colonialism and the postcolonial period. This has been a time when massive social upheavals have altered the nature of the African continent and of children's lives and their masquerades.

These features have created difficulties for the authors in this volume in categorizing children's pre-initiation masquerades. In recent years, children have been initiated into adult masquerade societies at earlier ages than previously,[2] which has resulted in the disappearance or weakening of children's pre-initiation masquerades. In some African cultures adolescent initiation has become briefer and of less significance than in the past, or it has disappeared, so that significant links between pre-initiation masking and adolescent initiation experience are less meaningful, or are lost. In African countries, such as Sierra Leone, Liberia, and the Democratic Republic of the Congo, civil wars over many years have eliminated almost all masquerading by children, as well as adults. In other regions of the continent, children's pre-initiation masquerades have declined as the lessening of secrecy in adult secret societies has come about. Adults, previously afraid to initiate young children for fear that they would expose adults' secrets, are no longer so concerned.

A consequence of Western influence in Africa through schooling and the greater wealth of some parents has been the initiation of children at an earlier age, if at all. This has discouraged the maintenance of pre-initiation masking.

On the other hand, in some African cultures in which children previously did not masquerade before initiation, they do so now. Children draw on Western images such as Mickey Mouse, and on Western dress and masking materials. The spread of Islam and Christianity in Africa has had a negative impact through religious disapproval of masquerading, leading to the disappearance or limiting of some childhood performances. Yet children's masquerades often appear in African Islamic cultures on Muslim holidays such as Ramadan, whether performed by children of Islamic or Christian families, or those that follow indigenous beliefs. And children's pre-initiation masquerades have become popular at Christmas and Easter in African Christian communities. This volume explores the constantly changing nature of children's pre-initiation masquerades.

Children's Masquerades and Adolescent Initiation

The acquisition of masquerade knowledge and performance skills in childhood helps prepare youths for their initiations, and for later adult masquerade activities and rituals. The child who has had some years of experience as a masquerader goes into his initiation, not as a naïve individual, but as one with useful skills, making use of these during his own *rite de passage* and his adult masquerading life; the child hardly enters initiation in a state of *tabula rasa*. Rather, initiation is a test of the skills that he or she has already acquired through previous masquerade experience. This is not to deny the significance of initiation to the child's maturation. This rite has both symbolic and practical value, bringing the child under the control of older persons, in a new and traumatic setting, often under physically stressful conditions. Yet studies of initiation that do not discuss what masquerading skills and abilities children bring to their initiation fail to present a true picture of their experiences in them.

Masquerading Children and the Learning Process

The editors view childhood masquerading experience in terms of children's growth over time and not as isolated behavior. Masking children often are creative and innovative. They acquire performance experience, ritual skills, dancing and musical abilities, and they learn to prepare their dress and their masks. They discover where their individual talents lie, whether in masking, singing, or in the playing of musical instruments. Some of them develop leadership abilities, which will carry them from masquerading on to other activities. Other children learn how to follow leaders successfully, often with interest and pleasure. Children's pre-initiation masking, particularly if it involves emulating adult masking forms, or taking part in adult rituals, assists the youths to understand something of the traditions and history of their culture. Through masquerading, children acquire an increasing understanding of the capabilities of their bodies, and of their emotional and mental capabilities. They have more freedom to make mistakes in masking—to push at the margins—than they will have during their adolescent initiation masquerades and while masking as adults. They develop skills in imitating humans, animals, and spirit forms, and they become sensitive to the reactions of viewers of their performances. Young masqueraders become skillful in teasing and provoking other children and in being humorous. Even if they do not actually play masking roles in their troupe, they acquire knowledge of masking skills through its members' activities. The children learn to view their masquerade performance as a whole, not just in its distinctive parts, a holistic conception of art and performance that will stand them well in adult life. They commence to develop aesthetic taste and sensibility in forms appropriate to their culture. These occur not only through their own masquerading experiments, but also through their keen observations of adult masquerades, if these exist, and of adult rituals. Occasionally, adults, particularly one or both parents of a child, increase his or her aesthetic awareness through direct teaching. Masquerade knowledge and aesthetics are also passed on from one child to another of similar and younger age as children in the troupes become informal instructors.

The editors of this volume view masquerading children as active agents in their own growth and development, not as passive followers of others, though parents and other older persons support their activities. Children's pre-initiation masquerades assist the young in developing a sense of cooperation with children their own age. They come to realize, if they have not already done so through other experiences, that their African society is age-graded. The children's age mates in masquerading often remain their age mates through their adolescent initiation and for a lifetime. They learn that the opposite gender is age-graded as well. They learn of gender differences through their allocation of roles in the masquerade troupes by gender. A sense of rivalry, within and between children's masquerade groups, assists them in developing competitive skills. Although the identities of children masqueraders are often known to other children and to adults, masking creates an air of illusion, which supports the imaginative life of children. Masking is a way of playing at secrecy. It becomes an avenue for children to learn something of secrecy's qualities, though children undoubtedly have secrets unrelated to masquerading. Masking is one introduction to the fact that many of the older individuals and groups that they know of hold secrets of one kind or another. In African cultures secrecy is common in the ritual and religious life, in adult masquerading, and in politics and land ownership. Unmasked members of children's masquerade troupes and the viewers of children's masking learn the play of secrecy as well. Through observing adult masquerade, the children commence to acquire a sense of the spiritual qualities of masquerading, which they may try to emulate in their own performances.

Through their performances, members of children's pre-initiation masquerade troupes acquire skills in obtaining gifts of money and food from adult viewers. As children, they have few other independent resources of gifts. Praise from children and adult viewers for their masquerading is often desired by the members of children's masquerading troupes; and gifts are seen as a form of praise, as well as for their intrinsic value. More than one male African adult has told the editors of this volume that the principal reasons that he masqueraded as a child was to obtain gifts. Children quickly learn who the wealthier community members are, and thus from whom they are most likely to receive generous gifts. In so doing, they acquire some knowledge of their community's social structure. They put this information to the test in decisions as to whose residences it is worthwhile to perform in front of. Gifts to masquerading children of food and indigenous forms of money, probably preceded the introduction of Western currency in Africa; the latter most likely accelerated children's interest in masquerading.

Masking children learn forms of non-verbal communication.[3] Whether or not they sing, shout, or talk while masking, they employ their heads, limbs, and body to portray animals, spirits, or other humans. And sometimes they do so in order to emulate adult masqueraders. The child masker can see his viewers and be guided by their reactions to him or her, but the viewers do not see the masker's true face, only the mask. The child's mask may or may not have the appearance of a face; it may be simply a piece of cloth or an undecorated gourd. The face and eyes of the masker are secret, even if viewers know who the masker is. If a child masker does not utter any sounds, and does not have other children with him who sing, he has to indicate what is being represented and acted out, not only through the mask and dress, but also through movement and gesture. Miming is involved; in non-verbal communication the masker must be creative for he or she cannot use his/her face and eyes for the viewers to know what he/she is communicating. Even if the masquerader employs his or her voice, his/her body and limb movements enhance whatever is being presented. Viewing the face and eyes of a person, an essential element of everyday human interaction, is denied during a masquerade performance. Since children's behavior is often very physical, albeit not always well controlled, an emphasis on non-verbal communication suits their world of masquerading. The change in the method of social communication while masked is one of its fascinating features. Acquisition of non-verbal masking skills, of course, is of help for children when they later masquerade as adults. However, it is not clear how else they may employ these abilities in adult life. Perhaps they are useful in ritual, political talk and debate, and in other social arenas where masking does not occur.

Masquerading children often learn something of their culture's rules toward aggression, not only in instances of masked boys chasing unmasked girls in play, and in mock stick combat among masked boys, but also through their satiric and humorous depictions of individuals. Child masqueraders are, in theory, protected against retaliation later on, since they are supposed to be unrecognized youths. In some African cultures, children also acquire knowledge of aggression, and of defensive skills against it, through being chased by adult masqueraders. Girls learn to permit themselves to be chased by masquerading boys so that no harm comes to them, and they develop skills in teasing boy masqueraders. But when boys' masked troupes fight one another, or when unmasked boys attack boy masqueraders, the rules of aggressive behavior occasionally break down, leading to chaos and to adult intervention.

The Limits of Childhood Masking

Childhood masquerading is framed[4] by cultural rules that are ultimately maintained by adults; children must learn these. Children's pre-initiation masking tends to occur before, during, and after certain adult rituals. It often is found during specified times of day or night, in designated sites, and is likely to be limited to one or two seasons, in farming communities to the ceremonial period following the harvest. Masking children generally prefer to have an audience of other children, of adults, or both. However, some children's masking occurs without any viewers; it is not usually a requirement. The latter may be the case for practice sessions, as children sometimes carefully prepare for their performances. Children may test the limits of the rules set by adults on their masquerading. If no negative response occurs from older children or adults, they may alter the length of their play, its content, and so on. Masking youths acquire knowledge of what is acceptable in their satiric and humorous performances. For example, they usually do not mock traditional religious figures, such as priests or diviners, who are believed capable of taking mystical retribution. Rather the masking youths are likely to satirize other children or foolish adults. Childhood masquerading in Africa, as well as adult masking, does not occur every day. Being infrequent in the span of a year's time, children's events are of special interest, and their emotional and symbolic impact on youths may be considerable. Yet since their performances do not occur frequently, there may be limits to their value in terms of learning.

Gender and Children's Masquerades

Boys' pre-initiation masquerades in Africa are more common than those for girls, though the latter are significant. The reasons for this disparity are not fully understood, though it follows the pattern that among African adults, male masquerading is more prevalent than female forms. However, both girls' and women's masking probably has been under-reported.[5] This difference in the extent of available information on African children's masquerades by gender, partially reflects past Western neglect in the scholarly research on African masquerading. However, even in Liberia and Sierra Leone, the regions of the most intensive adult female masquerading in Africa, where women scholars have been sensitive to gender issues, the evidence for girls' pre-initiation masquerading is minimal.

The preponderance of boys' masking over that of girls', relates to matters of adult power and control; patriarchalism, common in African cultures, is inevitably reflected in the nature of children's masquerading and adult controls over it.[6] Probably for this reason boys and girls rarely mask together in Africa. Adult male masquerade secret societies often attempt to control females through masking, as well as youths of both gender. The prevalence of male masquerading in contrast to that of females may also be related to the fact that many male adult performances involve wooden masks produced by male sculptors. These face pieces are sometimes created in secret from females, who only view them during performances. Females rarely sculpt in wood in Africa. However, men sculpt masks for female masquerade societies in Liberia and Sierra Leone,[7] so the fact of male mask production is not a conclusive argument in explaining gender differences in masquerading.

Though there are cases where boys mask alone, girls often play important roles in boys' masquerades. Girls may accompany boys in singing, playing music, and in dancing. They may suggest songs and acts to the boys, and they may assist in developing masquerade costumes, and with the cooking if a boys' troupe holds a feast after performing. Such an event is generally based on gifts of food and money received during the masquerade. Even if not directly involved in boys' masquerades, girls may form a significant part of the audience. It is not possible to discuss boys' masquerades without taking into account the complementary roles of girls. The reverse is true as well.

Since girls and boys generally play distinct roles in children's masquerade troupes, their activities are learning grounds in gender relationships that translate to other social situations. Where adult masking is strongly linked to gender separation, as is often the case in Africa, this will likely be reflected in the children's masquerades. Boys acquire skills in controlling girls through their masquerading, and girls learn to negotiate and manipulate boys. Girls try to ensure opportunities to be creative in the singing and dancing roles that they play in boys' masquerades.

Girls and boys in the same troupe may develop interest in one another as their own sexual awareness develops. Skilled child performers, whether in masquerade, or accompanying maskers as musicians, dancers or singers, are likely to attract the attention of the opposite gender. There have also been occasions when child masqueraders, like some adult masqueraders, imitate sexual motions. Child performers have plenty of opportunities to strut and prance about in expressing their egos, whether sexual attraction is involved or not. There is competition for attention among the children, to the delight of some of them and their observers.

Children's Masquerades as Play

Children's masquerades in Africa are generally forms of play, raising questions about the relationships of childhood masking to other types of play.[8] Members of a children's pre-initiation masquerade troupe often play together at other times, be it football (called soccer in the United States), wrestling, draughts (the British form of checkers), catching, roasting, and eating grasshoppers, or playing at being family members. These activities help to reinforce the solidarity of the masquerade troupe. However, if there is conflict or competitiveness during these activities it may be detrimental to the troupe. And children in a masquerade troupe may quarrel over leadership and who will mask in what roles.

Deeply into the analysis of children's masquerades, we should not forget how joyful and playful they are for those involved. Children's exciting and pleasurable attitudes towards being members of a masquerade troupe may carry over into adult life, if adult masking exists. African children are generally freer in their pre-initiation masquerades than when they later mask during initiation or as adults, if these also occur. Adult performances are frequently linked to spiritual beliefs and to strong cultural traditions, as to what is, and is not, proper masquerading. Yet some children perceive adult masquerading to be playful, as do some adults.

Social Relationships in Children's Pre-Initiation Masquerade Troupes

Whatever else African children's masquerading is about, it is about children's social ties with other children. Children frequently form masquerade troupes of some five to twenty individuals. These are sometimes ranked by age in a compound or a community; level of skill and age roughly coincide. Children in a troupe develop friendships that are reinforced by carrying out activities together. There is the sorting out of friends, and the beginning and ending of friendships. There are opportunities to talk about the attractions of individuals of the opposite gender, to gossip about sex, parents, and other adults, and the behavior of other children. There are opportunities to converse about the adult masquerades that children have seen, and to reveal masquerade secrets to trusted companions. Masquerading contrasts with the every day labor that children perform: farm work, carrying water, wood, and other loads, and acting as messengers for parents and other older persons. For girls, there is also cooking, washing, and tending to younger children. Much of the labor of children is not done in children's groups, in contrast to a good deal of the masquerading.

Children who form a troupe soon learn to cooperate and to compete with other children in their organization through masking. Who decides when and where to masquerade? What to do with gifts the troupe receives through its performances? Should it use them to feast together, divide the gifts among its members, or use them to obtain more masks, dress, and musical instruments? Who makes or obtains the troupe's instruments? Who owns them and who should play them at performances? Who will lead the masquerade? Who will play what particular roles in it? Children learn to make these decisions themselves.

The Classification of Children's Pre-Initiation Masquerades

African children's pre-initiation masquerades are often linked in significant ways to adult masking, if the latter exists, as well as to other relationships with parents and the parental generation. The linkage is particularly important for boys with fathers and for girls with mothers. For boys, masquerading is a mechanism that distances them symbolically from adult females, particularly their mothers and other female caretakers. For girls, masquerading symbolically associates them with fathers and other male adults, if they masquerade. Girls' masquerading gains them some independence from their mothers, yet the girls maintain a close association with them and with other older females, much more so than boys with these females.

The editors of this volume have developed a three-part classification of childhood pre-initiation masquerades on the basis of children's relationships to parents and other adults. We consider this to be a key issue in children's pre-initiation masking activities. Some of these masquerades are ritually linked to adult masquerades and rituals. Other children's pre-initiation masquerades emulate adult forms, for African children frequently "try out" acting as adults. In still other African cultures, the children's performances occur where adult masquerades do not exist, or where the children's masking bears no obvious relationships to adult masked forms. In these cases, child maskers emulate other aspects of adult behavior, taking their masquerading ideas from a variety of non-masking elements in their culture, or from outside of it, or they invent new forms of masking. It is also of significance whether a category of masquerade takes place in a rural or urban setting; each setting influences masking in specific ways.

It will become clear, as the cases of children's pre-initiation masquerades unfold in this volume, that our three categories are not rigid; rather they serve as guides in organizing data. An African culture may have masquerades that fall in more than one category, and a single masquerade may exhibit features of two or even all three categories. A masquerade may shift over time from one category to another. The matter is further complicated, for although the essays in this volume are detailed, the available information on other masquerades discussed in the introduction is sometimes incomplete. Thus, it is not always clear in what category a particular masquerade should be placed. Classification, in and for itself, is not our aim. It is of value in understanding the particular features of each masquerade, and in contrasting them. We begin with the category where the links of children's pre-initiation masquerades to adults are strong. In the next category they are weaker, but still significant. In the third, the ties between children masqueraders and adults are the least important. This arrangement does not imply that any category is more significant than any other one.

Integrated Masquerades

In these masquerades, children who are, not yet members of adult masking groups play important roles in certain adult activities. Children may mask with adult masqueraders of the same gender, or with adults taking part in unmasked rituals. The links of child masqueraders to adult activities are direct and publicly evident. There may sometimes be relationships between the children's performances and adult religious beliefs, even if the youths understand only a little of their significance. These children's masquerades are goal-oriented in terms of the needs of the larger society, albeit the children involved may view their activities as play.

Emulating Masquerades

Children's pre-initiation masquerading in this category exhibit greater independence from adults than in the Integrated Masquerades. Masquerades of this type occur in one or two ways, or both. In one, with or without adult assistance, children emulate adult masquerades, generally boys those of male adults, and girls those of female adults. Emulation is usually limited, as there are often restrictions placed by adults on children precisely copying adult masking. In the second form of this category, children may be advised, encouraged, and aided in their masquerades by one or more adults of either or both genders. For example, men may assist boys in mask and costume preparation. Masking boys or girls may carry out their own religious rituals involving masquerade activities, in imitation of adult rituals. These, however, are performed separately from those of adults. Both types of Emulating Masquerades are heavily play-oriented, although they do have the ultimate purpose of preparing boys for adult masquerading and ritual experience.

Independent Masquerades

These masking events are distinct in artistic quality from adult masquerading, and they are carried out with almost complete independence from adults and their activities. If adults also masquerade, children emulate the idea of masking, but not adult's dress, masks, and performances. In some cases the children mask but there are no adult masquerades at all. Some of these children's performances develop through urban influence and popular culture. Independent Masquerades of this type are generally secular, having little or no religious content, although they may appear at Christmas, Easter, Ramadan, and traditional religious holidays. They are usually oriented entirely towards play. Where masquerades of this category occur in rural areas, they may have spread from urban regions. However, there are also rural forms that do not appear to have been stimulated by urban influences, where a local evolution of masquerade style and content appears to have occurred. Both urban and rural Independent Masquerades are found where there is considerable freedom of children from parental controls, and where there is greater ethnic and religious diversity than in the other two categories. Some of these masquerades have now existed long enough to have developed their own traditions. The children put these masquerades together out of the bricolage of their past experience,[9] with whatever objects are at hand. The sources of influence on the creativity in the masquerades do not lie in adult performances but elsewhere. The urban masquerades derive ideas and materials from the cinema, from video, magazines, newspapers, cartoon strips, posters, television, and radio, among other sources. The rural children's pre-initiation masquerades draw from traditional elements, put together in new forms, and from neighboring cultures. There is a strong interest of children's masquerades in the acquisition of gifts through performances.

We will first consider boys' pre-initiation masquerades, and then the girls' performances.

Boys' Integrated Masquerades

We have excellent records of this form of masquerade in West Africa, among the Bamana and the Dogon of Mali, the Bobo of Burkina Faso, and the Yoruba of Nigeria.

The Bamana Ndòmò *Masquerades*

Traditional boys' *Ndòmò* masquerades of the Bamana of Mali have almost completely died out in recent years. They involved multiple horned masks, with a complex symbolism, and they were unique to boys, the masks differing from all adult forms of the several men's associations. Yet, the boys' masquerade troupes were organized by residential areas in a manner similar to those of the men's societies. The internal social organization of the boys' troupes also largely replicated that of the men's societies and, to a certain extent, the boys' troupes were under the control of male adults. The Ndòmò troupes controlled certain material objects that had important symbolic qualities, distinct from other objects of the men's societies. Each boys' troupe had its own shrine with its spirit, where the youths carried out sacrifices for their own welfare. These religious activities were not quite the same as those of the men, although the underlying concepts were similar.

Drawing from extant publications on Ndòmò,[10] we note that masquerading boys played useful roles in agriculture. Boys cultivated the adults' grain fields through prearrangement with adults, while girls provided water, some labor, and sang to encourage the work.[11] At harvest time each Ndòmò troupe visited the sacred threshing area with a masquerader and two boy drummers. The masqueraders performed a special dance in front of each pile of millet to bless it. They chanted and then plunged the horns of the mask into the grain, an action suggesting fertility, with undertones of sexual symbolism.[12] Adults considered this ritual to be essential for the successful growth of millet, a major Bamana crop. Boys' pre-initiation masqueraders played an essential role in Bamana life and welfare.

On other occasions, unmasked boys fought against whip-carrying Ndòmò masqueraders. These conflicts, which occurred both within and between boys' troupes, mainly went on during Bamana ritual occasions. Both masked and unmasked youths attempted to exhibit skill, courage, and strength. These were much admired qualities among adult male Bamana. We will note again and again in this volume the presence of boys' secular fighting contests involving masked and unmasked youths. The boys' troupes appear to have had considerable autonomy, although there was some adult guidance by males in their masquerading activities. The boys chose their own leaders, and learned the culture of Ndòmò through other boys, rather than through adults. Nevertheless, the prevalence of adult masquerade societies acted as an incentive and model for the boys.

Bamana boys' masquerade troupes exhibit qualities of all three of our masquerade categories, which forces us to note the complexities in any attempt at masquerade classification. The ritual blessing of the millet by masking youths is an excellent example of an Integrated Masquerade. But there are suggestions that we are also dealing with Independent Masquerade forms. Fighting among the boys, some of whom were masked, was not an activity carried out by adults, except in past times during warfare when it occurred with serious intent. The boys' masks differed from adult forms, and the boys' troupes were relatively independent of adults. Yet the emulation of male adult Bamana societies in the internal organization of the boys' troupes, and the boys' expression of adult values of male strength and bravery, suggest elements of the Emulative Masquerade category.

Mary Jo Arnoldi's essay in this volume describes what exists today of Bamana boys' masquerades. Ndòmò has largely disappeared, only occurring as play at the secular festival of *Sogo bò*. This traditional annual event involves a theater employing a variety of puppet masks worn by adult males. Arnoldi describes an imitative component of the theater organized by secular masquerade associations of boys, aged four or five years to adolescence. She notes the existence of further secularization since the Ndòmò mask has become one of Mali's national symbols. Elsewhere, she writes[13] that after the January millet harvest in the Segou region, boys five to seven years of age create miniature masks of millet stalk and cloth, and emulate cows, giraffes, and other animals. While they play their miming games, mothers and older sisters may provide a singing accompaniment. These masquerades imitate animal forms in the puppet theater, and Bamana men's animal masks. All of these contemporary boys' masquerades are Emulating Masquerades and forms of secular play.

Over time, the boys' masquerades of the Bamana have continued to have qualities of one or more masquerade categories. Since the 1930s, when early reports of Bamana boys' masquerading appeared, there have always been forms of children's masking. As Bamana life and culture have altered, so have their children's masquerades.

Dogon Masqueraders

The Dogon of the Bandiagara cliffs of Mali are well known to Africanist art specialists, collectors, and museums with holdings in the continent's art. They are also familiar to the frequent groups of tourists who enter Dogon country to visit and photograph its spectacular masquerades.[14] But until Walter E.A. van Beek's essay (chap. 2 in this volume) little has been published on Dogon children's masquerades. His first example, the role of boys in the revival of an adult diviner's fox image, allowing the latter to continue his work, is a good case of an Integrated Masquerade. The masked activities of the boys are a necessary part of this ritual.

The rite raises an issue that we will meet again later on in this volume. When is a mask a mask? Do we accept the usual Western convention that something is a mask if it covers at least a part of the face, particularly the eyes? In the diviner's fox renewal ceremony, boys only hold a piece of bark clamped between their teeth. Yet the Dogon consider this to be a mask, calling it by their term for mask. We will accept "native" definitions of masks in this book, since they are meaningful to the individuals and groups involved. But we will not completely discard Western conceptions, since a great deal of African masking involves non-verbal communication, as we have already stated.

Dogon boys' interest in masquerading is intense, which is not surprising considering its extent in the adult male world. At funerals, without actually masking, boys go through the motions of male adult masqueraders. They assist masked adult dancers at memorial services.[15] At some adult masquerades, boys wear masks similar to adult ones, a case of Emulative Masquerading. At other times they appear at adult rites in their own full body masks, where girls taunt them. These performances have sexual associations, a feature that is again noted in this volume. Van Beek also cites the intense curiosity that boys have for adult masqueraders, which is fundamental to much of African children's behavior.

The Dogon do not have a distinct initiation into adulthood that clearly distinguishes boys from men. Rather there is a gradual increasing involvement of boys in masking and in other adult ritual matters. There appears to be little tension between boys and men; rather there are mostly positive and helpful relationships. Among the Dogon, circumcision is only a small rite; it is not part of a major initiation. This contrasts with some African cultures where initiation and circumcision occur together, and there is some tension between uninitiated boys and initiated men. While Dogon culture presents problems in defining what are boys' pre-initiation masquerades, it is clear that young boys are involved and that the boys are in the early stages of their experience with masking.

Bobo Boys' Masquerades

Guy Le Moal[16] has reported on boys' masquerading among the Bobo in the Duma villages of Burkina Faso. He writes of leaf costume masquerades worn by uninitiated boys accompanied by boy followers, who appear for a brief time in a village and then go to a boys' tree shrine (*dwo*), equivalent to the adult one. There they sacrifice a chicken, assisted by an adult blacksmith, who breaks the general Bobo rule of the autonomy of the children's masquerade groups. Afterwards the masqueraders dance about and return to their community. A Duma Earth Chief, observes the sacrifice from a distance and the next day he orders the adult male society to prepare for its annual masquerade. The boys' masquerade is clearly linked to adult affairs. The youths, roughly five to nine years of age, arranged in pre-initiation troupes, are free to organize as they wish, drawing on childhood custom. However, their youthful leaders are drawn from the patrilineal lineages of the Earth Chief, the adult dwo priest, and the blacksmiths, reflecting adult social distinctions.[17]

Le Moal[18] provides a myth that the Bobo believe explains the existence of the boys' masquerades, and their priority in time over men's masquerading. An infant, Prakoro, had the earliest knowledge of masquerades, so that before men masquerade boys must repeat the myth by masquerading and sacrificing at their dwo shrine. Bobo adults are concerned that the boys' masquerade be performed, without interfering with what appears to be the largely spontaneous activity of the boys.[19] The myth, and the boys' masquerade, relate to Bobo beliefs that all their cults were first developed by children. Children are the sages, a reversal of the usual African youth-elder situation. The myth differs strikingly from the commonly held view among peoples that masquerading and secret societies originated with women.[20] The Bobo belief is supported by their views of the very close link of boys with their grandfathers. There is a condition of equality between them; the child innovates and the adult imitates. This conception is consistent with a social theory of the positive relationship of male members of alternate generations to one another, in contrast to the more antagonistic ties of contiguous generations.[21] The Bobo conception gives considerable importance to the boys' groupings and their masquerades. It reminds us of van Beek's essay, where he indicates that pre-initiate Dogon boys have important spiritual qualities associated with the bush.[22]

Yoruba Boys' Masquerades

Many examples of boys' masking abound among the numerous Yoruba of southwestern Nigeria. It is not rare to find boys' masking at Yoruba male adult masquerade festivals. This may occur before the festival begins, shortly before the adult masqueraders appear, or during the festival itself. Or it may happen at the festival's end, or immediately following it. Boys are sometimes organized into troupes. At other times they appear at the same time as adult masqueraders without being organized as a troupe, or there may be only a single masquerader. When masquerading boys are quite young, they are likely to be guided by their fathers, mothers or other older relatives.

The Yoruba are explicit in viewing boys' masquerading in terms of performance training, in a culture where masking is highly valued. While the boys' masking is considered to be part of a festival, it is not the major aspect. The Yoruba, like the Dogon, do not usually have a single adolescent initiation that socially differentiates boys from men, This is unlike many African cultures. And as in the case of the Dogon, among the Yoruba, there appears to be little tension between boys and men, at least over masquerading. Each adult Yoruba masking society is usually associated with a specific god, an *Orisha*, into which organization there is the gradual incorporation of boys' through masquerading and other activities. There are numerous Orisha, many of which have their own masquerade festivals. Adult male masquerading among the Yoruba is widely practiced, extremely varied, and elegant in appearance. Thus, it is not surprising that there are many instances of boys' masquerading. The population of the

Yoruba, is probably some 15 million persons, a people with a high population density, where many persons reside in indigenous urban centers. These features make possible a rich variety of adult masquerades, which are reflected in the Yoruba boys' masking. However, we should note that the village-centered Dogon achieve similar results in masquerading with a smaller population.

John R. O. Ojo's essay (chap. 3 in this volume) describes a Yoruba boys' Ōjija masquerade, where the boys wear mother-and-child sculpted headpieces of wood, as well as face coverings. Beginning at the end of the two-day adult *Elefon* festival, and lasting for five days, the boys' activities are considered a part of Elefon. Each boys' troupe erects an enclosure modeled after male adult ones. This is used for meetings, storage, and dressing for performances. It is not rare for boy masqueraders in Africa to have a dwelling of some sort, though not always in the style of adult males. Girls involved in the boys' Ōjija, and even the boys' mothers, are allowed to clean and prepare the Ojija masks for use. This is not surprising, as the Yoruba are generally less sensitive over females handling men's masks than are many African peoples.[23]

Ojo's essay suggests the richness of an Ōjija performance.[24] He also describes a like-named ceremony for girls in a nearby Yoruba town, where girls hold similar mother-and-child headpieces on their heads with their hands, but do not employ face coverings. Their performances exhibit some analogous features to that of the boys Ōjija, including singing in public. The boys' songs are generally about human fertility and the need for healthy children, while the girls sing of the greater need for Western education and for jobs, and of a desire to develop their community. Nevertheless, the girls carry sculptures that symbolize fertility. A Westerner, imbued with stereotypical views of Africans, might expect the reverse to be true, seeing males as playing major roles in social and political affairs, and females in child care. That Yoruba females can touch the masks and that they sing of issues of the day is consistent with their strong role in Yoruba society, as leaders, traders, ritualists, and in many other capacities. The songs of both boys and girls make use of metaphor, analogy, and proverbs, which they learn at young ages in a society rich in oral culture. The Ōjija rituals are training grounds in teaching Yoruba children how to vocalize in an elegant manner. The girls' Ōjija, similar in many ways to that of the boys except for the lack of face covering, raises the issue that we will discuss below, as to what exactly is a masquerade.

Gelede is a major Yoruba festival involving numerous adult male masqueraders, which honors females and their power.[25] It frequently includes boy masqueraders. Andrew Frankel[26] filmed a video showing three masked boys dancing at Ajilete, near Idi Iroko, a small Yoruba town that holds its Gelede festival every two or three years. The boys, dressed in rich appliqué cloths, as were the adult maskers, performed to a pair of drummers wearing Gelede-style headpieces, one carved in the form of a monkey, the other a mortar. At times the boys danced alone, while at other times they did so with adult maskers. Sometimes the adult masqueraders performed by themselves. The event, while planned in outline, was quite spontaneous in the manner in which it was acted out.

Henry and Margaret Drewal[27] describe a very different Gelede performance in western Yoruba country, where a masker of about five years of age holds the mask in his hands to keep it on his face. He is followed by teenage masqueraders who move more skillfully, and then by adult performers. "Thus a son whose father was a dancer could begin to perform at the age of four or five. By the age of 12-14 his instruction would be strictly disciplined as he mastered the complex rhythm."[28] Elsewhere, they write[29] that children inherit the right to perform Gelede, but whether they do or not depends upon talent and interest. Those who do not inherit it may do so if advised by a diviner for health or other reasons, or simply because the Orisha is calling them. Learning is largely by emulation, though some adult instruction occurs. "With regular sustained exposure to performances a young child can assimilate *Gelede* dance technique, structure and drum phrases and, by learning to make simple drum patterns with his feet, can begin to perform *Gelede* by the age of three."[30] Young maskers must not wear complete costumes, and an adult coach is likely to be present behind the scenes. With older children the latter may be more evident. He "watches from the side but does not hesitate to rush forward to correct a mistake or scold his dancers, putting them back on the right track. Thus spectacle functions as a training ground for novices in Yoruba society."[31] The explicit teaching of boys' masquerading by adults is not something that occurs in many African societies. As the boy improves, he learns about other aspects of the Orisha society, as he is gradually becomes absorbed into it.[32]

Boys mask at another major Yoruba adult masquerade society, *Egungun*, which is associated with the ancestors. The art historian Rowland Abiodun,[33] when a boy at Owo in about 1946-1947, took part in the *Ijamje* part of an Egungun festival. The boys in the masquerade troupe wore green raffia dress with no stockings, and cloth masks. Unmasked boy musicians played makeshift instruments of cans and rattles. The troupe went to the bush, chose their masqueraders, planned their performances, and practiced their songs. Then they came to town dressed up, going to the houses of relatives and other persons. They sang for gifts, receiving coins, bananas, plantains and yams, on which they later feasted. Other boys taunted them, whipping at the masqueraders.[34]

In 1986, Andrew Frankel[35] filmed a video of an *Egungun Apidan* troupe in Oyo, called *Ajan Gila*. It consisted of two masked dancing boys, one about four years of age, the other of about fifteen years. The younger boy wore a knit hood with eye-holes, the older youth a raffia mask and a long-robed costume that he elegantly flipped about and tucked between his legs as he danced. Acrobatics were involved, as occurs in some other Yoruba boys' and adults' masquerades. The boys danced alone, or with five adult maskers. In another Frankel video,[36] taped the same year, an Egungun Apidan troupe performed at Erin Osunin, outside of Oshogbo. Six adults and two boys of about eight or nine years of age, performed with three adult drummers. They appeared before a chief at his compound with his followers, testimony to the chief's interest in the performance. The boys alternately danced alone or together, and at times with the adult masqueraders, two of whom were fathers of the boys. Several styles of music were played. Though associated with Egungun, a serious men's religious society, this was a secular, vaudevillian performance with acrobatics and the satirizing of social types.

Although a variety of boys' masquerades are associated with various Yoruba festivals and Orisha, not all have child masqueraders. Where these occur, the boy maskers are probably less concerned with religion than with play and learning how to perform. Nevertheless, the boys' activities introduce them to the spiritual side of Yoruba life. Ulli Beier[37] has published the text of the Yoruba "Song of Egbe," associated with a children's masquerade society, whose words suggest an affiliation with a Yoruba spirit. One line, "Companions must know each other," states the desired peer-group solidarity of boys. The final line: "Nobody shall dare to mock us," suggests the children's self-confidence. Masquerading skills are gradually acquired by young boys, and there is usually no requirement that as adults they must continue to mask.[38]

Incorporating Children into the Adult World

The Integrated Masquerades described here display a variety of relationships of boys' masquerading to adult masking and behavior, in which the boys' activities are of importance to the adults. In the Dogon boys' masquerade, boys must perform to ensure the continued work of the diviner. The Bamana masquerade blesses the society's grain, while the Bobo boy masqueraders are a catalyst for a major adult masquerade ritual. Among the Yoruba there is the gradual incorporation of boys into adult religious masquerade associations. In the Bobo instance, and sometimes among the Yoruba, boys' masquerading precedes that of adults, symbolically accurate in terms of people's life experience with masking. The Bobo case also involves an unusual myth of the origin of masks with boys, not prevalent elsewhere in Africa as far as we know,[39] a tale closely linking boys to adult males.

It would be interesting to know whether in those cultures having Integrated Masquerades the close association of boys and men in masquerade activities is part of a general social pattern of close boy-men ties. Or whether these are exceptions, in that other boy-adult male relationships are more distant. Unfortunately, the editors of this volume were not in a position to gather data on this point. We note that this masquerade category exists among traditional, politically centralized, urban cultures, particularly the Yoruba, but also in non-centralized rural cultures, as among the Dogon, the Bamana, and the Bobo. Evidently the nature of a culture's larger political structure is not a determining factor as to whether Integrated Masquerades exist or not.

It is worth noting that non-masking boys sometimes participate in adult masquerades. The boys may be chased by adult maskers, or the youths may dance and play about the edges of adult performances, or they may simply be interested observers. Ruth Phillips[40] mentions the ugly, secular, adult male *gongoli* mask of the Mende of Sierra Leone, whose performances satirize individuals. She quotes a Mende chief: "When it's dancing it will take young boys to blow a horn behind him as if he's a chief, just to make people laugh." Phillips goes on to write that there are "troops of little children who follow him about singing songs that poke fun of his antics."

Boys' Emulating Masquerades

In Emulating Masquerades, the boys' behavior is more autonomous from adults and their masquerade performances than in the Intergraded Masquerades. Boy masqueraders are not involved with adult rituals deemed necessary for the community. Rather, the boys' carry out masquerades for themselves, and their performances are largely secular in nature. Yet the boys are still linked to men through their emulation of adult masquerades, as well as by the occasional advice and assistance of men. There is both a distancing of boys from men and some cooperation, suggesting the presence of ambiguous relationships and tensions between the two. Emulating Masquerades occur in both rural areas and in urban centers of colonial origin. They are found in a wide variety of indigenous political systems.

Kuba Boys' Masquerades of the Democratic Republic of the Congo

David A. Binkley's essay (chap. 4 in this volume) considers the emulation of men's masquerades by pre-initiate boys. Though the Kuba strongly distinguish the activities of uninitiated boys from initiated men, boys still emulate adult masqueraders in behavior, dress, and mask form. The boys also emulate lower status initiations and funerary masquerades, though not higher status ones. Adult Kuba males sometimes make masks for the boys (figs. I.1, I.2). These and other features that Binkley describes suggest that in terms of masquerade activities, matters are not as sharply drawn between boys and men as they are between males and females. Since boys eventually become members of men's masquerading groups, there is a somewhat relaxed attitude toward the boys' emulation of men's masquerades, something that is true in some other African cultures.

Kuba boys' masking, mostly occurring on an individual basis, involves learning to hold secrets, mostly from girls and other boys. This occurs in a culture where, when boys grow up and become members of adult secret societies, they will be expected to do likewise. In Africa, boys' masquerading often involves holding secrets, a skill that when boys become men carries over into the political and ritual life, as well as elsewhere.

Binkley reminds us that boys' masking among the Kuba, in contrast to its absence among girls, is only one aspect of the growth of gender differentiation among the children; many other behaviors are also involved. Nevertheless, the equation of masking and its absence with gender probably has high symbolic value in the development of children's gender identity in Africa.

Binkley mentions Kuba boys' drawings of masks and masquerade figures on paper (fig. I.3). Van Beek also collected boy's drawings of adult masqueraders among the Dogon (fig. 2.4). It is likely that before pencil, pen, and ink were available in Africa children drew images of masquerade figures and masks in the dirt or sand, as Cameron and Jordán mention in their essay (chap. 13) on the children's masquerades of the North-Western Province of Zambia. Through the act of drawing, children explore their own observations on masquerading. They reflect on masks, dress, performances, styles, and the meaning of masquerades as they develop keen observational abilities.[41]

The Afikpo Masquerades

Simon Ottenberg's essay (chap. 5) describes boys' masking at Afikpo, a group of Igbo villages in southeastern Nigeria.[42] These masquerades have almost totally disappeared today, though they existed when he first carried out field research at Afikpo in the 1950s. As in the case the Kuba boys' masquerades, the Afikpo youths emulated mask styles and performances of the men's secret societies. Only in the satiric skits and songs of the boys' masked play, *Okumkpa*, did they display almost total originality in performance. But this was still emulation, since masquerades of the men's Okumkpa also strove for originality. The organization of the boys' masquerade societies into troupes, unlike the more individualistic masquerade activities of Kuba boys, mirrored the organization of Afikpo men in their secret societies. Many of the boys' troupes had their own priest, and a house with a shrine inside, similar to those for the village men. Of course, the boys' shrines were simpler, and the activities of its priest less elaborate. Some boys' troupes also had a special enclosure where they dressed for masquerades, in emulation of the adult form. Boys spent time among themselves at their house, away from girls and older persons, in what Schwartzman calls "child-structured play,"[43] that is, play of their own devising, not involving adults. The boys shared similar taboos as those of adult men regarding females. It was forbidden for boys to wear masks made of wood, of which the men's face pieces were made. However, the youths often attempted to imitate the men's masks in style, employing gourds, coconut tree bark, or other materials. As in the Kuba case, men encouraged boys to be active in masking. Some boys had had as much as ten years masquerading experience by the time they were initiated and masked as men. The activities of the Afikpo troupes were consistent with some other African boys' troupes that we have already discussed, in that masking represented only one of the boys' activities. The whole range of a troupe's actions helped to create strong bonds among its members, which reinforced cooperation in its masquerades.

Adult masquerading is still important at Afikpo, though it has changed. But boys' masking largely gave way under the onslaught of Western education, a money economy, the movement of children away from home, and Christian religious beliefs. It may be that boys' masquerades in Africa are more sensitive to change than adult ones, since they are less likely to be associated with deeply held religious beliefs and ritual practices.

The Omepa *and* Onyeweh *Masquerades of the Igede of Central Nigeria*

In chapter 6, Robert W. Nicholls describes the *Omepa* masquerade, which emulates an adult form called *Aitah*.[44] Omepa, played by children between the ages of five and sixteen, has adult input in that a patron acts as secretary and director of the group. Boys sprinkle sanctified water on the dance area as do the men for their performances. For their music, similar to that of the masquerading men, the boys employ the same kind of drums, to which they add their own whistles and basket rattles. The boys' masks emulate those of the men, but have younger faces, appropriate for children. Boys learn to perform Omepa through emulation, and from talented peer-group boys, as well as directly from adults, who treat the boys' masquerades with respect. Unlike the boys' masquerades of the Kuba discussed above, but similar to those formerly found at Afikpo, Omepa involves boys' troupes with some regular organization. The Kuba, Afikpo, and Igede examples suggest that when boys' emulate adult masquerading, there is likely to be some assistance provided the boys by men. And, in any case, masquerade emulation would not occur without the men's tacit approval.

Nicholls also describes *Onyeweh,* an Emulating Masquerade, in another Igede village, which appears during holidays so the boys can gain pocket money. This involves performers with gourd masks that differ from all men's masks in Igede. Nicholls believes that Onyeweh has affinities to a children's music and dance group, *Ogbete.* Here boys emulate other children's forms, not those of adults.

Kalabari Masquerades

Anna A. Hlavácová's essay (chap. 7) raises the issue of children's emotional response to adult masquerading, in describing how a young child encounters *Mgbula*, a fearsome adult masquerader among the Kalabari of coastal Nigeria. This leads to a different reaction among child onlookers than those previously mentioned for the Dogon and the Kuba, where boys are very curious about adult masking. Here there is fearful astonishment, probably leaving a lasting impression on the child. Both responses to adult masking occur among African children; curiosity and fear may also occur in a child at one time.

Hlavácová relates the tale of a young Kalabari boy who masks with an old, discarded, men's *Ekine* mask. This suggests that children's masking troupes sometimes obtain their masks directly from existing or discarded adult masks. She also believes that emulative boys' masking is a way that a boy learns about his culture and its traditions, important in the growing awareness of his identity as he matures.

Robin Horton's Kalabari researches[45] shed a different light on boys' Ekine masking. He indicates that they are encouraged by adults to imitate the men's Ekine masquerades, though the boys omit certain spiritual aspects. Boys' performances are supervised by the drum master of the adult masquerades, and men look for promising boy performers to sponsor into the adult society. Ijaw boys, neighbors of the Kalabari,[46] play at emulating an adult *Owumo* masquerade, though with less elaborate costume and no drumming. "Adults believe that the games prepare the youths for eventual participation in the adult *Owu* dance and therefore encourage their imitation to the point of carving play masks for them."[47]

Other Masquerades of Southern Nigeria

G. I. Jones[48] provides examples of emulating masking from Igbo and Ibibio societies. He mentions a small boys' *Ekpo* masquerade of the Ibibio,[49] a form given up by adults that children took over. This again suggests that some children's masquerades derive from adult ones as "survivals," to employ an old-fashioned anthropological term. Sarah Adams,[50] in December 1994 at Eha-Alumona in Igbo country, observed a boy wearing a northern Igbo men's mask, but with a much more elaborate costume than is usual in Igbo boys' masking (Figure I.4). Perkins Foss[51] describes a boy *àkpàrákpà* masquerader at an Ohworu festival at Evwreni, among the Urhobo. According to the Evwreni, this was originally a male adult form, but its spiritual power was so great that its adult dancer went berserk. Divination revealed that it should be performed by a young boy. John Boston[52] mentions the *ulaga* mask of northern Igbo boys, also an adult form.[53] There are a considerable variety of boys' Emulating Masquerades in southern Nigeria, as there are adult masquerades.[54]

Mende Boys' Masquerades in Sierra Leone

Loretta Reinhardt[55] writes of the eastern Mende, that "[C]hildren are always present at festivities, doing their best to join in the singing and dancing. Little boys will get together and fashion their own spirit costumes. These are most often of relatively minor [adult masquerade] spirits, and are usually well received, provided they do not come round to the resting places during the rest breaks for the adult dancers." She describes the adult forms of the secular *nafali* and *falui* masquerades of the male adult Poro society, "the two which are also most often copied by children,"[56] While it is rare in Africa for boys to emulate sacred adult masking forms, Reinhardt[57] mentions boys who masquerade as the sacred adult *Goboi* of the men's Poro society.

African Accounts of Boys' Masking Experience

One of the few accounts by an African of the personal experiences of a boy masquerader is that of the poet, art critic, curator, and artist, Olu Oguibe, of Igbo background. He masked in the 1960s, despite some doubts about his doing so on the part of his Protestant minister father. In poetic fashion his account reads:[58]

> In the dry season after the harvest the ancestors in their masquerades tearing down huge palm trees and spitting fire from their mouths. I dusted my little wooden mask and dressed in dry plantain leaves and Odogwu led our group of uninitiated maskers around the village dancing for copper pennies, or trudged behind the ever-swelling cortege of elder maskers across towns and villages to distant duels where dangerous masquerades loosened the very soil of the earth in their match of charms and scattered the shreds of rivals to the four ends of the world. Occasionally, my father brushed aside the tenets of his gospel forbidding dancing as a sin and dressed me in wax-print cloth and shoved me into the group of the uninitiated forerunning the fiery ancestor Ebengu, he who departs with the harvest of me.

A fuller account of a Nigerian's experience as a boy masquerader is found in chapter 8 by Chika O. Okeke, an Igbo artist, art critic, and art historian. He took part in boys' masking both in his rural home and in an Igbo city where different masking forms existed. This is probably not an unusual experience for African boys, a good number of whom live away from home, but return for the holidays. Okeke had a wider experience in masking and in his observations of adult masquerading than if he had remained in a single community for his entire childhood. The masquerades he was involved with were based on adult types; chasing masquerades at home, and *Ékpó* presentations in the city. Despite the interest Okeke and his brothers had in boys' masquerading, they looked forward with excitement to their adolescent initiations. Or perhaps it was because of their childhood masking experience. It is uncertain whether Okeke was influenced to move toward his present interests in art through childhood masquerading or not. His art is not preoccupied with Igbo masquerades.

The available information on children's masquerading in Africa is generally lacking in detailed reports on what the experience has been like for those who have been involved in it. What were the emotions, the thoughts and beliefs that were aroused? What was the sense of pacing, of comradeship and competition? What was learned through the experience? This failure to obtain insight into children's masquerades also exists in studies of adult masking in Africa.

Learning and Tensions in Emulative Boys' Masquerades

Boys' Emulative Masquerades more commonly occur in Africa than Integrated Masquerade forms. Why this is so is not clear. Possibly it is because of the tendency of adult masqueraders to keep children away from their own activities and secrets until the boys grow up. Yet the adults wish the boys to acquire skills in masquerading so that they will later perform well as adults.

Further, the nature of Integrated Masquerades suggests the existence of adult dependence on children, which contradicts the importance of age distinctions in many African societies, where adults rule.

A more powerful explanation may be that much of childhood learning in Africa is carried out through emulation. It is basic to a child's education.[59] Children observe the behavior of older children and adults, and they begin to emulate what they have seen. Perhaps, then, their actions are corrected by their parents, older siblings, or other persons. But children are not usually taught by adults in sessions lasting long periods of time, as Western children are. As a consequence, the child does much of the work of self-education, using older persons as role models. This emulative process leads to raising his or her curiosity level, which we see so clearly in African children's interest in adult masquerades. The style of children's learning in masquerades is only one aspect of a more general emulative pattern in their education.

There are two distinct tensions embedded in Emulative Masquerades. One of them concerns ambivalent attitudes of boys and men towards one another in some of the cultures where both ages mask. While boys are linked to men through their'emulative masquerading, or through some adult support, or both, they are not as intimately involved with men socially and ritually as they are in the Integrated Masquerades. On the one hand, men want their sons, other youthful male relatives, and sometimes other youths, to acquire masquerade skills so that they will mature into skilled adult performers. Men wish this to occur for their own status and prestige and because of their own joy in the masquerades, sometimes taking delight in the masquerading of their sons and other young relatives. This may remind some men of their own youthful performances. Men also realize the importance of having skilled masqueraders in the next generation, in order to carry out the community's masquerades and its related rituals. Otherwise the adult masquerades will become stale. And communities wish to fair well in masquerade competition with other communities. So men may encourage boys to emulate adult masking, sculpt masks for them, and assist them with their dress and music. Men do these things in African cultures where outwardly there are marked social distinctions between boys and men in terms of the adult masquerade societies and other adult matters.

Yet men also wish to keep boys socially at some distance from themselves, to isolate the young from adult masquerade practices and secrets, as well as other rituals. Men desire to maintain social and ritual differentiation from youths. This desire exists, whether from fear of being replaced by the youths, from fear of loss of their secrets, or simply because they conceive of their society as best functioning in this manner. Men have a need to maintain control over youths, to keep boys as boys.

From the boys' viewpoint there is also ambivalence. In some ways they desire to emulate their fathers and other adult males and are delighted to copy their masquerades, even if only partially doing so. The boys enjoy receiving praise for their masquerading from their fathers and other adult males. Some boys probably perceive their symbolic association with fathers and other adults through their masking as a positive value. But boys also want to make their own mark in the world, including through their masquerades. They desire to have their own identities recognized. And boys may fear possible restrictions or retribution from fathers and other adults for their masquerade behavior. This fear is symbolized in the manner in which aggressive adult masqueraders sometimes swoop down on children, chasing them, threatening to thrash them, and even to capture them. Tensions between the two ages is, of course, only one aspect of the tensions among them that occur in other social situations. Thus, Emulating Masquerades express the sometimes ambivalent attitudes of men and boys towards one another. In contrast, Integrated Masquerades, with their closer relationships of boys and men, at least outwardly, appear to suppress potential tensions through cooperative activities.

The second area of tensions in Emulating Masquerades is between emulation and creativity. We have written extensively about boys' emulation of adult masquerading. From this it may appear that there is little creativity in the boys' performances, that it is only a question of emulating adult masking. But boys modify adult masquerade forms, rather than strictly follow them. To the outside observer, it is not always possible to tell why they do so. Is it done deliberately to introduce their own masquerade ideas, an effort to create something different which they can claim as their own? Are the boys simply not at the stage of maturation to fully emulate their elders' masking performances? Or do the boys not fully remember or comprehend the qualities of men's masquerading? In any case, boys sometimes introduce to their masquerades their own dance and body motions, songs and music, as well as modified dress. Is this because they do not have the physical materials, the skill, or the interest to fully emulate adult masquerades? Boys create make-shift musical instruments out of tins, gourds, and bits of wood. They improvise dress from pieces of cloth obtained here and there, and use raffia strips or leaf costumes that they themselves prepare. Masquerading boys, who, at times, endeavor to emulate adult forms, on other occasions, just romp about among themselves, perhaps chasing and whipping unmasked boys or other youths with masks. At these times they are in their own world, largely unconnected with adults, where they create their own forms of masquerade play.

Boys' Independent Masquerades

Boy's Independent Masquerades bear little or no relationship to adult masking. The boys' masquerades differ markedly from those of the men, and the boys' troupes are autonomous from adults. In this category we also include cases where boys mask, but there is no adult masquerading. Since adult masquerades are common in West and Central Africa, cases of boys' masking where men do not, are not common, although the literature about this is sketchy.

When boys' Independent Masquerades occur in Africa, there are often other cultural experiences that boys do not strongly share with parents and other older individuals, pointing to a separate culture for boys from adults, what Philippe Aries calls the culture of childhood.[60] This condition is unlikely to be found in Integrated Masquerades, where the boys' masquerades form a part of adult culture, or in Emulating Masquerades, where the boys attempt to emulate adult masking and culture, or where they are sometimes closely supported by adults in their masking endeavors, or both. It should not be surprising that a fair number of the cases of Independent Masquerades occur in urban centers that began under colonialism, and today are still centers of Western influence. These cities present the best African conditions for the growth of a separate culture of childhood, so characteristic of the West. Yet there are also a number of rural cases of Independent Masquerades.

The Alikali *Devils of Sierra Leone*

Boys' *Alikali* masquerades in Bo, Sierra Leone described by Jeanne Cannizzo in chapter 9[61] no longer exist. There have been virtually no masquerades in the country as a result of the bitter ten-year civil war there, which have recently come to an end. Whether these delightful boys' masquerades return to Bo and other parts of Sierra Leone is yet to be seen.

Bo is an inland city that developed under colonialism, first as an upcountry railway stop, and later as an educational and trading center. Unlike a good many boys' masquerades in Yoruba urban centers in Nigeria, the Bo forms were secular. The Alikali masquerades at Bo were an end-point of a long history of masquerade migration, a phenomenon becoming more common in Africa. They drew from men's masking in Freetown, the country's capital, rather than from that of the men at Bo, which was traditional and of Mende origin. The Freetown masquerades, in turn, derived from individuals of Yoruba, Igbo, Ibibio, and other West Africans backgrounds, descendants of persons who came from Nigeria and Ghana.[62] At Bo there was little connection between adult and child masquerading; they belonged to different performance worlds. Most of the troupes were multiethnic and multi-religious, and well organized, each with its own football team. A troupe was able to present up to four different masquerades, all derived from Freetown. Some of the boys had traveled to that city, or lived there for some time. They had seen the masquerade performances and festivals there.

Since the boys' masquerading was emulative, this suggests that they were Emulating Masquerades. However, it was emulation of distant elements many miles away, not of adult masking in Bo. Thus, the editors of this volume have placed them with the Independent Masquerades, as there was autonomy of the boys' masking activities from parents and other adult males.

Cannizzo, attracted to Aries's study of the history of the growth of a culture of childhood in Europe,[63] contrasts masquerading in Bo with that of a nearby rural Mende community. In the rural village, children's masking emulated traditional adult forms, and children had a variety of ties to adult masqueraders. On the other hand, the boys at Bo had developed a culture of childhood, with quite different masquerades and other activities from those of the adults and the rural village. The boys did not emulate traditional adult Bo masking. Cannizzo attributes the differences to schooling and other Western influences. The Bo children had developed a culture of their own. This distinguished them from their parents and other older persons and their masquerades.

Cannizzo was able to elicit well-developed aesthetic concepts from the well-organized Alikali masqueraders. Established performance standards existed, of which the boys were quite conscious. Clear masquerade aesthetic criteria held by children undoubtedly occur elsewhere in Africa, though they have rarely been studied in detail. However, some children's masquerades are so irregularly performed, or are so casual, that aesthetic factors cannot be clearly voiced by the participants. Since boys in African masquerade troupes often pass through them in a few years, special efforts have to be made to pass down rules, aesthetic concepts, and masquerade culture.

Alikali masquerades also existed in other upcountry areas of Sierra Leone, as in the multiethnic town of Kabala in the north. Irregularly organized troupes were also observed by Simon Ottenberg in 1978-1980, in the nearby Limba chiefdom of Wara Wara Bafodea. He saw different troupes at a memorial rite for a village chief, at the public aspect of girls' initiation ceremonies in another community (fig. I.5), and at Christmas in the chiefdom capital of Bafodea Town. At Wara Wara Bafodea, the masqueraders were not only called Alikali, but also *kumandegiri*. The performances probably represented a blending of an older traditional children's masquerade form with the contemporary Alikali style.

Children in the Bissau Carnival

The multi-authored chapter on carnival in Bissau, edited by Simon Ottenberg, explores the influence of modernity on children's masquerading in the capital city of Guinea-Bissau. This annual pre-Lenten event, which lasts a number of days, has prominent roles for masking children in it, as well as for adults. The children parade, dance, and prance, often in papier-mâché masks of their own invention and construction. However, some children's masks and performances are traditional or neo-traditional, drawn from indigenous cultures in the city, and in the surrounding rural areas. There is considerable emulation of elements drawn from carnivals and festivals in Brazil, Portugal, Cuba, Goa, and elsewhere. This is another case, like the Alikali masquerades of Bo, of the extensive migration of masking ideas. The children draw from videos, movies, posters, magazines, and from a well-known Bissau newspaper cartoon character. Government controls on carnival over the years, which have varied among socialistic, democratic, and militaristic styles, have influenced the nature of children's masking. In this, Bissau carnival resembles the later phases of the *Dodo* masquerades of Ougadougou (see below).

In the Bissau carnival, girls make masks, help boys and men prepare theirs, and sometimes mask themselves. Female masking is probably the consequence of a secular environment, influenced by the socialist ideology that existed in the country at one time. Otherwise, girls only occasionally make or wear masks in Guinea Bissau. Multicultural and multiethnic, Bissau carnival is one of a series of festival events that have sprung up in African cities in recent years, albeit with a stronger emphasis on children than most.

Dodo *Boys' Masquerades at Ougadougou, Burkina Faso*

Dodo or *Dodogo* masqueraders employ white-painted, horned calabash masks, which are found in Burkina Faso, Côte d'Ivoire, and Mali.[64] This masquerade probably originated as an adult form in the Nigerian Plateau region. It came to Burkina Faso through Hausa, traders and migrants, along with Islam.[65] However, non-Islamic boys' masquerades existed in these countries prior to Islam.[66] In the Bamana region of Mali and the Bobo area of Burkina Faso, adult Dodo masquerades often appear during Ramadam, despite Muslim strictures against the representation of animal and human forms. Dodo has also become a generic term for masquerades and masks throughout the West African Savannah, particularly on the part of Muslims.

Priscella Baird Hinckley's chapter on the popular boys' Dodo in the capital city of Ougadougou, makes it clear that now it is often considered a traditional masquerade there, despite its foreign origin. The two boys' forms of Dodo were originally almost entirely child-organized. The boys in the troupes are often from Muslim, Christian, and traditional backgrounds. The troupes are frequently multiethnic and made up of schooled and unschooled boys. Through time Dodo at Ougadougou went from an adult to a children's form, from the sacred to the secular, from secrecy to openness, from the frightening (particularly to females) to the familiar. They have gone from having only performances in the family courtyard to more public ones, and to a greater inclusion of girls as unmasked accompanists. As in the case of Bissau carnival and Bo masquerades, there is some history of the development of Dodo, accounts which are much more difficult to obtain for rural children's masquerades.

Dodo is unusual in having been taken over by the Ougadougou government, so that it has come to be presented annually by numerous boys' troupes at a government hall in the city. However, its preliminary activities are still staged in the city's quarters. The government awards prizes for the best performances and masks, and encourages the development of new mask forms. Except for the preliminary boys' masking in the city's compounds, the government's interest in Dodo is reminiscent of what occurs in Bissau carnival, where child masking serves the government's interests in social and political solidarity, and in tourism.

Elsewhere, Hinckley writes of Christian boys in Ougadougou who at Christmas time create street nativities.[67] She writes: "That children do so rather than adults is a departure, but more and more these children are becoming mediators between their families and the urban modern world. In the process of making a crèche they explore the nontraditional areas of their own individuality, Western concepts of space and design and modern technology." This is similar to what occurs in Dodo masquerading. It suggests that in urban situations, children, through masquerades and other activities have become active agents in negotiating change vis-à-vis older generations, even when under government supervision. This is also true of the Bissau and Bo boys' masquerades.

Another Independent Masquerade has been described in the Igbo city of Aba, southeastern Nigeria, by Ola Balogun.[68] At Christmas time in the late 1960s, he discovered boys' masquerades emulating those of adults, and other boys dressed as cowboys. The youths "came from the city-like elements of the population and were usually youth whose parents were from Sierra Leone or Fernando Po. They wore light masks over fancy dress and danced to the music of a brass band, whipping each other."

Rural Boys' Independent Masquerades

Nicolas Argenti,[69] employing play theory, has recently written a detailed study of boys' Independent Masquerades in the kingdom of Oku, though there are echoes of Emulative Masquerades. Rural, Oku is in a highly politicized region of Cameroun, boy maskers known as *kesum-body* present political themes. These concern the white man, and the country's opposition political party, which exists at Oku, in the anglophone part of a predominantly francophone Cameroun. The boys' performances serve as a means of engaging with the rapidly changing and increasingly violent world of Oku.

In pre-colonial Oku children masqueraded in the areas between the farms, away from village and forest, where boys chased birds and monkeys and played games. After the missionaries came at the turn of the twentieth century, these masquerades moved to the settlements, where they exist today. They are generally not controlled or initiated by adults, who only marginally participate, mostly as viewers. The maskers' dress is similar to that in adult masquerades, but the materials differ. The boys use jute cloth or nylon coffee bags, and their masks are created from aluminum sheets, plastic containers, and occasionally cardboard or paper. They do not perform in wood masks, as these are reserved the men. The boy's masks are embellished with colored strips of paper, chicken feathers or glossy paint, unlike those worn during men's masquerades. Not all men masquerade, for it is restricted to selected individuals, while the boys' troupes are open, fluid, and acephalous. The choreography of the boys differs from traditional adult forms, often changing from year to year, as does their dress, their masks, and their musical accompaniment.

The Oku masquerades indicate that it is not simply a question of urban in contrast to the rural sites, which determines whether Independent Masquerades are found or not, but the extent of modern social and political influences. Oku is an area where modernizing forces operate, while still largely rural. Argenti emphasizes the politicization of children through their masquerades. We have noted this in Bissau carnival, and the Dodo masquerades of Ougadougou, though at Oku it is in reaction to the government, rather than in acceptance of government influence. The issue of political involvement of children in masquerading and in other forms of play is a topic that needs further exploration.

However, not all rural boys' Independent Masquerades are associated with modernity in Africa. Frederick Lamp[70] states that among the rural Baga of Guinea, there are very well organized boys' associations with their own activities, including masking. Boys have sacred bush meeting places private from the elders, who do not like the masking and sometimes chase the boys away. The youths make their own masks, which differ from adult ones. While the idea of masking is related to present and former men's adult masquerades, the boys' groups are autonomous. Van Beek, in his essay in this volume, mentions that certain boys' masquerades among the rural Dogon of Mali differ from adult forms. Christian K. Hoejbjerg,[71] briefly has seen a boys' masquerade among the Loma of Guinea called *anibhèlèkoi*, which consists of worn pieces of cloth covering the wearer's entire body (fig. I.6), which was not a dress worn by men masqueraders. (There were also two Loma girls' masquerades that are discussed below.) Warren d'Azevedo,[72] before the civil wars in Liberia, saw boy masqueraders dressed in elaborate Santa Claus costumes. He notes that the masqueraders were spreading from urban to rural areas. In 1952, at Afikpo in Igbo country, then a rural area, Simon Ottenberg,[73] at his home during the Christmas holiday, viewed a boy wearing an Ibibio-style mask. He was accompanied by a group of non-masked singing boys, some of whom were playing simple musical instruments. This type of mask, either made at Afikpo or in Ibibio country, was sometimes employed by men at Afikpo in their masquerades. The boys made the rounds of the homes of Europeans and prominent Africans, receiving gifts of money.

Ruth Phillips[74] mentions a *nafali* masquerade in Sierra Leone (fig. I.7), in sharp contrast to those of the men's Poro society, which "in the 1970s among the central and western Mende...enjoyed the reputation of the Mende dancer *par excellence* and was usually performed by young boys of ten or twelve who were not yet full Poro members."[75] Nafali originally came from the eastern Mende, where it was performed by a boy as a herald to the men's masquerade, *Gbini*.[76] But among western and central Mende, it became a boys' performance, not associated with any adult masking. As a consequence of its migration it changed from an Integrated Masquerade to an Independent Masquerade.

Kenji Yoshida's essay (chap. 12) describes rural boys' masquerades among the Chewa in south central Africa. The *kalumbu* boy's associations possess their own songs, masks, costumes, and secret terms (fig. I.8). All of these differ from those of the men's *nyau* masquerade societies. The boys' activities are secular, while the men's masked associations have secret and religious ends, linked to ancestors and funeral rites. Nevertheless, boys' initiations into their own troupes, and their masquerades, are similar to initiations and some other behavior in the men's societies. The boy masqueraders are viewed and cheered by adults; they are praised by parents and other relatives at the end of the performance. Adult men consider the boys' activities training for adult masquerading. Thus, among the Chewa, there is part emulation of adults and part differentiation from them, part separation from them and part adult encouragement. These masquerades should probably be classed as intermediate forms between Independent and Emulating Masquerades.

Yoshdia quotes a riddle of the adult nyau society that suggests that the boys' associations are "bigger" than the adult one, since "even elders started up to masquerade with dancing *kalumbu*."[77] He writes that "we may as well say that the *kalumbu* is a model of the *nyau* as say that the *nyau* is a model of the *kalumbu*," which questions where the origin of masquerading lies. This sounds similar to the idea behind the Bobo myth, which was discussed earlier, that masquerading originated with boys and was only later taken on by men.[78]

Yoshida mentions a new mask and masquerade dance with its own name, which was created by a boy in kalumbu in 1984. Later, as a member of the men's society, he developed other new masks. That boys have talent in devising new masks, and continue to do so into adult life, is not surprising, although accounts of this kind are rare in the masquerade literature on Africa. For the Chewa, this suggests that neither boys nor adults are rigid over the rules of masquerading. Chewa girls also have masquerade groups (discussed below). These share some similarities with those of the boys.

Thus, autonomous, or nearly autonomous boys' masquerading groups, do not always arise out of conditions of modernity, but occur in rural, more traditional cultures, where the masking groups are under few influences of modernization. Why they exist in traditional settings, rather than only in urban centers, is not clear. It suggests that Western influences and urbanization are not the only factors involved in the growth of a culture of childhood, which can exist in rural areas—unless there has been further modernizing influences in these rural cases than we know about.

Independent Masquerades with Little or No Adult Masking

René Bravmann[79] refers to three Akan terms used by both the Asante and Bron in Ghana, in reference to masks made by children of cardboard or palm fronds, and employed in play. These cultures have little or no men's masking. The terms appear to be the only native ones for masking among them, whose language is otherwise rich in artistic terminology. This suggests that they are probably of recent origin.[80] At Elmina in coastal Ghana, a region with virtually no men's masking,[81] boys' Fancy Dress masqueraders appear in human and animal masks. They wear brightly colored cloth costumes,[82] whose colors link them to the Fante banners found there. The term "Fancy Dress" derives from a form of British ball, which undoubtedly came to the former British colony during the colonial period. Peter Pipim, a Ghanaian formerly in the Education Department at the National Museum of African Art in Washington, D.C., has told Simon Ottenberg that as a child he took part in Fancy Dress masquerading in the city of Kumasi, in inland Asante country. He believes that the masquerade came to the coastal Fante from Caribbean carnival. It then moved inland in the 1960s to Kumasi. There it existed in mixed Fante-Asante sections of the city, with boys from both cultures taking part in it. He believes it has now died out in Kumasi, although he is not certain why. At first, the boys' club that Pepim belonged to employed papier-mâché masks and then masks of fiber screens, both of which they made themselves. They performed the day after Christmas and at Easter. If a child wished to follow the club members when they were masquerading about Kumasi, he had to pay the boys something. Otherwise the club members chased him away. Its members did not ask for or receive gifts, unusual for children's performances in Africa; it was just to take part.

Growth of Independent Masquerades

The essentially secular Independent Masquerades are found widely in Africa. They exist in urban areas and modernizing rural regions, and at other times in more traditional rural areas. In the latter case, their presence may be the consequence of influences from the cities, or it may be the result of other factors. In urban centers, Independent Masquerades are sometimes linked to the government of the country and the city where they are located, as at Ougadougou and Bissau. Here, there is actually a kind of return to the Integrated Masquerade form. But instead of elders and adult secret society members having an interest in the boys' masquerades, it is the more socially distant national and urban governments who do so, integrating the performances into their activities. At times, Independent Masquerades have been influenced by external cultural features, including transatlantic ones. Many masqueraders and masking ideas in the urban forms have a long history of migration from distant places, particularly in the Bissau carnival, and the Ougadougou and Bo masquerades. The Independent Masquerades are closest to Aries's concept of a culture of childhood of the three masking categories. There is much fluidity and experimentation in Independent Masquerades, and less so with the Integrated and Emulative Masquerades. Independent Masquerades in the cities appear to have something to do with identity, with masquerading children trying to find their way in a multicultural worlds. While struggling to do so, they also enjoy the possibilities of choice, alternative activities, and new forms of creativity. Urban children may simply be playing when they masquerade, or they may be trying to locate themselves socially through performances (as well as in other ways). They live in a world of differences. They may be involved in schooling in a European language, while speaking one or more African tongues. They may be watching TV or the cinema, viewing Westerns, Kung Fu, Mickey Mouse, and films from India, and may read magazines and books, often in a European language. They may visit their parents' rural homes, where they experience traditional rites and customs, while in the cities they may live an urban street existence. They may masquerade at Christian and Muslim holidays in the city or at their rural homeland. In any case, boys performing Independent Masquerades are not as closely linked to parents and other seniors as those taking part in the Integrated and Emulative Masquerades. Rather they attempt to establish their identities in a much broader social and cultural climate. In the Integrated and Emulative Masquerades boys strive to act as, or to emulate adults. They achieve something of their identity in these ways.

Girls' Pre-Initiation Masquerades

Girls' pre-initiation masquerades in Africa are not as commonly reported in the literature as are those of boys. Greater attention to girls' masking will undoubtedly produce further examples. The underreporting of girls' masquerades is similar to what has occurred in the case of women's masquerades. Recent research indicates they women's masking is more widespread than the well-known cases in Liberia and Sierra Leone.[83]

Girls have masquerade roles in the Bissau carnival, as discussed in this volume. Boys and girls masquerade together, as well as separately. Children of both genders create new masks each year. Under what conditions is joint masquerading by boys and girls likely to occur? In Bissau it may be due to the modernizing social climate of Guinea Bissau. But there may also be some influence from rural areas, for among the Bijogo of Guinea-Bissau, not far from the city, girls ten to twenty years of age wear wood masks representing cows, other animals, and fish forms. These masks are usually smaller in size than those worn by men.[84] Girls and boys from surrounding rural areas come to Bissau to take part in the carnival. Thus, some rural masking traditions may influence girls' masking in Bissau. Of course, this occurs with boys' masking as well.

Girls' involvement with masquerading at the carnival is the only clear instance of girls' Independent Masquerades that we have discovered. It may be that under conditions of change in Africa, girls have tended to be less independent, particularly of mothers and other females, than boys of parents and older males. However, this issue has to be carefully evaluated in every case.

The essay by Elisabeth Cameron and Manuel A. Jordán (chap.13) on masquerading in the North-Western Province of Zambia also raises questions concerning the role of gender in masking. Women masquerade as well as men.[85] Boys and girls masquerade together rather than in separate organizations, as in Chewa children's masquerading (see below). Adult's cooperate in the children's activities, but they maintain the fiction that children's performances are merely "play," and not serious. The adults consider that play and ritual do not overlap, a commonly held view of children's activities worldwide. Yet the Africans in this study recognize the value of children's play in preparation for adolescent initiation, and the children often take their play seriously. We have encountered this ambivalent adult attitude toward children's masquerade play before.

Girls, as well as boys, may wear masks like those in male initiations. Even if the girls lack masks or headpieces, they still dress and dance in styles appropriate to adult masqueraders, though their movements are simpler. Children draw masquerade figures in the sand and not on paper, as among the Kuba (discussed above). The authors indicate that initiation rites into adulthood have been drawn from children's songs. We have already mentioned that at times adult masquerades appropriate elements from those of children.

J. R. O. Ojo's essay (chap. 3) contrasts Yoruba boys' Ōjija masquerading in one community with a girls' rite of the same name in another Yoruba town. The girls' performance exhibits similarities to boys' masquerading, though the girls' faces are not covered. In both cases there is the carrying of wooden sculptured headpieces, the extensive use of songs, and the presence of both girls' and the boys' masquerade performances at a men's festival.

The girls' Ōjija performance raises the question as to whether there are not a whole range of situations where girls' performance are quite similar to those of boys' masquerading, yet without the girls' wearing face covering? Are there not also like instances among women in African cultures?[86] The girls' Ojija performance would not be considered masquerading if a stricter definition were applied, that the key element in masking is the covering of the eyes and at least part of the rest of the face.[87] Even if the girls' performance is not considered to be masquerading, cases such as this one represent phenomena that require further investigation. What do similarities in separate performances for each gender tell us about female-male relationships in a culture? Are the similarities a consequence of the desire of females to equate their gender status to that of men, or an expression of that condition? A more traditional anthropological approach might ask whether the similarities are but the product of a culture's tendency to unify, simplify, and to make consistent its various elements.

Similar gender issues are brought forward in a discussion of female masquerades in the ancient Wuli State in Senegambia by Peter Weil.[88] In the nineteenth and early twentieth century there were two forms that were originally for girls and remained so over time. There were also eight adult female masquerade forms, which in later times either died out, or moved down in age to younger women, and then down again in age until they were performed only by girls. This is another instance, in addition to those already discussed in the introduction, of adult masquerading being taken up by children as the adult forms declined or disappeared. All of the female masquerades involved elaborate dressing in cloth, including the face, with a gourd of symbolic import sometimes attached to the body. The costumes were said to represent animals and birds, such as baby leopard, ostrich, heron, and *kurukupaa*, a spirit associated with senior women's divination rites. Female masqueraders were involved in important women's rituals associated with major religious beliefs. The masquerades were a "means of socializing girls to adult status by playing out female roles in Mande society."[89] Weil believes that female masquerading at an earlier time indicated that the status for women was virtually equal to that of men. In the former Wuli state today, female masquerades of any age rarely occur, if at all. Weil states,[90] "[T]he elimination of women's masks or their secularization as they were converted into little girls' entertainments prior to elimination, is part of the dramatic decrease in the status of women in public life that occurred throughout the twentieth century." Thus, Weil suggests that the presence, or the absence, and the nature of female masking in a culture reflects female and male gender and status. This is a similar issue that has been raised with the Bissau carnival.

In Kenji Yoshida's chapter on Chewa children's masquerades of south-central Africa, which was discussed in the section on boy's Independent Masquerades, there is mention of girls' masking. The girls' form can be viewed more or less as Emulating Masquerades. It is similar to those of the boys, in that they have an organized group, their own initiation, and secret terms like those of the boys. Furthermore, they have similar procedures for keeping secrets from adults. However, the girl's employ simple cloth face coverings, most of their songs differ from those of the boys, and several of their songs are similar to those found in female adolescent initiation. It is not certain how ancient Chewa girls' masquerades are, but they appear to have been well developed by the time of the research in the 1980s. We do not know why girls' masquerades developed among them.

Christian K. Hoejbjerg[91] calls attention to the existence of two girls' masquerades among the Loma of Guinea. We have already mentioned *Anibhèlèkoi*, a Loma boys' masquerade in the section of the introduction on Independent Masquerades. One form for the girls, *kpenyigbaï* (fig. I.9), consists mainly of a body dress of sliced green leaves. This masquerade figure resembles the *zadégiti* costume, including the type of headdress and the body painting worn by girls at the coming-out ceremony concluding their initiation into adulthood. However, kpenyigbaï is fabricated from different materials and colors than zadégiti. The other girls' "masquerade," *digibaï* (fig. I.10), has the same headdress as zadégiti, though the body painting differs (white arrows, horizontal stripes on the legs, and white spots on torso, arms, and face), but there is no mask. Digibaï is performed by a single girl, while kpenyigbaï appears in pairs. Adult Loma masquerades are not present in connection with seasonal changes, nor do they mark the agricultural cycle. However, the appearance of both boys' and girls' Loma masquerades at the end of the rice harvest suggests to Hoejbjerg that they may represent a first fruit ritual. While these girls' masquerades are considered to be play, there are "rules of the game." Women offer rice and rice flour in exchange for performances as the players pass from house to house in the early night, preferably by moonlight. In response to questions concerning the nature of the disguised performers, the leaders among the children respond that the boys' and girls' forms are masks (*aniwolaiti*: pl.) coming out of the bush to visit the village, and they are themselves cult masters (*kalamoiti*: pl.). The playing at masking of the youths is a means to learn of the practice and organization of Loma cult associations. Again, we have a case where girls do not actually wear a face mask, but they consider themselves to be masked.

Priscella Hinckley,[92] drawing on her research into Ougadougou masquerades, briefly mentions two girls' Dodo troupes, one dancing with a troupe of older boy masqueraders, the other organized by an older male. However, it appears from her comments that female Dodo masking groups are uncommon. There does not seem to be any prohibition on girls' masquerading in Ougadougou, and it is possible that other girls' troupes have existed or exist.

Outside of Liberia and Sierra Leone, where men make wood masks that women wear, a number of the cases of female masking involves the use of cloth to cover the face, rather than wood. This appears to be logical, since women do not usually carve wooden objects. While cloth in Africa, with significant exceptions, is made by men, both genders trade in commercial cloth and females make much use of it in dress. Using their own cloth, rather than relying on male mask makers, frees from a dependence on men.

Some instances of girls' masquerading in Africa involve them in important relationships with their mothers and other women. Girls also sometimes emulate their mothers' masquerade activities. But there is also girls' identification with fathers and other males, in so far as they emulate men's masquerading and the organization and activities of men's associations. This is probably important to them, as they will likely become intimately involved with a male in marriage at an early age, while boys do not marry until they are much older, and they need to break with mothers and other older females in order to establish their identity with men.

Notes

1. Ottenberg 1982b.
2. For examples among the Bamana of Mali, see Dieterlen 1951, 170; Imperato 1980.
3. Ottenberg 1982b.
4. Bateson 1972, 186-190.
5. But see Kasfir and Franco (eds.) 1998.
6. Murphy 1980.
7. See d'Azevedo 1973a and b, for a thoughtful account of male sculptors creating masks for senior females of the women's Sande masquerade society of the Gola of Liberia.
8. Bateson 1972; Huizinga 1949; Manning 1983; Piaget 1951; Schwartzman 1978, 1983; Sutton-Smith 1997; Sutton-Smith and Kelly-Byrne 1984.
9. As at Bobo Dioulasso. See Bravmann 1983, 66-67, figs. 51 and 52.

36   Playful Performers

10. Often N'tomo or Ntomo in the literature. Some basic sources on these boys' troupes in addition to Arnoldi's chapter in this volume are Arnoldi 1986a, 1986b; Dieterlen 1951; Fellous 1981; Imperato 1980; McNaughton 1979; Paques 1954; Tauxier 1927.
11. Dieterlen 1951, 174-175.
12. Zahan 1960, 99-103, Plate VIII.
13. Arnoldi 1986a, 12.
14. For example, Ezra 1988; Griaule 1938; Imperato 1978; Laude 1973.
15. Often called "second funerals" in the literature on Africa.
16. Le Moal 1980, 1981.
17. Le Moal, 1980, 242-243, mentions other boys' masquerades, one that mimics the dances of young girls, another appears as a blind woman; another acts as an unlucky child, and there is a comical acrobatic form that imitates a mouse's movements.
18. Le Moal 1980, 267-271; 1981, 246.
19. This is unlike the case of two Bobo children's possession cults, which are quite separate from adult activities, and which indicate other religious involvements of children.
20. For example, Cameron 1998, 58-59; d'Azevedo 1973a; Pernet 1982, 1992; and for the Dogon, see the explanation in van Beek's chapter in this volume. This also argues against a scholarly view, based on European data, that children's games, songs, and dances are sometimes derived from those abandoned by adults. See Opie and Opie 1960. But see an example of such cases in Africa in Hlavácová's chapter in this volume, and also in Weil 1998.
21. Epstein 1978.
22. See van Beek in this volume.
23. For example, there are restrictions on females touching the Ndòmò masks of the Bamana discussed by Mary Jo Arnoldi, as well as for the traditional Afikpo Igbo boys' masquerades of Nigeria described by Simon Ottenberg; both authors have essays in this volume. African boys sometimes place taboos on their masks and some of their activities, exacting fines from girls, and even, on occasion, from women who violate them.
24. vander Heyden 1977 discusses Yoruba boys' masking as part of an Epa masquerade at an Elefon festival at Iloro, which differs in appearance from Ojo's description. The boys wear headpieces of a stylized human face with horns, colored with black dots on a light surface, and with raffia hanging from the headpiece to the waist or knees.
25. Drewal and Drewal 1975; Lawal 1996.
26. Frankel 1986a, 1991.
27. Drewal and Drewal 1975, 36, and figs. 1 and 2.
28. Drewal and Drewal 1975, 36.
29. Drewal and Drewal 1983, 105-106.
30. Drewal 1979, 220-221.
31. Drewal and Drewal 1983, 106.
32. Also see Harper 1970, 71-72, and Ibitokun 1981, for brief accounts of boys' masquerading in Gelede festivals.
33. Rowland Abiodun, personal communication to Simon Ottenberg, 1991.
34. Aremu 1983 mentions an Egungun children's masquerade, Kundoke, which entertained in semi-tight costumes of hand-woven traditional cloth, prepared in such a way as to allow intricate steps and acrobatics.
35. Frankel 1986b, 1991.
36. Frankel 1986c, 1991.

37. Beier c. 1963, 13.
38. Several instances of boys' masquerades in Burkina Faso that fall into our Integrated Masquerade category are cited by Roy (1987a, 138-40, 140, 218, and fig. 110; 1987b, 42). The most interesting one is in a Nunuma masquerade. "At most Nunuma performances one or two monkey masks are worn by young boys who had shown special talent as performers. They provide crowd control, and like monkeys in the wild, mimic human actions in ribald performances that move the audience to laughter and loud applause" (Roy 1987a, 218; also see Roy 1987b, 42).
39. But see N. Leis 1982, who indicates where children among the Ijaw of southern Nigeria are believed born with power, gradually losing much of it as they mature.
40. Phillips 1995, 68.
41. Other Congo boys' masquerades are briefly discussed by Merriam 1978, 98-99; 1982, 29-31 for the Songye, and Petridis 1999, 46, for the Beena Luluwa.
42. Also see Ottenberg 1975, 57-60, 186-187, figs. 28 and 68; 1982a; 1989a, 62-81.
43. Schwartzman 1983.
44. For further references to both of these masquerade forms see Nicholls, 1984, 1985, 1986, 1988, n.d.
45. Horton 1963, 100-101.
46. P. Leis 1972, 27, 62, 64.
47. P. Leis 1972, 64.
48. Jones 1984, 61-62, 138, 209, fig. 13; 1989 62-63, fig. 52.
49. Jones 1984, 61-62.
50. Personal communication to Simon Ottenberg.
51. Foss 1973, 25 and fig. 4.
52. Boston 1960, 56-57.
53. Cole and Aniakor 1984, 118, and figs. 217-218.
54. For other examples of Igbo boys' masquerades, see Cole and Aniakor 1984, 112-113, who mention boys' masking that imitate adult types, including Okoroshi. Also see Anon 1957, in the city of Aba. Aniakor 1978 discusses Igbo boys' masquerades at Nsukka. Nicholls, in his chapter in this volume, mentions two Igbo boys' masks that appear to derive from adult forms.
55. Reinhardt 1976, 30, and fig. 31.
56. Reinhardt 1976, 41. Also see the section on the Integrated Masquerades in our introduction, where Ruth Phillips discusses the boy's nafali masquerade among the central and western Mende. There its place in the masquerading culture differs from that of the eastern Mende described by Reinhardt.
57. Reinhardt 1976, 30-31.
58. Oguibe 1989.
59. For example, see Erny 1973; Hollos and P. Leis 1989; Gelfand 1979; Lancy 1996; P. Leis 1972: Lijembe 1967; Read 1959. These publications provide numerous examples of emulative learning, although they do not necessarily employ that term.
60. Aries 1962: Jenks 1996, 62-67.
61. Also see Cannizzo 1978, 1983.
62. For Freetown masquerading, mostly adult in nature, see Kreutzinger 1966; Little 1951; Nunley 1981, 1982, 1984, 1987, 1988a, 1988b.
63. Aries 1962.
64. Béart 1955, 577, 580-583, figs. 425, 619; Kam Sie 1986, 93, 103; Hinckley 1985, 1986. Bravmann 1983, 66-67, figs. 51 and 52, discusses Dodo among the Dyula of Bobo Dioulasso.
65. Meek 1925, vol. 1, xvi, and vol. 2, 18-20; Hinkley 1985, 1986; Kam Sie 1986.
66. Kam Sie 1986, 93, 98-99.

67. Hinckley 1983, 42.
68. Balogun 1969, 44.
69. Argenti, 2001.
70. Personal communication to Simon Ottenberg. Also see Lamp 1996.
71. Christian K. Hoejbjerg, personal communication to Simon Ottenberg.
72. Warren d'Azevedo, personal communication to Simon Ottenberg, 1991.
73. Ottenberg 1975, 89, fig. 29.
74. Phillips 1995, 61-62, and figs. 3.11 and 3.12a-d.
75. Phillips 1995, 61.
76. Alldridge 1910, 196, calls it "nafari." Also see the plate on the opposite page, where nafali is clearly a child masquerader accompanying an adult Gbini. See the discussion of nafali among the eastern Mende by Loretta Reinhardt in the Emulating Masquerades section of the Introduction.
77. Yoshida, 235 in our text.
78. Also see the essays in this volume by Cameron and Jordan, where children's songs are adopted by adult male initiators. Ottenberg 1982b further discusses this matter.
79. Bravmann 1979, 44, 46.
80. See Warren and Andrews 1977, where charts I and V list the Akan aesthetic terminology.
81. Although there is a general belief that no adult masking occurs in coastal Ghana, an animal form, usually called Bush Cow, is occasionally found. McNaughton 1991, 42-44, and fig 5, and Doran Ross, personal communication to Simon Ottenberg.
82. Cole and Ross, 1977, 179-186, and Herbert M. Cole, personal communication, 1992.
83. For Sierra Leone, see Boone 1986; Phillips 1995; for Liberia, see Adams 1986; Harley 1950. Kasfir and Franco, 1998, have edited an issue of *African Arts* that provides further evidence of women's masquerading. Weil 1998, presents cases of nineteenth- and early twentieth-century women's cloth masquerades. Also see Biebuyck 1985, for an example of wives of members of the men's Bwami society among the Lega of the Congo. Women masqueraders among the Bokyi of Cameroun are described in Nicklin 1974, among the Chokwe of Angola by Bastin 1993, 84, and Fancy Dress masquerades among the Fante, by Cole and Doran 1977, 179. Michelle Johnson reports (personal communication to Simon Ottenberg) a female masquerade called *ulo* existing among the Mandinga of Guinea Bissau. Cases of possible temporary women's masquerades are discussed in Weston 1984, and in Staschewski 1917.
84. Philip J. Havik, personal communication.
85. Also see Cameroon 1998.
86. Röschenthaler (1998) describes a situation among the Ejagham of southeastern Nigeria and Cameroun when there was a time that problems so bothered women that they dance naked at night while the men were required to stay behind closed doors. He argues that this was a form of masking. Ottenberg's unpublished researches on the Limba of Wara Wara Bafodea Chiefdom in northern Sierra Leone indicate that during one point in the girl's initiation rites the girls and women appear in the village, and men must stay behind locked doors and shutters so as not to view the rite. Following Röschenthaler's logic this would be considered a form of masking. Arguments have been made by Cameron (1998, 58-59) and others that woman's face painting at rituals can be equated with masking, equivalent to actual masks employed by males. She argues while women do not cover their faces in North-Western Zambia Province, their initiation activities are similar to those of the men's masking societies, and women think of their rites as masquerades. These cases raise issues of what constitutes masking; definitions appear to be broadening in recent

years, and the interpretive skills of researchers are becoming more sophisticated (See Cameron 1998, 57-58). During some Yoruba male masked festivals in southwestern Nigeria, women wear headpieces, some elaborately carved, though without face coverings (Lawal 1996, 43, 44, 54-55, figs. 3.1, 3.6, 3.7, 3.8, and plate 2). Women do likewise in the funerary rites of the Bangwa of Cameroun (Brain and Pollock 1971, 111-113). Lawal 1996, 287, fn. 2, suggests, without elaboration, that the origin of some masks used by males among the Yoruba, the Ijo of coastal Nigeria, the Mende of Sierra Leone, the Senufo of Côte d'Ivoire, and the Dogon of Mali may lie with women. Beliefs that women were the originators of men's societies, including masking ones, are worldwide among indigenous peoples (Pernet 1992, chap. 7). Girls' and women's masking in Africa and their relationships to male masquerading clearly need further thought and research.

87. Ottenberg 1982b. Also see the discussion on the nature of masks in Cameron 1998, 57-58.
88. Weil 1998.
89. Weil 1998, 24.
90. Weil 1998, 90.
91. Christian K. Hoejbjerg, personal communication to Simon Ottenberg. See also Goepogui 1975.
92. Hinckley 1985, 88-89.

Bibliography

This bibliography includes some titles that are not referred to in the Introduction. It represents a survey of the extant literature on the subject of African children's masquerades, as well as references cited in the text.

Adams, Monni. 1986. "Women and Masks Among the Western Wè of Ivory Coast." *African Arts* 19:2, 46-55, 90.

Alldridge, T. J. 1910. *A Transformed Colony: Sierra Leone As It Was, and As It Is. Its Progress, Peoples, Native Customs and Undeveloped Wealth.* London: Seeley and Co.

Aniakor, Chike. 1978. "Omabe Festival." *Nigeria Magazine* 126-127, 3-12.

Anon. 1957. "Asaba." *Nigeria Magazine* 54, 226-242.

Aremu, P.S.O. 1983. "Spiritual and Physical Identity of Yoruba Egungun Costumes: A General Survey." *Nigeria Magazine* 147, 47-54.

Argenti, Nicolas. 2001. "*Kesum-body* and the Places of the Gods: The Politics of Children's Masking and Second-World Realities in Oku (Cameroon)." In *Man: Journal of the Royal Anthropological Institute* 7:1, 67-94.

Aries, Philippe. 1962. *Centuries of Childhood: A Social History of Family Life,* translated from the French by Robert Baldick. New York: Knopf.

Armistead, P. R. 1969. "Bete Masked Dance: A View From Within." *African Arts* 2:3, 37-43, 76.

Arnoldi, Mary Jo. 1986a. "Becoming a Performer. Notes on Children's Play and Aesthetic Expression Among the Bamana of Mali." Unpublished manuscript.

_____. 1986b. "Puppet Theatre: Form and Ideology in Bamana Performances." *Empirical Studies of the Arts* 2, 131-150.
_____. 1991. Personal communication.
Balogun, Ola. 1969. "Christmas at Aba in the Early 1950's." *Nigeria Magazine* 101, 436-443.
Banton, Michael. 1957. *West African City: A Study of Tribal Life in Freetown.* London: Oxford University Press.
Bastin, Marie-Louise.1993. "The Akishi Spirits Among the Chokwe." In Frank Herremann and Constantine Petridis (eds.), *The Face of the Spirits: Masks from the Zaire Basin.* Ghent: Martial & Snoeck; Tervuren: Musée Royal de l'Afrique Central, Sciences Humaines, 140.
Bateson, Gregory. 1972. "A Theory of Play and Fantasy." In Gregory Bateson, *Steps to an Ecology of Mind.* New York: Ballantine, 177—193..
Beart, Ch. 1955. *Jeux et Jouets de l'Ouest Africain.* Dakar: L'Institut Francais D'Afrique Noire, Memoires, 42.
Beier, Ulli. C. c. 1963. *The Moon Cannot Fight: Yoruba Children's Poems.* Ibadan: Mbari Publications.
_____. 1964. "The Agbegijo Masquerades." *Nigeria Magazine* 82, 189-199.
Biebuyck, Daniel. 1985. *The Arts of Zaire.* Vol. 2. Berkeley: University of California Press.
Blier, Suzanne P. 1976. *Beauty and the Beast: A Study in Contrasts.* New York: Tribal Arts Gallery Two.
Boone, Sylvia A. 1986. *Radiance of the Waters. Ideals of Feminine Beauty in Mende Art.* New Haven: Yale University Press.
Boston, John S. 1960. "Some Northern Ibo Masquerades." *Journal of the Royal Anthropological Institute* 90:1, 54-65.
Brain, Robert, and Adam Pollock. 1971. *Bangwa Funerary Sculpture.* London: Gerald Duckworth.
Bravmann, René. 1979. "Gur and Manding Masquerades in Ghana." *African Arts* 13:1, 44-51, 98-99.
_____. 1983. *African Islam.* Washington, D.C./London: Smithsonian Institution Press/Ethnographica.
Cameron, Elisabeth L. 1998. "Women-Masks: Initiation Arts in North-Western Province, Zambia." *African Arts* 31:2, 50-61.
Cannizzo, Jeanne. 1978. "Alikali Devils: Children's Masquerading in a West African Town." Ph.D. diss., University of Washington.
_____. 1979. "The Alikali Devils of Sierra Leone." *African Arts* 12:4, 66-70, 90.
_____. 1983. "The Shit Devil: Pretense and Politics Among West African Urban Children." In Frank E. Manning (ed.), *The Celebration of Society.* Bowling Green, OH: Bowling Green University Press, 125-141.
_____. 1984. "Play, Performance and Social Commentary: The Alikali Devils of Sierra Leone." In Brian Sutton-Smith and Diana Kelly-Byrne (eds.), *The Masks of Play.* New York: Leisure Press, 17-23.
Cole, Herbert M. 1986. "Children of the Clouds: Igbo Boys' Okoroshi Masking." Unpublished manuscript.
_____. 1992. Personal communication.

Cole, Herbert M., and Chike C. Aniakor. 1984. *Igbo Arts: Community and Cosmos*. Los Angeles: Museum of Cultural History, University of California, Los Angeles.

Cole, Herbert M. and Doran Ross, 1977. *The Arts of Ghana*. Los Angeles: Museum of Cultural History, University of California at Los Angeles.

Crowley, Daniel. 1987. "Pan-Portuguese Carnivals on Three Continents." Unpublished paper presented at a meeting of the Anthropological Association for the Study of Play, Montreal Canada, March 25-28.

d'Azevedo, Warren L. 1973a. "Mask Makers and Myth in Western Liberia." In Anthony Forge (ed.) *Primitive Art and Society*. London: Oxford University Press for the Wenner-Gren Foundation for Anthropological Research, 126-150.

_____. 1973b. "Sources of Gola Artistry." In Warren L. d'Azevedo (ed.), *The Traditional Artist in African Society*. Bloomington: Indiana University Press, 292-340.

Dieterlen, Germaine. 1951. *Essai sur le religion bambara*. Paris: Presses Universitaires de France.

Drewal, Henry J. 1979. "Pageantry and Power in Yoruba Costuming." In Justine M. Cordwell, and Ronald A. Schwarz (eds.), *Fabrics of Culture*. The Hague: Mouton, 189-230.

Drewal, Henry J., and Margaret T. Drewal. 1983. *Gelede: Art and Female Power among the Yoruba*. Bloomington: Indiana University Press.

Drewal, Margaret T., and Henry J. Drewal. 1975. "Gelede Dance of the Western Yoruba." *African Arts* 8:2, 36-45, 78-79.

Enry Pierre. 1981. *The Child and His Environment in Black Africa: An Essay on Traditional Education*. Nairobi: Oxford University Press.

Epstein, A. 1978. "Identification with the Grandparents and Ethnic Identity." *Ethos and Identity: Three Studies in Ethnicity*. London: Tavistock, 139-156.

Ezra, Kate. 1988. *Art of the Dogon*. New York: Metropolitan Museum of Art.

Fellous, Michele. 1981. "Socialisation de l'enfant bambara." *Journal des Africanistes* 5:1, 201-215.

Foss, Perkins. 1973. "Festival of Ohworu et Evwreni." *African Arts* 6:4, 20-27, 94.

Frankel, Andrew. 1986a. Videotape of *Gelede* masquerade in Ajilete Town, Ogun State.

_____. 1986b. Videotape of *Egungun Apidan* masquerade in Oyo, Oyo State, called *Ajan Gila*.

_____. 1986c. Videotape of *Egngun Apidan* masquerade in Erin Osun, Oyo State.

_____. 1991. Personal communication.

Fyle, Clifford N., and Eldred D. Jones. 1980. *A Krio-English Dictionary*. Oxford: Oxford University Press.

Gelfand, Michael. 1979. *Growing Up in Shona Society: From Birth to Marriage*. Gwelo, Rhodesia: Mambo Press.

Gilmore, David D. 1998. *Carnival and Culture: Sex, Symbols and Status in Spain*. New Haven: Yale University Press.

Glaze, Anita J. 1981. *Art and Death in a Senufo Village*. Bloomington: Indiana University Press.
Goepogui, Marc. 1975. *L'art en pays loma*. Conakry: Archives nationales du Guinée.
Griaule, Marcel. 1938. *Jeux Dogons*. Paris: L'Institut d'Ethnologie, *Travaux et Memoires*, 32.
Harley, George W. 1950. *Masks as Agents of Social Control in Northeastern Liberia*. Cambridge, MA: Peabody Museum.
Harper, Peggy. 1970. "The Role of Dance in the Gelede Ceremonies of the Village of Ijio." *Odu* n.s. 4: 67-94.
Hinckley, Priscilla B. 1983. "Street Nativities in Ougadougou." *African Arts* 16:3, 47-49.
———. 1985. "Let Them Dance Before You." The Educative Role of Performance in a West African Children's Masquerade. Ph.D. diss., Boston University.
———. 1986. "The Dodo Masquerade of Burkina Faso." *African Arts* 19:2, 74-77, 91.
Hollos, Marida, and Philip E. Leis. 1989. *Becoming Nigerian in Ijo Society*. New Brunswick, NJ: Rutgers University Press.
Horton, Robin. 1963. *The Gods as Guests*. Lagos: Nigeria Magazine.
———. 1963. "The Kalabari *Ekine* Society: A Borderland of Religion and Art." *Africa* 33:2, 94-114.
———. 1965. *Kalabari Sculpture*. Lagos: Department of Antiquities, Federal Republic of Nigeria.
Huizinga, Johan. 1949. *Homo Ludens: A Study of the Play-Element in Culture*. London: Routledge & Kegan Paul.
Ibitokun, Benedict. 1981. "Ritual and Entertainment, the Case of Gelede in Egbado Ketu." *Nigeria Magazine* 136, 55-63.
Imperato, Pascal J. 1978. *Dogon Cliff Dwellers: The Art of Mali's Mountain People*. New York: L Kahan Gallery.
———. 1980. "Bambara and Malinke Ton Masquerades." *African Arts* 13:4, 47-55, 82-85, 87.
Jenks, Chris. 1996. *Childhood*. London: Routledge.
Jessup, Lynne. n.d. "Mandinka Mask Traditions. Banjul: Oral History and Antiquities Division, Office of the Vice President." Unpublished manuscript.
Jones, G. I. 1984. *The Art of Eastern Nigeria*. Cambridge: Cambridge University Press.
———. 1989. *Ibo Art*. Aylesbury: Shire Publications.
Jordán, Manuel. 1993. "Le Masque comme Processus Ironique. Les Makishi du nord-ouest de la Zambie." *Anthropologie et Société* 17, 341-61.
Kam Sie, Alain. 1986. "Le Dodo au Burkina." *Cahiers du LUTO (Laboratoire universitaire de la tradition orale), Universitaire de Ougadougou* 4, 89-95.
Kasfir, Sidney Littlefield. 1998. "Elephant Women, Furious and Majestic: Women's Masquerades in Africa and the Diaspora." *African Arts* 31:2, 18-27, 92.

Kasfir, Sidney Littlefield, and Pamela R. Franco. 1998. *Women's Masquerades in Africa and the Disapora. African Arts* 31:2 (whole issue)
Kreutzinger, Helge. 1966. *The Eri Devils in Freetown, Sierra Leone.* Vienna: Osterreichische Ethnologische Geselschaft, *Acta Ethnologica et Linguistica*, no. 9.
Lamp, Frederick. 1996. *Art of the Baga: A Drama of Cultural Reinvention.* New York: Museum for African Art; Munich: Prestel.
Lancy, David F. 1996. *Playing on the Mother-Ground: Cultural Routines for Children's Development.* New York: Guilford Press.
Laude, Jean. 1973. *African Art of the Dogon: The Myths of the Cliff Dwellers.* New York: Brooklyn Museum.
Lawal, Babatunde. 1996. *The Gèlèdè Spectacle: Art, Gender and Social Harmony in an African Culture.* Seattle: University of Washington Press.
Leis, Nancy B. 1982. "The Not-So-Supernatural Power of Ijaw Children." In Simon Ottenberg (ed.), *African Religious Groups and Beliefs: Papers in Honor of William R. Bascom.* Berkeley: Folklore Institute; Meerut, India: Archana Publications, 151-169.
Leis, Philip E. 1972. *Enculturation and Socialization in an Ijaw Village.* New York: Holt, Rinehart and Winston.
Le Moal, Guy. 1980. *Les Bobo: nature et function des masques.* Paris: OSTROM.
_____. 1981. "Les activites religeuses des jeunes enfants chez les bobo," *Journal des Africanistes* 5:1-2, 235-250, and Plate XIII, opposite p. 281.
Lijembe, Joseph A. 1967. *East African Childhood*, ed. by Lorene K. Fox. Nairobi: Oxford University Press.
Little, Kenneth L. 1951. *The Mende of Sierra Leone.* London: Routledge and Kegan Paul.
Manning, Frank. E. (ed.). 1983. *The World of Play: Proceedings of the 7th Annual Meeting of the Association of the Anthropology of Play.* West Point, NY: Leisure Press.
McNaughton, Patrick R. 1979. *Secret Sculpture of the Komo: Art and Power in Bamana (Bambara) Initiation Associations.* Philadelphia: Institute for the Study of Human Issues, *Working Papers in the Traditional Arts*, 4.
_____. 1991. "Is There History in Horizontal Masks?: A Preliminary Response to the Dilemma of Form." *African Arts* 24:2, 40-53, 88-90.
Meek, C. K. 1925. *The Northern Tribes of Nigeria.* 2 vols. London: Oxford University Press.
Merriam, Alan. 1978. "Kifwebe and Other Masks Among the Basongye." *Africa-Tervuren* 25, 3:57-73, 25:4, 89-101.
_____. 1982. "*Kifwebe* and Other Cult Groups Among the Bala Basongye. In Simon Ottenberg (ed.), *African Religious Groups and Beliefs: Papers in Honor of William R. Bascom.* Berkeley: Folklore Institute; Meerut, India: Archana Publications, 19-34.
Murphy, William. 1980. "Secret Knowledge as Property and Power in Kpelle Society: Elders versus Youth." *Africa* 50, 193-207.
Nicholls, Robert W. 1984. "Igede Funeral Masquerades." *African Arts* 17:3, 70-76, 92.

_____. 1985. "Music and Dance Guilds in Igede." In Irene V. Jackson (ed.), *More Than Drumming: Essays on African and Afro-Latin American Music and Musicians*. Westport: Greenwood Press, *Contributions in Afro-American and African Studies* no. 80, 91-117.

_____. 1986. "The Omepa and Onyeweh Children's Masquerades of the Igede of Nigeria's Benue State." Unpublished manuscript.

_____. 1988. "African Dance." *The World and I: A Chronicle of Our Changing Era* 3:10, 458-469.

_____. n.d. "How Do Igede Children Learn Music and Dance?" Unpublished manuscript.

Nicklin, Keith. 1974. "Nigerian Skin Covered Masks." *African Arts* 7:3, 8-15, 67-68, 92.

Nunley, John. 1981. "The Fancy and the Fierce: Yoruba Masking Traditions of Sierra Leone." *African Arts* 14:2, 52-58, 87-88.

_____. 1982. "Images and Printed Words in Freetown Masquerades." *African Arts* 15:4, 42-46, 92.

_____. 1984. "Urban Odelay Masquerades of Sierra Leone: A Theoretical Explanation of Failure, an Answer to Success." *Sierra Leone Studies at Birmingham 1983, Proceedings of the Third Birmingham Sierra Leone Studies Symposium, July 1983*. Birmingham: Centre of West African Studies, University of Birmingham, 363-382.

_____. 1987. *Moving with the Face of the Devil*. Urbana: University of Illinois Press.

_____. 1988a. "Purity and Pollution in Freetown Masked Performers. *The Drama Review (TDR)* 2:2, 101-22.

_____. 1988b. "Take It to the Streets: Urban *Ode-Lay* Masquerades of Sierra Leone." In Sidney L. Kasfir (ed.), *West African Masks and Cultural Systems*. Tervuren: Musee Royal d'Afrique Centrale, *Annales, Sciences Humaines*, vol. 126, 195-220.

Nzekwu, Onuora. 1960. "Masquerade." *Nigeria Magazine* 66, Special Independence Issue, 135-144.

Oguibe, Olu. 1989. *Statements: Recent Art and Poetry*. Olu Oguibe. The Author.

Ojo, John R. O. 1986. "Öjija: Children's 'Masked' Dance in Two Ekiti Yoruba Towns." Unpublished manuscript.

Opie, Iona, and Peter Opie. 1960. *The Lore and Language of Schoolchildren*. Oxford: Clarendon Press.

Ottenberg, Simon. 1975. *The Masked Rituals of Afikpo: The Context of an African Art*. Seattle: University of Washington Press.

_____. 1982a. "Boys' Secret Societies at Afikpo." In Simon Ottenberg (ed.), *African Religious Groups and Beliefs: Papers in Honor of William R. Bascom*. Berkeley: Folklore Institute; Meerut, India: Archana Publications, 170-184.

_____. 1982b. "Illusion, Communication and Psychology in West African Masquerades." *Ethos* 10:2, 149-185.

_____. 1989a. *Boyhood in an African Society: An Interpretation*. Seattle: University of Washington Press.

_____. 1989b. "We Are Becoming Art Minded: Afikpo Arts 1988." *African Arts* 22:4, 58-67, 88.
Paques, Viviana. 1954. *Les Bambara*. Paris: Presses Universitaires de France.
Pernet, Henry. 1982. "Masks and Women: Toward a Reappraisal." *History of Religions* 22:1, 45-59.
_____. 1992. *Ritual Masks: Deceptions and Revelations*. Columbia: University of South Carolina Press.
Petridis, Constantine. 1999. "Luluwa Masks." *African Arts* 32:3, 32-7, 91-94.
Phillips, Ruth B. 1995. *Representing Women: Sande Masquerades of the Mende of Sierra Leone*. Los Angeles: Fowler Museum of Cultural History, University of California.
Piaget, J. 1951. *Play, Dreams and Imitation in Childhood Play*. New York: Norton.
Primus, Pearl Eileen. 1978. "An Anthropological Study of Masks as Teaching Aids in the Enculturation of Mano Children." Ph.D. diss., New York University.
Read, Margaret. 1959. *Children of Their Fathers: Growing Up Among the Ngoni of Nyasaland*. London: Methuen.
Reinhardt, Loretta R. 1976. "Mende Carvers." Ph.D. diss., University of Southern Illinois.
Richter, Delores. 1979. "Senufo Mask Classification." *African Arts* 12:3, 66-73, 93-94.
Ritzenthaler, Pat. 1967. *The Fon of Bafut*. London: Cassell.
Röschenthaler, Ute M. 1998. "Honoring Ejagham Women." *African Arts* 31:2, 38-49, 92-93.
Roy, Christopher D. 1987a. *Art of the Upper Volta Rivers*. Meudon: Chaffin.
_____. 1987b. "The Spread of Mask Styles in the Black Volta Basin." *African Arts* 20:4, 40-46, 89-90.
Schwartzman, Helen B. 1978. *Transformations: the Anthropology of Children's Play*. New York: Plenum Press.
_____. 1983. "Child-Centered Play." In Frank E. Manning (ed.) *The World of Play, Proceedings of the 7th Annual Meeting of the Association of Play*. West Point, NY: Leisure Press, 200-214.
Segal, Daniel A. 1990. "Trinidad's Carnival and the Absence of Nationalist Substantiation." Unpublished manuscript.
Staschewski, F. 1917. *Die Banjangi. Baessler Archiv,* supplement 8.
Sutton-Smith, Brian. 1997. *The Ambiguity of Play*. Cambridge: Harvard University Press.
Sutton-Smith, Briand, and Diana Kelly Byrne (eds.). 1984. *The Masks of Play*. New York: Leisure Press.
Tauxier, Louis. 1927. *La Religion Bambara*. Paris: Librarie Orientalist Paul Geuthner.
Thompson, Robert F. 1973. "An Aesthetic of the Cool." *African Arts* 7:1, 40-43, 64-67, 89-91.
Ugonna, Nnabuenyi. 1984. *Mmonwu: A Dramatic Tradition of the Igbo*. Lagos: Lagos University Press.

Vander Heyden, Marsha. 1977. "The Epa Mask and Ceremony." *African Arts* 10:2, 14-21, 91.
Warren, D. M., and J. K. Andrews. 1977. *An Ethnosceintific Approach to Akan Art and Aesthetics.* Philadelphia: Institute for the Study of Human Issues, *Working Papers in the Traditional Arts* 2-3.
Weil, Peter. 1998. "Women's Masks and the Power of Gender in Mande History." *African Arts* 31:2, 29-37, 88-91, 94-95.
Weston, Bonnie E. 1984. "Northesstern Region." In Herbert M. Cole and Chike C. Aniakor (eds.), *Igbo Arts: Community and Cosmos.* Los Angeles: Museum of Cultural History, University of California, 145-162.
Zahan, Dominque. 1960. *Sociétées d'Initiation Bambara. Le N;domo, Le Kore.* Paris: Mouton, *Le Monde d'Outre Mer Passé et Present*, Premiere Serie, Etudes VIII.
_____. 1974. *The Bambara.* Leiden: Brill, *Iconography of Religions*,VII:2.

Part 1

Integrated Masquerades

1

Ndòmò Ritual and *Sogo bò* Play: Boy's Masquerading among the Bamana of Mali

Mary Jo Arnoldi

Masquerading among the Bamana, a Mande-speaking group living primarily in south central Mali, has a long history and it remains vital in many communities, today. Masking is a predominantly male activity and its production intensifies the separation between men and women in Bamana society. Adult men own, organize, and perform the majority of masquerades in the community. Their masquerades are an integral part of initiation associations' rituals, young men's public festivals, celebrations honoring local rulers, and entertainments by master performers.[1]

Pre-adolescent Bamana boys engage in masquerading in two differently defined contexts: ritual and play. The boys' ritual masquerades are performed within the context of the Ndòmò association, one of a whole series of male *jow* or initiation associations once widespread in Bamana communities. The masquerades that boys use in play activities are inspired by masquerades performed in the *Sogo bò* festivals which are under the auspices of the *kamalen ton,*, the young men's association. These masquerade events are defined as *nyenanjéw*, entertainments and amusements. In the formal context of ritual and as part of informal play boys' masquerades are intimately related to adult men's masking in their respective communities. Both Ndòmò ritual masking and the Sogo bò masquerade games are important sites for the transfer of knowledge about Bamana aesthetics, the moral universe, gendered personhood, and the practices of everyday life.

In the Bamana world personhood and social identity are gendered and a man's identity is emergent throughout his lifetime. One dimension of identity derives from a man's membership in a patrilineal clan and in one of three socially articulated social strata: freeman (*hòròn*), craft specialist (*nyamakala*), or descendent of former slaves (*jòn*). An equally important dimension of identity is tied to an individual's uninheritable and randomly distributed qualities such as his intelligence, luck, and charisma. Additionally, the evolving status of age (boy, male youth, adult man, and elder) plays a distinct and shifting role in shaping a man's relationships to other men and women in the community.[2] It is the intersection of all of the dimensions of gendered personhood that forms the matrix within which a man organizes, negotiates, and interprets his and others behaviors.

Knowledge and action are conceptually linked in Mande worldview. In the last several decades scholars have analyzed this essential link between knowledge, ethos, and practice in a variety of contexts including daily work activities, rituals, and entertainments.[3] In Kris Hardin's discussion of learning and socialization among the Kono, a Mande-speaking group living in Sierra Leone, she states that "Part of socialization for the Kono, then, implies learning how to act appropriately in specific situations and how to accurately gauge one's authority and social position relative to others. Learning also implies how to physically incorporate categories of emotions that underlie social interaction, how to use action to demonstrate particular capacities and knowledge, and how to resist the demands of those more powerful in acceptable ways."[4]

As part of this socialization process, a Bamana boy begins to learn that control over his body, that is, control over his actions in interactions with others, is the outward manifestation of control over his interior state, his mental and emotional being. The act of masking within Ndòmò rituals and in Sogo bò masquerade play inaugurates formal and informal processes that lead to a boy's acquisition of social knowledge of self and others. The very aesthetic judgments rendered about the mastery of expressive skills necessary for successful masquerading are related to wider Bamana concerns for control and mastery of self through the mastery of one's body in every other domain of production.

Ndòmò Boys' Ritual Masquerading

A Bamana aphorism states, "The head is nothing without the foot." Elders interviewed by Zahan in the 1950s referred to the Ndòmò association as the "foot" within the larger body of adult men's initiation associations and explained that just as the foot is the pivotal support for walking, so Ndòmò plays a critical role setting boys on the path of self awareness, a process that will continue throughout their entire adult life.[5]

According to the Bamana, children are born as androgynous beings and it is only through circumcision or excision that a child becomes wholly male or female. Circumcision removes a boy's female substance allowing him to become wholly male and subsequently capable of sexual reproduction. Oral testimony suggests that in the distant past uncircumcised boys, the *bilakorow*, were initiated into Ndòmò just prior to puberty, but since at least the beginning of the twentieth century boys have been initiated as early as the age of four or five.[6]

Boys spend three to five years as members of the Ndòmò association. At the end of their final year they are circumcised, move out of the association and attain a new social status as circumcised, male youth. As male youth, the boys leave their mothers' houses and begin to share a house with some of their age mates within the exnded family. Later, as they mature and become sexually active they build their own houses and begin to refer to themselves and are referred to as *kamalen*.

During Ndòmò's annual festival, sacrifices are made, new classes are initiated, the masquerade is danced, and the boys participate in a flagellation ritual that tests their stoicism and endurance. The boys, themselves, are responsible for planning, organizing, and carrying out these rites and adult men serve only as advisors to the group as needed. Through their participation in Ndòmò, the boys begin experimenting with and becoming proficient in various roles that ensure the successful execution of both ritual and daily activities in an adult world.

Dominique Zahan has provided the most complete exegesis of Ndòmò rites, the masks, masquerading and the sacred emblems. His work is based on research he conducted in Mali between 1948 and 1958.[7] Ndòmò masks are formally distinct from most other types of Bamana masks used by the various adult men's associations. They are, like the adult men's masks, made by blacksmith-carvers and this accounts for the high quality of the carving and the finesse of the surface decorations found on many of these young boys' association masks that have been collected over the past century.

The mask represents a human face atop which sits a wooden superstructure of horns numbering from two to eight. The eyes, nose, and mouth of the mask are always prominently articulated and refer to the knowledge of others and of the world acquired through the senses. The mask is sometimes called *Ndòmò suruku* or *Ndòmò tara*, the hyena of Ndòmò. Among the Bamana the hyena figures prominently in adult men's masquerades and is a frequent character in folktales. In the context of the Ndòmò association, the hyena is a symbol of ferocity and clairvoyance. A few examples of the Ndòmò mask housed in museum collections have carved feet at the base of the Ndòmò face and symbolize the status of Ndòmò as the first of the Bamana men's initiation associations.

The number of horns on the superstructure of an Ndòmò mask indicates its gender. Masks with three or six horns are considered male; those having four or eight horns are female; and those with two, five, or seven horns represent androgynous beings. The various configuration of horns, also known as *ma kolo*, bones, symbolize various dimensions of experience. According to elders interviewed by Zahan, three horns symbolize impulse and desire while four horns refer to passivity and sufferance. A mask with five horns refers to the need for man to work in order to live. Six horns symbolizes the senses through which a man comes to know the world. Seven horns, a joining of four (male) and three (female) horns symbolizes marriage and society, while eight horns refer to reincarnation.[8]

Each individual Ndòmò chapter generally owns only one mask, although in large communities there can be several active chapters which are organized by residential quarter, each possessing its own mask. In discussing the mask symbolism Zahan makes the point that knowledge of the complete repertoire of masks and their different symbolism is decentralized with boys only being exposed to the particular mask used in their own chapter or to masks used by the chapters of their immediate neighbors.

Ndòmò masks are performed on several occasions and at various different locales during the association's annual rites which take place during the dry season and in the harvest period between November and January. The masked dancer is accompanied by drumming and singing and except when the masquerade appears at the temporary initiation camp built by the boys, its performances are open to men and women in the community. The masquerade appears publicly on the threshing grounds adjacent to the fields, at the village crossroads, and in the village streets when the boys greet each household accompanied by the Ndòmò masker.

Each chapter is organized into three to five classes depending on local custom. In ascending order they are the lions (*wara*), the toads (*ntori*), the birds (*kònò*), the guinea fowl (*kami*), and the dog (*wulu*). Each class owns a special sounding instrument which is its sacred emblem. The first class, the lions, symbolizes education and the opening of knowledge. Its primary emblem is a rhomboid-shaped wooden bull roarer whose fearsome sound recalls that of the lion and alludes to the animal's intelligence, force and ardor of spirit. The second class, the toads, symbolizes reincarnation and resurrection and its sacred emblem, a small friction drum, emits a sound that mimics that of the toad. The birds class symbolize thought and the interior life of a person and its emblem is a millet stalk flute whose high pitched sound is likened to that of a bird. The fourth class, the guinea fowls, alludes to vitality, energy, and fecundity and its emblem is an iron hoe struck by an iron key. The resulting sound mimics the screech of the guinea fowl. The fifth and most senior class is the dog and its sacred emblem is a perforated gourd which when swung through the air emits a sound resembling a dog barking. Domesticity, fidelity, and the movement from nature to culture are associated with dogs in nature and this class symbolizes man as a social being.[9] At the end of their year as members of the wulu class, the boys are circumcised after which they move out of the Ndòmò and into a new social status as circumcised, male youth.

The structure and organization of the association reproduces that of the community at large and of the adult men's associations. The head of the association, known as the *Ndòmò tigi*, owner of the Ndòmò, is chosen from the senior class and takes on a role similar to that of his adult counterpart the *dugu tigi*, the village chief, or any of the men's association leaders who also take the title of *tigi*. The *murakalatigi*, literally the owner of the knife handle, is a position that is chosen from among the senior boys, but generally reserved for a boy from a craft specialist family. This boy officiates at the sacrifices, taking on the same role as the ritual leader in the village at large. Sacrifices include blood offerings of red roosters and goats and millet gruel, or masticated kola nuts that are poured over or spit onto the various altars or objects. Each chapter possesses several types of altars and objects on which the sacrifices are made. These include sacred trees, stones, and constructed objects known as the *bilakorow kolosiba*, protectors of the uncircumcised. Sacrifices can also be made over the group's Ndòmò mask and over each class's sacred emblems.[10]

While the boys understand that the rites, the mask and the various emblems are sacred, they do not fully comprehend Ndòmò's complex symbolism. The full meaning of the various Ndòmò masks, the sacred emblems, rites and songs are something the boys will only learn much later, if they are initiated into the adult men's associations. What Zahan emphasizes in his study of Ndòmò is that the association incites within the boys a philosophical curiosity that launches them on the search for esoteric knowledge, a search that will continue for some of them throughout their lifetimes.[11]

Yet at the level of praxis, I would argue that young boys participation in the Ndòmò does more than just incite a philosophical curiosity. It also provides the boys with the performative means to imagine and enact their nascent social world and to discover its moral, including aesthetic, dimensions. In his study of men's initiation rites among the Kuranko, a Mande-speaking group in Sierra Leone, Jackson demonstrated how "what is done with the body is the ground for what is thought and said...bodily practices mediate a personal realization of social values, and immediate grasp of general precepts as *sensible truths* " (the emphasis is mine).[12] Sensible truths are generally not open to verbal exegesis but are practical habits and truths. In Jackson's words, "Bodily self-mastery is thus everywhere the basis for social and intellectual mastery."[13]

Through their participation in sacrifices, endurance rituals and masquerading, Ndòmò initiates begin to apprehend that control over their bodies is the outward manifestation of control over their interior states, their mental and emotional beings. Ndòmò activities reinforce the values and attitudes that organize and sanction gendered behavior in Bamana society. The boys' introduction to Mande esoteric knowledge, the authority they are given to conduct sacrifices, and their ownership of masquerades and sacred emblems foregrounds their male identity and clearly separates them from women in Bamana society. As Maria Grosz-Ngate has noted, "The ndòmò society...appears to have played a role in the actual creation of male identity. All young boys were initiated and remained members until circumcision. They were thus set apart from girls in the acquisition of knowledge and self-control at a time when they were still considered to be androgynous beings."[14]

Participation in Ndòmò rituals gives Bamana boys a practical knowledge which is grounded in adult men's organizational strategies and plans, and which is informed by key cultural values. Within Ndòmò boys begin to embody moral values, differentiate among various social contexts, and gain confidence in the organization and structuring of behavior that leads to successful action. They begin to act upon those qualities associated with individual aptitudes and talents and even at such a young age, the boys achieve some proficiency in harnessing these talents to successfully discharge their annual festivals. Through practical experience, rather than any verbal exegesis of the Bamana moral universe, the boys begin the process of developing those social skills that are deemed critical for men to function as socially competent actors in the community.

The important role that the Ndòmò association once played in socializing boys into adult men in Bamana communities is well documented in the ethnographic record. Even as late as the 1950s, a survey conducted by Dominique Zahan in the Bamako region revealed that between 80-90 percent of this region's Bamana communities still had active Ndòmò chapters.[14] A generation later, however, the association has undergone a rapid decline, although there are still active chapters in some communities. While Ndòmò's decline parallels a similar decline in men's initiation associations, it cannot be ascribed to any single factor. Rather, it reflects broader changes in contemporary community life. For example, state-sponsored primary schools have taken over some of the educational functions of the Ndòmò. In addition, over the past twenty-five years there has been widespread conversion to Islam in many Bamana communities that once supported Ndòmò and other men's initiation associations. Adherence to Islam and participation in Ndòmò or men's initiation associations are rarely seen as compatible.

Even as the Ndòmò has gone into decline, its memory and power as a cultural resource remains strong in Mali. For example, in the Segou region where I had conducted research between 1978 and 1987 on the adult Sogo bò masquerades, the Ndòmò masquerade was incorporated into the repertoire of some of these troupe's masquerade festivals. In 1979 I attended a festival that included a reenactment of the Ndòmò rites. The community had an active Ndòmò chapter that had thrived up into the late 1950s, but was abandoned before independence in 1960. During the 1979 Sogo bò performance, a Ndòmò masker led a group of male and female dancers drawn from the younger age sets of the youth association into the arena. The young men wore costumes which they identified as once having been worn by Ndòmò initiates and many of the young men carried the signature reed whips associated with Ndòmò endurance rites. The dancers (both the young men and women) followed the mask into the center of the ring and then they sat in a semicircle facing the masker, who danced before them. Periodically, one of the male "initiates" would jump up and begin to dance with the masker. Even though young women were now included in the play, the play's interpretation was still heavily weighted towards the central role that Ndòmò once played in the making of men. The song that was sung for the mask, made references to the Ndòmò association, to heroic male behavior, and to boy's mastery of self through the endurance rites of flagellation:

> eee Ndòmò, here is a branch of the *balasan* tree
> *Ndòmò*, the branch of the *balasan* tree
> a man does not run from under the whip

In the late twentieth century, the Ndòmò mask and by extension its performance had become a potent symbol of both Bamana identity and an even broader Malian cultural patrimony. The National Museum of Mali has a number of Ndòmò masks in its collections and they are on display in the permanent exhibit. Ndòmò masks have been featured in performances by the Malian National Theatre troupe and in the 1980s the mask appeared as part of the official design logo for the Semaine de la Jeunesse, the week-long national youth sports and arts festivals. It was also used as part of a design on a textile produced to celebrate the Journée Internationale des Musées. The mask with its various associations with boyhood, Bamana patrimony, and Malian national identity has now been incorporated along with other Bamana, Dogon, and Senufo masks into a pan Malian visual vocabulary and regularly appears in a variety of popular and commercial contexts.

Boys' Sogo bò Masked Play

While the Ndòmò and other men's initiation associations have gone into decline throughout the Segou region, the kamalen ton, the youth association, and its Sogo bò masquerade theater have retained a strong presence in rural communities. Like Ndòmò, the *kamalen ton* has a long history in these same communities. In a footnote in his study of Ndòmò, Zahan recognized the kamalen ton and its Sogo bò masquerades as an equally important avenue through which young men and women gain access to knowledge and instruction in Bamana beliefs and values.[15]

Unlike attitudes towards Ndòmò or other men's initiation associations, most Bamana communities rarely see participation in the kamalen ton or its Sogo bò masquerades as violating Islamic precepts and values. The young men's association is organized around the principle of mutual aid and it continues to play a central role in organizing labor in both the agricultural and fishing sectors and for local public works projects. The Sogo bò masquerades, which are performed under the auspices of the association, are defined by the community as entertainments and play.

The Sogo bò, the animals come forth, include an extensive repertoire of grass, cloth and carved wooden masks and puppets which represent a wide variety of theatrical characters including bush animals, humans, and spirits. Grass and cloth masquerades are considered the oldest masquerade forms in this theater. However, over this past century carved wooden masks and wooden rod puppet masquerades have gradually come to dominate the masquerade repertoire. Today, the most ubiquitous masquerade form and the Sogo bò's signature form is the rod puppet masquerade.

Most of the rod puppet masquerades consist of two parts: a large carved wooden head and a costumed armature that represents the character's body. On the underside of the head a cavity is hollowed out and a wooden rod several feet long is attached to the sculpture which allows the dancer/puppeteer hidden within a costumed armature to manipulate the puppet head. The armature for the body is covered with grass skirting and/or cloth. These "bodies" are often over five feet high and are several feet wide and four or five feet in length.

The rod puppet heads, themselves, average from two to three feet in height and often support superstructures that extend vertically another several feet. Some of these larger puppet characters also have additional miniaturized rod puppets attached to them which may or may not be independently articulated. Masks and puppet heads are called *sogo kun*, while the entire construction is called *sogoba*, the big animal, whether the character represented is an animal, human or spirit (fig. 1.1).

Smaller rod puppets sometimes appear out of the back of the larger animal masquerade and are independently articulated by rod and string apparatus. These puppets are called *sogoden*, children of the big animal, or *maani*, little people. One of the most interesting features of the Sogo bò theater is that its repertoire has continued to expand over time. In some communities' theaters, as previously mentioned, the Ndòmò boy's mask is now played within the Sogo bò event.

While researching the adult Sogo bò theater I often gained important insights about masquerading and the social and aesthetic values that support it from observing children's play activities and from discussions with children about their impressions and understanding of the Sogo bò theater and its artistic forms. One of the primary ways that young children acquire knowledge of masquerades and begin to develop performance proficiency prior to entering the association at the age of fourteen is through informal play activities. For generations Ndòmò, its rituals and masquerade performance was one of the most important formal contexts within which young boys could begin to explore the nature of Bamana male personhood. Today, boys' masquerade play, which imitates the adult Sogo bò theater, continues to provide pre-adolescent boys with an informal context within which they can begin to imagine themselves as adult men.

During research in 1978-80 I had the opportunity to live in the Diarra household and to observe play activities of the children. Many games the children played involved dance, drumming and song and a number of these games were directly related to the Sogo bò theater. The Diarra children's interest in the theater was piqued by their own fathers' and older brothers' active participation in the annual masquerade events. A number of the adult men in the Diarra household were or had been active in the theater either as musicians, maskers or inventors of masked characters. Adult men provided important artistic role models for young boys in this household. Their wives also play critical roles in actively encouraging their sons and daughters interest in the theater. These women prior to their marriages had been active members of the women's section of the kamalen ton. Following their marriages they continue to sing in the chorus for the masquerade events. These women, as the primary care givers for their children, were key figures in instructing their children in the songs and dances performed in the theater.

Masking (for men) and dancing (for men and women) are important cultural arenas in which gendered personhood is constituted and expressed. The acquisition of performance skills and a person's grasp of what constitutes appropriateness for the Bamana have important implications for understanding aesthetic action and judgments. Appropriateness as defined by Bamana involves how action fits with the group's definition of the context and the definition of the social actor which includes considerations of gender and relative age.

The process of becoming a competent performer and by extension a socially competent man or woman begins at a very early age in a Bamana household. Infants are introduced in the first years of their lives to basic musical rhythms that are defined as Bamana by the group and which are drawn from a variety of performance events including the masquerade theater. In informal play situations, an adult woman or a child's older female sibling, will hold a child on her lap and clap the child's own hands in basic rhythm sets. Later, when the child has gained a modicum of dexterity and is old enough to sit on its own, women will place an overturned container—calabash, tin can, plastic bucket, etc.—in front of the child (both boys and girls). The adult first beats out a rhythm on the makeshift drum and then encourages the child to imitate it. These games are informal, constructed as play, and last only until either the toddler or the adult loses interest. There seems at this early stage to be no gender differentiation in the acquisition of basic performance skills and both boys and girls are encouraged to learn to reproduce the same sets of rhythms.

In a similar manner at this early age both male and female children are introduced to dance patterns in a household setting and through their association with specific rhythms, which are beat out, clapped, or sung, they begin to experiment with particular dance movements and rhythm sets as single units. Once a child has gained even a perfunctory competence in these dance movements, he or she will be encouraged to experiment with embellishing these basic patterns without destroying them. James Brink suggests that artistic expression for the Bamana implies sustaining equilibrium between the cultural identity of the form and embellishments that play upon that form. He states, "Maintaining this interplay in the performing arts is often expressed as *keneya*, a word denoting 'suppleness' but referring to artistic virtuosity in general." Keneya in music and dance, for example, consists of improvising within the format provided by the given rhythms and dance steps, in such a way that the aesthetic identity of these configurations is never lost even though they are broken down, played with and otherwise submitted to the creative "cleverness" of the performers.[16]

Learning to perform proceeds initially from the direct manipulation of a child's body. Later the child self-consciously imitates other performers whether they be older children or adults. Mauss describes this second stage in the learning process as "prestigious imitation," stating that:

> The child, the adult imitates actions which have succeeded and which he has seen successfully performed by people in whom he has confidence and who have authority over him. The action is imposed from without, from above, even if it is an exclusively biological action, involving his body. The individual borrows the series of movements which constitute it from the action executed in front of him or with him by others.[17]

It is within these play contexts that children's musical and dance skills emerge and are refined. Perhaps more importantly for understanding the affective nature of dance and masking in these communities, children not only learn to generate form, but they begin to embody the culturally specific framework that makes these forms and movements meaningful and relates them across contexts to other domains of experience and action. As Bateson and Mead noted in their studies in Bali, mimetic learning is not all form, but to a great degree involves the mastery of content.[18]

Through "prestigious imitation" and not direct verbal instruction, children slowly begin to embody the formal principles that organize the production of various Bamana expressive forms. Because dance and masking are gendered activities children not only learn to generate specific expressive forms, but they begin to master content, which includes a realization of the gendered content and meanings associated with specific forms and the recognition of the formal patterns in others' movements and actions. Learning through "prestigious imitation" is not restricted solely to the mastery of artistic forms. It is employed in teaching children all manner of skills, from farming to domestic activities and from culturally appropriate postures and gestures in daily social interactions to ritual activity.[19]

In the realm of expressive forms, men's and women's dances are associated with different rhythms and with specific gendered contexts. My initial impressions of gendered dances were that men's and women's dances embodied different skills, that is, that men's dances were more acrobatic and their selection of gestures were more forceful. Conversely women's dances placed a high value on graceful and fluid movements. More recently I have become aware of the complexity of the notions of gender complementarities and the values associated with them in Bamana society. Particular dance skills are not exclusive to one gender or the other. In fact, men's and women's dances often embody similar constellations of gestures, movements, and skills. Specific dances performed by both sexes emphasize graceful and fluid movements, while others require extensive acrobatic skills. Yet the mastery of these different skills by men and women has different meanings within specific gendered dance contexts.

Since mastery of the body among the Bamana implies mastery of an interior self, both a man's and a woman's dance performance is read as the overt expression of his or her character and an indicator of his or her future potential. For example, while there are many men's dances that emphasize acrobatic skills, stamina, and strength, the men's *Bara* dance places an emphasis on grace, elegance, and finesse, rather than any overt display of acrobatic ability. In a recent thesis on arts festivals by Younoussa Toure, he described the men's Bara in Segou as a "a dance of seduction." In the performance, young men dance to be observed and admired by young women. Within the Bara women praise the exceptionally graceful male dancer and they interpret his mastery of the dance as an indication of essential character traits—gentleness and benevolence—traits that young women look for in a future husband.[20]

Similarly, there are a large number of women's dances that emphasize this same grace and fluidity of movement that men master in the Bara. In 1998 I attended a performance of the popular women's dance, *Ko file*, which demands acrobatic skills, overt strength, and vigor. The young women gather around a circle and their dancing is accompanied by a young men's drum team. Individuals are encouraged to step into the circle and perform. The dance requires strength and agility in order to maintain one's balance while twirling to increasingly faster drumming at the same time as the dancer flings her arms backwards over her head in a sweeping arc. Like the men's Bara dance, the Ko file is characterized as a seduction dance. While individual dancers win praise from their female peers, young men watching from the sidelines also praise those young women who can perform the Ko file. They see a young woman's mastery of this dance as a mark of her energy, vigor, and health, an indication of her future success in her role as wife and mother. As one young man in Segou, who Toure interviewed about the import of the Ko file stated, "It is not unusual to see young men compete with one another for the affections of an ugly woman who is strong and vigorous."[21]

It is my impression from watching the younger Diarra children and their friends that through a variety of play activities young boys and girls gain a practical knowledge of all of these dances, that is, those that embody graceful, elegant movements and those that foreground acrobatic and more overtly athletic skills. At the same time they are learning these skills they are also learning the specific gendered contexts in which one skill or another is valued and judged to be appropriate. This shared universe of dance skills and the growing understanding of social appropriateness has implications for thinking about how adult men and women make judgments about the others skill in a variety of dance and masquerade performances. Men's and women's knowledge and practical mastery of a wide range of dance skills, movements, and gestures and their knowledge of drumming and song does have implications for understanding how aesthetic evaluations are made about performances in the Sogo bò. As Jackson noted for the Kuranko, a Mande speaking group in Sierra Leone:

...the principle of sexual complementarity in Kuranko society can only be viable if Kuranko men and women periodically recognize the other in themselves and see themselves in the other. Mimesis, which is based upon bodily awareness of the other in oneself, thus assists in bringing into relief a reciprocity of viewpoints.[22]

In the Sogo bò theater, women who praise the drumming or dancing of a male performer are basing their aesthetic evaluations on their practical knowledge of Bamana drumming and dancing. These are skills that they have acquired beginning in childhood and thus their evaluations are not as untrained observers. The reverse is also true. Men's evaluations of women's dancing and their imitation and sometimes parody of women in the theater demand a practical knowledge of a variety different women's dances. Two examples from a 1979 Sogo bò performance stand out in this regard. In the performance of *Jobali*, a beautiful masked woman character, two masked male dancers competed with each other while imitating an elegant woman's dance. In the latter half of the two maskers' performance the young women's section put forth two of its own highly regarded women dancers to perform alongside the male masqueraders, implicitly engaging the maskers in a dance competition. Later in the same event, a male masquerader appeared as the female character, *Taasi doni*. He launched into a parody of a woman's dance by exaggerating the upper body and hip and pelvic movements to give a heightened sexuality to the performance, much to the delight of young men in the audience. But, again, as in the Jobali sequence, a young woman entered the ring to dance with the masker. She pulled him back from the parody by playfully challenging him to match or exceed her mastery of the original dance. In this case in order to create a successful and credible performance and to meet the young woman's challenge the male masker was expected to have mastered the basic movements of the original dance from which he had originally built his parody.

Each year following the millet harvest in January, young boys between the ages of five and ten often make miniature Sogo bò masquerade toys from millet stalks and bits of scrap cloth for the costumes (fig. 1.2). Girls rarely participate in making these toys. The boys work diligently on their toy masquerades with older brothers advising or lending a helping hand. The boys pay close attention to capturing what they understand to be the critical visual elements that identify particular masquerade characters. Giraffes have long necks and short ears and bush buffalos have broad sweeping horns. Once they have completed the toys they incorporate them into mini performances. Their mothers and sisters will sometimes pause from their household chores to join in the performance for a few minutes to provide the vocal accompaniment to the boys' masquerade play. These games would continue sporadically for several weeks until the fragile millet stalk toys were thoroughly broken and the boys' interest in the toys was spent. I noticed that once the boys had abandoned their masquerade toys, their young sisters might rescue the toy and begin to play with it, but theirs was generally a solitary play. Older women did not actively discourage the girls' play, but they did not join in as they had done during the boys' play since masquerading is not the purview of women in these Bamana communities.

Some boys also own scaled-down versions of wooden masks that are used in the adult Sogo bò theater. Most of these masks were carved expressly for them by adult smiths and the character the mask represented was clearly identifiable. However, in a few cases, a young boy, who was himself from a blacksmith family and was an apprentice carver, would make his own small-scale mask to be used during the Sogo bò game. These young blacksmiths modeled their own masks on those made by adult blacksmiths for the adult theater. While the skill in execution was variable, it was far from rudimentary, and often quite accomplished. Even I, a novice to this masquerade world, had little trouble in recognizing the characters being portrayed.

Children generally brought out their masks in the weeks just prior to the adult masquerade performances when anticipation of the coming event was high. Groups of young boys would organize their own masked performance and they exhibited a surprisingly thorough understanding of how the performance was structured and an understanding of performance roles appropriate to men and to women at these events. Because adult men own the masquerades, it was always boys who took the role of masqueraders. Women are the singers for the adult masquerades and young girls took the role of chorus during the children's masquerade play.

I observed a number of these mini performances which were held in front of one of the boys houses. An older boy always emerged as the leader and chief organizer of the play and he assigned the other boys and girls to appropriate roles. In preparation for the event, the boys would organize the dance space by dragging out benches or chairs from the house. The boys would then direct the girls to be seated together in a group to take the role of chorus. Toddlers would be relegated to the role of audience and were seated, sometimes with great difficulty, in a circle on the ground. One of the boys, generally the owner of the mask, would take the first turn as the masquerader accompanied by one or two other boys as his attendants. As the game progressed, other boys took their turns dancing the mask, although girls were never allowed to do so. Adults did not participate in the games, although they often stopped to watch the children from the sidelines. They noted which of the boys emerged as the leader; how well the different boys danced the masquerade; which girls demonstrated particular talents for singing.

Young boys also engaged in short spontaneous performances on the day of the Sogo bò festival itself. They were always the first to arrive at the dance plaza and they were always in high spirits. The boldest of the boys would pick up the association drums which were lying near the meeting house and they would begin to play and their mates would begin to dance and sing. A few of the boys wrapped themselves in discarded bits of grass skirting that they had salvaged from behind the scenes and would create makeshift costumes and dash around the dance circle imitating one of their favorite masquerades, *Gòn*, the Baboon. As the adults slowly began to take their seats and the association drum team arrived, the boys' play was abruptly brought to an end. The drummers reclaimed their instruments and the boys were sternly directed to leave the circle. As the audience gathered for the Sogo bò performance, minicircles quickly formed and reformed on the sidelines as toddlers and young children were thrust forward to dance, encouraged by the clapping and singing of their peers, sisters, and mothers.

Through their attendance at the annual masquerade theater and through their participation in masquerade games organized and dominated by the boys, children begin to experiment with reproducing these events, with conceptualizing particular constellations of drum rhythms, dances and masquerades as single units and associating these expressive forms with particular masquerade personae in the theater. Throughout childhood boys and girls experiment with performance forms. Out of these play experiences their own judgments about skills emerge and are refined. More importantly, for understanding the affective nature of art in these communities, children not only learn to generate form, they also embody the culturally specific framework that makes these forms and movements meaningful and relates them across contexts to other domains of experience and action. Children, who are in the process of learning songs, drum rhythms, and dances in Segou communities, learn not only to reproduce more and more complex formal configurations, they learn to reproduce them in culturally appropriate ways and in culturally appropriate contexts. They are not only learning to sing, play music, or dance, but they are also learning through praxis the culturally specific evaluative criteria applied to these expressive forms.

I became aware of the sophistication of children's knowledge of the Sogo bò theater when I showed photographs of the masquerades to the children in my household. Already at the age of four or five, the children responded to each image by launching into the masquerade's song and dancing its dance. A similar response was elicited from the children if I played a tape recording of a particular masquerade song. The group always responded to the song by jumping up to dance often overlaying the dance with hand and body gestures that imitated the movement of the masquerade. For instance, they would generally raise and lower one arm in imitation of the Giraffe mask. To imitate Bush Buffalo they would bend over and lumber around the courtyard, while for any of the antelopes they would move swiftly, often leaping as they danced.

One afternoon in 1980, after I had played a series of masquerade songs, Kogo Diarra, who was then twelve, brought me a series of drawings that he had made of the different masquerades. The characters were immediately identifiable and the drawings exhibited his knowledge of the critical visual elements that identify an individual character for the audience in the theater. For example when he drew the character *Bilanjan*, a bush masquerade, he made it appropriately tall with long extended appendages. His drawing of *Waraba caco*, a wild cat, captured the masquerades distinctive barrel-shaped body, its large teeth and its beard (figs. 1.3, 1.4). His *Misi*, Bull, had large curving horns and his drawing of *Mali kònò*, a large fishing bird, captured its distinctive beak and its elaborate crown feathers.

By the time that boys and girls reach adolescence and become members of the kamalen ton and are expected to perform publicly, most already have a working knowledge of the structure and content of the Sogo bò theater. This knowledge is gained both through nearly a decade of their attending the adult theater and through practical experience which they gain in the games that they devise to imitate these performances. In the context of play activities, boys experiment with the various theatrical roles reserved for men in the adult theater; while girls attend to those reserved for woman. It is out of this experiential knowledge of gendered performance that skill develops and judgments made about skill emerge.

Mastery of the masquerade theater involves much more than a mastery of its form. Acquiring knowledge of the culturally appropriate ways of acting, thinking, and feeling in specific contexts is an essential part of becoming a competent social actor. It involves an individual's understanding of how theatrical action fits with the definition of the Sogo bò as ludic. It includes an awareness of the social identity and the nature of relationships among actors and between performers and their audience that is based on culturally defined notions of gender and relative age. It calls for the recognition and reproduction of appropriate behavior within the theatrical setting. Adults encourage children to become involved in masquerade play not because they see these games only as a fertile training ground for future maskers, drummers, dancers, and singers, but because they know that these games play an important role in moving boys and girls towards becoming socially competent men and women within a larger social field. Young boys as maskers, musicians, and dancers, and young girls as singers and dancers, begin to gain a measure of competency as theatrical actors and as social actors and they begin to acquire a practical knowledge about the Bamana social world and the moral values and emotions that support it.

Masquerading, like many gendered activities in everyday life in Bamana society, is so sanctioned by tradition and has become naturalized over time that I never found that either men or women questioned its ownership by men in the formal contexts of ritual or entertainment, or even in the informal context of children's play. Boys' masquerade activities—whether ritual or play—foreground the categories of social status and gender, at the same time that they contribute to each boy's growing self-awareness and the development of his personal skills and attributes. How boys learn to perform masquerades and how they learn to organize masquerade events provides important insights into the production of adult masquerading and the ways it is evaluated and interpreted.

It also provides ways of thinking about the processes through which Bamana personhood and male and female identity are constructed.

Successful masquerading demands that boys in their roles as owners of the masks, organizers of the events, masqueraders, musicians, and dancers and girls as singers and dancers orient their individual actions towards cooperation, stability, and expressions of respect. Simultaneously, masquerading provides an arena within which Bamana boys and girls can begin to exercise, develop, and experiment with their individual capacities, which they ideally put to the service of organizing and successfully carrying out this collective action. This orientation guides masquerade events in much the same way as it guides successful community governance and agricultural production. Bamana boys ritual masquerading and children's masquerade play provide formal and informal contexts in which emerging social competency is effected through budding performance competency.

Notes

1. Arnoldi 1995; McNaughton 1988, Zahan 1960, 1980.
2. Grosz-Ngate 1989, 173.
3. Bird and Kendall 1980; Brink 1980, 1981; Grosz-Ngate 1986, 1989; Hardin 1987, 1993; McNaughton, 1988.
4. Hardin 1993, 206.
5. Zahan 1960, 51.
6. Dieterlen 1951, 170.
7. Zahan 1960.
8. Zahan 1960, 85.
9. Zahan 1960, 52-73.
10. Zahan 1960, 88-91.
11. Zahan 1960, 87.
12. Jackson 1983, 337.
13. Gosz-Ngate 1989, 174.
14. Zahan 1960.
15. Zahan 1960, 12, n. 3.
16. Brink 1981, 12.
17. Mauss 1979, 102.
18. Bateson and Mead 1942.
19. Hardin 1987, 180-191.
20. Toure, 1996, 59.
21. Toure 1996, 60.
22. Jackson 1983, 336.

Bibliography

Arnoldi, Mary Jo. 1995. *Playing with Time: Art and Performance in Central Mali.* Bloomington: Indiana University Press.

Bateson, Gregory, and Margaret Mead.1942. *Balinese Character: A Photographic Analysis.* Special publication no. 2. New York: New York Academy of Sciences.

Bird, Charles, and Martha Kendall.1980. "The Mande Hero." In I. Karp and C. Bird (eds.), *Explorations in African Systems of Thought.* Bloomington: Indiana University Press.

Brink, James. 1980. "Organizing Satirical Comedy in Kote-talon: Drama as a Communication Strategy among the Bamana of Mali." Ph.D. diss., Indiana University.

_____. 1981. "Dialectics of Aesthetic Form in Bamana Art: An Introduction." Unpublished paper. Presented at the University of Wisconsin, Milwaukee.

Dieterlen, Germaine. 1951. *Essai sur la Religion Bambara.* Paris: Presses Universitaires de France.

Grosz-Ngate, Maria. 1986. "Bambara Men and Women and the Reproduction of Social Life In Sana Province, Mali." Ph.D. diss., Michigan State University.

_____. "Hidden Meanings: Explorations into a Bamana Construction of Gender." *Ethnology* 28, 2 (1989): 167-183.

Hardin, Kris. 1987. "The Aesthetics of Action: Production and Re-Production in a West African Town." Ph.D. diss., Indiana University.

_____. 1993. *The Aesthetics of Action: Continuity and Change in a West African Town.* Washington, D.C.: Smithsonian Institution Press.

Jackson, Michael. "Knowledge of the Body." *Man* (n.s.) 18, 2 (1983): 327-345.

Mauss, Marcel. 1979. "Body Techniques." In his *Sociology and Psychology.* London: Routledge and Kegan Paul.

McNaughton, Patrick. 1988. *The Mande Blacksmiths: Knowledge, Power and Art in West Africa.* Bloomington: Indiana University Press.

Toure, Younoussa. 1996. "La Biennale Artistique et Culturelle du Mali (1962-1988): Socio-anthropologie d'une action de politique culturelle africaine." Doctorat Nouveau Regime, Ecole des Hautes Etudes en Sciences Sociales, Marseille.

Zahan, Dominique. 1960. *Sociétés Initiation de Bambara, le Ntomo, le Komo.* The Hague: Mouton.

_____. 1980. *Antilopes du Soleil: Arts et rites agraires d'Afrique noire.* Vienna: Editions Schendl.

2

Boys and Masks among the Dogon

Walter E.A. van Beek

A Fox Funeral

Aninyu, one of the fox diviners of the Dogon village of Tireli in Mali, has a problem. The wild desert fox that used to come at night to the small patch over in the bush where he did his divination does not show up any longer. Or so it seems. For several weeks now there have been no traces in the neat rectangular pattern in the sand each morning, dotted with symbols; when Aninyu goes out to inspect the result of the previous evening's divination *yurugu* has not been there. In consultation with Meninyu, one of the main officiators in sacrifice, a renowned lineage elder, they conclude that the fox must be dead. A funeral is due, as foxes and cats receive the attention that is bestowed on adult men. However, this funeral of a fox spells work for the boys of the village. Meninyu's son-in-law Dogolu, who happens to be present when the two men discuss the problem, offers his welcome help. As one of the leading younger men in the village, and father of a great number of sons, he will have a pivotal role in the ritual. They decide that the fox burial will be held after the next market.

When the sun nears the western cliff in the later afternoon, the three men set out, some twenty children trailing them. Dogolu carries an hourglass drum, Meninyu a sack with some ritual paraphernalia; the boys carry sorghum stalks; one larger boycarries a jar of beer. The group of boys stretches out in long Indian file behind the older men. They arrive at the *yurugu mine* (fox field) way out in the dunes, though still in view of the village. Responsible for this spot, Aninyu takes off his shoes and enters the fenced enclosure, which is filled with three parallel sand beds, a meter wide and some five meters long. He squats down at the altar stone of the fox, a small flat stone near the entrance. His right hand brushing some *sadele* leaves over the stone, Aninyu intones his usual invocation:

> *Lèwè*, good evening, good evening
> *Lèwè*, greetings in the evening
> *Lèwè* his evening be greeted
> *Yurugu,* good evening
> *Yurugu*, greetings in the evening
> *Yurugu*, this evening be greeted
> greetings in coming
> greetings in going
> give us the traces of your feet
> speak the truth
> tell us the truth
> do not tell any lies
> do not tell fables
> do not tell me things that are not correct
> do not cover anything
> remove your bad things
> your spoiled things
> tell us the truth
> *Lèwè*, call your people.

This time, this standard invocation will serve as the start of the funeral, not the divination. The others do not enter, but prepare for the festival. With great care the boys prepare their "guns," the intricate and fragile contraptions they usually fabricate from sorghum stalks: the bent fibers should give enough pressure on the ultra-light "bullet" that a minute shake (through the "trigger") sets off the charge. Meninyu takes some strips of bark from a small focus tree growing near the fox patch, and cuts it into small pieces. Dogolu, with one of the boys, assembles two bundles of twigs, ties them together into two miniature "biers," and then ties a roll of white cotton band onto each of them: the burial biers. When the preparations are completed, Meninyu, as the ritual master, taps his iron ring to summon all present. With all sitting in a circle, he softly intones the first greeting of the dead, as done at an ordinary funeral:

> *Lèwè* the things are spoiled
> *Lèwè*, they have arrived.
> We humans have no means,
> the people of old told us
> to leave it to God.
> Greeted God,
> things are spoiled, greeted.
> The head has died
> the feet are still not in.

This is the start of a long ritual invocation in which all gods and spirits are addressed. In the case of the fox, the text is slightly shorter than normal, as here only *Lèwè*, the chthonic spirit is invoked.[1]

Just as in other funerals, the deceased are greeted as well:

> *Yurugu* the day has come,
> your big evening has come.
> Greeted with thanks,
> greeted with sorrow.
> *Yurugu yanu* [wife of the fox]
> the day has come,
> your big evening has come.
> Greeted with thanks.

The arrival of death thus announced, the boys jump up, shout and shoot their straw "guns," dancing and jumping in the sand. Their high shouts and loud howls imitate the loud booms, so characteristic of Dogon flint lock guns. When all guns have been fired, the boys quietly recharge their "ammunition." Meninyu appoints the four largest boys as "bearers": in two pair they take the miniature biers on their heads and with great mimicry of carrying heavy loads, their heads shaking to and fro, they run up into the dunes. After traveling a seemingly tortuous trail, they place the tiny bundles under a shrub, dig a shallow hole, and lay them to rest in their *onjay* (grave). Meninyu and Aninyu each take a stick and from farther in the dunes, mark trails in the sand leading towards the divination place: the road for the next foxes to take when they come to foretell the future. Back at the divination ground, the dances are due: first the war dance. Directed by Dogolu's drumming, the boys take their straw guns and start prancing around, mimicking mock battles, which is the first social highpoint of any funeral. With a loud *"tshadak,"* they fire away, to the immense amusement of the men. Then the rhythm of the drum changes, when Dogolu "calls the masks." Meninyu hands out his pieces of bark to each of the children. Clamping the bark between their teeth, their mouths closed, the boys file up in strict order of age, and start the first mask dance, the arrival of the maskers. Twirling, jumping and striding like real masks, they enter the improvised dance ground and make an reverse-clockwise round, until all have arrived. Then the other dance sequences are initiated by Dogolu's expert drumming; each dance is enthusiastically performed by the boys. After the four obligatory dances, the boys settle down to receive the greeting due to them. In *sigi so*, the ritual mask language, Meninyu thanks them for coming, exhorts them to be fierce to outsiders (women!). And he gives them his blessings:

> God has seen you, has seen a good thing. Something big is there,
> something small,
> if anything is wrong, it is with God. Greetings, good heads, who
> came running, all
> The women are afraid.

After the short peroration in the mask language, the boys shout the high-pitched mask cry *"hée, hée, hée,"* and sit down. They take the bark that marked them as masked out of their mouths, and wait for the real praise. Aninyu thanks them in normal Dogon:

> *Sagatara* [strong men]
> you have danced well.
> You have fired your guns well.
> Thank you,
> thank you so much,
> this all depends on you.

Finally, everyone joins in drinking the beer that they brought along, enjoying the bitter taste in the growing dark of the evening.[2]

Such a burial for the fox is essential for the return of a new fox to the divination grounds; without the funeral the *yurugu mine* would still be a place of death, not a place of the future.

Dogon Boys and the Èmna Masks

The fox burial just described may not look like a masked dance, but for the Dogon it is in fact is. The boys dance as maskers, even if only the little piece of bark they clamp between their teeth distinguishes them as such. Thus, during the dance the boys are considered masked for all ritual purposes. They are called *èmna* (mask), are addressed in mask language, and dance all collective dances of the masks. They are not a specific type of mask, as they do not differentiate between various types of masks, neither in their extremely simple outfit, nor in the dance; the boys are just "masked."

This masked performance for a dead fox, which mingles a serious role with intense amusement for all, reflects much of the involvement of Dogon boys with masks. The first major category is the adult *èmna* masks, the masks well known in anthropological literature, and which are collectors' items all over the world. The èmna perform at two occasions; funerals (of old men) and the masked festivals (*dama*), which can be considered the first and second burials for the Dogon.[3] In the fox's funeral the boys danced just as the masqueraders dance at the funeral of a lineage elder. During such a funeral in which an old man is mourned, the boys watch the real *èmna* perform, which come out to usher the old man towards his new status an ancestor. In funerals of other people for whom no masks come out, the war dances are concluded by a general performance by all participants, in which the general dances of the masks are practiced. There the boys join in and without pretense of being masked, without any costume, go through all the dancing routines of the mask, following the adult, initiated men through all the steps until nightfall: for this they are praised and exhorted by their fathers and older brothers. At this funeral, unlike that of the fox, the boys' performance is not essential, just a welcome addition to the long list of performers that hold the stage for most of the day.

The funeral mask dance is only one item on a long list of rituals in the funeral proceedings. As such it is a pale reflection of the larger, longer, and intense performances of the maskers during the *dama*, the masked festival of the second burial. At that time, all masks of the village turn out in full force, dozens and dozens of them, and perform for over a month on many occasions. In these masked dances,[4] the role of boys is marginal. Some boys may assistan older brothers in their performances. For example, the young men who dance the stilt masquerade, *tingetange*, representing a water bird, have a younger brother carry their stilts, wrapped in cloth, towards the dancing grounds. Masked themselves, the dancers cannot carry anything in their hands other than the dancing sickles and sticks that form a part of their outfit. Yet, during a masquerade festival they are vulnerable, for anyone with evil intent might use part of the dance outfit to perform magic with.[5] So they rely on their kinsmen, especially on younger brothers that are looking for their elder siblings to introduce them to masquerading later on.

For the rest of the dance itself, the young children are continuously chased away. Being the most ardent and curious spectators, eager to view and even imitate the dance steps themselves, the lithe boys sneak through the throngs of spectators and easily get out in front. Two masks have the special task of keeping spectators in check, the antelope and the monkey. Whenever spectators crowd in on the dance area they charge ferociously, chasing them back to their proper place. Women are afraid of the masks, even though they are well aware of the masquerader and usually keep a respectful distance. Young boys, on the contrary, are more curious and daring; they tend to challenge the masqueraders, surefooted and fast on the rocks as they are. Though awed by the spectacle, the young boys have a sort of joking relationships with the masks, aware of the fact that their older brothers are dancing, aware of their own future participation as maskers, but still in awe of the imposing spectacle of a fully adorned mask storming towards them.

The term "mask" may at first glance suggest a headpiece that disguises the natural head. Tourists, art dealers and museum curators routinely call Dogon head coverings "masks." For the Dogon, however, the notion of èmna is the whole person dancing in a costume, including a headpiece. Masks are not worn, but masks dance, perform and shout. The total outfit consists of red and black fibers for skirts and arm adornments, a pair of very wide Dogon trousers, a head piece with cotton bands for attachment, plus any odds and ends belonging to a particular mask, like a dancing stick, a rattle or a bronze ax. The essential element in this ensemble, are the fibers; sometimes a few are tied on a stick and are used to prohibit women from entering a water hole: these, too, are called *èmna*. The headpiece defines the type of mask, but the fibers define the outfit as a mask.

The *dama* performance is for the boys a dividing line between childhood and manhood; in fact, it is the second one, after circumcision (see infra), and eventually the third will follow, when the boys see the *sigi*.[6] In principle, after dancing a *dama* a man should build his house and his fiancée comes over to live with him. In practice, with the limited number of *dama* festivals these days, this does not hold any longer. Recent droughts have played havoc with the time schedule of the *dama*, as in many villages the years have gone by without enough harvest to have a large festival.

Still, having one's first *dama* is an important even for a boy at any age. They eagerly look forward to their own initiation in it, that is their first performance, and actually prepare for it. They practice the dances any time that they can, be it at the above mentioned funerals, or also at less official occasions—after a market, after a bout of wrestling in the sands–when they test their strength against the other wards. Still very young, they know each other's dancing skills, and so do their parents and older brothers. As competition, this is an important venue for them. The four general Dogon dances are not all they have to master. In order to arrive at some prominence among their peers, some of the more difficult specific dances have also to be mastered. The most difficult ones among these are the stilt dances and the "tree" or "big house." The first, the *èmna tingetange* is danced on long stilts to resemble the strutting gait and jutting head of the water bird. The costume itself is not very special (either a Dogon girl or a Mossi/marabout, two types of head cover and dress that are fairly popular), but the two-yard-long stilts are quite another matter. The dance requires perfect balance, a sure gait and the ability to stand still on one leg as well. A good dancer not only has actually to dance with the stilts, but should also be able to stand on one leg, clicking the loose one against the other. This, of course, takes practice–a lot of practice. Young boys start by fabricating very short stumps for themselves in some field at the village's rim, and tie these on, hoping no one sees them fall (fig. 2.1). They try to keep their practice bouts to themselves, often practicing unobserved, at least trying to have as much privacy as the very communal and compact Dogon social life allows them. The other mask, the "tree," takes skill plus strength, as the 4-meter long mask rests on the head but is kept and maneuvered by one's teeth, gripping the mouthpiece. The swinging and turning of this demands great strength, which is much admired by spectators. Young boys practice with smaller pieces of wood, but usually at a later age.

Mask making is practiced as well by the boys. During the dry season, after the harvest, they make masks similes out of the light interior of sorghum stalks. Though they may fabricate any mask, the *kanaga* (stork) is the most popular one, in its habitual form (fig. 2.2), or in one of the many more fanciful versions the boys dream up.[7] These play masks, however, are not just children's play; these types of children's versions do function in proper mask dances as well, and, in fact, all kinds of materials may be used. For example, while spectators waited for an adult mask dance to arrive in Tireli village square, suddenly from a house at the opposite end a figure appeared, a small boy wearing a mask made out of a blue sugar box. With only some holes for eyes and a tiny baton to hold the mask in the teeth, this type of carton is ready made for a "mask." As on cue, the boy ran down the steps to the square, and performed the proper kanaga dance, making two full-circles at center stage, to the delight of the crowd. Just before the "real" masks appeared, he made a quick getaway, disappearing to the other side of the square.

In the *dama* performance a definite slot is reserved for the young performers, boys of 11 and 12 years old, just after their circumcision, using a special mask, the hare or rabbit (*jou*). The boys also wear the masks that all initiates have to dance with, like the "pupil" (*bèdyè*) mask, during the period before the main performance, when they hone their skills each night in the bush. The young performers then differ from the older ones only in height. But in the public performances, when all dancers put on their masks of choice, the boys will dance with hare or rabbit masks. Especially reserved for the young and small performers, this is the one type of mask that operates in a group.

In one case, the boys were dressed in the usual indigo trousers, cowry shell shirts, strings of beads, and of course, the wooden head covers. They thronged onto the dancing ground, the largest among them in front, aged somewhere around 14. The old men at the far end of the dancing ground picked up the rhythm, starting with the special drum exhortation of the *èmna jou*. Awkward and shy, as fits their dancing role, the boys slowly moved about in the small square the sides of which were packed with spectators. Huddling closely together in one corner of the square, they turned their heads to look at all sides. Then they spotted the danger. From behind the bystanders, a mask appeared, a large spear in hand, with a terrible head–huge, black, bulging forehead, the teeth fiercely protruding. It was the hunter (*èmna dananu*). His hand above his eyes, he scouted the place for game; suddenly he spotted the youngsters, threatened the scared masked rabbits with his spear and took long menacing strides in their direction, chasing them from corner to corner. After some rounds, the hunter and the rabbits cleared the dancing ground, leaving the stage for a new type of mask. When well executed, this can be a splendid performance, and the spectators love it. If no hunter mask is available, one of the old men who lead the dance, may take his role.

Though these young boys do have their own place in the *dama* ceremonies, they are essentially on a par with masks that demand more skill and strength, like the *èmna kanaga*, stilt, *modibo* and other "adult" masks. Even when only rabbits the boys are still masking, still part of a ritual that is absolutely essential for the well being of the Dogon village. The fact that they play a minor role, does not diminish in anyway the fact that they are initiated as maskers, and that their masks are just as potent and powerful as any. Their youth in no way diminishes their ritual functions; on the contrary the symbolic message of the masquerade festival fits in well with their social position. A short excursion into the masks' symbolic content makes this clear.

The masks clearly express male superiority. In speech the expression "Hit the women," is a normal exhortation in *sigi so*, in the behavior of the masks as well in the symbolism of the masker's outfit and paraphernalia, for example a short stick with rounded top used for beating women. Also, the central taboo of the masks concerns women: they should not come into close contact with masks—headpiece, the paraphernalia and especially the red fibers. Above all, women are not supposed to know that masks are costumed men, though of course they are perfectly aware not only that men are inside but who is inside. Women are not supposed to comprehend the mask language (*sigi so*), though of course they do, and women who are "sisters of the mask" understand the language without receiving any specific instruction in it. The myth of mask origin balances the roles of men and women.[8]

The myth goes like this: Once upon a time the shirt of the *yènèu* (a spirit) was dirty, so he washed it and put it in the sun to dry. From on high the buzzard mistook it for meat, swooped down and picked it up. Up in the sky he saw his mistake and dropped the red shirt near the village of Yougo, where it fell in a field of couch. One Yougo woman in the field to gather some leaves, noticed the thing, took it home and kept it in her granary, well under lock. When a few days later her husband made problems with her, she donned the shirt, took two sticks and scared her husband He fled. Any time she wanted to get back at her husband this happened again. After a while an old woman called the man: "Come, I'll explain. What frightens you is a thing of your wife, red with two sticks. She is in the bush now, go and look into her granary. Take it and when she comes to you put it on and beat her with the sticks. she will run away. But do not give it back to her." "Thank you, thank you, I do understand," the man said. He saw the red thing, stole it, put it on, and when his wife came he beat the sticks together; she fled in great fright.

The man divulged his secret to the village elders, who decided that henceforth this was to be a thing for men. "How do we give it to the youngsters?" "Let everybody who wants this thing, these masks, cultivate tobacco, sesamum, and have his millet sprout and brew beer. Then we will give the masks to the young men." So the old men guard this thing: "If you see a child or a woman, beat them! This is for the old men and the *sagatara* (strong young men). Stow it away safely, not in the hut, but in the caverns. Let no woman see it, this is something good."

The èmna masks, with their head pieces, fibers and paraphernalia are somewhat female; the pointed breasts, skirts, maybe the red color, the jewelry (female beads and jewelry); they feminize the men. Together with the *sigi*, the *dama* address fertility. After a *dama* crops should be abundant, and the *sigi* should lead towards numerous offspring, to a splendid new generation. In both instances the women are absent and men do the performing; the whole mask-

sigi complex is ritually marginalized, and men, by transforming themselves, become self-sufficient in procreation. In the masks the men proclaim their control over the sources of fertility, of power and of life.[9]

The source of that power is the bush, *oru*. Masks are bush-things, representing the power and wisdom of the bush, also the source of fertility.[10] Masks arrive in the village from the bush, first "naked" from the "west," from the direction of Yougo, then in complete outfit from the plains where the spirits dwell. At the end they leave towards the "east" for the next village, and finally for the bush again, back to their place of origin. The central masks for the ritual, the *bèdyè* and the *adyagai*, do represent the bush as such: simple hoods with just two, four, six or more eyes. Many masks are animals, like the antelope, monkey, buffalo, water bird, and hare. One human mask, the *sadimbe*, refers to the mask myth, the woman who originally found the masks. Other human masks are associated with the bush, like the hunter, the shaman and the healer.

Language is a key to this interpretation. Masks do not speak; they shout a meaningless, high-pitched cry, but whatever may happen, they never speak. even when unadorned; speaking is forbidden. They do shout, as animals, but without words, without sentences. Masks are not people: thus they are never addressed or exhorted in Dogon; they are spoken to only in the ritual language. This *sigi so*, a derivative language with a simple syntax and a 20 percent overlap with Dogon,[11] is used in the mask, funeral, and *sigi* rituals, and then only in a one-way communication: long texts, exhortation, and greetings. The old men speak, but nobody ever answers. Also *sigi so* is never spoken, it is nearly always shouted at the top of the voice, even when the recipient mask is quite close. *Sigi so* is a form of linguistic non-communication. People speak to masks as people speak to animals, without expecting any response, shouting in a language that stems from bush spirits who taught the first *sigi* initiate. One indication of the ambivalent position of the boys toward the *èmna* masks is exactly their use of language. The boys will never dare to speak out in *sigi so*, not because they cannot, but because they dare not. Speaking the mask language is the prerogative of old men, of the ones initiated and even of the initiators.

Now, this wildness, with its concomitant power and fertility favors young dancers. They can exemplify these traits just as well as more adult performers. Young boys are less domesticated, more "bush-like" than adults; as such they can easily represent the world of the bush. They do have a privileged position versus the gods anyway, whether associated directly with the bush or not. One example is the fox funeral. Another is their role in home sacrifices, collective or familial. There they are the ones that have to finish to leftovers of a sacrificial meal. Also, when the lineage elders give their blessings, either the very old or the very young are appointed receivers of the small gifts that accompany the reception of the blessings As for the bush, the fact, that the boys are not yet sexually active (or not considered to be so) puts them apart from the dividing line between men and women, not yet party to the opposition between genders.

This makes their intermediary role in the masquerades all the more powerful: they are not yet fully male, and thus an apt vehicle to express the male self-sufficiency in ritual fertility.

Masks for the Boys: Sagiri

Thus far the masks have been called *èmna masks*, seemingly a needless pleonasm, as the Dogon word *èmna* is routinely translated as "mask." However, the Dogon insist that these masks are of relatively recent origin, that is, were "found" in Yougo and from there spread out over a fair part of the Dogon area. Specialists and dancers alike stress that they are not the oldest mask forms. The coming of the èmna masks, of course, cannot be dated, but according to indirect oral evidence and some archaeological finds, this occurred over two centuries ago. Whatever the above-mentioned myth tells, the fact is that the Dogon know and appreciate an older mask type that has been displaced by èmna. This is the *sagiri* or *sanakurey* mask, made only of branches and leaves.

At the end of the dry season, a quiet afternoon is suddenly ruptured by loud whoops and the rustle of dry leaves. More whoops follow, like the cries of the red-beaked hornbills that roost in the valley trees. Three green-clan figures dart between the rocks, hiding behind boulders and huts. Walking bushes, more or less, they are the sagiri masks, the leaf masks of the ritual that marks the changing of the season. The boys who have donned these leafy costumes (fig. 2.3) costumes try to scare–and if they can–catch young children and especially young girls.

This apparently relaxed and funny, frolicking behavior is in fact an essential part of the ritual to start the *buro,* or rite of the year. No sagiri mask, no festival of the year. As with the other masks, each of the adults easily recognizes some of them as their own boys or their neighbor's children, but signaling this would not only be impolite and disrespectful, but even dangerous. The Dogon not only consider sagiri as older than the wooden and plaited masks that have become collectors' items throughout the world, but it is more widely spread. In fact, not all Dogon villages have masks, but most of them have *sagiri*. Any boy can dance in them, provided his father gives millet flour and beer to the lineage elder that is in nominal command of the *sagiri*. It is not just a cover of leaves, but a real mask, and the boy should be up to it. First of all, the boy has to be circumcised (on circumcision see below).[12] Then, not just any kind of leaf is used; it should be from *wènyé*, a tree important in the Dogon symbolical system. If no *wènyé* is available, the *sa* (fig tree) might furnish the branches and leaves, and in some villages the leaves of the *yuro* (*néré*) might be used. Also, each day the *buro* lasts–at least a week— the leaves have to be freshly cut. Rain should not touch the *sagiri*. If rain threatens to spoil the festival, the *sagiri* will dance on a specific rock and the clouds will recede. Any connection with the planting season should be avoided: *sagiri* may never tread on millet and it avoids millet chaff.

As often happens, the ritual element is over when the dance starts, which is mainly fun. But before coming out the sagiri dancers gather in the house of their chief, where they dance to the rhythm of a split drum beaten by the chief, and they drink beer from an old jar "straight from the ancestors." This ritual chieftaincy, of a type usual in Dogon villages, implies that the lineage in question has–or happens to have–the responsibility over a shrine of some sort, either a statue or an earthen altar, a heap of stones, or in this case a jar. His chiefdom does not extend much beyond the yearly ritual drinking around this jar, and the blessings he imparts to the gathered boys. All children who want to dance in the sagiri next season will present him two balls of flour, a calabash with millet and a jar of beer.

For the proceedings of the sagiri, other old men hold responsibilities as well, that is, the numbers eight through fourteen in the social age system. In each Dogon village, or in the case of some larger villages each village half, the oldest men are ranked by relative age. This provides the basis for most economic and ritual power in the village. First of all, the major fields in or near the village are parceled out according to age; the oldest gets a set of fields, then the next oldest.[13] Among them, the oldest in actual age is the *primus inter pares*, the Hogon. Ritual tasks also devolve on these elders. The oldest seven are in charge of the èmna masks. Each new dancer or would-be initiate has to give them gifts of millet, sesamum and tobacco before starting his mask. This ordering according to age does not automatically imply that the men command a lineage. Besides this age-ranking the oldest men of the respective lineages have their ritual obligations in terms of the members of their kin group.[14]

With the seven oldest men in charge of the èmna masks, the next seven oldest occupy themselves with sagiri. Just as in principle the dancers are the younger brothers of the ones who dance the "real masks," the elders in charge of sagiri are the younger brothers of the seven èmna elders. Also the cries of the masks indicate this: the èmna have a three-pronged cry, *hée hée hée*, while the sagiri cry is just *hée hée*.

Nowadays the order of succession in the masks is disturbed in many villages as too many years have passed since the last dama, and almost three generations will have to dance together. However, the new generation of dama dances, who with the next dama will have "graduated" to the èmna masks, will have beer brewed by their sisters who cook a meal and invite their younger brothers. Before drinking and eating the older boys then address the younger ones: "This is your day now. Now the sagiri is yours, till you dance the dama." This will be done by all new *èmna* initiates at the same time. If the rains are early, this transfer of sagiri will be postponed until next year. If the rains are late, handing over the sagiri will occur after the dama, which usually precedes the rain. One reason is that omitting the transfer when the rains allow for it, may keep the rain away.

The sagiri have a clear association with fertility and agriculture. Their caverns where they play are close to the women's menstrual huts, and as indicated they should avoid touching millet or being touched by rain. Yet during the growing season they might be active, if the boys and their sagiri chief decide this. They can perform until the harvest ritual in November, when the first harvest is tasted, the first beer brewed with the new millet, and the blessings are bestowed upon the village, thanking *Ama* (god) for the new year that has safely passed. After this first taste until the buro ritual, the sagiri should not perform. That is the time for the dead, for burials, funerals, and for all of the èmna masks. The sagiri are part of the cycle of sacrifice and fertility, not of the death cycle.[15]

With the coming of the buro ritual the leaf masks appear. The term *buro* is a general one for sacrifice at any of the many types of Dogon shrines the villages possess. In principle each echelon in the kinship and ward system has its own altar or shrine and sacrifices at irregular intervals are made at them. Sacrifices are made at all the shrines, though during the buro, just before the wet season.

The complicated buro rite lasts about a week, starting one afternoon when all people with an altar perform a sacrifice. In principle the lineage system dictates sacrifices: clan and lineage houses always have set altars, small lineages portable ones, while for family heads having an altar is optional. Of course, Christians and Muslims do not engage in these practices. The performance of sacrifices on the first day of buro is strictly ordered. The oldest village man starts the cycle in the early afternoon, with a chicken presentation on his *Léwé* altar, which functions as the village shrine. When he is finished the lineage next in age does the same on the altars of the village halves, after which the clans, lineages and finally the individual family altars are sacrificed to.[16] For any altar sacrifice the meat is just nibbled during the ritual itself, then divided among officiators, old men and young boys.

The day after these sacrifices the *buro* announces itself with the appearance of the leaf masks. Most people are too busy to mind their kids antics inside the leafy envelopes, however, as the *buro* is well under way. This first full day is the first of the greeting days. All men and women put on their best garments. In the morning women of the wards visit all the men, all married women visit their husbands and son, their paternal kinsmen and their sister's compounds. In small groups or alone the women thank the men with loud voices for the year the village has lived through. "Thanks for the way you have guarded the village, keeping it well provided, healthy and in harmony with the gods." Beer is plentiful and the greetings quickly fade into the usual small talk at drinking.

The next morning the men reciprocate the gesture. In their best attire they look up their wives and female relatives. The men thank the women for their work, food ("fire") and especially their fertility. "Thank you that you have given birth to new people, that you have suckled babies, that you have fed the village. Thank you that there is a village at all." The male thanking party gets larger in the afternoon, when the men visit their in-laws. All men of the age set that has started to build their own houses gather at their ward meeting place. Their attire is peculiar. Their "market day best" pandouble, large gowns, hats, and the occasional umbrella and sunglasses, are supplemented by unusual adornments: red necklaces with plaited hair, pendants of red glass, and with sashes around their waists. The ones playing drums and flutes, especially, sport such female attire, borrowing the jewels from sisters. They also put pictures in the rims of their hats, if possible of themselves with their girlfriend or wife; if not, any picture will do. Gathered on the village dancing ground, close to an altar specifically geared for *buro*, one of the elders welcomes the new *kanaga* (age group), speaking as predecessor.

A hush falls upon the eager crowd, when the ritual elder, who is in charge of the altar, gives a lengthy invocation calling on the gods–like in the sacrificial invocation–to bless, protect and fertilize the men. With the eldest of the age group in front, the young men make their way to the other village half, in an Indian file that meanders like a huge colorful serpent through the rocky trail leading east. Drumming, fluting and chanting, happily showing off their rich clothes and marvelous umbrellas, the young men arrive at the compound of the father-in-law of their "chief," the eldest of the age set. Dancing and singing, they enter the compound and profusely thank the master of the house for the wonderful gift he has given to their leader: his daughter. His age mates join him in the greetings, and give some money to the bride's mother and the musicians. One of them serves as town crier; and at the top of his voice he shouts the amount given: 50 francs is hailed as 5,000 francs, a 100 franc coin becomes 10,000 [17]cfa. In the rear of the long procession the young married wife in question enters the compound, dressed in great and splendid robes, with sunglasses and necklaces, to show off her headgear. Her husband has covered her scarf with banknotes; his father-in-law can rest assured that his daughter has married a wealthy man and is well cared for. Like all old men, the father-in-law has not dressed up, and acts very subdued, almost embarrassed with the huge crowd of supporters his son-in-law has managed to turn out. "Welcome, welcome. Sit down. I do not have much in the house," he says.

The visit takes about an hour and when all pots are empty from drinking the troupe moves on to the next father-in-law compound. By now the people of the ward with close links to the visitors acknowledge the visit with large shouts: "The mothers have come, the mothers have come." Visiting, dancing, giving, cajoling go on till well after sunset, and all pots are emptied and the whole troupe, somewhat less strictly organized, returns home, content with good work well done.

The next day people from that ward reciprocate the visit and parades in neighboring villages occur. Comparisons between the number of people and the riches they display inevitably are made. This benign rivalry is capped on the buro's final day, with "parading the market." This is the largest of all occasions, the real test of riches between the two village halves. From early afternoon onwards, people gather in the market place. Spectators from neighboring villages make a huge arena for the procession to follow. The westernmost, "oldest" of the two village halves comes first. Youngsters install two rows of brightly decorated bicycles, draped in gaudy blankets, adorned with everything that shines, for this staging of the final procession, which outdoes all previous showings in length and color. All men and all young women participate, each not only adorned to the brim, but carrying whatever riches one has to show off. Under the approving roar of the crowd, with the blessings and exhortations yelled by older men, the first village half shows off. A troupe of six motor scooters appears, their heavy fumes followed by a throng of decorated bikes pushed by the younger boys. The young women at the end of the line carry their riches: blankets, horsetails and an occasional plastic doll. The older women shriek and sing, shouting praises to their kin. Then the eastern village half comes out with two scooters, seemingly the lesser of the two, but counting on three horsemen in high backed saddles hung with tassels, to carry the day. However much Dogon admire horsemen, the western part is sure to come out first, with its scooters and bikes.

Rain should be imminent now, but some ceremonies may have to be performed first.[18] "Throwing the millet" is one of them, only done the year before a new age set is formed in some villages, but each year in others. The day after the market parade young men gather at the clan house where the oldest, the Hogon, lives. Each carries a millet stalk, accompanied by drums and flutes. The Hogon is frail, so his son gives a benediction and then flings a handful of millet cobs into the waiting and waiving crowd, where next years new *kanaga* members stand out in front. In a general shuffle everyone tries to get as much of this millet as he can: mixed with one's own seedlings this is believed to guarantee a good crop. Drumming, dancing and singing, the crowd then moves on, waiving the stalks, to the next clan house, just around the corner. Finally, all return to the first house, where the Hogon's son gives a last blessing to usher in the rainy season.

> Let salted rain fall on your heads
> you are small bushes now.
> Let *Ama* make you big trees.
> Who has no wife, will get one,
> who has no child, will get one.
> May you all enter into the new year,
> May you all have a next *buro*.
> *Ama* give you health, *Ama* give you peace.

So much for the general ritual, but what of the boys' leaf masks? During these days the sagiri have been in the background, coming into the village each day, trying to catch some still younger children, drinking at their *sagiri* chief's compound each day. By now the girls have grown wise, and taunt the running bushes in song: *"Sagiri, sagiri,* dance, *sagiri* dance, catch me, *sagiri,* catch my cowry." This oblique sexual reference can be repeated in less covert terms:

> *Sagiri,* come and hit me
> come from the bush, lazy one.
> Come and rub my thing,
> come for my thing,
> rub me with your stick:
> with your stick rub my back
> old hyena with the leaves.[19]

The maskers may hit the girls with the sticks they carry, or throw stones. Girls and young men flee and sometimes throw dirt and sand over the players, but no stones. Only during the tour of the market do the masqueraders leave their leafy costumes at the caverns and join in with the spectacle at the foot of the cliff. At the time of the "throwing the millet" they are there again, close to the proceedings, just watching, while at the final blessing they almost mingle with the crowd, for this is their blessing as well.

They may continue wearing sagiri masks until the first rain, or in some villages until the sacrifice on the bush altar (*pegu*) that precedes the cultivation season after the buro rites.[20] These days, the *sagiri* usually call it a day after the march to the market at the end of buro, and finish as they have started, with a sacrifice and a drinking party at the compound of their chief.

In some villages the sagiri have to be present at the yearly sacrifice on the altar for the age group. At that sacrifice, usually done each year in the dry season, the oldest of each age group are present, and the one representing the linage in charge of the altar, performs the actual sacrifice. The sagiri cry out loud when the chickens are killed; after this ritual these leaf maskers run through the village. No strangers, that is persons from another village or the village half, are allowed at this time. Young women present at their in-laws for cooking and the evening meal have themselves escorted home that night, to avoid a confrontation with the *sagiri.*

Circumcision: The First Step into Manhood

In order to dance the *sagiri* boys have to be circumcised. In Dogon society circumcision is not among the large rituals, but still forms an important step of the boys into the society of masks, first *sagiri,* later *èmna*. In principle after circumcision a boy is considered old enough to function as a youngster; ideally this moment coincides with his first girlfriend. After the operation boys normally stop sleeping at their parents home, but take their sleeping mat to a boys' house in the neighborhood, usually an older friend of the same lineage.[21]

Boys are circumcised in principle every other year, alternating with years in which girls are excised. Within the dry season a ward or village half can decide on any date for the boys coming of age to be circumcised. The presence of a dispensary in Sangha has seen the local "docteur" replace the blacksmith who used to perform the operation.[22] As a consequence, the dispensary has replaced the bush as the operating theater. The boys are notified a week in advance, and a paternal relative guides each boy through the operation, assisted by one of the boy's elder brothers, if possible someone from the group circumcised last time. The day before the operation the fathers sacrifice at their altar on behalf of the boy's good health, often following instructions from the fox diviner. With the older brothers and the paternal uncles the boys flock into the dispensary the next morning, cautious that no women cross their path. Following the order of their respective age, the boys are circumcised,[23] the foreskins taken by their "fathers" to be buried under the male washing place in the compound. The boys put on a small contraption of millet stalks to keep the penis free, and dress in a loose hanging long skirt that they will wear until the wounds heal. Ground rabbits' droppings are considered a good means to stop the bleeding. As a group the boys roam the bush around the village during the day. Usually some millet cream without salt (bad for healing) is waiting for them to eat. On the roads leading to the village the boys beg any passerby for money, singing the songs of the circumcised:

> May God heal you and bring you back
> This has given you thought.
> The children of the circumcision have entered the deep
> May God heal you and bring you back.[24]

Any passerby should give a few coins, lest evil fall upon him or her. In the evening they return home and eat as much as they can. During the healing period the boys are very careful not to be addressed by a menstruating woman (bad for both, the wounds would not heal). Nor should their healing penis be seen by any woman, relative or not.

The following days the boys roam the bush to beg and sing. Their older brothers help them to fabricate their rattles to accompany their songs. The last night before their return to the village, a fortnight after the operation, each of their fathers brings them some sesame balls, sesame oil and new clothes, most importantly a new *ponu*–a short white version of the ubiquitous Dogon wide trousers–so important a mark in growing up.[25] The boys rub in the oil considered to be a purification, eat the sesame, throw the millet suspensories away (often burned with the rattles) and put on a splendid white outfit.[26] Their return home that evening is festive and joyful, and may be marked with a sacrifice on the family altar.

The first great collective entry of the boys is at the next market day. First, they assemble at the house of their oldest and dress up. The market is well under way when a white flurry of movement at the north entrance catches the eye. In long Indian file a dozen small boys march into the market, immaculately dressed in white trousers, white shirts and shining white caps with long tassels dancing around their dark faces. The new "young men" have come to drink. One of them, beating a little drum, they show their new status at market. The oldest boy buys the beer, usually from one of his women relatives, and they all sit down just like adults, just like the grand old men, to chat and drink. They take quite a while to finish one jar, and also invite bystanders to join them, just like grown-ups. The circle of white-clad boys, their earnest dark faces in full contrast to the shining white of the clothes, is a delight to the eye for the Dogon who love the display of the spunky youths. Some men offer them "bonbons axe," the throat clearing sweets found all over West Africa, and others offer them kola nuts to chew, just like for the old. Self-conscious, they stay together, hardly moving through the market as most men do, while they thoroughly enjoy the attention given them.

Circumcision marks the end of childhood. Now they are entitled to dance the *sagiri*. This also implies that they have to leave the things of children behind them. One of these, a game leading toward the leaf masks, is called the "old hyena" (*ta pey*) in some villages. Just before their circumcision their younger brothers, still small of course, have cut *néré* branches. Clothing themselves in the leaves more or less like *sagiri*, these small boys dance and sing before their family, begging money:

> Old hyena,[27] who walks here
> roams over there
> who eats anything
> not very good
> not very bad.

In other villages this playful dance is called *taragolugolu* (a creeping plant), but it is danced in the rainy season.

Conclusions

Boys' masquerading activities in Dogon society are well integrated with the main masking endeavors of adult men. The boys learn the dances of the masks at a very young age, in performances that are part and parcel of the main ritual cycle. Burying the divination fox, concluding public dances at the funerals, the boys form the rim of public festivals. Also, their role as the sagiri, with their very own masquerade, has similar characteristics. Where the èmna masquerades can be interpreted as the bush coming into the village, within the masking complex boys are among the first to interact with these masks. As semi-initiated, they are the ones that know a little, dance a little, speak a little, intermediaries for intermediaries. The fox funeral holds the same characteristics. The fox is the essential intermediary in the relations between man and destiny. His death is a threat to this relationship and is mediated by boys, as they stand between men and women, and between men and little children. The boys mediate the transitional phase of the mediator. When the *èmna* maskers arrive in the village the boys are the first to see them, the first to be chased away, the first to sneak up to them again. During the dances they can help out the maskers with small errands, indispensable little helpmates, who one day will be maskers themselves. Their transitory stage is exemplified by their silent and often lonely exertions to master the steps, the stilts and the cries of the masquerade. Curious and eager, they form the buffer between the silent powers of the bush and the learning capability of the village. They do not speak *sigi so* themselves, leaving that to their elders, but they do comprehend a lot. Between the elders shouting their exhortations in ritual speech and the animal cries of the maskers, the boys form the silent rim that links bush and village together.

The boys' own mask, sagiri, is not part of the death-mask complex. Still, their intermediary function between bush and village is clearly evident here. The association of *sagiri* with the fertility of the bush, with agriculture and rain, gives them a comparable position between village and bush, even though the focus is less on human fertility.

The mask itself is a fair example of a "*gusunkenes Kulturgut*," a tradition that has been marginalized from the center to the periphery of the boys' culture. It may share this aspect with other elements in their culture. Some of the songs boys and girls sing during *buro* seem to have been more important in adult renderings of burial songs. For instance, some songs of the first night's wake at a funeral appear to be transferred from the adult group to the younger generation, probably with the introduction of the *baja ni*, the central song of funeral nights.

As for typology, using Ottenberg and Binkley's classification in this volume, the Dogon case combines the Integrated and Emulative masquerade categories, not uncommon in societies with a central masquerading tradition. One reason for the variety of the boys' experience with masking of course, is the intense occupation of Dogon men with masks and masked dances. It is their main interest, their favorite occupation their almost morbid fascination. Nothing interests them as much as a mask dance, nothing offers as productive a topic for conversation as masquerade performances. Children draw masks when presented with a piece of paper and crayon, boys and a fair number of girls as well. Boys make masks out of all things and materials.

When a famous Dutch painter visited the Dogon a few years ago, he distributed paper and pencils in the school. A large majority of the children immediately began to draw masks, and the painter was deeply impressed by the draftsmanship of the youngsters. The realism of their drawings and the meticulous rendering of small details astonished him (fig. 2 .4). In return, he made a drawing on the blackboard, producing one of the many bird and tree drawings that have made him famous. Politely, the children admired his handiwork. After he left they wondered what kind of bird and what tree species he had drawn, as his bird and tree did not look like any species known to them. So, when he was out of sight, they immediately wiped out his drawing, replacing it with one of a masker. Of course, the irony that if they had preserved it, it might have brought enough money for a roof on the classroom, escaped them.

Initiation into masking is a gentle one for Dogon boys. No harsh initiation here, not rites of endurance (these are only for the masters of the *sigi so*, the *orubaru*). Relations between male generations are not fraught with tension, nor very competitive. On the whole, competition is not a central issue in Dogon society. In fact, the masked dances are one of the few things in which boys can excel amongst themselves, but this is made anonymous by the maskers for the most part.

Secrets, in the sense of previously unknown information, are not imparted in Dogon initiations, neither in circumcision, nor in the first masked dance, nor for that matter in the *sigi* initiation. What the boys learn is previously well known, save perhaps the exact route the masqueraders have to take, round this tree, overstepping that particular stone. The only ones for whom a substantial cognitive learning is due, are the *orubaru*, the young men initiated to become the ritual speakers of the village.[28] They are the ones who have really to master the mask language, know the songs and texts by heart, who have to be able to perform the recitations without a minor glitch.

What the boys learn, though, is a strengthening of communal values, peer group dependency, the gentle ways in which competition is possible without becoming disruptive. They hone their aesthetic skills, their dancing abilities and their sense of theatricality. Within their peer group the various rankings become clear. Age is a major structuring principle, but also performance qualities, drumming and dancing skills, and the fabrication of masks. The general cover of anonymity during the performances ensures that competition is palatable with the communal orientation of Dogon culture. Aggression, also easy to hide under the cloak of anonymity, is less obvious. If present, it is directed not so much against older men, but towards women. The discourse in the ritual language is surprisingly severe on women. This may stem from two sources.

First, some competition in sexual matters exists between generations. When boys reach puberty they are expected to sleep outside their parents' compound. the same holds for girls. One reason is that parents are not supposed to be aware of the sexual activities of their children among the Dogon. Though the rule is widespread, for a Dogon man awareness of his son's sexuality would mean that he would have to scale back his own sexual activities. No two generations, ideally, should be sexually active at the same time. For old men in the lineage houses this rule is absolute. If they have a grandson who is sexually active they have to abstain themselves. having the boys sleep out of the house gives leeway, for the parents in this respect, for they do not have te aware of their children's endeavors.

Secondly, the link between masking and sexuality, which boys enter into at the same time, is obvious. The taunting songs of the girls vis-á-vis the sagiri maskers, the feminization of the èmna masks and the not so latent sexual metaphors in the speeches surrounding the masks, all indicate a definition of young adulthood in which masks and sexuality are intertwined. The masks form one of the few arenas for boys and girls to collectively engage the other gender. The ritual appropriation of female fertility the masqueraders embody may be seen as an outlet for frustrations of dependency that are not allowed expression in the politeness dominated interactions of daily life.

All in all, the boys' involvement in masks does form part of a Dogon culture of childhood.[29] Though the passage from childhood to the more adult phases is easy, there is a definite "world of the youngsters," both a concept of childhood and of a youth culture. The children's plays and their masked performances, may be some kind of anticipatory socialization, as they do form a prelude to adult life. The forms they take and the place they have in the children's lives gives the world of the young a distinct flavor. In a culture that is as age conscious as the Dogon, this insistence on a proper culture for the young might be astonishing. Still, it may be seen as a balancing mechanism. The ritual attention given to the young, the admiration for their dressing up (as masqueraders, or as youngsters during dances and the *buro*), sharply contrast with the simple, shopworn outfit of the old men and their place in the curtains of Dogon ritual theater. Though old men are the ones in power, all eyes are upon the newest generation. Still, even if the children hold stage and they are publicly and openly admired, this happens within the bounds of performance, within limits set by the old men. The mutual dependency of old and young finds it expression in the old men exhorting the young maskers, thus reestablishing their own eminence while focusing on the indispensable role of the youngsters in procuring new life.

Notes

1. For the Dogon, the relation between Ama, the high God, and the fox has been fraught with problems, at least according to myth. It appears that the fox was too cunning for the likes of Ama. Therefore, the main god of the fox is the earth god, *lèwè*.
2. After the death of a cat a similar ritual follows, though less elaborate. The bier is made with the white cotton bundles, buried near a senge, or in its hollow (in the case when the corpse of the cat is not available). The boys make "war" with their sorghum guns in the case of a tomcat, and dance with girls in the case of a female cat. In the former instance the boys dance a few masked dances; in both instances they finish with drinking some millet cream, with some *sa* (*pegu*) fruits.
3. Van Beek 1991b.
4. Van Beek 1991b.
5. Van Beek 1994.
6. Dieterlen and Rouche 1971.
7. Griaule 1938, 39-41.

8. Griaule 1983; Dieterlen 1989.
9. Van Beek 1992.
10. Van Beek 1992.
11. Leiris 1983.
12. According to Griaule (1938, 269-72), before World War II only boys just circumcised wore these masks. At present, older boys also wear them.
13. Van Beek and Banga 1992.
14. Also see Paulme 1940.
15. Thus, the leaf masks used in the Hogon funeral are considered something quite different from *sagiri*. Not only are they never called *sagiri*, for they are *èmna*, but they are also worn by young women in a ritual characterized by a series of symbolic reversals (Bouju 1984; de Ganay 1937).
16. van Beek 1988.
17. French West African currency (except Guinea) at the time of this particular event.
18. Paulme and Lifchitz 1936.
19. See Griaule 1938, 269-270; Béart 1955, 624-625.
20. Griaule 1938, 269-270.
21. van Beek 1992.
22. Leiris and Schaeffner 1936.
23. For a description of the former bush procedure see Leiris 1936.
24. See Leiris 1936; Calame-Griaule 1987 (1965), 127; Baudoin 1984, 115-120.
25. Van Beek 1992.
26. The spiral ornamented stick they formally took on has not been spotted lately.
27. The hyena is considered immortal in Dogon culture. An old hyena never dies from old age. it either is shot by a hunter or may die if when drinking water it eats its whiskers.
28. Van Beek 1992.
29. Aries 1962.

Bibliography

Aries, Philippe. 1962. *Centuries of Childhood: A Social History of Family Life,* trans. from the French by Robert Baldick. New York: Knopf.

Béart, C. 1955. *Jeux et jouets de l'ovest Afrcain* Dakar: Institut Francais d'Afríque Noibe, *Memoire* 22.

Baudoin, Gérard. 1984. *Les Dogons du Mali.* Paris: Armand Colin.

Bouju, J. 1984. *Graine de l'homme, enfant du mil.* Paris: Société d'Ethnographie; Nanterre: Service de publication du Laboratoire d'ethnologie et de sociologie comparative, Université de Paris X, Société africaines, 6.

Calamé-Griaule, G. 1965. *Ethnologie et language; La parole chez les Dogon.* Paris: Gallimard.

———. 1987. *Des cauris au Marché.* Paris: Presses Universitaires de France.

Dieterlen, G. 1982. *Le titre d'honneur des Arou (Dogon-Mali).* Paris: Musée de l'Homme, Société des Africanistes.

———. 1989. "Masks and Mythology among the Dogon." *African Arts* 22:3, 34-43, 87-88.

Dieterlen, G and J. Rouche. 1971. "La fête soixantenaires chez les Dogon." *Africa* 41, 1-11.

Ganay, S. de. 1937. "Note sur le culte de Lébé chez les Dogon du Soudan français." *Journal de la Société des Africanistes* 7, 203-212.

Griaule, M. 1938. *Masques Dogon.* Paris: Institut d'Ethnologie, Université de Paris,

Travaux et Mémoires de l'Institut d'Ethnologie, 33.
Leiris, Michel. 1948. *La langue secrète des Dogon de Sanga (Soudan français)*. Paris: Institut d'Ethnologie,, Université de Paris, Travaux et Mémoires de l'Institut d'Ethnologie, 33.
Leiris, Michel and Schaeffner, André. 1936. "Les rites de circoncision chez les Dogon de Sanga."*Journal de la Société des Africanistes* 6, 141-161.
Paulme, D. 1940. *Organisation sociale des Dogon (Soudan français)*. Paris: Editions Domat-Montchrestien.
Paulme, D. and D. Lifchitz. 1936. "La fête des Semailles in 1935 chez les Dogon de Sanga."*Journal de la Société des Africanistes* 6, 95-110.
Pern, S.B., B. Alexander and W.E.A. van Beek. 1982. *Masked Dancers of West Africa: the Dogon*. Amsterdam: Time-Life Books.
Van Beek, W.E.A. 1988. " Functions of Sculpture in Dogon Religion." *African Arts* 21:4, 58-66, 91.
———. 1991a. "Harmony Versus Autonomy: Models of Agricultural Fertility among the Dogon and the Kapsiki." In A. Jakobson-Widding and W.E.A. van Beek (eds.), *The Creative Communion: African Folk Models of Fertility and the Regeneration of Life*. Uppsala: University Press, 285-306.
———. 1991b. "Dogon Restudied: A Field Evaluation of the Work of Marcel Griaule." *Current Anthropology* 32:2, 139-167.
———. 1991c. "Enter the Bush: a Dogon Mask Festival." In S. Vogel (ed.), *Africa Explores: 20th Century African Art*. New York/Munich: Center for African Art/Prestal, 56-73.
———. 1992. "Becoming Human in Dogon Mali.: In Göran Aijmer (ed.), *Coming into Existence*. Götenborg: Institute for Advanced Studies in Social Anthropology, University of Götenborg, 47-69.
———. 1994. "The Innocent Sorcerer; Coping With Evil in Two African Societies, Kapsiki and Dogon." In T. Blakely, W.E.A. van Beek and D.L. Thomson (eds.). *African Religion:Experience and Expression*. London: James Curry, 196-228.
Van Beek, W.E.A. and P. Banga. 1992."The Dogon and Their Trees." In D. Parkin and E. Croll (eds.), *Bush Base Forest Farm*. London: Routledge, 57-75.

3

Gender Differences and Performance Styles in *Öjija* among Children in Two Ekiti Towns

John R. O. Ojo

This contribution deals with Yoruba performances by children in two towns of Ekiti State in southwestern Nigeria. Most field researchers concentrate on what adults do unless the actions of children are too obvious to be ignored. As Audrey Richards noted,[1] researchers fail to record what children do, consequently, there is little material on how skills and knowledge are transmitted; and at what stage of childhood and adolescence the deeper levels of meaning associated with symbols are passed on to the younger generation, especially in the context of rituals and ceremonies.

In the following pages, the role of children in ritual activities with special reference to masked performances will be discussed in relation to the socialization process and the training ground for adult performances.

The place of children in religious and ceremonial activities varies from culture to culture, so also do adults' attitudes toward their presence. Attitudes can range from outright intolerance to encouragement to full participation. But whatever the attitude of adults towards children, singing, dancing, and drumming, these three basic elements of ceremonial activities are learned through initiation as children watch adults either as part of the crowd of adult spectators in public performances, or as toddlers and young children accompanying their parents during esoteric ceremonies.[2]

Available data on the acquisition of performance skills by children in the context of masking can be grouped into three: children's masking as part of adult performances; as part of initiation ceremonies; and lastly as separate performances in the annual ceremonial and ritual calendar.

Examples of the first group include Balinese children using coconut shell face masks in order to be Balinese so as to perpetuate the culture,[3] and the Yoruba of southwest Nigeria, where adolescent maskers participate in the an-

---

Note: ë for e with a dot at the bottom, (e): ö for o with a dot at the bottom (o).

nual cycle of masking rituals, constituting the lowest level in the hierarchy of masking types.[4] Henry and Margaret Drewal[5] have also documented the appearance of young children, fully masked, being guided and critically watched by dance masters during the Gelede masquerade performances among the Egbado Yoruba. And among the Ekiti and Igbomina of northeast Yorubaland, participants in Ëpa, Ëlëfon, and other masking performances include small boys of eighteen months to as many years.[6]

Children's masking as part of initiation ceremonies has been documented and include the Poro and Sande masking societies among the Mende of Sierra Leone and the Mukanda among the Chokwe. In an unparalleled study of Afikpo Igbo masking, Simon Ottenberg has shown that children emulate adult performances by organizing their own displays. But as soon as the boys are initiated and start using masks, which form part of the Afikpo corpus, they abandon the make-believe displays.[7] As participants in the adult performances, the boys grow up and wear adult masks and stage more elaborate performances, as is the case with Öjija and other children's masking rituals among the Yoruba, the subject matter of this chapter.

Öjija Performances

The etymology of Öjija, like those of the adult masquerades, *Ëpa*, *Ëlëfon*, and related masquerades such as *Okorotosha* and Eritu, is very obscure. But like them, the term refers to the carving as well as the ceremony in which it is used, whether performed by boys (as at Ido and Igbole), or by girls (as at Ire). As with Ëpa and Ëlëfon headpieces, each Öjija carving has a name, as we find in Ire. This may have been so in Igbole. The names, as in adult masquerades, are based on the motifs on the headpieces.[8] But while the motifs on Öjija are concerned with fertility, those on Ëpa and Ëlëfon include concern with physical and spiritual well-being (symbolized by Osanyin priests, devotees of the deity associated with medicine), and war (represented by equestrian motifs), a reflection of the bellicose history of the area.[9] And in Ire, the mythical burial place of Ogun, the deity associated with war, Ogun is represented during the annual festival by a masker using an Ëpa/Ëlëfon type of headpiece of a hood mask surmounted by the superstructure of a mounted warrior.[10]

Öjija at Igbole

Igbole was one of the satellite towns of the former Ido kingdom. Ritual cooperation existed between the various towns and villages in the performance of some adult festivals such as Ölua. There are also similarities in the performances of other festivals, such as Öjija, which I have witnessed at Ido and Igbole. In the former, it is one of two masking performances by children. The other is *Eigun ömöde* children's masquerade, which is performed after the adult version in February/March.[11] Both make use of palm leaf costumes, but have no carved headpieces, unlike Öjija, which is performed after the adult Ëpa cycle in March/April.[12]

I took some photographs of an Öjija performance in Ido (fig. 3.1), but carried out more detailed studies of the performance in Igbole, where, as in Ido, the boys were costumed in green palm leaves, rather than yellow palm fronds,[13] carrying wooden figures on their heads representing women carrying babies on their backs, or kneeling women carrying carved bowls. They danced to improvised percussion sounds of sticks, broken calabashes, old tin cans, and enamel plates.

In Igbole, Öjija is part of the annual Ëlëfon festival that takes place during late February or early March, just before the rains. The two-day festival opens with a brief parade at sundown on the first day. The second day's performance starts in the early afternoon and ends just before sundown, after which the Öjija performance begins.

The major performers are eight- to fourteen-year-old boys assisted by younger boys and a few girls of the household. These girls assist in repainting the carved headpieces, which consist of mothers with children on their backs and kneeling female figures carrying bowls or combinations of these in the best tradition of Ekiti carving.

In preparation for the performance, the boys construct elaborate palm leaf enclosures, *ule öjija* (Öjija's house), making ingenious use of the walls of adjacent houses or compounds (fig. 3.2). Each enclosure has three or four compartments, the outer one of which is called *ule ömöde* (children's house), for girls and also boys younger than the principal performers. Another compartment is for bean cakes and other food items provided for the occasion by their mothers. In the innermost recess, reserved for "elders" (*agba*), the headpiece and palm frond costume of the maskers are kept. There the choicest food is consumed by the older boys, the agba or elders.

In planning the enclosure, the children are already imitating the adult practice of having outer, inner, and innermost recesses in their sacred groves. In these adult groves, the outer precincts are also for the non-initiates and the degree of seniority in the group determines which area one can reach in the inner recesses. In the past, very young uninitiated boys accompanied their parents and grandparents to the shrines, just as Margaret Mead observed for the Balinese. As to how these young children acquire such knowledge, more often than not some of the boys performing Öjija may have been initiated into the *Oro* bull roarer cult, but can be trusted to keep secret what they saw or were told.

In preparation, the headpieces are washed and repainted by girls (fig. 3.3), sometimes older women (mothers of the performers), in imitation of the way in which women wash and repaint the headpieces used by Ëpa masqueraders.

The performance starts as soon as the adult Ëlëfon masqueraders return to the shrine house. The younger performers having earlier in the day offered salt and tiny bits of food to the headpiece and consumed the rest, and put on their masks and costumes in the outer recess of their enclosures, having driven out girls and younger children. The maskers emerge from their enclosures in the various compounds and go to the streets, followed by retinues of children of both sexes, who constitute the chorus. There is an orchestra made up of assorted, improvised musical instruments already described, to which the maskers dance. Children, and especially older boys who are not taking part, tease the performers by shouting at the maskers:

O-o-o-o-le: o-o-l-e-e-s-oro
Thief—you cannot harm (flog)

Though the young maskers do not carry whips and are not allowed to flog with the small palm leaf brooms decoratively tied with spliced cane used earlier during the Ëlëfon performance, they chase away persistent hecklers so that they can concentrate on their main task of going to the various compounds where they sing, dance, and receive monetary rewards.

The songs are few and standardized, of the call-and-response variety, in complete contrast to that of the Öjija of Ire.

1. Solo: *Öjija a gbe ö*: Öjija will aid (help) you
   Chorus: *Ömö alakergbe ko*: Child (or children)
   of the gourd (*ko* is a sound)

In the past, boys in the farm were sent to brooks to fetch water with portable gourds. This may be a prayer that the compound head will have children to send on errands.

The next three songs deal directly with the issue of fertility.

2. Solo: *Olule e*: Owner of the house
   Chorus: *In a b'mö ye*: Your children will (be born to) live

It means that the children will be not stillborn, and those that are born will grow up into healthy children.

3. Solo: *Ömö ju s'aribi:* It is impossible not to think of bearing children
   Chorus: *Ömö ju s'aribi o e:* It is impossible not to think of bearing or having children
4. Solo: *Ömö kubukubu*: Plump, plump children
   Chorus: *Ömö kuruba eusa ömö*: Babies plump like giant rats

Eusa (*okete*), the pouched rat,[14] is believed to breed rapidly, giving birth to healthy offspring. This song echoes one of the songs that marks the final stages of Ëlëfon, when the singers sing *E-e-e-kubu* several times. The sounds are reminiscent of playing with healthy babies.

The maskers, with the aid of assistants, put their monetary gifts in bowls, which form part of the figures on the headpieces. But in compounds where they are not offered anything, they round off with this abusive song: He cooked soup with crab oil, that is why he is smelling like *asin*.

Asin is a carnivorous, smelly, long-snouted mouse that sucks eggs, bites chickens to death, and exudes a pungent odor alive or dead. The red algae on the surface of shallow stagnant pools and on muddy riverbanks where there are crab holes is believed to be oil made by crabs. The crab is one of several animals who can make things similar to man's products, but which humans will not use. The crab makes oil, the toad makes beads (eggs), the woodpecker carves, but their products are not suitable for human use.

The young maskers perform from late afternoon to dusk for the next five days, at the end of which there is a grand finale when they dance to the rhythm of the *Ösanyin* (medicine god) orchestra of bells and a pot drum beaten by adult devotees of the Ösanyin cult. The best dancer and the most beautifully painted headpiece are supposed to be chosen by the elders. But invariably the children are all told that it is difficult to choose the best because they are all very good.

Öjija at Ire

In complete contrast to the Öjija performance in Igbole, the principal actors in Ire are girls rather than boys, and the face of the carrier of the Öjija sculpture is not concealed. Instead of the palm leaves of the boys, a girl wears a wrapper tied round her chest leaving the shoulders and arms bare. She carries the Öjija on her head as one would a head load (fig. 3.4). The common denominators are the name Öjija, the motifs on the carvings, which include a woman carrying a baby on its back, and the fact that both performances are by children, albeit of different gender.

The exquisitely carved Öjija figures are in the form of a mother with child, resting on a round base, which sits on the carrier's head. Each ward had one, so there used to be five, most of which have been stolen. They are all individually named; my informant remembered two,[15] but could not recall which ward the names belonged to. They are: *Ariyunkë*, "the one who has costly beads" (*iyun* meaning "to take care of"), and *Ömörotimi*, "the child stays with me," a reminder of *abiku*, that is, spirit children who die and are believed to keep coming back.

The performance, which takes place every other year, is organized by girls aged five to fourteen years, around February or March, at the height of the dry season when there is little agricultural activity. Three months before the performance the girls compose and rehearse songs that reflect what has happened in the town, the district, and the nation since the last performance. The actual performance is very competitive, as each of the five groups from the five wards of the town try to outdo one another in their songs as they go around the town. There may be fights between two groups if one feels that the songs of another ridicule them or their ward. In the course of such a fracas, the Öjija carving may be broken. Then the girls generally end up in the king's palace for reconciliation. The performance is supposed to be competitive, but since there are no adjudicators, each group congratulates itself for giving the best performance!

The carrier of the Öjija sculpture is the lead singer, but the carving can be dispensed with, as happened during the fiftieth anniversary celebrations for the King of Ire in 1985. The carved Öjija was used only at the insistence of the announcer and compère of the program, when he discovered that I had followed the first set of singers home in order to photograph their Öjija, which they did not bring to the arena.

The singing and dancing are not accompanied by a musical instrument. Each song is in three sections: an opening passage consisting of homage, a long middle section which contains the subject matter, and a closing portion which contains pleas about what should be done by the elders to remedy certain intolerable conditions; the song then ends in a call and response manner.

It is in the long middle section that the singers, in a sort of social commentary, sing of all the various things that have transpired in the previous year in Ire, in their immediate environment in Ekiti, which is their home state, and in Nigeria. The wide ranging and almost inexhaustible subject matter touches on the 1982 drought resulting in the burning of coca farms, thus depriving the owners of the means of paying school fees for their children and providing other goodies. The crux of the matter was that some "big guns" were shielding the arsonists. Other subjects include child kidnappers, political hoodlums who destroy the property of their victims, even when heavy ransom money has been paid, and how six lorry loads of soldiers came to destroy a cannabis farm. On national issues, they sing about the change of the national currency from the British pound sterling to the Nigerian *naira*, as well as the change in traffic regulations from driving on the left to driving on the right. There was also the issue of unemployment among secondary school dropouts and eventually university graduates.

Whenever the girls touch on very controversial issues, they include lines to the effect that they are the mouthpiece and spokespersons of the community, since what they are singing about affects everyone in the town and beyond. And to protect themselves from any backlash, not physical but spiritual, they sing lines of protective incantations.

Below is a free translation of one of the songs:

Opening:

> My fellow Öjija performers keep silent
> Chorus singers keep silent
> Keep silent so I can speak
> You keep silent so I can talk
> Adediwura's father I am greeting you
> I am greeting you as in a household ceremony

> I am greeting you as in a children's festival
> Which of your cognomens do I not know
> Your lucky head like a bagful of beads
> Slim one like an eel
> The spring does not dry up
> I am greeting you fervently
> (18 lines of cognomen)
> Those sitting, those standing, do you hear me?

Subject Matter:

> Adediwura's father are you listening?
> The amount of suffering we are undergoing
> Is most intolerable (more than two hundred)
> Those sitting, those standing are you listening?
> The bosses in Lagos
> The bosses in Öyö
> The bosses in Ibadan dun[16]
> We do not know what they are doing
> The same type of school children attended in
> Lagos
> The same type of school children attended in Öyö
> The same type of school children to Ibadan dun
> Is the same type of school we sent children to in
> Iremoko
> People standing and those sitting
> When they leave school they cannot find jobs.
>
> The children in our house in Lagos
> The children in our house in Öyö
> The children in our house in Ibadan dun
>   Cannot find jobs
> Is this what you call a good life?
>
> Those sitting and those standing
> The children in our house in Iremoko
> Will, as if it is all a joke, not find jobs
> When we write to them
> They will reply we are still looking for
> employment

Invocation:

> May *àsé* [skewer] not *sé* [skew] my mouth
> *Sèsé* [a climbing bean] does not *sé* [miss] the top of
> the tree stake
> A rain drenched singer knows the way home

A hen does not lay without hatching her eggs
When *ògan* [a thorny creeper] grows, it knows
where to twine
A needle is never harmed in Ifëland
I will talk with my mouth today
No one can conspire against a parcel
One wraps it; the other unwraps
When the giant rat uses mud to seal its entrance
He will remove it with its own head.

Subject Matter:

Well, we decided to write them [unemployed
school leavers]
As soon as they get the letters they burn them
And say *vèrì sörì* [very sorry] we have not got jobs
yet
Those standing and those sitting down
All the elders in (our house at) Ire
Help us to find a powerful force
So that children who will make us famous
Children who will transform Ire
Will be sent to us by *Olodumare*[17] in Ire
Death will not snatch our children.

Adediwura's father are you listening?
All the strangers in Ado
Have brought progress to Ado
Ibadan people in Uyin, brought progress
Those standing and those sitting
Those who will make us famous
Children who will transform us
Olodumare will choose them for us in Iremoko.

Closing Section:

Leader: Elders of Ire, good tidings
Chorus: Greetings elders of Ire, pray that children who will
transform us will arise in Ire.

The chorus leader sings several one-line solos of truisms and impossibilities, to which the chorus repeats their lines. Three of the solos are:

Salt is forever sweet.
The needle is never hurt in Ife (the mythical origin place of the
Yoruba).
A small [baby] snake is never used to tie a parcel.

From other songs we hear that

> The brown monkey has no time to rub camwood paste on its young
> [it's too busy looking for food, and in any case it already is the
> color of rubbed camwood].
> A dog does not lose its teeth however fiercely it barks.
> A cockerel does not mate with a hen and sigh with grief.
> The kola nut tree is never used as a house post.
> The maize can never be so angry with humans to grow out half a
> cob.
> And when the maize brings out its cob, it never forgets to bring out
> the tassel as well.

The main theme of the songs above is unemployment among secondary graduates, a condition that has spread to university graduates.

Before this problem, there was the issue of placement in schools, which was linked with the coming of the white man. They came from Imësi and Ado to Ire. Everybody wondered whether they were going to stay. The elders did not allow them, so they all left to settle in Ado and Imësi. Very soon Ado had pipe borne water, electricity, good roads, three doctors (with their own hospitals), and four high schools.

So every year Ire children go to Ado to take their high school entrance examination, but Ado and Imësi admit only indigenes of their towns. Are the children in Öyë, Itapa, and Ire so dull? The singers then implore the elders in the closing song to bring good things to Ire.

In another verse, the *Onire*, the chief, was praised for having his crown restored and for providing good roads. The singers also asked for pipe borne water, which was in progress. At last, the girls sang, they have been able to spend their money on worthwhile projects.

The matter discussed in the three paragraphs above is documented in British colonial as well as local archives. It dates back to 1905, when a health official who came to Ire to provide vaccinations lodged in a chief's house without paying the usual courtesy call on the Onire, who then prevented the vaccination. The king was accused of obstruction "in the lawful discharge of duty." Because his predecessor was too old to travel to register at Odo Ötin when Yorubaland was finally "pacified," he was held responsible for the offense of the previous king, fined 50 pounds and his crown seized.

When he realized it was a serious matter, the Oniri went to the governor in Lagos in 1911. Lagos upheld the decision of the district commissioner, then based in Ilesha. The matter dragged on until 1964, when a former employee of the Survey Department became the Onire. Apart from effecting the restoration of the Onire to full *Öba* (king) rather than *Baalë*, he fought an uphill battle for the establishment of a school in Ire. According to Msgr. A. Oguntuyi,[18] because the elders had invoked a curse on anyone who established a school, the king had to get the elders to sacrifice a cow in order to revoke the curse, so that that school could be built.

At the national level, the girls sang about the changing in driving from left to right:

> About twelve months ago
> The road we used to drive on
> We are told has changed
> They say *kìpù raìtì* [keep right] is here.

They go on to the currency change:

> About six months later,
> They said it is the naira that has come
> I will use the naira that has just come
> To send my children to school
> Like a joke he will go to America
> Willy nilly he will buy a car there.

The reflection of social events was also evident in the performance in Onire's palace towards the end of 1985. The singers were worried about the government's war against indiscipline and the resultant pulling down of kiosks and the order to dig pit latrines, an impossible task in some towns situated on laterite terrain.

Differences in Performances

In the context of masking, it seems rather strange that Öjija, a children's mask type, should be performed by boys in one area, and girls in another, bearing in mind that except for less than half a dozen documented cases, masking is a male preserve. But from the material discussed, the boy maskers are almost completely concealed except for hands and feet, following the example of adult maskers, while the girls are not concealed as they carry the Öjija on their heads.

Whereas in Igbole and Ido the boys' Öjija is a continuation and part of Ëpa and Ëlëfon masked performances, in Ire, there is no connection with any other ceremony or ritual. The Ogun festival, in which the Ëpa mask is used, is performed in August, and like Öjija in Ire, cannot be described as a training ground for any adult performance, except in the area of singing and public performance, which gives the girls confidence for future public appearances.

In Igbole, however, there is a direct link between adult performances in which maskers emerge from shrine houses, or "sacristy" adjoining open spaces in the middle of the forest.[19] In these secluded areas, maskers dress out of the sight of the spectators. This is the type of sacred space created by the boys for their Öjija performances.[20]

But in Ire, no enclosures are needed: since it is not a masking ceremony secrecy is not necessary. After putting on their clothes, all the other girls' preparations are made on the verandah in front of the lead singers' houses. It may be mentioned here that the shrine house of Ogun is out of bounds except to the Ogun priest and a couple of elders, and that the finale of the public outing takes place in a forest clearing some distance from the town. The access road to the venue is closed to all strangers. But since Ogun is not a masking ritual, although represented by a masker, and the girl Ōjija performers are not masked, there is no basis for comparison. The only point that can be made is that the Ogun performance is a re-enactment of a culture hero's warlike exploits and that Ōjija is a social commentary on current and not so current events.

Indeed, the most important features of the girl's Ire performance are the songs, while in Igbole attention is focused on the masked dances, the enclosures, and the adult-assisted closing ceremony. Also, in Igbole the boys go round the town as in the adult performance, but follow no prescribed route as do the adults. Unlike Ire, there is no rivalry between performing groups at Igbole.

Even though there is an element of competition in the performances—in Igbole it is in the dances by various groups that round off the performance; and in Ire, it is the content of the songs—no group is declared a winner. In Igbole, everyone is the best; in Ire each group declares itself the best.

There is sharp contrast between the songs in the two cases. In Igbole (and also in Ido), the boys' songs follow the adult pattern and deal with fertility, but do not go on to other concerns of the adult performers—protection against wars and strife, safety from malevolent forces, as well as physical and spiritual well-being. The songs are fixed and do not vary from year to year, nor does the subject matter change.

In the case of Ire, the girls' songs deal with social well-being, but of a more immediate nature, the here and now, matters that affect the youths and townspeople. The fact that only comparatively recently schools were built in Ire may account for the content of the songs. As far back as the early 1940s, boys and girls in Igbole were attending school in Osi, a mile away, and by the early 1950s, there were Anglican and Catholic mission schools in Igbole. Western education opens doors for employment and other opportunities outside the immediate community, and the presence of educated indigenes can pull strings to bring "goodies" to the community.

It is worth noting that Ire is off the beaten track. The road leading to the town starts from Ōyë, which is on the main road linking the west with Kabba and Lōkōja at the confluence of the Niger and Benue rivers. The road to Ire terminates there, thus militating against the supply of social amenities such as water and electricity, which are often connected to existing networks. Luckily, for Igbole, the high tension cables of the national grid bypass the town, while an 18-inch main supply pipe from a World Bank loan assisted water scheme passes through the town from Igede via Ado.

Even if all the community requirements are supplied, these ceremonies will still continue to be performed, since they are part of the annual cycle of festivals in each town. As the girls in Ire sing: "Ojija performers never miss the annual performance." In this, they are fully supported by the adult population, apart from releasing them from whatever chores they should perform so that they can prepare for the performances. Parents provide food in Igbole, fine cloths in Ire, and in both cases, adults and other children turn up to watch the young ones aspiring to one day perform their own Ojija.

It is worth noting that once the ceremonies are over, no one queries the children about abusive songs addressed to a person or persons in the course of the performance. This makes interesting comparison with masqueraders who flog spectators in other types of masked performances. In fact, there is no redress in customary law and in the criminal code as long as there is no grievous bodily harm. After all, it is just a festival, *odun*, best translated as "celebration." The word play will trivialize the issue because masquerading, or the use of the mask-like carving, whether by adults or children, is a serious matter. That is why Ojija in Igbole addresses basic human issues that need intervention, while Ojija in Ire addresses current social issues that call for the attention of all levels of government—local, state, and national as well as community progressive unions made up of the educated sons and daughters.

Notes

1. Richards 1969, 9, 12.
2. Mead 1930, 38-39.
3. Mead and Wolfenstein 1955, 40-45.
4. Olajubu and Ojo 1977, 288-289.
5. Henry and Margaret Drewal 1983, 30-33.
6. Clarke 1944, 92; vander Heyden 1974, 14, 17-19.
7. Ottenberg 1975, 184-188. Also see his article on the Afikpo children's masquerades in this volume.
8. Ojo 1978, 456.
9. Ojo 1978, 461-467
10. Ibigbami 1977, 1978.
11. Although festivals have their fixed places in the annual cycle of each community, dates and periods of performance vary from year to year, a few days to as much as a fortnight in some cases (Ojo 1974, 149; 1996).
12. Ojo 1974, 97-114.
13. It is believed that the use of yellow palm fronds by small children can attract smallpox, normally prevalent in the dry season, the period when Ojija is performed.
14. *Cricetomys gambianus*, otherwise known as the "big rat." The pouch refers to the expanding, elastic skin on both cheeks that enables these pesky rodents to carry palm nuts, cob corn pieces and other farm products to their holes or burrow for storage or for feeding to their young.
15. The five wards in Ire are coterminous with the original five settlements from which people moved to the present site beginning in 1929 (Oguntuyi 1979, 86).
16. "Ibadan is sweet."
17. The supreme Yoruba deity.

18. Oguntuyi 1979, 84-88.
19. Ojo 1974, 80, 105; Carroll 1956, 64.
20. Ojo 1974, 94.

Bibliography

Abrahams, R. C. 1958. *Dictionary of Modern Yoruba.* London: London University Press.

Carroll, Kevin. 1956. "Yoruba Masks: Notes on the Masks of North-East Yoruba Country." *Odu: Journal of Yoruba and Related Studies* 3 (old series), 2-15.

———. 1967. *Yoruba Religious Carving: Pagan and Christian Sculpture in Nigeria and Dahomey.* London: Geoffrey Chapman.

Clark, J. D. 1944. "Three Yoruba Fertility Ceremonies." *Journal of the Royal Anthropological Institute,* 74, 91-96.

Drewal, Henry J., and Margaret T. 1983. *Gelede: Art and Female Power among the Yoruba.* Bloomington: Indiana University Press.

Ibigbami, R. I. 1977. "The Sacred Images of Ogun in Ire Ekiti." *Odu* (new series) 18, 104-110.

———. 1978. "Ogun festival in Ire Ekiti." *Nigeria Magazine* 126/127, 44-59.

Mead, Margaret. 1928 (1961). *Coming of Age in Samoa: A Psychological Study of Primitive Youth in Western Civilization.* New York: Apollo Editions.

———. 1930 (1965). *Growing Up in New Guinea.* Harmondsworth: Penguin Books.

Mead, Margaret, and Wolfenstein, Martha. 1955. *The Child in Contemporary Cultures.* Chicago: University of Chicago Press.

Oguntuyi, A. 1979. *History of Ekiti: (From the beginning to 1939).* Ibadan: Bisi Books.

Ojo. J.R.O. 1974. "Epa and Related Masquerades among the Ekiti Yoruba of Western Nigeria." M. Phil. thesis, University of London.

———. 1978. "The Symbolism and Significance of Epa Type Masquerade Headpieces." *Man* (new series) 13, 455-470.

———. 1981. "Masked Dances of the Yoruba Peoples." *The World of Music* 23:3, 37-51.

———. 1988. "A Cross-Cultural Study of Some African Masquerades." In A. I. Asiwaju and B. O. Oloruntimehin (eds.), *African Unity: The Cultural Foundations.* Lagos: Centre for Black African Arts and Civilization, 119-133.

———. 1996. "Doing Year: Performance Patterns in Some Ekiti Yoruba Festivals." *Kurio Africana: Journal of Art and Criticism* 2:2, 28-40.

Ölajubu, Oludare, and J.R.O Ojo. 1977. "Some Aspects of Oyo Yoruba Masquerades." *Africa* 47:3, 253-275.

Ottenberg, Simon. 1975. *The Masked Rituals of Afikpo: the Context of an African Art.* Seattle: University of Washington Press.

Richards, A.I.R. 1967. "Socialisation and Contemporary British Anthropology." In *Socialisation; The Approach from Social Anthropology.* London: Tavistock, 1-15.

vander Heyden, Marsha. 1977. "The Epa Mask and Ceremony." *African Arts* 10:2, 14-21, 91.

Part 2

Emulating Masquerades

4

From Grasshoppers to Babende: The Socialization of Southern Kuba Boys to Masquerade

David A. Binkley

The ritual structure of rites of passage in West and Central Africa place uninitiated boys and girls in direct opposition to the institution itself. Following initiation, successful novices are not only differentiated from the uninitiated by a status change (from boyhood to manhood) but also by the secret knowledge acquired in the initiation process. While the degree of exegesis imparted to the novices varies in field reports of initiation practices, it is clear that the process imparts some knowledge to the novices that must be kept secret from the uninitiated. Indeed, the very words *buadi* and *nkaan* employed in Southern Kuba culture mean "men's initiation" as well as "secret."

In many African societies, mask fabrication and display are an integral part of the secret knowledge acquired during initiation rites. These experiences are often regarded by adult initiated males as the first culturally sanctioned foray into the complex world of mask fabrication and display. While this view is in some ways accurate, it is increasingly clear that it is also outmoded. My own field research as well as evidence by Herbert Cole (1985), Simon Ottenberg (1982, 1989), Anita Glaze (1981), and others, clearly indicates that long before initiation, young boys are intensely interested in mask making and through observation and imitation they acquire many of the skills necessary to participate in this activity.[1]

While my field research in the Southern Kuba region of the Democratic Republic of the Congo did not include a sustained program of daily observation of child play activity, it did make it apparent that there are distinct differences between how girls and boys are socialized.[2] By the age of five years or even younger, girls tend to interact more frequently with girls of their own age than with boys and tend to congregate in areas where older girls and women gather to work or relax, especially in areas associated with food preparation. These include areas near the household kitchen where cassava and corn are pounded into flour. During the day, when older girls and adult women are in the fields, younger girls spend their time either caring for their younger siblings of both genders or engaging in play-acting modeled on activities associated with food preparation. For example, young girls may take hot coals from their mother's hearth and start a small fire of their own made of twigs. A discarded tin can, serving as a receptacle, is set on the fire. Sand is then sifted into water placed into the tin can recalling their mothers sifting cassava and corn flour into a pot of boiling water in the preparation of *kot/bidia* the staple food of the Kuba region.

When girls are a little older, they accompany their mothers to agricultural fields during the day and gather firewood or fetch water from nearby streams for use in food preparation. These various activities are categorized as women's work and always take place in the company of older girls or women.

Socialization for boys differs and is in many ways more unbounded. After the age of four or five, they begin to move away from the family homestead and the watchful eyes of their mothers and older sisters and gravitate to those areas in the village that are dominated by male work activity. In most Southern Kuba villages this occurs under the blacksmith's enclosure where hoe blades and other tools are produced or under the enclosure where the weaving of raffia cloth takes place. Virtually the only individuals present at these work activities, even if they are young children, are males.

During more active play periods, young boys consistently fashion their play on adult male activity. This includes building miniature blacksmith furnaces in the sand, making tools or models of tools and hunting paraphernalia such as bows and arrows. On several occasions, I observed a group of small boys construct a raffia palm frond house, exact in many details to a typical Kuba full-size house built to house either gender, but on a miniature scale. In communities located near motor vehicle routes, young boys often construct models of trucks or Land Rovers; and in riverine communities on the borders of the Kuba region in the north and the south, models of boats or canoes are often made in miniature form. Many young boys demonstrate surprising skills at an early age in selecting appropriate raw materials and utilizing tools such as large knives to fashion the various wood and fiber materials into technically sophisticated models of the desired objects.

Young Southern Kuba boys are also intensely interested in masks and their fabrication. These interests translate into a variety of creative activities. Young boys may make pencil or ink drawings of masked dancers and their entourage (fig.I.3). They also may construct models of masks made from wood, raffia fiber, feathers, and other materials they have found nearby (fig. 4.1*)*. Boys also may fabricate entire masquerade figures that they wear during play activity in the community (see figs. I.1). These impromptu performances may include one or more masked dancers who are often accompanied by other boys who serve as musicians and helpers who may adjust the costume from time to time but who also serve as a ready-made audience. These are loosely organized group play activities that may occur spontaneously at any time. During the boys' masquerades I have witnessed, the masks are not arbitrary or experimental in form and style. On the contrary they are based on mask types the boys have observed firsthand in the community during funeral and initiation rites.

The Organization of Play Activity

All Southern Kuba communities are governed by a village-based council (*malaang*), which is composed of fifteen to twenty titled individuals, presided over by one or more headmen or chiefs.[3] The council convenes at least once a week, but may meet daily for short periods of time for important matters that demand the attention of council members. Council meetings are always public proceedings. Given that on most days men who are not council members and most women are busy away from the community (either hunting or working in their fields/gardens, respectively), the potential audience for council meetings may consist almost entirely of children. As titleholding is the means by which adult men organize themselves as members of the village council it is not surprising that title taking becomes an important organizing principle for the group play activities of young boys. Based on the village council model, each boy selects a title in imitation of adult titles and roles. This appears to be an entirely informal activity with no other justification on the part of the boys than the desire to act out adult roles.

This aspect of child play activity took on added significance when I interviewed an elderly Northern Kete titleholder from the village of Mombo Munene. In our conversations he described the various titles he held in his life including both actual conferred titles as well as those "unofficial" titles he held when he was a child. The first group he belonged to (at the age of nine or ten) was called *Bena Mapopu* (grasshopper people), a name chosen by the boys because, as he described it, the primary activity of this group was hunting insects, especially grasshoppers in the grassy areas just beyond the edge of the community. But even at this early age he held a title appropriated from the adult world, that of *diyulu mbengi*, a warrior title. The second informal group he belonged to called themselves *Bena Manyanga*. The primary activity of the second group was hunting, but owing to the older age of its members, group activity often ranged farther away from the community and included setting traps and hunting in the forest. As in the earlier group, he had taken a title but this time it was a higher rank. He was promoted from *diyulu mbengi* to *mbengi* that elevated him to a title associated with the *bakolomu*—the highest level of titleholders in the community. This, of course, was not a sanctioned title but one modeled on village titleholding. He held informal titles in other groups, but eventually after his own initiation he received a title from village council members that allowed him to participate officially at its meetings. A number of years ago, he was appointed to the important title of *mbambi*, which placed him among the most influential members of the council. He still held this title when I interviewed him in 1982.

Interviews with other Southern Kuba elders suggest similar informal group affiliations during childhood that are also based on the village council prototype. These group activities often extended into early adulthood and included the initiation process itself as the village council also provides the model on which the novices in the forest initiation camp are organized (see Binkley 1987a, 1991).

Clearly the village council serves as an important model for the creative exploration of boys and young men into the highly competitive world of adult titleholding, but does this same institution also sustain their creative interest in mask making and masquerade? Observations in a number of Southern Kuba communities suggest this is not the case. Neither the village council nor these informal groups of boys based on the village council model are the impetus behind mask making and performance. Unlike the Afikpo case, as discussed by Simon Ottenberg in chapter 5, where young boys organize themselves into secret societies that support children's masquerades, the playful experimentation with mask making and masquerade on the part of Southern Kuba boys is solely an individual creative pursuit and is divorced from any age grade or other formal youth organization. I suggest that Southern Kuba boys are not aware of the fundamental connection between titleholding and masquerade because the extensive planning necessary to prepare for masked performance is never a topic of discussion during village council meetings. These discussions are the purview of initiated men and are held secretly in a secluded forest location away from the watchful gaze of children. Consequently, children do not see a public validation of mask making and performance by the village council. Children do occasionally witness masquerades in the community, but an understanding of the inner workings of the initiation society that organize these performances must wait until boys are much older. It is only later during initiation rites that older boys and young men are introduced to the governance aspects of adult masked performance.

Modeling Masks and Behavior

As previously mentioned, it is individual initiative and creativity thst spurs children's mask making in the Southern Kuba region. This interest is sustained by the periodic masked performances in the community by the adult initiation society. Principally, there are two contexts for masked performances in the region: during initiation and funeral rituals. Initiation rites for young men are called buadi in Northern Kete villages and nkaan in Southern Bushoong villages. These two forms of initiation are very similar as Southern Bushoong nkaan is based almost entirely on the Northern Kete model. Both forms erect an initiation wall during the rite and fabricate identical types of masks and costume regalia. They also employ similar initiation songs and other verbal lore.[4]

Initiation Masks

While initiation rites occur infrequently in the region, the rites do last six weeks or longer.[5] Therefore, Southern Kuba boys have a number of opportunities to observe masked dancers perform. During initiation rites, dances are held on three occasions. The first dance occurs as soon as the initiates (*babende*, pl.; *mubende*, sing.) fabricate their dance costumes and several raffia masked figures with the help of participating elders. The raffia figures produced during the initial period of buadi include the male figure Munyinga and several examples of the female figure Kamakengu. When completed, the babende accompanied by the masked dancers perform their individual dances (*keke*) before family and friends on the principal dancing ground in the community, demonstrating the knowledge and skill they have acquired during the initial period of seclusion in the forest camp. Following a dance at midpoint, the final dance in the community coincides with the conclusion of the rite.

There are other occasions during buadi when small boys observe initiation masks close at hand. While the babende are required to remain in the forest initiation camp most of the time, on occasion they are given license to wear the Kamakengu masked figures and to enter the community to chase uninitiated boys and girls. During initiation at the Northern Kete community of Kambash in 1981, boys who were too young to be initiated anxiously waited at the edge of the village near the path leading to the forest camp to see the babende and the Kamakengu masked figures emerge from the forest. Following the taunts of the young boys, the Kamakengu figures began to chase them. The figures also chased older girls they knew and were only stopped when those being chased found shelter in a house or under an enclosure where the large size of the Kamakengu figures prevented them from following.

When the masqueraders had returned to the forest encampment, several young boys in Kambash constructed drums made with large leaves stretched over discarded tins or sections of bamboo. Their dances imitated the special initiation dance steps they saw the babende perform. On occasion, a boy would also fabricate a copy of the female figure Kamakengu. The body of the initiation Kamakengu figure is made in the forest camp entirely of split raffia palm frond with a head constructed from an old basket or alternately from tree bark formed into the shape of a cone. The completed Kamakengu masked figure is quite large and heavy. The masked dancer performs distinctive rocking back and forth and spinning movements during the performance (fig. 4.2). The voice of this mask is also distinctive—a high-pitched twittering sound that is created with the aid of a special whistle.[6]

On one occasion, three Kamakengu masks entered Kambash to chase uninitiated boys and girls. Within an hour after the masks had returned to the forest camp, a small boy dressed in a leaf costume resembling Kamakengu began to chase children younger than himself. During his performance, he attempted to create the twittering "voice" of Kamakengu. which is produced by a whistle whose construction is an initiation secret. Although his figure was not made from raffia palm fronds and was therefore different in both color and texture than the "official" Kamakengu figure and the vocalizations of the boy were only a feeble attempt of the original, the basic form and movements of the official Kamakengu were closely followed. Both the official Kamakengu made in the forest initiation camp and the copy made by the young boy were functionally identical within the context of buadi. During the periodic forays into the community, the babende wearing the Kamakengu mask are given free reign to assert their status over the uninitiated by chasing them. In turn, the young boy wearing his own version of Kamakengu asserted his dominance over still younger boys. The reward for the boy who made his own Kamakengu mask was license to chase still younger boys in the same way he had been chased several hours earlier.

There are other initiation-masked figures that also mediate between the babende residing in the forest camp and the playful nature of young boys residing in the community. The most ubiquitous initiation masked figure in the Southern Kuba region is Munyinga, which represents a fierce warrior and also a fool. The raffia cloth head of the mask is distinctive with its projecting basketry eyes and a nose made from a large hornbill's beak. Among this figure's most distinctive characteristics is its rapid falsetto voice that speaks incessant gibberish during performance. The words uttered by Munyinga are often ribald and nonsensical and are interpreted by elders as the words of a fool. On the other hand, Munyinga's performance attracts uninitiated boys who invariably follow Munyinga through the community accompanying it in song.[7]

Other masked figures stylistically similar to Munyinga are also found in the Southern Kuba region. In certain communities a masked figure such as Kinguita or Kalengula may perform the function of crowd control to enlarge the dance area needed by other masked figures, dancers, and musicians. On these occasions, the figure is usually taunted by uninitiated boys until it chases its tormentors and attempts to trip them up or wrestle them to the ground, much to the delight of boys who are not caught. When a boy is occasionally caught, he may be frightened but not seriously harmed. As Simon Ottenberg (1989) has noted, pertaining to similar encounters during Afikpo masquerade, young boys both learn and test the limits of their relationship with adult masks. While initiation masqueraders may chase and occasionally catch the uninitiated, the masked performers are also paying attention to the boys. This attention peeks their curiosity and motivates their play and imagination.

There are other initiation-masked figures that are also favorites of uninitiated boys, of which Kayeke is among the most popular (fig. 4.2). Kayeke represents a Cwa person and this masked figure is invariably worn by an individual who is short in stature in keeping with its characterization. The face of the mask is carved from wood and polychromed red with other details such as the eyes pigmented in white. The top and back of the mask are covered with long raffia "hair" that has been dyed black. The Kayeke mask carries a short hocked stick with which it feigns to trip anyone who ventures too near. The appearance of the Kayeke masked dancer, its short stature, and its gentle and non-aggressive nature during performance as compared with more aggressive types make it more accessible to the numerous small boys who surround the dancer whenever it performs and sings its song: "Kayeke, our brother of lighting."

Funeral Masks

As initiation rites occur infrequently in the Kuba region, the most typical occasion for masquerades is in conjunction with funerary rites for initiated men.[8] There is a hierarchy of funerary masks in the region and depending on the community and the rank of the deceased, different types of masks may appear during funerary rites. In the Southern Kuba region, well-known mask types such as Bwoom and Ngady Mwaash may perform on the day closing the funerary rite, just before and immediately after the body of the deceased is buried. The most senior mask in the region is called Inuba. Its appearance is mandatory at the funerals of certain key senior titleholder (fig. 4.3).[9] The performance of Inuba is always preceded by the appearance of another masked dancer named Bishuadi, which is considered to be the herald for the senior figure Inuba.

After the appearance of funerary masks such as Bwoom, Ngady Mwaash, Bishuadi and Inuba, young boys quickly initiate mask-making activity. These activities may include making pen or pencil drawings of the masks and the retainers and musicians that accompany the masked performance. I was given a small ink drawing made by a boy the day after a mask appeared in the community of Kabao. That the boy understood both the performative and economic aspects of funerary masquerade are clearly demonstrated in his drawing as he includes musicians as well as a retainer who is collecting money from someone in the audience who appreciates the skill of the masked dancer (fig. I.3).

Boys also make small models of masks complete with costume details or create the head of the mask from leaves, flowers or a discarded piece of gourd (fig. 4.1). Other boys will make the mask and its entire costume and than perform impromptu masquerade performances much to the delight of family and friends who witness these activities. While cowrie shells, parrot or eagle feathers, and leopard pelts are not accessible to the boys and skilled woodcarving techniques are beyond their technical abilities, creative substitutions are often made in order to simulate the basic form and materials of the masks they wish to imitate. I once heard a commotion behind a house and discovered two small boys who had crawled into a chicken coup (much to the disapproval of the chickens) to obtain feathers to utilize in the construction of a mask they were planning to make. That this occurred in the Ngongo community of Bulongo in the Northern Kuba region clearly indicates that children's mask making is not an activity isolated to the Southern Kuba region.

Mask making is often left to a boy's own creative energy and imagination, however, I have encountered older men who have actively helped their sons to create masks. Because of this experienced help, the quality of the resultant masks is often much higher than that of the quickly made and quickly discarded masks constructed completely by the children themselves (see fig. I.1).

Secrecy and Masks

While uninitiated boys see public masquerades, they are often prohibited from witnessing the preparations that take place before masks perform in public. However, there are occasions when they may catch a glimpse of mask dancers dressing prior to the performance. The relationship of masks and secrecy is directly related to the masquerade hierarchy in the Kuba region. Preparation for the appearance of senior masquerades such as Inuba take place in the forest far from the curious eyes of uninitiated children. Masquerades of a lesser stature such as Bwoom, Ngady mwaash, and Bishuadi are often prepared at the edge of the village and often within view of uninitiated boys.

In 1982, I witnessed several initiated men prepare Bwoom and Ngady mwaash for their appearance at the funeral of a Southern Kuba initiated man. Preparations took place in a grove of trees at the edge of the village in full view of a number of uninitiated boys. On another occasion, I observed a Bishuadi masked dancer dressing prior to a funeral masquerade. While preparations for the appearance of Inuba took place in the forest, the individual who was to dance Bishuadi and several retainers dressed under a grove of trees behind a house at the edge of the village. Several uninitiated boys were present during the entire process. When men noticed the boys, they shooed them away but they soon returned. They were told to leave again but remained at a safe distance and still observed the entire proceeding. These examples clearly indicate that through firsthand observation of these activities, uninitiated boys learn the collaborative nature of masquerade and acquire some specific details related to the preparation of the masks and costumes prior to masked performance.

The degree of secrecy surrounding the preparations for Inuba, as compared to that surrounding Bishuadi, is also articulated publicly when Inuba and Bishuadi perform. While Inuba enters the village surrounded by senior titleholders and performs at the home of the deceased's family accompanied only by initiated men, the Bishuadi masked dancer circulates through the village, followed by young uninitiated boys who sing the masked dancer's praises (fig. 4.4).[10] The relationship between Inuba and initiated men on the one hand and between Bishuadi and uninitiated boys on the other seems both to reinforce as well as contravene the boundaries between categories—the initiated and the uninitiated. I suggest that the interaction between certain masked dancers and uninitiated boys is purposeful and important. The hierarchy of masking reinforces the authority of elders at the higher levels of masking activity, but creates avenues for interaction between the uninitiated and certain masks at the lower levels of masked performance. The grading of Southern Kuba masks into a hierarchy allows certain masks to be more accessible (and approachable) to children. Interviews with Southern Kuba elders clearly suggest that fathers want their sons to experience, learn, and succeed within the adult initiation organization. However, adults declare that this process is a gradual and lifelong pursuit that begins before the initiation rites when boys are quite young. There is certainly a different level of expectation on the part of adults toward children and uninitiated youth. While boundaries are always maintained, there is at least a bending of the rules. Initiation and masquerade-related sanctions are more lax for the uninitiated then for initiated young men. After the initiation process, the enforcement of rules by elders and peer pressure become important means to maintain distance. Anger directed toward initiated young men is evident if youth do not respect the authority of elders or mock initiation activities. This slackening of rules for the uninitiated is vital to the socialization process and is both understood and sanctioned by the adult male community. It certainly whets the boys' appetites for the mysteries that lie ahead.

An example of this formative socialization took place following the closure of initiation at Kambash in 1981. After the babende performed their last individual dances (keke), wearing a special skirt (*mukele*) signaling the close of buadi, they dressed in long, undyed raffia skirts to symbolize the close of the initiation process and their new status as adult initiated men. Immediately following this celebratory closing dance, several older, initiated men selected small boys to perform the same individual dances the babende had just completed. The boys stripped off their clothing and put on smaller versions of the mukele skirt. Then they began to dance their own keke dance in imitation of the dance they saw the babende perform earlier. The keke dance performed by the boys symbolized the end to their own pretend initiation that could only be experienced in an active way when the group of babende and the masked figures came from the forest camp to the community for food or to dance. The pride on the face of an elder who was instrumental in training babende in the forest camp as he watched his grandson perform the keke dance, illustrates the point succinctly (fig. 4.5). While initiation secrets are jealously guarded by initiated men in Southern Kuba culture, some avenues are left open for the acculturation of the young boys into mask making and masquerade performance.

Conclusion

Published field reports seem to suggest that initiates enter the forest camp as culturally and intellectually empty vessels ready to be filled with the knowledge and wisdom of the elders. However, my research experiences suggest that long before initiation takes place, young boys are actively pursuing their individual interests that often include honing their skills in dance, musicianship, mask making, and performance. Some Southern Kuba boys and young men enter buadi with a degree of skill and accomplishment superior to other members of the forest camp. Therefore, they are able to take advantage of opportunities in the camp that less experienced boys may be reluctant to attempt. For example, they may actively observe and then help elders to fabricate initiation masks. They may also wish to dance a mask such as Kamakengu when given the opportunity. An elder who carved two wooden masks, which eventually performed at the last initiation dance at Kambash, had been given the opportunity to carve a mask during his own initiation almost thirty years earlier. He subsequently carved masks for another initiation prior to his participation at Kambash in 1981. He told me that his active participation during his own initiation was instrumental in his development as a carver.

Just as not all boys enter buadi with the same abilities and skills, not all initiates who belong to the initiation groups are "recreated" equally by the process.[11] The boys and young men who actively participate in forest camp activities clearly get more from the experience. William Least Heat-Moon in his book, *Blue Highways, A Journey Into America* (1982, 17) notes that "...a man becomes his attentions. His observations and curiosity, they make and remake him." This insight seems apt for Southern Kuba boys and young men as well. It is not only the creative vitality of the initiation experience, but also the imaginative explorations of boys as they hone their observational and mimetic skills during childhood. These imaginative explorations help the boys to achieve the technical skills, aesthetic competence, and self-confidence to participate more fully during initiation and to take advantage of each opportunity as it arises as they prepare themselves for the highly competitive world of Kuba adult masquerade and titleholding.

Notes

1. Research in 1981-1982 was made possible by grants from IIE-Fulbright-Hays, Samuel H. Kress Foundation and the Wenner-Gren Foundation for Anthropological Research. In 1989, research was made possible by research funds from the University of Missouri—Kansas City.
2. Various peoples including Northern Kete, Bushoong, Dulungu, and Cwa are also called the Southern Kuba as they reside in the southern portion of the Kuba region. For a discussion of Southern Kuba culture, see Binkley 1987a, 1991; Vansina 1964.
3. See Binkley 1987b; Vansina 1978.
4. See Vansina 1955; Binkley 1987a, 140-145.
5. See Binkley 1987a, 27-28, for a discussion of the frequency of initiation rites in the Southern Kuba region.
6. The Kamakengu dancer wears a series of whistles individually tied to a necklace made from a strand of raffia suspended around his neck. When a whistle no longer produces the appropriate sound other whistles are readily at hand to create the distinctive voice of Kamakengu.
7. The boys at Kambash did not make a copy of the Munyinga mask. It may be that the falsetto voice of this mask, which is among its most distinctive features, was determined to be beyond the scope of the boys to imitate.

8. Interviews with Southern Kuba elders suggest that Inuba and Bishuadi may appear on several occasions during the year at funerals for senior titled officials.
9. See Binkley 1987b for a discussion of masks at funerals for senior titleholders in the Southern Kuba region.
10. The song sung by the boys is, "Father Bishuadi, you are here; Inuba is not far away."
11. This insight came during conversations with Woot David—headman of Boganciala in 1982.

Bibliography

Binkley, David A. 1987a. "A View from the Forest: The Power of Southern Kuba Initiation Masks." Unpublished Ph.D. diss., Indiana University.

———.1987b. "Avatar of Power: Southern Kuba Masquerade Figures in a Funerary Context." *Africa* 57:1, 75-97.

———. 1991. "Masks, Space and Gender in Southern Kuba Initiation Ritual." *Iowa Studies in African Art, Volume III, Art and Initiation in Zaire*, University of Iowa, 157-176.

Cole, Herbert M. 1985. "Introduction: The Mask, Masking, and Masquerade Arts in Africa." In Herbert M. Cole (ed.), *I Am Not Myself: The Art of African Masquerade*. Museum of Cultural History, UCLA Monograph Series, 26.

Cole, Herbert M., and Chike C. Aniakor. 1984. *Igbo Arts: Community and Cosmos*. Los Angeles: Museum of Cultural History, University of California.

Glaze, Anita J. 1981. *Art and Death in a Senufo Village*. Bloomington: Indiana University Press.

Heat Moon, William Least. 1982. *Blue Highways, A Journey into America*. Boston: G. K. Hall.

Ottenberg, Simon. 1976. "Childhood of African Art." *Ufahamu* VI, 2.

———.1982. "Illusion, Communication, and Psychology in West African Masquerade." *Ethos* 10:2.

———. 1989. *Boyhood in an African Society: An Interpretation*. Seattle: University of Washington Press.

Vansina, Jan. 1955. "Initiation Rituals of the Bushong." *Africa* 25: 138-53.

———. 1964. *Le royaume Kuba*. Musée Royal de l'Afrique Centrale, Anthropology and Ethnography, no. 49. Tervuren.

———. 1978. *The Children of Woot: A History of the Kuba People*. Madison: University of Wisconsin Press.

5

Emulation in Boys' Masquerades: The Afikpo Case

Simon Ottenberg

In a group of twenty-two Igbo communities in southeastern Nigeria called Afikpo, children's learning in past times was largely through emulation of adult behavior. This was evident in farming, fishing, household duties, hunting, and in many rituals. There were important adult men's secret societies, which still exist today, in which masquerading played significant roles. It is not surprising then, that boys should have masqueraded in emulation of men's masking societies. Data for this essay was gathered in 1952-1953 and in 1959-1960,[1] when the boys' masquerades were dying out. They are rarely performed today.

The Afikpo, a tropical forest farming and fishing people, unlike many other Igbo, live in highly compact communities, composed of densely packed compounds. The population density at the time of the research was over 400 persons per square mile. This allowed for impressive rituals of all kinds to be held, usually in the central clearing of each community. Large numbers of participants and substantial audiences were involved. The high population density also allowed for the formation of numerous children's informal and formal groupings. Among these were boys' societies that emulated the men's secret societies, and which held their own masquerades.[2] These boys' troupes were active during the ritual season, from about September to March. This was after the harvest, when food was plentiful, and there was a leisure time before the next farming period began.

At the time of my research there were sharp distinctions of gender roles at Afikpo, with men claiming the high ground, even if not always holding it. The men's secret societies, through their spiritual forces, attempted to control female behavior.[3] Females did not wear masks, though they might be involved in the masquerades in other ways. Training in gender distinctions in childhood occurred through the boys' masquerades, as well as in other ways.

There were three levels of boys' societies in the larger Afikpo communities, while in the smaller settlements the boys were grouped into one or two. Called *ohia omo ena* (bush children uninitiated), the societies were only for boys who had not yet joined a men's secret society. Once initiated they no longer took part in a boys' group, although they continued to play with both boys and girls in other contexts. The youngest level of these societies was for boys roughly five to ten years of age. The next one included boys of some ten to fifteen years of age, and the senior level was for boys fifteen years and older in age. The societies at each age level were organized by compounds in a community. If the compounds were small in numbers, the boys in several compounds might be grouped together, or by a larger ward, or the whole community. Through initiation, boys could join an adult society at any age, according to their parents' wishes, or sometimes the incessant demands of the youth. However, boys most frequently joined up when they were in the senior level.

In the decades before my research at Afikpo, joining a boys' society was obligatory, as it was also necessary for every male to later on initiate into at least one of the men's secret societies. Through time, the age of initiation gradually was lowered. Circumcision was not an issue in the boys' groups; some had had the operation while others had not.[4] Boys learned a good deal about punishment and control as members of a society, mostly from other youths rather than from adults. Each society was autonomous from others at its age level, and from those of higher or lower ages. All of them emulated the men's secret societies.

For the first two years or so of a boys' life, he was breast-fed by his mother, the father being a more distant individual, involved with other wives and matters. By the time a young boy joined the lowest boys' society level he was becoming weaned socially from his mother. The strong emotional bond between mother and boy was gradually eased by a series of activities.[5] An early one was the creation of a shrine for the boy by his father. Located in the compound patrilineal ancestral shrine house, this allowed the boy to visit and eat there. He joined other boys there at this convenient meeting place, which excluded girls. These events provided some early spiritual input for a boy. About the age of three to five, a mother pushed her son out of her house (the father usually lived in a separate home nearby). The boy moved to a dwelling in the compound where boys and young men of various ages were living, including some males who had been initiated into a men's society, but had not yet married. His entrance into the lowest level of the boys' societies and its masquerades occurred not long afterwards.

These events were designed, although persons at Afikpo rarely put it this way, to begin to separate a boy emotionally from his mother, and to move him more closely into the male world. Afterwards, a boy had less close contact with his mother, sisters, and other females, and he became more closely associated with his father and with ideas of maleness. If he still hung around his mother,

other boys' might tease him, calling him "mother's tail," or by some such phrase. However, he was still fed by her and contact with her was not forbidden.

Boys in the youngest society level were generally not well organized, often centering their activities around the compound patrilineal ancestral shrine house. They staged their own brief initiations with a small fee of perhaps some papayas or groundnuts. The youths made crude masks of leaves, cloth, and coconut shell. Sometimes naked and sometimes in simple raffia or leaf dress, they hopped around imitating adult masqueraders and older boys. New members learned to do this from older ones in the society. They also played a variety of games as a group. Leadership was unstable and there was roughhousing, chasing, and the flogging of other small boys who were not yet members of the society. Older boys looked upon these youths with amusement as being unsophisticated in masquerading and other activities, and as lacking real knowledge of what boys' societies were about. But the boys enjoyed themselves immensely, in this major move away from parents.

When the boys moved into the second level of their societies, as they wished, or through pressure from their fathers, they joined a well-organized group. Initiation into it was more expensive than to the first level, and parents sometimes helped out with some support. Each society had an elected or a self-chosen leader, and a rest house of its own, with a shrine in back of the compound. Nearby was a cleared space for games and masquerades. Some boys' societies had a roofless, fiber-walled enclosure (*ajaba*) close to their own shrine house, where boys dressed in private for their masquerades (fig. 5.1). If they had no dressing place they used their rest house. Both structures were constructed by the boys and kept in repair by them. All of these features emulated those of the men's secret societies.

During the ritual period of the year at Afikpo, boys spent little time at the compound ancestral house or in their male quarters in the compound. They would be at their own rest house for many hours. One boy was the priest of the shrine, which was similar to the adult male *Egbele* shrine of the men's secret society. The boys' house was taboo to females. Girls and women were not allowed to touch anything there, nor certain forms of the boys' masquerades, or to see the secret activities of the boys. If they violated these rules they had to have a sacrifice done for them by the boys at the shrine to purify them, and to prevent barrenness or illness when they were older. Girls often feared to break any of these taboos, as they believed in the power of the boys' shrine, and in the sacredness of its masqueraders, even if they knew the identities of the masking boys. This was similar to the action taken if females violated the rules of a men's society and its shrine spirit. Everything about the boys' societies smacked of maleness. The boys had their own titles and title ceremonies, which emulated adult ones. A boy who had not taken at least the first few titles by paying fees and performing certain acts, could be punished. He might be required to fetch water, sweep the cleared area, and be forbidden to use certain seats in the boys' house. The boys' societies were training grounds in developing male relationships, particularly peer group relationships. They were good preparation for a strongly aged-graded adult world. Masquerading played a part in these developments.

A major activity of the boys' societies was to put on a number of masquerades, which greatly delighted the boys. At an early time, each society of the second level produced its own masked events, but in later years, as membership declined, a number of boys' societies in a community, or all of them, joined together to do so. The boys made their own costumes and masks, often in simple imitation of those of the mens' societies. Wood, used in many adult society masks, was not permitted in the boys' masks, by a standing rule of the men of Afikpo. This clearly differentiated the masquerades of the two ages. Boys constructed masks out of calabashes, coconut shells, coconut tree fiber, cardboard, cloth and other materials, or occasionally had them made by an adult sculptor (fig. 5.2). They made drums and wooden gongs to use in their performances, similar to those employed in the adult societies, only simpler. They taught themselves to play them, or they learned from older boys, or by watching adult musicians play.

Girls and women were not supposed to know who the masqueraders were. They were expected to believe that they were spirits, as they were expected to believe this about adult masqueraders. In fact, they often recognized the boys as they did some of the adult performers, but they kept this information to themselves among the females, for fear of being punished by males if they revealed it. Boys learned at an early age that girls knew who they were and that they were not spirits. This was training in masquerade illusion for both genders. It enhanced the interest in the boys' performances. The illusion carried over into adult life and masking.

Okumkpa, a popular adult masquerade that the boys emulated, was a humorous and satiric calypso-like adult performance.[6] In its adult form a variety of masqueraders sang and acted out humorous and scurrilous events that had occurred in the community within the past year. The masqueraders impersonated and named individuals, ridiculing them, often making moral comments on their behavior. For the boys in the societies of the second level, Okumkpa was also a major production, requiring some twenty or more masqueraders and several boy musicians. It took place in the society's clearing ground, or sometimes at the edge of the commons in the community, an area reserved for children to play. Boys' Okumkpa masquerades were well attended by men, women, and children, as were the adult ones. The boys' play was said by some Afikpo to have been better produced at times then that of the men. The boys satirized one another, as well as girls and adults, dwelling on any behavior that seemed odd, humorous, or unusual to them. Some performers masked and dressed as girls or women, imitating them in dancing and behavior. This was always popular with the audience in both the boys' and the men's masquerades. At its best this play, which might last for several hours, was a sophisticated popular form of boys' theater involving song, instrumentation, dance, and acting. It required skill and imagination to create and perform, requiring time and energy to prepare and rehearse.

During the ritual season, boys who were members of a society at the second level, occasionally played games while in masquerades. These were chasing events, whose adult forms were called by similar names.[7] One popular masquerade, *Logholo*, involved a number of boys dressed in raffia body costumes, wearing a variety of masks (fig. 5.3). Each carried a stick, as they moved as a group through the compounds of the community, or as they played at the edge of the community commons. Unmasked boys, who could be younger or older boys acting alone or in coordination, chased and attempted to knock down the masqueraders, while the latter tried to fend them off. The only rule was that the attackers could not yet be members of a men's secret society. Other boys watched the action, as well as girls and some adults; bystanders encouraged either the attackers or the defenders. A boy who threw a Logholo masker to the ground took great pride in this act, and was envied by other boys. When a group of Logholo masqueraders traveled through compounds other than in their own community, it was an open challenge to the boys living there. Fights broke out and there was fierce hitting and whipping.

The boy masqueraders of Okumkpa and Logholo each carried the leaf of a certain tree in their headpiece as a protective charm, as adult maskers did. In both cases, this meant that the masquerader could not be touched by females, on pain of illness or barrenness occurring to them. The night before performing either masquerade form, the boys slept in their society rest house in order to avoid contamination from females, for contact with them was believed to spoil their performance. Adult masqueraders refrained from sexual activity the night before their performances for similar reasons.

For two other boys' masquerades, *Otero* and *Okpa*, the special leaf was absent and there was no taboo on girls touching the performers. Boys planning to mask in one of these forms could sleep in their regular male home in the compound, rather in their society rest house. Both these masquerade forms played with, and chased girls, as well as other boys. The dress for Otero was constructed of banana leaves, with a metal bell around the waist and a raffia headdress covering the face. Otero appeared as a single masker, or two or three together, but not usually more. Its players pranced around the compound chasing boys and girls. Girls would hide in their homes, where masqueraders were not permitted to go. The girls sometimes taunted the maskers, darting out to shout "slave," or "wicked," or like terms, egging them on. If a girl touched a masquerader, or was touched by him, nothing unfortunate was believed to happen to her. However, if she knocked off his mask to reveal who he was, she had to have the purifying sacrifice performed for her at the boys' shrine. This also had to be done at the men's shrine if a female knocked down a man's Otero mask. Sometimes small boys were frightened of either a boys' or the men's Otero. They would run away to the amusement of older persons, who might try to get them to face the masquerader.

Okpa, a less common masquerade, was only occasionally performed in the boys' societies, though it was more often seen in adult performances. Its dress of a looped-string form, with some raffia attachments, covered all of the body but the hands and feet of the masker, who carried a stick in his right hand. The adult form of costume was not made at Afikpo, but in nearby Igbo groups, such as at Amaseri, where it was purchased at considerable expense. Boys sometimes prepared makeshift ones at home. A boy Okpa masquerader, usually acting alone, also chased uninitiated boys as well as girls, but in a gentler, less fearsome manner than Otero. It mostly pranced about the masquerader's compound, and was enjoyable to observe. Since adult Okpa and Otero also chased and played with boys, who would run away, hide, and the come out again, the boys were quite familiar with their style of behavior, and could readily copy their actions. The boys were also keen observers of the more complex Okumkpa masqueraders, which were not as simple to emulate. All boys' and men's masquerades discussed above were public; the secrecy was supposedly in who the performers were.

It is not surprising, in this Christian region of Nigeria, that boys' troupes, based on their societies, or informally organized, performed at Christmas time. They would move from home to home through a number of communities, making a point to stop at the residences of prominent Afikpo families, where they generally received small gifts of money for performing. Sometimes the boys' masks were of styles that indicated that they came from outside of Afikpo (fig. 5.4).

Masquerading was one of the high points of the boy's activities. There was a sense of creativity, and sometimes of mystery about them, and the boys were pleased when they received positive responses from viewers. Masquerading allowed for publicly aggressive actions on the boys' part in their Otero and Okpa performances, and for various forms of assertion in the satiric skits of their Okumkpa masquerade. Obtaining gifts of money or food from watchers through masquerading was not a major aspect of the activities, as it sometimes has been in other African cultures.

The boys' masks and costumes, following the men's pattern, were kept in their rest house, or in the compound ancestral shrine house, if that of the boys was not in good repair. But these materials usually did not last long and had to be replaced frequently. Boys sometimes became quite skilled at mask and costume making, later using these abilities during initiation into an adult society and even afterwards as members.. Sometimes a capable boy would make a mask or costume for another youth for a small fee. Some of the best Afikpo carvers developed their skills as children.

Physical strength was one criterion for leadership at Afikpo for status among boys as well as young men. Thus, boys willingly engaged in fighting without any of them wearing masks. Sometimes they fought one another within their society, but some of their fiercest contests were with boys in other compounds or communities. They developed strong whipping abilities, and in not flinching when others hit them. Whipping occurred, and still does, through the men's secret societies, in a more organized fashion. This sport was supposedly secret from boys who had not been initiated into a men's organization; women were also forbidden to watch the contests. Boys' whipping was much in the same style, though simpler.

Adults did not normally interfere in the masquerading or the other activities of the boys. Nor did they direct, or guide, the boys' societies, or act as their sponsors. However, sometimes a father advised a son over some aspect of his activities in the boy's society, or assisted him with his costume. Only if boys interfered with adult activities would the latter step in. The boys' societies and their masquerades stressed independence from parental autonomy, while emulating male adults, their activities, and values. Despite the fighting and whipping that went on within each society, the members valued cooperation. Since the particular level of a boys' society reflected age, strong peer-group relations existed among boys of similar ages, who lived within a well-delineated residential areas. In contrast, there was hostility to boys outside of their age and place of residence. The importance of both age distinctions and of place of habitation in Afikpo life became imprinted on the youths.

The activities of the third and highest level of the boys' societies were very much like those at the second level though the youths possessed greater skill and were more experienced. Their activities served as models for younger boys, and they often had the best masquerades. There was a greater degree of organization within the societies at this senior level, though also a good deal of fighting within and outside of them. The older youths had developed a good deal of experience in activities that would stand them in good stead in their initiation into the men's societies, and in the years afterward.

Conclusion

Afikpo boys' masquerades were but one aspect of a broader emulative pattern with reference to men and their activities. This was evident in the existence of boys' rest houses and shrines, the *ajaba* masquerade dressing sites, and the taboos on girls. In the boys' activities there was not a great deal that was original, except in the Okumkpa skits and songs, which usually involved fresh material every year, though its general form followed that of the men's Okumkpa. However, it was all new and often exciting for each boy going through the process of joining and taking part in the boys' societies.

The fact that the boys' masquerades took place during the same ritual season as the men's reinforced a sense of emulation. It is not surprising that boys gained many of their masking ideas from men's masking in a culture that prizes masquerading so highly. It was always popular entertainment and a source of male symbolism and power. At Afikpo, the ritual period has always been a season of change, when many feasts and festivals are held. It has been a time of settling land disputes, as well as other legal issues, before the next farming period. It has been the period of title taking, both within and outside of the men's secret societies. It has been the time that initiations into the men's societies have occurred. It is a period when there are numerous marriages, and also some divorce settlements. It has always been a season of social activity at the community level, as well as in the smaller residential groupings within it. In the remainder of the year people are active in farming and fishing, in which the older boys play useful roles. Life becomes more family-oriented, and it involves smaller numbers of individuals who work hard at productive labor. The boys' masquerading and their other activities helped provide them with a sense of seasonal change, of the swing of life between work and play.

The ritual period was also a time of social change for boys: they held the initiations into their own societies, moved upward in the ranks of these organizations, and finally into a men's society. As boys this occurred when they moved in social orientation from the compounds to the larger community level. They went from activities with other boys, who were very likely patrilineal kin, to the larger sphere of community life, where many individuals were unrelated to them. They went from unsophisticated masquerades to more skillfully performed ones.

Since the boys' societies and their masquerades were well developed in the 1940s, it is likely that they existed in the nineteenth century, a time when there was warfare at and near Afikpo. Afikpo men hired out as mercenaries to fight elsewhere, and slave trading and child kidnapping occurred. In this context, the whipping and chasing masquerade activities of boys, duplicated in the more organized and elaborate forms of men's whipping contests, can be seen as preparation to become fighters. This orientation was also evident in the physical hardships and stress of the initiations into the men's societies. The boys' active physical life was to prepare them to be able to attack outsiders and to defend their own communities. One probable explanation for the gradual decline of boys' masquerades and their societies by the time I carried out research at Afikpo, is that after the British conquered its communities in 1902, warfare and slaving gradually died out.[8] Training to be warriors lost its meaning, although emphasis on physical skill and strength did not completely die out. These were to some extent retained for their value in farm work, and because strong men attract females.

Afikpo men did not know the origin of most of their masquerades, except for several men's forms, which were clearly derived from neighboring Igbo and non-Igbo groups. It is likely, however, although Afikpo men do not state it, that some of the masquerades that Afikpo men know to be quite old, derived from one or more non-Igbo groups who were probably the first inhabitants in the area. In any case, Afikpo men assumed that their masquerading commenced as an adult activity, and then boys came to emulate it. However, the reverse is possible, that adult forms gradually grew out of children's masking. To bring forth this alternative is not to suggest that the Afikpo men's adult masquerades are childlike. In any case, it is likely that men masqueraders, in their performances, linked emotionally with their past childhood masking experience. After all, they had had masquerading experience from childhood to adulthood over a number of years. For adult male masqueraders, the past was folded into the present, but in more sophisticated forms.[9]

The boys learned something about humor, the nature of performance arts in their culture, and about what was attractive or not to others in their masquerades. They gradually developed an aesthetic sense, which would serve them well in the future. They acquired control over their own bodies through masquerading and other society activities. When the boys were finally initiated into an adult society they were no longer novices. The initiation was partly a test of their abilities and past experiences. Of course, in their initiations they also encountered new, and often traumatic, experiences.

The boys' activities in masking and with their own shrine were introductions to spirituality, a beginning of religious experience. However, these activities were probably viewed more as play than as religion. Whatever religious feelings were developing in the boys were likely to have been reinforced by their exposure to the compound ancestral house and its shrine, and to sacrifices that they took part in with their parents.

On a more somber note, one has to realize that even at the time of my research at Afikpo, the death of children through illness, accident, and the killing of twins[10] was not a rare event. This certainly was common in earlier times. Life expectancy was low, and a boy's parents might die while he was still young. Children lived in a world of considerable uncertainty about life. In this context, the boys' societies, with their masquerades, provided stability and regularity that must have been welcomed. Those were joyful periods of group cohesion and friendships, in contrast to the probability of individual loss and sorrow.

Secrecy was an element in the boys' societies, although some of it was a kind of play secrecy, certainly not as serious as that of the men. Boys learned how to hold secrets, learned to whom they could reveal that they were masqueraders and to whom they could not. They had a sense of privacy from others in their boys' rest houses. What they did there was their own business, away from the public world, even though older boys and men know perfectly well what went on.

While the boys' activities stressed male bonding, their masquerading, especially the chasing forms, were ways of relating to girls. This suggests that there were interests developing between the two genders. However, other matters, such as the taboos on girls and the punishments for violating those taboos, which were discussed above, and the fact that they did not masquerade, tended to move girls and boys apart from one another. Also, the models for girls were their mothers and other adult females, while for boys it was fathers and other adult males; this drew them apart. However, although girls did not masquerade, they were certainly involved in some of them, and, of course, they also viewed the boys' masking events. I believe that the girls were keen observers of masquerade activities and took delight in watching them. Girls had their own singing and dancing organizations, which employed women's songs and others verses that they themselves created. They were also organized into groups to keep their compounds clean.[11]

Notes

1. The 1952-1953 research was supported while I was an Area Research Fellow of the Social Science Research Council, with a grant from the Program of African Studies, Northwestern University. The 1959-1960 research was undertaken with the support of a National Science Foundation Grant. My former wife, Nora Ottenberg, made thoughtful comments on an earlier draft of this chapter.
2. For further information on the boys' masquerade societies, beyond what is presented here, see S. Ottenberg 1975, 1982a, 1989.
3. P. Ottenberg 1958, 1959, 1982; S. Ottenberg 1989.
4. Excision usually occurred between the ages of five and fifteen. It was, however, a requirement for admission to adult men' societies.
5. S. Ottenberg 1989.
6. S. Ottenberg 1972, 1975.
7. S. Ottenberg, 1975.
8. Another reason is that because many boys are going to school they cannot spend as much time in the boys' societies as boys formerly did. Some boys are living away from Afikpo, either for their education, or because their parents have moved away. Also, some fathers have acquired sufficient wealth at an earlier age than before, thus they can initiate their sons at an earlier time.
9. S. Ottenberg 1989.
10. Until the 1960s, the killing of newborn twins at Afikpo was common, as it was at various earlier times throughout much of Igbo country. The rate of twin births was and is high at Afikpo, as it is throughout southern Nigeria.
11. P. Ottenberg 1958.

Bibliography

Ottenberg, Phoebe. 1958. "Marriage Relationships in the Double Descent System of the Afikpo Ibo of Southeastern Nigeria." Ph.D. diss., Northwestern University.

_____. 1959. "The Changing Economic Position of Women Among the Afikpo Ibo." In W. R. Bascom and M. J. Herskovits (eds.), *Continuity and Change in African Cultures*. Chicago: University of Chicago Press, 205-223.

_____. 1982. "Sex Polarity among the Afikpo Igbo." In Simon Ottenberg (ed.), *African Religious Groups and Beliefs: Papers in Honor of William R. Bascom*. Berkeley, CA: Folklore Institute, Meerut, India: Archana Publications, 79-94.

Ottenberg, Simon. 1968. *Double Descent in an African Society: The Afikpo Village-Group.* Seattle: University of Washington Press, American Ethnological Society, Monograph no. 47.

_____. 1971. *Leadership and Authority in an African Society: The Afikpo Village-Group.* Seattle: University of Washington Press, American Ethnological Society, Monograph no. 52.

_____. 1972 (1996). "Humorous Masks and Serious Politics Among Afikpo Ibo." In Douglas Fraser and Herbert M. Cole (eds.), *African Art and Leadership.* Madison: University of Wisconsin Press, 99-121. Reprinted 1996 in Roy Richard Grinker and Christopher B. Steiner (eds.), *Perspectives on Africa: A Reader in Culture, History and Representation.* Cambridge, MA: Blackwell, 423-449.

_____. 1975. *The Masked Rituals of Afikpo: The Context of an African Art.* Seattle: University of Washington Press.

_____. 1982a. "Boys Secret Societies at Afikpo." In Simon Ottenberg (ed.), *African Religious Groups and Beliefs: Papers in Honor of William R. Bascom.* Berkeley, CA: Folklore Institute; Meerut, India: Archana Publications, 170-184.

_____. 1982b. "Illusion, Communication, and Psychology in West African Masquerades." *Ethos* 10:2, 149-185.

_____. 1989. *Boyhood Rituals in an African Society: An Interpretation.* Seattle: University of Washington Press.

6

Omepa and *Onyeweh* Children's Masquerades

Robert W. Nicholls

Masquerade genres unique to children, would appear to be a long-standing African tradition and not as rare as their omission in the literature might imply. Within children's masked dance groups, children entertain themselves, and on special occasions may perform for adult audiences in exchange for gifts. In Africa, the tradition of children performing for adult approbation is pronounced. Carrington,[1] for example, recalls that youngsters of the Mbole people of Zaire would make a talking whistle out of a spherical forest fruit. These were used to solicit gifts by serenading older relatives and reciting their drum names. During the 1970s and 1980s children's masquerades could regularly be seen in Otukpo Town, Benue State, seeking pocket money at Christmas. In Orlu, Imo State, about 1976, I witnessed two different Igbo boy's masks called by the generic term *Agaba*. They toured family compounds with a troupe of boy dancers during the Christmas season and danced in return for gifts. One wore a humanistic face mask, while the other had a long snout (fig. 6.1). My sense is that Agaba masks, especially the one with the snout, are distinctly the province of children and are not replicated in adult society, but my stay in Orlu was short and I learned little about them. I did, however, study the *Omepa* and *Onyeweh* boys' masquerades of the Igede of Nigeria's Benue State and learned they represent not only two different types of boy's masquerade but two distinct conventions. I also documented costumed girls' dances of the Igede such as *Ogbete*. In addition to firsthand observation and interviews, photographs were taken and tape recordings made. Omepa and Onyeweh tunes are included on *The Igede of Nigeria album*.[2]

Through songs and costumed dancing, individuals in Igede are exposed to the values and qualities that their society deem important. Within Igede oral traditions verbal proficiency is a valued attribute, and song texts serve as mnemonic devices for the storage and transmission of information, and also as a means by which young people are initiated into the mores and conventions of adult society. Masquerade songs establish group identity, instill pride, and foster social integration. Other dance songs disseminate local news, critique behavior, and comment on the ills of society. Dance similarly provides a meaningful form of symbolic communication that can demonstrate normative behavior both directly and metaphorically. The gestures, stances, and locomotion manifest fundamental worldview principles such as fertility, egalitarianism, innovation, respect, reciprocity, solidarity, and competition. Dance is social behavior, which on the level of the individual serves as a medium for self-expression by revealing character traits, attitudes, aesthetic sensibility, physical prowess, and the extent of enculturation. It provides a forum for nonverbal communication between individuals including admiration, derision, praise, and rivalry. It offers an opportunity to impress, woo, confront, flatter, challenge, and provides a means to enhance social status. Masked dancing is concerned with the enactment of power. Manifesting ethnic norms, a traditional masquerade invests a ceremony with ancestral authority and serves to ratify rites of transformation, whether seasonal rituals such as New Yam Festivals or life-cycle rituals such as a funerals. It follows that the Igede perceive that the enculturation of young people into music and dance traditions is critical.

I became interested in the expressive culture of the Igede during my tenure at Ahmadu Bello University in Kaduna State, Nigeria. The Igede of Nigeria (formerly known as Egede) are an Idoma-related group who occupy Oju Local Government Area in Benue State, bordering Anambra State at the southwest and Cross River State at the southeast. It should be noted that there are cultural similarities between the Igede and the Idoma, and other ethnic groups in the region such as the Iyala, Igala, Iyachi, Ukele, and Igbo. Although Benue State formed part of the Protectorate of Northern Nigeria in colonial times, the Igede resisted northern Islamic influences, which impacted on some Nigerian music and dance. Musicologist Akin Euba[3] notes that "Igede music preserves many distinctive features and has been little affected by Hausa-Fulani musical traditions...[for example, it remains] rich in vocal polyphony."

Many of the men's associations of the Igede past were connected to war. However, with the cessation of institutionalized warfare, such music lost much of its status. Commenting on this situation, Ranung[4] states: "The expanding sector of Igede associational life today is that of the mixed dance groups. In this respect we can talk of a 'feminization' of Igede music." Having raised this tantalizing point, which in Ranung's terminology applies to the complete music and dance complex (*ayilo*), he does not pursue it. However, the "feminization" of Igede music and dance, and how it might be conceptualized, is explored below. This chapter concludes that in response to changing times one might talk not only about the feminization of Igede music but also the "youthization," since some adult masking practices in the modern era such as *Iboma* seem to reflect the conventions of young people's masquerading rather than those historically associated with adult male genres.

In order to locate Onyeweh and Omepa children's masquerades within the universe of Igede music and dance, this chapter compares not only the visual arts—the masks and costumes—but also examines dance choreography, song texts, musical styles and instrumentation as a means of distinguishing between different types. Music and dance genres may be similar in some respects but not in others. For example, Onyeweh is comparable to some girls' associations in musical instrumentation and, to a lesser extent, costume and choreography, whereas its song texts are more typically those of boy's associations. For the Igede, a costume, or some element of one, is a necessary indication of the dancer's special status, short-lived though this may be. Often it consists simply of a cloth tied around the waist, or alternatively around the head or wrist. During a funeral, the deceased's relatives, both male and female, wear special cloths such as *ejenta* and *eturubabah*, which are recognized as burial shrouds.[5]

Discussing the visual appearance of dance in terms of dance costumes, rather than simply "masks," reduces the disparity between the genders. Mask wearing in most of Africa is strictly the province of males. Exceptions include a version of the *Ogbodo Enyi* masquerade that is danced by women of the Izzi Igbo, neighbors to the Igede, and the *Zooba* masquerade of the *Sande* society of Liberia.[6] Ranung[7] states of the Igede: "Women master dancers may never wear a carved mask or a costume belonging to it. Instead they dress up in colorful clothes, and disguise their features with the help of facial painting functioning as a kind of equivalent to masking." These days costumed dances of adult Igede women are rarely seen and one must look to adolescent female dances for examples of women's costumes. It is worthy of note that Kasfir, who observed the *Babangida* costume-dance performed by "some little girls" in the Uwokwu district of Igedeland, comments: "It comes as close to a 'masquerade' as anything I have seen girls do."[8]

Children's Music and Dance

With regard to costumed dance there is a flexible continuum between sacred and secular, and to describe any dance performance, whether by children or others, as merely "play" is to underestimate the role of dance in Igede society.[9] Most performances are thought to conduct supernatural beneficence to some degree or another, irregardless of whether the performers are men, women, or children.[9] In Igede, as elsewhere, dance provides a common ground of shared experience between human and supernatural realms. *Alegwu*—the spirits of the dead (*Alekwu* in Idoma)—are thought to have a particular penchant for music and dance, and during public celebrations and festivals they assemble with the living to be entertained. Moreover, as with the Kalabari, the deity's propensity to help the community is proportional to the quality of the entertainment provided.[10]

In many ways Igede children's dance cannot be viewed as separate from the adult world, for children get co-opted into adult activities and their music making is important to Igede communities for a number of reasons. The Igede's belief in reincarnation engenders a cyclical view of time. In most societies that feature ancestor worship, elders are revered both as links to the past and for their proximity to the forebears. By the same token, children, as recent arrivals from the other-world, are considered near the life-force and in close rapport with the spirits. The Bobo of Burkina Faso also have a cyclical time sense; Le Moal[11] suggests that Bobo adults attach significance to children's imitation of adult ritual because in a sense the children are the parent's own ancestors. Exemplifying this view, Ojo[12] reports that among the Yoruba of Ekiti, groups of young girls took to singing incantations, an expression even denied to adult women, as a vehicle to criticize adult society. When challenged they denied responsibility, attributing the songs to the ancestors. Thus excused they were allowed to continue. Armstrong[13] shows that in the ancestral songs of the Idoma of Otukpo, the terms "father" and "child" are interchangeable and that the hallowed Alekwu ancestral mask is referred to as "The Child." He states: "Throughout these songs, long departed ancestors and their *Alewku* masks are referred to as 'child.' The ancestor is the child of some still earlier ancestor."

According to Erny,[14] who examined the symbolic meaning of childhood in Africa, the child participates in society as: (1) a symbol of growth and transformation, (2) a being close to the ancestors, (3) an example of the endless reincarnation of the lineage, and (4) an innocent, a symbol of divine wisdom. Representing the last of these attributes among the Igede young, uncircumcised children are considered the embodiment of purity and sometimes symbolize this quality where purification is required. For example, because of the association with menstrual blood, a woman's death is traditionally thought to defile the compound, which requires purification as a result. One purification ritual involves passing objects associated with the deceased through the smoke of the blacksmith's fire. According to Idikwu[15] (1976, 18), "this important ceremony is carried out by a boy of about six years of age, who has not yet been circumcised. He is regarded as being very pure and without any blame." The special status awarded children in Igede society is encapsulated in the chorus of a song rendered by teenage Agidi Obaike and her younger sisters:

> *Anyanjwo ichiche mweje*
> *Anu mweje nyamu*
> *Anu ja bwo olegwu bioka ee*
> *Anu mweje nyamu*
>
> Little children sing
> Sing with them
> Nobody knows what their spirit (*olegwu*[16]) tells them
> Sing with them

In the past the *Adiya* dance was performed by two young virgins as a fertility ritual connected to the New Yam Festival. The two girls, the Adiya dance queens, were transported from the Adiya compound to the dance arena on a mat, in order that their purity would not be defiled by contact with ordinary ground. It is significant that little girls were chosen to perform a dance that celebrated a ritual reunification in the Uwokwu district of Igede. This event was described by Sidney Kasfir, who characterized the installation of a new district head in Uwokwu district in 1986 as an "emotional reunification of the district," settling a feud between three warring factions. She states, "Some little girls had invented a costume-dance which they call (appropriately) '*Babingida.*'"[17] The name was borrowed from the status of the then Nigerian head of state, Ibrahim Babangida, to symbolically seal the reunification.

Each Igede village encourages young people to form children's music and dance associations to insure that the society of the future will have accomplished performers at funerals, New Yam festivals, and other ritual or social occasions. Adults, in particular parents and older siblings, encourage children to engage in music and dance from an early age. In the questionnaire distributed by this author, 43.5 percent of the respondents indicated that specific individuals influenced their induction into music and dance. These included fathers, other family members, and expert musicians.[18]

In a community where children traditionally spend long hours working alongside adults, time for recreation away from the compound is necessary. This author's observations of the Idikwu household confirm that more of a youngster's leisure time is spent drumming and dancing than with any other form of recreation. On moonlit evenings, boys and girls may steal away to the *ojiya* (village meeting ground—not to be confused with the *Ojiya* girls' ensemble of the Ekiti Yoruba[19]) to interact with their peers and play those universal games such as tag, hide and seek, or dance such dances as *Ogbete, Oge, Olalah,* or other dances performed spontaneously. Ogede[20] notes, "moonlight play situations are occasions when older Igede children invent songs." The music making of children on these occasions is somewhat undifferentiated with regard to gender, and until the age of nine or ten, boys and girls tend to sing and dance together.[21] No special costumes are worn, although when children perform for adult approbation their mothers will dress them in their best clothes.

When they are nine or ten, boys and girls tend to separate into gender-specific groups. Young girls, although not excluded from the mixed teens-and-twenties associations such as *Ijo* or *Odege,* usually prefer to form their own *Imere* or *Ogbete* associations. Unlike such dances as Oge and Olalah, which are basically games and do not appear to have an associational structure, the organization of children's societies parallels that of adult groups. For example, like adult music associations, Omepa and Onyeweh boys' associations each operate under the patronage of an influential and respected adult leader, who becomes their *Ada-ilo* (father of play). Children's associations also elect from their ranks managing functionaries such as *Akiraa* (secretary) and *Alijwoh* (directors), who play a vital role in organizing the group and arranging public performances.

Boys' Masquerade Ensembles

In Omepa, the youngest member of this boy's association of Obohu village is about five years old, while the upper limit includes a few eighteen- or nineteen-year-olds who round out the harmonies by contributing voices in a lower register. The present author observed a performance of Omepa. Drummers played the *ubah, egbong,* and *okpirih,* and *icheche* maracas were shaken. Recalling the warrior societies of bygone times, one of the drummers of the Omepa ensemble wore a skull cap decorated with a dozen or more feathers. A series of solo dances and a trio dance were performed by individuals wearing the requisite cloth as described above. Although all of the instrumentalists were male, two females were included among the solo dancers. The Omepa masquerade danced alone and wore a raffia *onyunwunyu* costume with a humanistic wooden face mask painted black with red rims around the eyes and mouth. In Igede fashion, the dances of the Omepa masquerade concluded the ensemble's performance (fig. 6.2).

The membership in the Onyeweh (Something New) Boy's Ensemble of Andibla village is younger, on average, than the Omepa Ensemble, and few, if any, teenage boys are members. The Onyeweh association has two masquerades that dance as a duo. This author observed a performance that commenced with a solo non-masked dancer wearing a matching red sweater and shorts. This was followed by two Onyeweh masquerades who danced to an instrumental number executed by drummers and an icheche player. Their dance was not so much in unison, rather their bobbing up and down and fluttering movements were in counterpoint to each other. Their costumes resembled short shift dresses, tied at the waist, and with elbow length sleeves. The material had a maroon background and was printed with green and cream foliage patterns outlined in black. Tassels of the same material were attached to the hem. One dancer wore a white sock on his left foot and a blue sock on his right. The other dancer was barefoot. Both dancers wore "jingle bell" ankle rattles. Their masks were not of carved wood but were simply hemispherical calabash halves. The smooth surfaces of the masks were daubed with silver paint and holes were pierced through for the eyes and mouth. Cloth and tufts of goat's mane covered those parts of the head not covered by the mask (fig. 6.3).

Girls' Ensembles

As an institution Adiya died out during the 1940s. Adiya was not so much a music association as a title, "Dance Queen," that was awarded to personable young women who, through formal training, acquired distinctive dance skills. These girls were chosen for their beauty and skills in dancing. One was fair in complexion (*Aloho*) and the other smooth black (*Omilonya*).[22] The elaborate decoration of Adiya dance queens included beads wound around the head, two white hemispheres painted around the lower side of the eyes, and vertical parallel lines painted on the legs.

The idea of paired dance queens continues in the *Imeri* association, a term for the name "Mary" which is danced by two adolescent girls in the center of a dance ring. There are conflicting versions of the provenance of Imeri. According to Ranung[23] this dance arose out of the earlier *Ijo* music type that was imported into Igede from the Ukelle of Ogoja in Cross River State. John Eriba Idikwu disputes this although he acknowledges that Imeri is of the same general dance genre as *Ijo*. He maintains that, "The *Imeri* dance is a modification of *Odege*. The modification was introduced by the Uwokwu clan," the clan which was the originator of Odege. He differentiates between Odege and Imeri in that "flutes" are played in the former but not in the latter and that Imeri features dance queens.[24] In Ranung's[25] photograph of Imeri dance queens, the two young ladies have white powder on their faces and wear black head scarves from which a profusion of red plastic threads dangle. The Imeri dance proved so popular that in 1975 it was selected by the Benue Plateau State Government to perform in the All Nigeria Festival of Arts and Culture.

Named after a sweet, intoxicating wine made from guinea corn, *Ogbete* songs and dances are strictly the province of unmarried girls. Originating in the late 1960s, it is a successor to Imeri and Ijo music, which it displaced to some extent. Following in the footsteps of the *Imwo* and *Ihih* women's association, the lyrics are often satirical and express social criticism. Ogbete songs are sung by participants as they dance in a circle around a lone male drummer. Each song is terminated by a fast, foot-stamping dance, which is initiated by intense drumming punctuated by blasts on a whistle (*aji*). The Ogbete costume consists of a gathered blouse, wrapper, and head tie. Leg rattles (*iworo*) are usually worn and pink powder may be put on the face. This author observed a performance by girls of Ibilla Primary School who simply wore their school uniforms. Such associations as Ogbete occasionally perform at funerals, for they provide an opportunity for eligible adolescent girls to be viewed for marriage. More commonly, they perform at festivals or during seasonal holidays when they may tour family compounds for pocket money.

How do such children's associations relate to the adult music and dance associations of the Igede? In order to explore the connections between Onyeweh and Omepa, and adult masquerades, it is necessary at this point to discuss briefly the music and dance conventions of adult Igede males and females. This chapter hypothesizes that Omepa is modeled on adult warrior masquerades such as *Aitah* and is an apprentice or "trainee" ritual masquerade. Relative to Onyeweh, although some similarities exist between Onyeweh and newer masquerades such as Ijo and *Iboma* of young adults, the music and dance Onyeweh performs, their masks and their costumes, are distinctively the province of children. Imeri dance queens echo the fertility cult of Adiya, which utilized the dance of virgins within an adult ritual. In contrast, the Ogbete girls' association ostensibly serves to train girls for membership in *Imwo* and *Ihih* women's associations. It is ironic that while the adult women's associations have declined, Ogbete has grown in popularity.

Adult Music and Dance Associations

Men's Masquerade Ensembles

In the past, male music ensembles would stage dances during warrior initiations, battle victories, and member's funerals. Warriors of renown were identified by the red *uma* feathers they wore, while the best dancer would be invited to wear the masquerade costume. The masquerades of Igede music of war (*ayilo nya ewu*) symbolize the force that protects society and are necessarily fierce and awe-inspiring. Even adolescents who were posted as lookouts at the village outskirts developed their own vigil dances. For example, two *Eworo* masquerades would perform in body-stocking costumes.[26] These days, with the cessation of internecine warfare, warrior masquerades perform principally within funerals. In itself the Igede warrior masquerade is ostensibly secular representing male power and is not a religious icon. It is the conjunction of warrior masquerade and funeral ceremony that leads to their characterization here as ritual artifact. Although festive, a funeral is a sacred event and special rites help insure its success. On the night preceding the funeral a chicken is sacrificed on the large *ogirigboh* (slit-drum) and the blood and feathers daubed on the instrument. This talking drum represents the voice of the ancestors and the offering is believed to improve the instrument's sonority. On the day of the funeral, elderly female relatives bring a burial cloth enclosed in a woven mat belonging to the deceased and place it in a tree as a mark of his presence. *Ilo* (sanctified water) is sprinkled around the dance arena as protection against witchcraft. The masquerader is required to handle special leaves before donning the mask, and special rituals are performed during de-masking, to "cool" his head and disperse the supernatural energies. Should the masquerader fall during his performance it is considered the equivalent of a curse and he is required to eat the neck parts of a goat to symbolically strengthen his own neck for mask wearing. During the funeral, the eldest son is given a pot to break, symbolically releasing the soul of the departed. Various groups may perform during a man's funeral including women's or adolescents' associations, however, the occasion is sealed by performances of warrior masquerades such as *Ogirinye, Onyantu, Abakpa* and *Aitah*.[27]

Three basic masquerade costume-types can be discerned. They are: a crocheted body stocking that covers the face as well as the body; a large, shaggy raffia costume that increases the illusion of monstrousness; and a colorful, billowing velvet costume that is showcased by the dance of the "female" masquerade (worn by a male dancer). Most Igede masquerades conform to one or other of these three categories. The body-stocking costume of Ogirinye, a masquerade of some antiquity that also is found among adjacent ethnic groups, is tight-fitting and, like the costume of modern American mythological figures such as Batman and the Lone Ranger, it accentuates the human torso and projects a heroic quality. Among the Igede this costume type is normally worn with a head crest effigy. A shaggy raffia costume (*onyunwunyu*) is worn by the male masquerades of Aitah, Abakpa, and Onyantu. It is commonly, but not invariably, worn with a large frontal face mask—Janus-faced in the case of Onyantu– with pierced eye-holes so the dancer can see out. The male masquerades of the Aitah of Adum-Owo and Aitah of Andibla each have a female partner with a "smooth" *ibelebele* costume made of colorful velvet that covers the dancer from head-to-toe. Eye-holes are cut in the velvet so that the dancer can see. Ibelebele does not wear a frontal face mask, but instead has a carved effigy of a human head set on top of the costume above the dancer's head. The female Aitah of Adum-Owo village has a reddish pink face, bulging yellow eyes, and a pair of vertical horns that are fluted in a spiral fashion. The masks of the Aitah association of Obohu village are both male, and are dramatic in appearance, with boldly chiseled features. One is painted bright yellow and has large silver-painted horns, prominent teeth, and a band of studs stretching across the forehead. The other mask is black with red rims to the eyes and mouth. Its large teeth are biting a black and yellow-banded snake that stretches around the face. The snake's tail lies beneath the right eye, while its head is on the forehead of the mask between the eyes. A small warrior clad in a loincloth stretches from the rear of the scalp and is frozen in the act of cutting off the snake's head, which probably refers to the historical custom of taking trophy heads.

The instruments used by an Aitah association include prestigious talking instruments such as the ogirigboh slit-drum (large and small) and the *opikeh* bugle horn. These are accompanied by ubah, egbong, and okpirih drums; metal gongs (*ojeh*); and maracas (*icheche*). Masquerade's song texts are short, repetitious, and dance oriented. The ostinato refrains often relate to the act of dancing, such as "*Ahi ka chewo*"—"We shall dance." Other texts sung by warrior associations foster group solidarity and are competitive or boastful in content. A song performed at a funeral by the Aitah ensemble of Obohu has the refrain "*Omurukpa dewu ju'be nyamu*"— "The wasp wages war because of its home." Additional paraphernalia included the ceremonial *ijachi* spear, *iworo* leg rattles worn by dancers, and war regalia such as the *ehwong* wrist-shield.[28]

Women's Ensembles

Women's funerals are less ostentatious than those of men; moreover, they take place not in the *ojiya*, but in the compound of the woman's husband or father. Either male or female dance groups may perform, but any masquerades that appear are those of the associations to which the husband or father belonged. On other occasions, women engage in ritual activities that may involve singing and dancing, although not at the level of a large public event. For example, *Apuruja* is a women's healing cult, in which the afflicted individual is dressed in various leaves and beats iron *ubeje* rods (traditional currency), while dances and incantations are performed around him or her. The role women play in the traditional sociopolitical life is articulated by their membership in women's societies such as *Imwo* or *Ihih*. In addition to safeguarding the purity of drinking water, Imwo functions primarily to regulate female conduct in public settings and protect the interests of its members. Okita[29] states that "*Imwo* could be regarded as the watchdog of respect and dignity for womanhood and...it was the source of sexual morality in *Igede*.... Members could threaten and impose sanctions on those who said or did anything that would lead to the undermining of female respect and dignity, and this applied to married men and young boys alike."

One means by which Imwo guarded against socially unacceptable behavior was through derogatory songs. The pointed and biting satire contained in the lyrics regulated the conduct of overzealous males. The threat of being derided publicly is an effective means of encouraging conformity to social norms. As a casualty of Christianity and encroaching Western influences, the Imwo society has largely died out in Igedeland.

According to Ode Ogede,[30] Ihih songs relish exaggeration and melodrama, and are mostly heard at village meetings, parties, funerals, and weddings. Ogede remembers performances at Uchenyim village; people would gather at a local dignitary's compound every two weeks. They were recreational events in which Ihih women sang and members and other individuals present danced. Food and drink were served including local *burukutu* gin. Igede women do not beat drums; men provided the instrumentation by playing the ubah and okpirih drums and the aji whistle. It was a secular occasion and no special libations or rites were performed. Costumes as such were not worn, but both men and women dressed in their best attire. For Ihih women this involved conventional wrappers and head ties. Ogede explains that it was an age-grade association and those members present would comprise the ensemble. There were no dominant lead singers, instead any member could break into song as inspired and extemporize on the spot. Local gossip and controversial issues, some involving marital disputes were aired and advice freely dispensed. Although the song texts were significant the event was very much a dance. Songs were not delivered in immobile positions since the dance context allowed tongues to move freely. According to Ogede, the last performances of the Ihih Association of Uchenyim village took place in the early 1980s.[31]

Dance, rather than song texts, is the primary focus of some women's music associations such as the *Abwo* (Bamboo) ensemble of Andibla village, which was observed by this author in 1979. For Abwo, named after the bamboo clapping sticks that the women use, male musicians provide drum instrumentation. The repetitive choral refrains are sung in the Ukele and Iyala languages, which are not widely understood, and feature hocket techniques, in which a lead singer traces the melody against a counterpoint refrain provided by a second soloist, while the ensemble repeat the chorus. As with Ihih, the participants wear their best clothes but no costumes.

Mixed-Gender Ensembles

In Igedeland, many associations, including those of children, have doubtless emerged and declined over the centuries, always conforming, however, to a continuity of traditional standards and aesthetic models. The colonial era discouraged some musical events, such as those connected with martial traditions, and encouraged others, notably those associated with the West and Christianity. Today, traditional ensembles are disappearing due to the impact of modernity. As a result there is no longer a great diversity of warrior associations and those that remain no longer celebrate battle victories or warrior initiations. In his study of Igede music and dance undertaken in the early 1970s, the Swedish ethnomusicologist Bjorn Ranung noted a decline and secularization of traditional music and characterized this as a "feminization" of Igede music. He states:[32] "The expanding sector of Igede associational life today is that of the mixed dance groups. In this respect we can talk of a 'feminization' of Igede music." How Ranung conceptualizes the "feminization" of Igede music is rather obscure. However, on his music album, which, incidentally, includes no purely female music associations, the only groups that meet the criteria of "mixed dance groups" are the tracks of *Ijo* and *Iboma* ensembles.

Ijo is a recreational dance type that is performed by young adults of both sexes, and its song texts are rudimentary. According to Ranung, who recorded a song by the Ijo ensemble of Andibla village, Ijo was adopted from the Ukelle ethnic group of Cross River State, and became popular throughout Igede during the 1960s. There are no masquerades, instead Ijo participants dance in a circle to the accompaniment of two egbong drums, two icheche maracas, and one ojeh gong and, "with the help of a whistle (*aji*) 'the head of the music' directs the performance."[33] Okita[34] (1973, 4) describes *Iboma* (*Ibwoma*) as recreation for adolescents and suggests that such playful dance occasions provide an opportunity to socialize with peers of the opposite sex. According to Ranung,[35] Iboma was created in 1957 by a woman of Ojenya, one of the major villages of the Oju clan, who had been compelled to take care of the baby of her sister who had died. The child had been crying for her mother and the stepmother had to soothe it and lull it to sleep by frequent singing. In the years that followed Iboma spread rapidly throughout Igedeland, but its center is still Ojenya village and its association there features Aleka Ominyi, a leading poet and singer. Instrumentation includes an egbong and ubah drum, an ojeh gong and icheche maracas. Unlike Ijo, the Iboma associations have masquerades, but do not use the aji whistle. The masquerade's costume varies. A "male" masquerade in a rough raffia onyunwunyu costume and a "female" in a smooth velvet ibelebele costume may appear together or, more commonly, masquerades dressed in body-stocking costumes topped by carved wooden effigies perform. The fact that no set masquerade costumes are proscribed gives a clue to the fact that these are considered "recreational" as opposed to "ritual" masquerades, and the masks that are worn are intrinsically less threatening than those of warrior associations. As is customary, the masquerade costumes are worn by male dancers, but females may enter the dance arena to dance with the masquerades, an act traditionally considered taboo. It is of interest that Ogede states that the texts of Iboma songs serve as a counterpart to Ihih (below). Unlike traditional masquerades it is the texts rather than the masquerades that seem to be the focal point of an Iboma performance.

Traditional Pedagogy

The picture that emerges from a review of traditional education in Africa is of a system that is weighted toward social learning and the development of vocational competencies.[36] Among the Igede, enculturation into music and dance possesses broad utility as a form of education and socialization. It is considered important that children learn to perform because it is pleasurable and encourages sociability, it develops their talent so they can become contributing members of society, and it preserves traditional culture. Studies of learning in traditional Africa show it to be largely self-directed, and direct experience and learning-by-doing occurs more often than teaching.[37] Pedagogical methods include role modeling, peer learning, and imitation.[38] Adult intervention includes both verbal instruction and reinforcement in the form of praise or criticism. Elsewhere, this author[39] discovered that both imitation and expert instruction are featured within Igede music and dance pedagogy, and that imitation (77.3 percent) occurs more widely than expert instruction (45.5 percent). It was also found that a significant amount of imitation and expert instruction occurs between peers and may not involve adults. An example of this is provided by the transfer of the *Ikpirigidi* dance, a costumed acrobatic dance performed by youths, which was introduced into Igedeland from the Utonkon Idoma of the Okpokwu area of Idomaland in 1965. "They were invited to play in Ikwokwu [a village in the Ito district of Igedeland] so that the youths in this area could also perform the music. The music was performed and through imitation it was mastered by the youths. From this village, the dance spread to other villages in Ito."[40]

Evidence of imitation in music and dance is readily apparent. During performances, whether children's, adolescent's, or adult's, young children are keen observers. During a funeral at Obohu meeting ground at which Aitah masquerades performed, young children were initially kept back to the outskirts of the crowd. However, during the course of the event most managed to squeeze their way to the front where they watched with rapt attention. The use of tin cans as a substitute for drums is common, and one creative boy stretched plastic over the open end of a dried-milk can in imitation of a membrane drum. Unhindered by the lack of appropriate costumes, Igede children are always ready to improvise. I photographed an infant boy who danced with a plastic bag headdress in imitation of a masquerade. Or during an informal Ogbete dance in a family compound, mango leaves were threaded around the ankles to mimic leg-rattles.

The Omepa masquerade copies adult masquerades of the overtly male Aitah and Abakpa warrior associations and is ostensibly an apprentice or "trainee" ritual masquerade since, in the sense that the proscribed behavior that accompanies masquerade performances is observed, it serves as a training ground for future ritual specialists. Although the prestigious talking instruments are excluded from the Omepa ensemble, the masquerade dances to the same music as adult masquerades, and ubah, egbong, and okpirih drums and icheche maracas are used to weave Omepa's lively rhythms. Evidence of imitation is readily apparent. At least for the sake of convention the Omepa masquerade is awarded the same respect as an adult Aitah masquerade. Before it appears, *ilo* (sanctified water) is sprinkled over the dance arena to protect it against witchcraft, just as with adult masquerades, and it is accompanied by an attendant with a cane switch who serves as a guard and a guide. With its rough raffia onyunwunyu costume and carved mask, the Omepa masquerade is a youthful imitation of an adult masquerade. A wooden mask of the adult Aitah masquerade of Obohu has gaunt black features and red rims to the eyes and mouth. The mask of Omepa has similar coloring, however, unlike the adult masquerade, its "younger" face is chubbier with rounded features and minus the snake that adorns the adult mask. The imitation factor is apparent in Omepa songs also (see below).

Unlike Omepa, whose masquerade is like a miniature Aitah, Onyeweh has no direct counterparts in adult society. Onyeweh costumes and masks are unlike those of any adult masquerade observed by this writer; cross-generational imitation does not appear to be a factor. Unlike Omepa no preparatory rituals were observed preceding their performance. Although similarities exist between Onyeweh and newer masquerades such as Iboma of young adults, the music and dance Onyeweh perform, their masks and their costumes, are the province of children. It is more accurate, therefore, to place Onyeweh within a category of recreational dance associations that exist among Igede children of both sexes. Like Imeri dance queens, Onyeweh perform as a duo. This affinity is apparent in Onyeweh's music also. The bursts of intense drumming accompanied by blasts on a tin whistle that initiates fast foot-stamping dances is shared by Imeri and Ogbete associations. Although tin whistles are not used by adult male ensembles, they are used by mixed-gender Ijo groups and, according to Ogede,[41] by the Ihih women's ensemble. In the case of Onyeweh it would seem likely that imitation occurs laterally between various children's groups rather than vertically through the generations as occurs when a child copies adult groups.

Song Texts

The lyrics of the songs associated with the various music types further clarifies the distinctions. The songs of young children constitute a melange of various music types and often reflect the songs of adults. The belittling of rivals, which is found in warrior refrains, also appears in children's songs, as in this song performed by young boys and girls of the Idikwu household:

A ya ya ee
Anyi nya Ainu la ori Imany?
Anyi nya Ainu la ori ita!

A ya ya ee
The children of Ainu have how many ropes?
The children of Ainu have three ropes!

Sarcasm is a major ingredient of songs of ridicule. In this song, the children of Ainu village are ridiculed for having so few ropes. Warrior songs are boastful and provocative, and/or dance oriented. Refrains are rudimentary and are repeated in an ostinato call-and-response fashion. The connection of Omepa to adult masquerades is apparent in their songs, some of which are calculated to reinforce group solidarity. An example is "*Al'Obohu ru inwa le-enu*"—"The people of Obohu collect honey in the afternoon." Collecting honey in the afternoon is considered an act of bravery since honey is normally collected at night when the bees are dormant. The Omepa song, "*Go ehwong ju abwo*"— "Put the *ehwong* on your hand," makes a connection between fighting and dancing. The *ehwong* is a goat's hide wrist shield that was traditionally donned for battle. Today it is worn by dancers, including masquerades, in the dance arena. Some of the lyrics of masquerade songs simply refer to the act of dancing. The refrain of an Aitah song recorded at a funeral held at Obohu is "*Ewoh, ewoh, ka'i chi*"—"Dance, dance, let's do it." The same song is part of Omepa's repertoire. It is of interest that the two recordings that I made of the Aitah and Omepa ensembles' rendition of this song are in the same key even though they were recorded on separate occasions.

Satirical commentary in song texts is often associated with the Igede chanteuse. As discussed above, the songs of women's groups such as Imwo and Ihih are directed at creating behavioral change and can thus be considered redressive. The intent is that listeners pay heed and correct objectionable behavior. Included among songs of the children of Uchenyim village documented by Ogede,[42] is a song by a group of little girls and boys that conforms to the social critique genre of Ihih and Ogbete:

O d'onu chim ka
M w'eje ka
O d'onu chim ka
M w'eje ka
Alikpa nyam a d'onu chim ka
M w'eje ka

Chorus

Inyi ki r'ichicheh
I pyeh-pyeh-pyeh, i pyeh-pyeh
Inyi ki r'ituka
I nmo-nmo-nmo

I nmo-nmo-nmo
I h'inu gbogbilo-gbogbilo
I h'inu gbogbilo-gbogbilo
Arichal h'inu gbogbilo-gbogbilo

She doesn't say hello
I don't mind a bit
She doesn't say hello
I don't mind a bit
My friends don't say hello
I don't mind a bit

Chorus

The skinny ones
Sneak quietly away
The big, fat ones
Rudely bulldoze by
Rudely bulldoze by
They perpetually twist their faces
They perpetually twist their faces
Aricha perpetually twists her face

Ogede[43] discusses how such a song is directed at creating behavioral change:

> The speaking voice belongs to a group of children addressing a particular girl, Aricha, whose individualism they evidently view as a source of danger to one of their society's most cherished values—group solidarity. They make a running commentary on Aricha's misbehavior in order to discourage any other person who might be inclined to behave like her from doing so. Since the singers know Aricha and see her daily in their midst, they may feel that their singing can directly influence her to change her bad habits. The rude comments that underlie their singing, then, are meant to serve an instructional purpose.

The special license enjoyed by Imwo and Ihih women's associations is extended to the Ogbete girls' association. The following Ogbete song focuses on a local dispute. Along with contested land claims, market disputes are a common source of discord among the Igede.

Ogo anyi ra chaji
Nyo ka la Onyike
A'Lukpa go anyi ra chaji
Nyo o'ka la Onyike
Ori odudu

They sold their own children
So as to own Onyike
Ukpa people sold their own children
So as to own Onyike
In vain.

Onyike is the largest market and is thought of as an Igede-wide market. Attempts by any single group to claim ownership is resisted. It is unlikely that the Ukpa clan "sold their children" in the literal sense. The most politically contentious song collected by this author was an Ogbete song.[44] At the time of the study, the Och'Idoma, the paramount chief of the Idoma, was the late Mr. Abraham Ajene Okpabi. He was a popular figure among the Igede and a source of pride in that he hailed from Igedeland. Nevertheless, the following song acts as a reminder that even celebrities should not forget who they are and where they came from:

> *Okpobuna l'Igede*
> *Ajene 'kpobuna l'Igede*
> *Oyi lomu ki Kpoto*
> *Ajene ye lomu li Kpoto*

> He comes from Igede
> Ajene comes from Igede
> He turns himself into an Idoma
> Ajene turns himself into an Idoma

(*Akpoto* is the old term for Idoma. Here it is abbreviated to *Kpoto*).

It is worthy of note that Ogede[45] links Iboma (*Ibomah*), the young adults' mixed-gender group, to Ihih woman's associations, at least as far as song texts are concerned. He states, "In content there is no dividing line between the two types, both focus on matrimonial problems; but while *Ihih* discusses such problems from the woman's angle, *Iboma* represented the artistic response by men." Ranung[46] recorded a song of the Iboma association of Ojenya village and provided a translation of the text. The song, which is sung by Aleka Onminyi, the composer, contains ninety-three lines of text that refer, either directly or metaphorically, to marital problems, male-female relationships, economic hardships, misogyny, and parenting. For example, "I am the neglected animal they drive away each day, but I stay with me eyes burning" refers to unrequited love. While "climbing a mountain is more difficult for me than pounding with a pestle" refers to the difficulty of marriage with Idoma (i.e., non-Igede) women.

Although the dance and music of the Onyeweh boy's association have been compared to Imeri and Ogbete, the lyrics of Onyeweh songs, unlike those of Ogbete, do not offer social critiques, but, similar to male dance music types, foster group solidarity, proclaim the emergence of Onyeweh as a modern ensemble, and contain oblique references to folk tales. For example:

> *Onyeweh, ahi a lee*
> *I ya ee, Ijwo m'onyi ka je onyi ka*
> *Eje ku ro ibailon*
> *Anyi nya Ibilla we le*

Onyeweh, this is us
I ya ee, Leopard bears no child so knows no child
Eje wears *bailon* (synthetic fiber)
The children of Ibilla have come

The "Feminization" and "Youthization" of Music and Dance

For the Igede, the ancestors in their conservative aspect are manifestations of "the dawn" or tribal beginnings. But because the dawn occurs each day, the ancestors also have a regenerative aspect that signifies rebirth and creativity. Omepa and Onyeweh reflect these two aspects of tradition. Omepa mimics adult masquerades of the overtly male Aitah and Abakpa warrior associations whose presence marks every respectable funeral, and through a process of imitation prepares young people for adult roles. In contrast, the Onyeweh masquerades have no traditional counterparts in adult society and are distinctly the province of children. Thus, while Omepa represents conservative aspects of tradition, Onyeweh represents those creative aspects of tradition that provide a new, modern vision of society. Although both categories of children's masquerade may provide the future community with performance specialists, associations such as Omepa overtly serve as a means to this end, while associations exemplified by Onyeweh are fully realized, but may have this result as a possible further consequence.

The question is raised, who copies whom? This chapter refutes the assumption that the adult music ensembles act as the only models for children to imitate and that children's masquerades are invariably small versions of adult genres. Instead, the Onyeweh masquerade can be seen to be a fully formed children's recreational masquerade that is not potentially anything beyond itself—"play for plays' sake." Rather than resembling adult masquerades it seems to have more in common with girl's costumed dance associations such as Imeri. The girls' Ogbete association, on the other hand, like the boys' Omepa association ostensibly provides training for adult roles, but Ogbete currently exists in limbo since adult women associations on which it is modeled have become extinct. A teenage girl, a member of a teacher's college choir, confided in me that she joined the choir because she felt she was getting too old for her Ogbete association.[47] The Ogbete genre may once have been influenced by Imwo and Ihih, but these no longer provide performances to copy. Instead, the Ogbete genre is spread among peers and such imitation and instruction that takes place is now strictly children's preserve.

In light of Ranung's pronouncement of an ongoing feminization of Igede music, a consideration of Ijo and Iboma provides some interesting conclusions. Both are non-ritual, secular associations performed for recreation; both are relatively new Igede dances, originating in the late 1950s-early 1960s; both are associations for young adults in which male and female dance together. But whereas Ijo is danced in a circle like Imeri and Ogbete, and like them uses an aji whistle to coordinate the dancers, it does not have set costumes or masquerades. Iboma on the other hand does have masquerades. The idea that Iboma, which originated in 1957, has song texts that serve as a counterpart to those of Ihih, a woman's tradition of some antiquity, is provocative. Moreover, a music that has its origins in lullabies is far removed from the fierce and aggressive music of war, typical of the masquerade traditions of Igede men. This, no doubt is what Ranung means by the feminization of Igede music.

Without knowing the history of Igede dance, it might be tempting to depict children's associations such as Imeri and Onyeweh as youthful versions of recreational associations of young adults such as Ijo and Iboma. However, the evidence suggests that the children's genres are historically antecedent to Ijo and Iboma, and, therefore, an inverse causality is more likely. Thus, it might be argued that in response to changing times and the impact of other cultures, one might not simply talk about the "feminization" of Igede music but also about "youthization," since some adult masking practices in the modern era such as Iboma seem to reflect in part the conventions of children's masquerading as represented by Onyeweh, rather than those traditionally recognized as adult genres. It would be overstating the case to suggest that the mixed-gender associations overtly mimic children's associations, but assuming that individual members may have belonged to children's ensembles in the past, it could be that they are simply reproducing behavior they learned as children, rather than progressing to adult associations as they would have in the past.

In order to remain alive and vital a community's expressive culture must adapt to changing circumstances. Traditionally, the Igede's belief in reincarnation engendered a cyclical view of time whereby children were considered close to the life-force and in close rapport with the ancestors. Evidence collected by Armstrong, Le Moal, and Ojo[48] suggests that as a result of the African cyclical sense of time, the adults of many African groups attach significance to children's performances and see ancestral expressions within them that are capable of providing new models and visions to society. As African societies like the Igede enter the twenty-first century it is important that new, creative visions of society are fostered. Perhaps it might behoove Igede adults of today and others to look closer at children's music and dance for the inspiration they can yield.

Notes

1. Carrington 1949.
2. Nicholls 1991.
3. Euba 1976, 398.
4. Ranung 1973.
5. Idikwu 1976, 47.
6. Cole and Aniakor 1984; Monts 1984, 53-59.
7. Ranung 1973.
8. Sidney Kasfir, personal correspondence 2/27/1986.
9. The term "play" is singularly important in discussions of West African enactments.

It is regularly used by native practitioners throughout Africa and less so by Western scholars. In common English, "to play" connotes lighthearted behavior such as the games and recreation of children. Certainly, Igede children's dance is a playful activity. The broader African usage also includes occasions of import such as rituals. Allen (1981, 233) discusses the difficulty in translating the Kiswahili term *cheza*, which variously means "to play, to play an instrument, to dance." He states: "As playing and dancing are more or less inseparable, it is often convenient to translate *cheza* 'dance.'" In Hausa parlance, "*wasa*" (play) describes a wide range of recreational activities most of which involve music and dance. The patron of an Igede music association, *ada'ilo* (*ada ayilo*) commonly translates as "father of play." Within Igedeland the *ojiya*, an open area at the center of each village, is described in the literature variously as the "town square" (Ikoni 1988, 30), "the central meeting ground" (Ranung 1973), and "Igede stadium" (Eru 1990, 7). However, the local people invariably refer to it as "the playground." This despite the fact that traditionally, serious activities such as trials, public trials, public deliberations, funerals, and ritual sacrifices take place there, as well as dance festivals and children's games. Within public rituals elements of recreation and entertainment are usually present. In her study of Idoma masking practices, Kasfir (1988, 3) discusses the blurring of boundaries between ritual and entertainment. She exclaims: "Indeed, it would do a disservice to the reality of African masking performances to polarize them in this fashion...[for] in the Nigerian village where I lived, masquerades were both a primary form of enactment of religious ritual and the most popular form of entertainment."

10. Horton 1960.
11. Le Moal 1981.
12. Ojo 1986, and see his chapter in this volume.
13. Armstrong 1969, 2.
14. Erny 1973.
15. Idikwu 1976, 18.
16. *Olegwu* is the singular of *Alegwu* and refers to an individual's soul.
17. Sidney Kasfir, personal correspondence 2/7/86.
18. Nicholls 1995.
19. See the chapter by John Ojo in this volume, who spells the term *Öjija*.
20. Ogede 1994, 116.
21. Ode Ogede, personal communication 5/29/1995.
22. Johnson Ochelle, personal communication, 1978.
23. Ranung 1973.
24. John Eriba Idikwu, personal correspondence, 4/1/1979.
25. Ranung 1973.
26. John Ochelle, personal communication, 1979.
27. Nicholls 1984.
28. In addition to Igede masquerade song texts, which are dance oriented, there is a genre of philosophical songs sung by males on social rather than ritual occasions. Associations featuring these songs are normally centered around an originator and lead singer such as Ibuh Okuobo of the *Iged'Agba* association; Micah Ichegbe of the *Adiya* association (a re-working of the traditional title), and Odeh Egban of the *Etuh* association. The songs of *Etuh* feature folk tales, wise sayings, and proverbs. Because performances are recreational and highlight song texts, such associations use neither the ritual paraphernalia nor the talking instruments of warrior music; however, members may wear costumes. At the Etuh performance I witnessed that a dozen or so members wore identical uniforms, consisting of sky blue kaftan shirts and trousers with red and orange patterns. A lone male dancer clad in this uniform

and flourishing the association's emblem danced sporadically, but dance was not the primary focus. Other men's associations may wear age mate or professional group uniforms on special occasions such as funerals or festivals. Professional hunters, "*imukpe*," for example, wear distinctive black costumes and special hunting charms and amulets.

29. Okita 1973, 14.
30. Ogede 1988, 131.
31. Ode Ogede, personal communication, 5/31/1995.
32. Ranung 1973.
33. Ranung 1973.
34. Okita 1973, 4.
35. Ranung 1973.
36. Adams 1982a, 1982b; Lema 1973, 146.
37. Evans 1970; Erny 1972, 131.
38. Hinckley 1985, and see her chapter in this volume.
39. Nicholls 1995.
40. John Eriba Idikwu, personal communication 1979.
41. Ogede 1988, 131.
42. Ogede 1994, 114.
43. Ogede 1994, 114.
44. Nicholls 1992.
45. Ogede 1988, 131.
46. Ranung 1973.
47. Oto'o Obaike, personal communication, 1978.
48. Armstrong 1969; Le Moal 1981; Ojo 1986 and see his chapter in this volume.

Bibliography

Adams, Milton. 1982a."A Modern Analysis of African Traditional Pedagogy: Implications for Contemporary Education." A research proposal sponsored by the Institut de Recherche, d'Enseignment, et d'Experimentation en Pedagogie, Ivory Coast, presented at the 1982 annual conference of the African Studies Association.

_____. 1982b. "Behavioral Objectives, Processes and Outcomes in African Traditional Education." A paper presented at the 1982 annual conference of the African Studies Association.

Allen, J. de Vere. 1981. "Ngoma: Music and Dance." In Mtoro Bin Mwinyi Bakari, *The Customs of the Swahili People.* Los Angeles: University of California Press, appendix III.

Armstrong, Robert Gelton. 1969. *Music of the Idoma of Nigeria: Edigwu Sings the Ancient Songs of Oturkpo, Nigeria.* Music album with notes. Smithsonian Institution, Folkways Library.

Carrington, John F. 1949. *The Talking Drums of Africa.* London: Carey Kingsgate.

Cole, Herbert M., and Chike C. Aniakor. 1984. *Igbo Arts: Community and Cosmos.* Los Angeles: University of California, Museum of Cultural History.

Erny, Pierre. 1972. *L'Enfant et son Milieu en Afrique Noir.* Paris: Petite Bibliotheque Payot.

_____. 1973. *Childhood and Cosmos.* Washington, D.C.: Black Orpheus Press.

Eru, Peter. 1990. "Igede Agba Agba Festival: A Time for Reflection." *The Voice* (Benue State Newspaper) September 1, p. 7.
Euba, Akin. 1976. "Review of *Music of Dawn and Day...*" by Bjorn Ranung." *Ethnomusicology* 20:2, 398.
Evans, Judith L. 1970. *Children in Africa: A Review of Psychological Research.* New York: Center for Education in Africa, Teachers' College, Columbia College.
Frampton, A. 1935. Intelligence Report on Egede District. MAKPROF:AR/IN/1/9, unpublished.
Hinckley, Priscilla B. 1985. "Let Me Dance Before You: The Educative Role of Performance in a West African Children's Masquerade." Ed.D. diss., Boston University.
Horton, Robin. 1960. *The Gods as Guests: An Aspect of Kalabari Religious Life*. Lagos: Nigeria Magazine Publication.
Idikwu, Simon Eriba. 1976. *Burial in Igede*. Oju, Nigeria: L.G.A.
Ikoni, John O. 1988. "Igede Indigenous Religion." In Ogwuna Oboh, Ogaga Agocha, Isaac Ode, John Adima, and John Aja, (eds.), *Igede Gedegede: Selected Essays on Igede Culture and Language*. Oju: Local Government Council, Benue State, Nigeria, 27-33.
Kasfir, Sidney L. 1988. "Masquerading as a Cultural System." In Sidney Kasfir (ed.), *West African Masks and Cultural Systems*. Tervuren: Musee Royal de L'Afrique Centrale, Tervuren.
Lema, A. A. 1973. "Black Civilization and Education." *Presence Africaine*, 87, 3eme trim.
Le Moal, Guy. 1981. "Les activities religeuses des jeunes enfants chez les Bobo." *Journal des Africanistes* 5:1-2, 235-250.
Monts, Lester. 1984. "Dance in the Vai Sande Society." *African Arts* 17:4, 53-59.
Nicholls, Robert W. 1984. "Igede Funeral Masquerades." *African Arts* 17:3, 70-76.
_____. 1991. *The Igede of Nigeria*. CD Album. Chapel Hill, NC: Music of the World.
_____. 1992. "Music and Dance Associations of the Igede of Nigeria: The Relevance of Indigenous Communication Learning Systems to Rural Development Projects." Ph.D. diss., Howard University.
_____. 1995. "Dance Pedagogy in a Traditional African Society." *International Journal of African Dance* 2:1. Philadelphia: Temple University.
Ogede, Ode S. 1988. "Igede Oral Literature: Preliminary Issues of Identification." In Ogwuna Oboh, Ogaga Agocha, Isaac Ode, John Adima, and John Aja (eds.), *Igede Gedegede: Selected Essays on Igede Culture and Language*. Oju: Local Government Council, Benue State, Nigeria.
_____. 1994. "Oral Performance as Instruction: Aesthetic Strategies in Children's Play Songs from a Nigerian Community." *Children's Literature Association Quarterly* 19:3, 113-117.
Ojo, John R. O. 1986. "Ojiya: Children's 'Masked' Dance in Two Ekiti Yoruba Towns." Paper presented at the Seventh Triennial Symposium on African Arts, Museum of Cultural History, University of California, Los Angeles, April 3.

Okita, Silas I. O. 1973. "The Historical Evolution of Religious and Related Ideas and Practices in Igede." B.A. thesis, Ahmadu Bello University, Zaria, Nigeria.

Ranung, Bjorn. 1973. *Music of Dawn and Day: Music and Dance Associations of the Igede of Nigeria*. Music Album with notes. No. LXLP 513/514. Helsinki, Finland: Love Records.

7

Three Points of View of Masquerades among the Ijo of the Niger River Delta

Anna A. Hlavácová
[For Amatu Braide and Jack Moses]

This chapter treats of young children's responses to adult masquerades as well as the boys' own masquerades. It is written in the context of changing conditions in masquerade performance in various Kalabari communities in coastal southeastern Nigeria.

Kalabari Children View Adult Masquerades

"*Afuru* is coming. *Mgbula* is around!" The tension of children rises as a masquerade approaches their homes, slowly and systematically, performing his duty for the whole community. Adults know that *Mgbula* will not forget their compound, and their curiosity is animated mostly by the thief masquerader *Afuru* (from *furu* to steal). Adults experience it again with their children, who are going through it for the first time.[1]

Mgbula appears on the last day of our calendar year, as if in approaching New Year's Eve he is carrying the community to safety and security into the new year. His nature is a preventative, cleansing, and curative one. Palm fronds around his neck, carrying a bent sword in each hand, he goes from ward to ward healing the sick by jumping over them and by the touch of the sword as they lie prostrate on the ground. All the children, boys and girls, receive Mgbula's preventative visit. Afuru looks like a "classic" Halloween ghost, with a hat and feathers. For him there is no special dance, unlike Mgbula, except that he acts like a thief and takes things.

Afuru performs from the morning, stealing what he calls "his father's property." He has the right to steal, to take, while Mgbula drives away disease, evil, and restores good health. Later in the afternoon there is an auction, where you can buy back what you have lost, if still needed. Afuru is assisted in his auction by some younger persons without masks.[2]

Between the rainy and dry seasons waters withdraw into the ocean. Nigerians in the southern coastal area worry that an upland evil may settle with the sediment and affect their delta. So, in the night, Mgbula is expected to deal with this, before his visible performance and after. As we went from Buguma to Abonnema between the two years, early in the first morning of 1994, we met Mgbula of Abonnema going home after his work was done:

> Where does he go?
> To the mangrove.
> How has he come?
> Now on a boat, but for the first time...

The myth is that Mgbula was introduced to the Kalabari by a prince of the royal lineage. He did not come through spying neighbors or through people who live at the waterside, but of his own accord. Prince Amachree pleased him so Mgbula decided to become his friend and taught the prince all about himself.[3] Through his royal connection Mgbula is linked not only with the environment, but with a kind of national or cultural consciousness. The masquerade is believed by Kalabari to have come from the water, but since the headpiece faces the spectators, as most masquerades of inland origin in the Kalabari area do, it is probable that it came from the land and the Igbo people to the north. Masquerades of coastal Kalabari origin generally have headpieces that face skyward.

Horton pictures one of these masks from Soku village, which is of wood.[4] But in Buguma today the top of Mgbula is made from woven basketry, keeping its cylindrical form of two inverted cones under palm fronds, signifying its curative nature (fig. 7.1). This masquerader carries two bent swords to show that strength may also be dangerous. But the Mgbula at Agbonnema has a conical shape decorated by palm fronds and leopard's teeth; the latter shows that he is dangerous as the swords are just two fresh boughs. The mask is worn on top of the head, facing the spectators, not the sky.

No child will forget the strange appearance of Mgbula jumping over his naked body, as is the practice. Often this experience will be one of his remembrances, if not the very first. And in his mind, life remains forever bonded to death, as well as to the two masquerade characters, Mgbula who heals and Afuru who steals. From the dark shadow of Mgbula's uncertain shape, there remains a visual memory of the masquerader's three white ovals shining from its face, ovals representing mouth and eyes, represented in connection with fertility in the shape of cowries.

> The recurrent image into preconscious terrors
> To explore the womb, or tomb, or dreams,
> all these are usual pastimes.[5]

At the age of a child's usual question of "Why?" it receives instead of an answer an experience in the form of a first touching of the world beyond everyday life. For the child the masquerade is without a background of understanding, in total illusion, since for the child there is no difference between dancer and mask. Whatever the child learns later on, this first concern with masquerade will have consequences for his understanding of it for his or her whole life. On New Year's Eve, as everywhere, people feel strongly about the passing of time. The masquerade performances personify the point in time when the existential "Why?" takes it place between the old and the new year, heaven and earth, earth and sea, life and death. These are celebrated with this question.

The stealing Afuru is reminiscent of someone trying to get everything from life, for he does no know how long he will live. At this time, people go to the river to throw in small objects with the words: "I am fed up with you. I don't want to see you again next year." In the recollection of the past they wish to give, to lose this day, since the one who will lose will eventually gain. As if to keep a chance for good luck for the next year, they clear even their unknown debts while performing this symbolical detachment. The sense of performance lies in holding past and future balanced. Mgbula's masquerade, including Afuru, has this as its raison d'être, which is at the same time the reason it is kept by the Kalabari men's *Ekine* masquerade society.

Children Playing at Masquerades

All over Nigeria new phenomena exist today. Young boys start to perform masquerades without previous entry into existing masquerade societies that were necessary for them to join in the past. Often, when they are cut from active participation in local traditions by various circumstances, they bring masks, headdresses, and dances from distance territories that remain unintegrated into the original local masquerades.

But in parts of the Kalabari area there has been a different experience. A child from the Kalabari seaport of Abonnema is masquerading, with a wooden face mask that probably once was a major mask of the adult Ekine society, which would have been worn facing skyward, not forward as this one does (fig. 7.2). The boys' ankles are wound with bottle covers that for him represent both rattles and Indian-bells that adult masqueraders use. He is wrapped in cloth with his large headpiece.

A masked boy has, of course, his followers, friends in the game. But the reaction of grown-ups is, if not anger, then a manifested ignoring of them, aimed at letting the children know their opinion of this activity. Indirectly this was expressed to me through an adult's words: "Why are you taking a picture of it? This is not a masquerade. It does not exist."

Of course, it is not a masquerade in the adult sense. The wood has old paint, there are no feathers on the costume, nor are there features of a communal event. However, it exists. Remarkably, while adults perform today in dashing new headdresses, the youngest play in the oldest masks.

In these riverine communities, a masquerade society is only open for men when they become adults, though there is no age-grade system here. In former times, Ekine society members used to seize all masquerades brought to the community from outside, a privilege they held from seizing masks of their enemies in war. Today people introduce so many new masquerades from distant places that the local masquerade society cares just to take over only if somebody performs what Ekine does. This attitude reduces the masquerades of strangers to the level of entertaining dances; to fully master the Ekine dancing is rare and deserves respect. Entry into Ekine is dependent on skills in dance and drum language, as well as financial considerations.

The existence of a *Fiasiri* dancing club at Buguma of young men, roughly between 15 and 20 years, reflects a certain tension between generations, but it is a sign of the community's health that there are still young men conscious of traditional culture and able to practice it, still respectful that the town's central square is Ekine territory. The Ekine society silently tolerates the Fiasiri masquerades, not impressed by the quality of its dancing. Slowly, masquerade dancing in Kalabari disassociates from the centralizing tendency of the past and toward pure performance. But in Buguma, as a rapidly changing society, local cultural identity is preserved, while in other Kalabari towns the youths often bring in alien masquerades, not always properly introduced, and with songs in languages that the spectators often do not understand.

At present many people just come home occasionally, which makes for the continual involvement in the traditional masquerade societies impossible. That is why the masquerade is partially left to boys that do not follow higher education. But this situation varies according to the location of the Kalabari town, how distant they are from Western influences. In Opobo, its elites, for the sake of the schooling of children and for employment, remain too far away to control the masquerades. Thus, the New Year's ones are reduced to secular entertainment. On the other hand, there is a feeling that something is missing. Young boys are unnecessarily violent, especially when not outstanding in dance. Similar signs can be found in Abonnema, where resistance to foreign impulses is not as strong as in Buguma, the capital of the Kalabari people.

In Igbo culture inland, unlike riverine societies, there is a long tradition of children's performance that prepares boys to play in real masquerades. Uninitiated boys play at *Okoroshi* with leaves or cardboard masks. Children imitate masquerades while they play and they may even be encouraged by adults, who help them to dress.

Coming to a second form of child's masquerade, it is well known that Opobo combines two distinct masquerade traditions, that from the riverine and that from the hinterland. This reflects historical events, with a population of both inland Igbo and coastal Ijo settlers. The carved lizard headdress carried by the boy in Opobo (fig. 7.3) faces skyward, typical of riverine people, and yet the attitude to it is taken from the hinterland. The age-grade system of the hinterland classifies masks according to their importance and releases only minor masks for the use of children. This means that serious masks are protected from children, so adults can cheerfully smile at the children's ones. Without this system the children might play at masquerades with a serious mask, which the adults could not smile at. Therefore, under these conditions in the hinterland, the masking of a child does not cause anger; in fact, it is even welcomed.

The Opobo child has probably been helped by adults to dress and to use the minor masks. Similar to the first example above of the Abonnema child's masquerade, this carved mask is not as recent as those employed in adult masquerades. Whether ignored or encouraged, Kalabari children are allowed by adults to touch abandoned objects, archaic objects of their society's culture. The youngest people approach the oldest objects. One is reminded of the Mgbula, where children are touched by the "old year." Or it recalls forgotten ancestral aspects with the Opobo Town masquerade, *Nwa Atam,* which has to be renewed to let new children be born into the community.[6] For a child, the opportunity to masquerade is a pathway to the past; for basically oral cultures it is often a way to transmit continuity. A male, while playing during childhood, goes through the history and culture of generations of his forefathers, and sometimes in this way he repeats the story of mankind, whether conscious of this or not. We find many cases in the world where the songs and dances originally belonging to adults have become those of children, or what may have formerly been a ritual has become child's game. In analyzing children's costumes we discover that archaic elements may be better preserved in children's dress than in adult wear. Age distinction is often stronger than aesthetic function.[7]

As for adult costumes, is the failure to wear older elements a desire to be "up to date?" A European example, probably closest to Kalabari masquerades, may be a transition within male costume, where peacock feathers, formerly worn by young men, came to appear only on little boys.[8] Among the Kalabari, plumes attached to an adult's headdress stand for the eyes of the masks. Children, as in Abonnema Town, can carry masks only without plumes. Such a child's mask is "blind." It would be difficult to imagine it otherwise in a society where a chief removes his feathers before approaching a woman to shake her hand. In some African societies, old carved masks are believe more powerful than newer ones, through the numerous performances they have undergone. Living in a society, such as Kalabari, that does not believed that, it is clear that in the rapid innovations of carvings these days, especially if they originate elsewhere, knowledge of specific cultural patterns can become lost.

In Africa, instead of spiritual architecture there is the masquerade. Instead of museums there are processions of masking children. What do children's masks, which are "blind," remind adults of in Kalabari society? Where is the inner eye of eyes? Where is the sense beyond senses? If then "la coiffure dangles sanctionne et commemore,"[9] masks without feathers used by children in Africa keep no element of power other than that of memory, a commemorative function of human desire for immortality of the community. While the wearer is part of the present the wearing prolongs a desire for immortality on the part of the individual human being.

In the final analysis, an attitude of a society towards the masking efforts of children depends on one of the two positions. In cultures with age-grade systems, the distinction is made *by the type* of headgear; if that of the children is regarded as harmless or powerless, there is no need to demonstrate it through the behavior of the on-lookers. On the other hand, riverine peoples, such as the Kalabari, have to distinguish *by taking a different attitude,* since for them the performance of children employs a carving from former adult masquerades that is probably still played by adults but with newer carvings. It looks as if among the Kalabari a preferable attitude of children is to respect the masquerade of adults. As an objective observer one can understand both attitudes. However, even if children themselves are not conscious that they remind others of a past, this message, on an existential level, happens through a performance that is a game. And that is the main reason why children's play at masquerade should not be disregarded.

Notes

1. There are at least three different important *Mgbula* performances, but the author witnessed only the described type. For information on *Mgbula*, see Iyalla (1983, 77) who regards *Mgbula* "as the most important of Kalabari masquerades."
2. Horton (1960, 44) depicts *Afuru* and in the caption he states: "When *Afuru* has picked a man's pocket, the stolen property can only be reclaimed by a payment to the members of the *Ekine* [men's] society–hence the mischievous amusement of the children."
3. Iyala 1983, 79.
4. Horton (1965, figure 35) calls the mask *Ngbula.* See Horton 1960, 31, for further discussion of this figure, which he describes as "the ugly, deaf and paranoiac water-doctor, whose masquerade stares at people as if to read their lips, then rushes savagely at them because he thinks they must have been insulting him in his infirmity."
5. Eliot 1944, 37.
6. Bell-Gam 1983.
7. Bogatyrev 1971, 77.
8. Bogatyrev 1971, 67.
9. Levi-Strauss 1984, 268.

Bibliography

Bell-Gam, Ruby A. 1983. "The *Nwa Otam* and Socio-Cultural Development in Opobo." In Nwanna Nzewunwa (ed.), *The Masquerade in Nigerian History and Culture.* Port Harcourt: University of Port Harcourt Publications Committee, 334-343.

Bogatyrev, J. 1971. *The Functions of Folk Costume in Moravian Slovakia.* Paris: Mouton.

Eliot, T. S. 1944. *Four Quartets.* London: Faber and Faber.

Horton, Robin. 1960. *The Gods as Guests.* Lagos: Nigeria Magazine.

Horton, Robin. 1965. *Kalabari Sculpture.* Lagos: Department of Antiquities, Federal Republic of Nigeria.

Iyalla, Bliss. 1983. "Concept and Functions of the Masquerade—*Mgbula.*" In Nwanna Nzewunwa (ed.), *The Masquerade in Nigerian History and Culture.* Port Harcourt: University of Port Harcourt Publications Committee, 73-82.

Levi-Strauss, C. 1984. *La chasses rituelle aux aigles: Paroles donnés.* Paris: Plon.

8

At the Threshold: Childhood Masking in Umuoji and Umuahia

Chika O. Okeke

One of the greatest mysteries of my childhood was knowing the home of the masquerades. In due season they would appear at dawn terrorizing or entertaining the village, depending on the nature of the particular masquerade. The war was on.[1] I was a barely three-years old. My hometown, Umuoji, is in today's Idemili Local Government Area of Anambra State, in Igbo country. The hostilities did not quite stop the seasonal rhythm of the masquerades, in part because, as I understood later, the sacred Python of the Idemili River, *Eke Idemmili*, kept the Nigerian soldiers away from Umuoji.[2] *Àyaka* and *Àjìkwù*, both night masquerades, continued to instill dread of the profoundest type in the dark dry season nights, and no one dared leave a lantern burning even in their inner rooms without drawing the ire of the masquerade. Perhaps the most terrible thing about Àyaka was its haunting voice that would sound so close when, as we were told, it actually was several miles away. And how was that possible? Only the initiated knew. The nights were dreadful, but by morning, everywhere it would be quiet (except for the distant thundering of mortar fire from the war and Ogbunigwe),[3] for the masquerades would have returned to their underground abode. On occasion, the only physical evidence of the nocturnal visits would be a table or chair—left by a careless trader in the village square—neatly anchored high up on the branches of the tall Indian almond tree. Who else but the superhuman Àyaka could perform such feats? For Àyaka, and indeed any other masquerade to return again, the initiated would perform necessary rites, pour palm wine into the ant hole, and the masqueraders would come forth, moving backwards from the belly of the earth, the abode of the spirits.

The war ended in 1970. We returned to Umuahia, the present capital city of Abia State, where I was born, and where my family had lived prior to the war.[4] It was a time for rebuilding, at least in the former Biafran region. But I was quick to notice that the masquerades in the Ndume-Ibeku community there were very different from those in my hometown of Umuoji. There were no *Àyaka*,

Ònyekulufá, Àjìkwù, or the mother of masquerades, Íjélé. But there was a thriving culture of children's masquerade especially during the Christmas or, less so, Easter season. We lived in a large tenement and most of the families came from outside the Umuahia area; most of the parents worked at the School of Agriculture, Umudike, at the Government College, Umuahia or the Rural Education Centre, which later became the Umuahia Campus of Alvan Ikoku College of Education.

At Christmas time, the girls would spend several nights learning new dances while the boys planned mask displays, often also including music ensembles. This way, the awareness of gender difference was subtly reenacted. The practice periods, therefore, were times for closer gender bonding. Although the adult masking tradition in Umuoji was different from that in Umuahia, children's masquerades in both were very similar, perhaps because they did not involve ritual. Rules of proper conduct hardly existed. There were no requirements other than being a young male living in the area—unlike in adult masking where one had to be a native of the given community to participate. Also young boys were not necessarily expected to appreciate the seriousness of masking—which at the childhood stage was mainly a means of entertainment. Because the children did not yet "know" the masquerade—which happened only during the initiation ceremony—they could get away with such things as removing their masks in full view of everyone without incurring any sanction.[5] This often happened after long hours on the road with the dry season afternoon temperature so high, the air still humid, and the costume stifling. Usually, when the masker was fatigued, he would signal his companions so they could find a secluded place to get some rest. Yet, certain procedures aimed at affirming the necessary secrecy of masking, though not enforced, were observed in children's masquerades. While, for instance, the girls would practice their new dances in the tenement courtyard, the boys preferred the backyard, keeping away from prying eyes, especially of the girls in the neighborhood. Similarly, to ensure sufficient anonymity, the masker would borrow some of the costumes from his peers so as not to easily give away his identity, but this was not always, if ever, successful. It is important to point out the two different types of children's masquerades: the aggressive, cane wielding type, and the dancer type usually accompanied by music makers. The first was more prevalent in the Umuoji of my childhood, the other more fashionable in Umuahia.

In Umuoji, the major masking period is the Uzo-Iyi festival season that usually takes place in March-April, but as a child I never had the opportunity to witness this event.[6] For me and my brothers, and cousins at Umuahia, Uzo-Iyi increasingly assumed mythic qualities, especially because as we were told, it was the occasion when the finest masks like Ógwùlùgwù and Ògòlò, and the most spectacular including Ijélé, Óbá Mmílí, and Nkénékwú, performed at the town square. But every two years when we traveled home to Umuoji for Christmas we had the opportunity take part in the children's masquerades, which usually took place on December 26, while the adult masks performed after that date. The children's masking day was dreaded by everyone because the maskers would go to absurd extents to corner their victim. Often, a child masker hides in the bush for several minutes patiently waiting for someone to come near enough before engaging the person in a chase, whip in hand. This way, one's chances of making a "hit" was increased. Needless to say, this unnerved girls and pre-middle-aged mothers, the usual victims of such stealth tactics. For this reason, such masquerades were derisively called *Mmonwu Ukwu Aja,*[7] and when spotted in the market square, an enthusiastic crowd of boys and girls taunted the masquerade, calling it *Opia-onye-kwu-akwu* (one-that-flogs-a-stationary-person). For these chaser masquerades, light costumes and non-cumbersome face masks are preferred to the more elaborate types that added a lot of drag, therefore impeding the masker's ability to race about. One particularly favorite type, called *Magbàdà*[8] or *Ògbá Mgbàdà,*[9] was made of a medium-weight woven cotton fabric, by weavers from the northern Igbo area, or bought from northern Nigerian traders. The costume covered the masker from head to toe, and sometimes a sparse raffia skirt was tied around the waist. Two small perforations in the face area allowed the masker an almost unhindered viewing field. Sometimes, however, the mask had a small wooden headpiece—like the one on *Ùlaga* or *Òji-onu,*[10] that was pushed to the masker's back when moving at full speed. Compared to costumes that included regular wooden face masks, the *Mgbàdà* child masker did not have to hold the face mask in order to stabilize it when engaged in a chase. It therefore enjoyed the reputation of being the most dreaded cane-wielding masquerade.

Apart from proving one's speedy prowess by the number of "hits" recorded before sunset, another significant part of childhood masking in Umuoji had to do with proving one's ability to endure pain. This took the form of engaging another masker by mutually flogging each other until one surrendered. For this, those who had the time, spent several weeks prior to the outing day in the bush searching for prime *Alo-anyasi*, a particularly popular shrub known for its toughness, and flexibility.[11] The youngest maskers used softer whips made from the mid-rib of the long leaves of a particular plant usually found in family shrines. Doubtless, this was one way of establishing one's place within the age group or circle of friends.[12]

The masking culture in Umuahia is not as elaborate as that of Umuoji. For the adults the major masquerade is *Èkpè*, which usually performs during the annual *Iri ji* (new yam) festival at the village square. The more prevalent masquerades are generically called *Ékpó*—often so huge and ugly that pregnant women are encouraged not to look at them, else their ugliness infect the child in the womb. Years later in art school I would learn that both Èkpè and Ékpó were derived from among the neighboring Ibibio-Efik who live in the Cross-River area. The children's Ékpó masks, however, are usually very colorful, with decorative patterns to enhance their attractiveness; they, too, are made elsewhere, perhaps also by Ibibio artists. The face masks, and raffia frills to complement the costumes are usually bought by the mothers as presents for their sons.

Occasionally, we prepared our own raffia skirt to be worn over the fabric costume. As part of the preparations, we also constructed our own drums. These were made from open-ended beverage cans covered on one end with a cellophane membrane tied down with dry strands from banana trees. The membrane was stretched taut by means of orange thorns carefully pushed in at the outside edges. With a few of these drums a bona-fide orchestra came alive to accompany the masquerade as we visited homes to perform for money and, less preferably, sweets. During the outing, it was often necessary to look out for menacing adult masks that usually carried machetes. At the sight of one we would make a tactical detour, and if the danger was very unambiguous we found the quickest route to safety.[13]

Older boys danced the more spectacular Òjì-onu.[14] This is the quintessential dance masquerade that requires a full complement of drummers, rattle shakers, and, most importantly, a flutist. The art of making the two-hole flute from bamboo sticks, like that of constructing cellophane drums for the younger boys, was a full-time hobby during the Christmas holidays. During this period also, the boys would carve the Òjì-onu head mask, which, technically speaking, is one of the simplest masks. Although, eventually, preference was given to the more refined and colorful ones bought in the Umuahia main market, which had a section where, on occasion, we would go with a parent to look at the masks and music-making paraphernalia.[15] Within any given group of boys, the best dancer was selected to perform with the mask since the success of the entire display depended largely on the masked dancer's ability to translate into dance, the lyrical song of the flute. Like Ùlàgà, Òjì-onu's performance was so popular that a competent ensemble was always assured of impressive gifts of money by appreciative spectators.

Through it all, the experience of childhood masking was, to say the least, complex, perhaps due to the different levels of the individual child's relationships with masking as peer activity, as social performance, and as personal experience. As peer activity, there was no doubt as to its use as measures of courage and strength, which translated to respect within the group. As social performance, it indicated whether the boy–as son or brother or friend to other members of the community–would develop into a fine specimen of manhood as constructed within that community. As a personal experience, it straddled various psycho-emotive states. The very first outing elicited anxiety and suppressed fear–anxiety about the known, such as being able to impress one's spectators by either dancing very well, or making numerous "hits," depending upon the nature of the masquerade. And about the unknown, such as finding out what it felt like to be behind the mask, *to be the masquerade*. Then there was the question of power inherent in masked performances. Behind the mask you could, if necessary, get back at another child with whom you had a score to settle, without fear of retaliation—especially if that other was a masked boy, or a girl from school or the neighborhood. The thrill of watching such a victim the day after trying to figure out unsuccessfully if you were the "merciless" masked one was one of the most memorable experiences of childhood masking.

In spite of all the excitement of Christmas masquerades in Umuahia, and the occasional thrills in Umuoji, it was with great anticipation that we–myself and my two older brothers[16]— looked forward to *Ikpu ani* or *Ima mmonwu*[17] back in our hometown. For as yet, we were but children, far removed from the secrets of the masquerade; nothing prior to the induction process prepared anyone for the *real* thing. Naturally, it happened at different times for each one of us since we had to do it with our age-grades. I still remember that very day, in 1978, the day, in Umuazu, Umuoji, when in the eyes of my kinsmen, women, and friends, I ceased to be a child. That day I finally learned how the masquerade emerges from the belly of the anthill. And the source of Àyàkà's fearful voice.

Notes

1. Nigeria-Biafran (civil) War, 1967-1970.
2. The majestic python, whose beautiful skin patterns are said to have been painted by the creator at the dawn of the world, is revered in Umuoji and other Idemili towns.
3. Ogbunigwe (Mass Killer) was the dreaded, mysterious explosive device invented by Biafran engineers during the war.
4. The often-misunderstood concept of "hometown," in Nigeria at least, refers to where one's father comes from and not necessarily the town where one was born. The idea, of course, is that the individual maintains active contact with the ancestral home, often through town unions, age grades, kindred meetings, and other socio-cultural organizations operative within the given community. Although I was born and spent most of my childhood in Umuahia, where my father and mother come from, Umuoji, remains my hometown. The situation is complicated by "documentary evident," like a birth certificate that often names one's place of birth, which in the scheme of the individual's life matters very little.
5. In Umuoji, for instance, *itikpo isi mmuo*–an untranslatable concept that defies mere description, but which for the sake of textual *convenience* might be called "the coming out of the adult mask in public"–would receive great sanction, including heavy fines imposed by the masking society. This usually happened during occasional violent fights between rival groups of boys from neighboring villages. As such moments, the burden was on the uninitiated males and women to avert their eyes from the sacrilege. Nevertheless, the "errant" child masker, who knew very well it was wrong to do so, would often be at the receiving end of harsh jokes days, even weeks, after the event. For this reason, many a child endured discomfort in his costume, even sobbing behind the mask, while struggling to keep his dignity and reputation intact.
6. Uzo-Iyi is the most popular annual festival in Umuoji. Unlike so many other ceremonies that have been adversely affected by Christianity, it remains the most important cultural activity for Umuoji people. It is the occasion when the town's twenty-four villages display their most important masks. But individual masks perform in the weeks leading to the Uzo-Iyi ceremony.
7. "The mask the lurks behind walls." The implication of this nomenclature is that agile, confident maskers come out to the village square and take challenges from race-ready spectators, while the lazy maskers get to their unwary victims by stealth.

8. *Mgbàdà* is a small antelope-like animal known for its quickness in the bush.
9. The *Mgbàdà* dancer or masker.
10. *Òji-onu* is described below.
11. Those of us who came home only about two weeks before Christmas brought with us our own cache of *Alo-Anyasi*, or we relied on the generosity of home-based peers for supplies.
12. This consensual flagellation was not restricted to child-maskers, for young boys often participated in this as part of the displays for spectators. Initiated adults, along with their masquerades, had their own more brutal version of this activity. However, as a test of manhood, it was not as elaborate as the groom-eligibility *Sharo* performance among the Hausa-Fulani of northern Nigeria.
13. It was perhaps in order to avoid these kinds of encounters that the children and adult masquerades were and are danced on separate days in Umuoji, although it was more likely a way to separate the "real thing" from the foibles of children.
14. The equivalent of *Òji-onu* in Umuoji is the *Ùlàgà*.
15. This market at Umuahia is not a typical "tourist" market, as the buyers are mostly people from the town or neighboring communities. Also the traders, such as my mother, who sell masks and musical instruments, also sell materials used for herbal medicine and religious rituals.
16. I was the third of five boys in a family of nine siblings. My mother had three sons after the first girl. And with two sisters separating me from my younger bothers, the latter could not share with the older boys, their boyhood experience.
17. Both terms refer to the process of induction into the adult masquerade society. The first means "entering the earth," the second "knowing the masquerade." These terms indicate an ontological connection between masquerades and the earth, which in Igbo cosmology, is the abode of the ancestors. So entering the earth to know the masquerades means also, by implication, connecting and communing with the ancestors.

I.1. The mask was made by the boy's father in imitation of the adult mask *Kalengula*. Northern Kete peoples, Democratic Republic of the Congo. Photograph by David A. Binkley & Patricia Darish, 1982

I.2. Adult *Kalengula* mask. Northern Kete peoples, Democratic Republic of the Congo. Photograph by David A. Binkley & Patricia Darish, 1982.

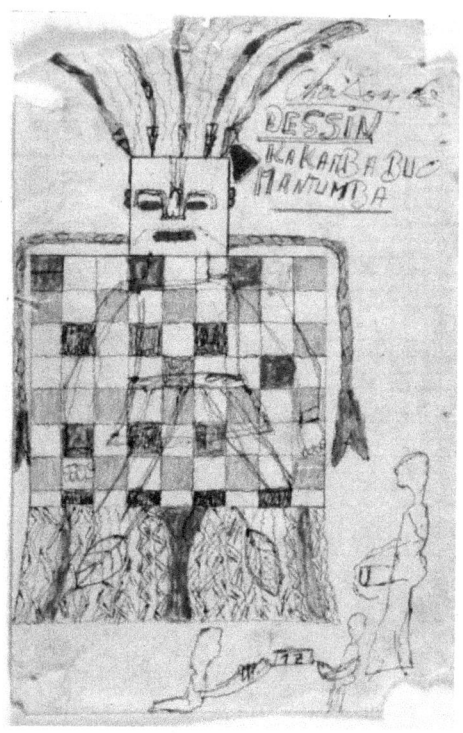

I.3. Drawing made by boy after a funeral masquerade, Democratic Republic of the Congo. Collection of David A. Binkley and Patricia Darish, 1981.

I.4. Boy masquerader wearing a northern Igbo style mask at Eha-Alumona, Nigeria. Photograph by Sarah Adams, 1994.

I.5. "Devil" dancer at girls' initiation rites, Kakoya village, Wara Wara Bafodea Chiefdom, Limba peoples, northern Sierra Leone. Photograph by Simon Ottenberg, 1979.

I.6. Boy *anibhèlèkoi* masquerader. Loma peoples, Guinea. Drawing by Anne-Sophie Helger.

I.7. Boy Nafali masquerader. Mende peoples, Bo, Sierra Leone. Photograph by Ruth Phillips, 1972.

I.8. Boy's Kalumbu masks. Chewa peoples, Kaliza, Zambia, Photograph by Kenji Yoshida, 1993.

I.9. *Kpenyigbaï* girl's masquerade. Loma peoples, Guinea. Drawing by Anne-Sophie Helger.

I.10. Girl *Digibaï* performer. Loma peoples, Guinea. Photograph by Christian Hoejbjerg.

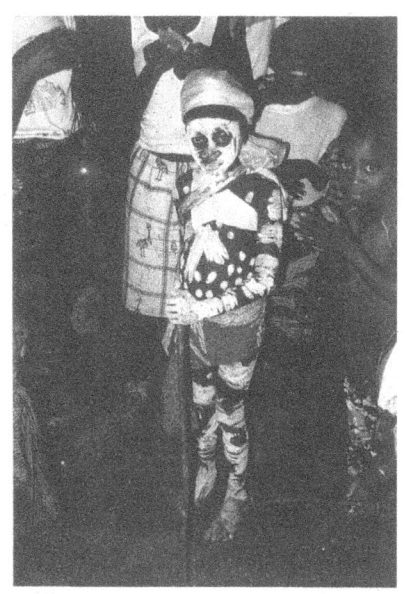

1.1. Preparing the roan antelope rod puppet masquerade for performance. Bamana peoples, Kirango, Mali. Photograph by Lynn Forsdale, 1979.

1.2. Baisu Diarra with his millet toy masquerade representing the roan antelope. Bamana peoples, Kirango, Mali. Photograph by Lynn Forsdale, 1980.

1.3. A drawing of the *Waraba caco* masquerade (center) by Kogo Diarra, age 12. Bamana peoples. Photograph by Mary Jo Arnoldi, 1980.

1.4. The *Waraba caco* masquerade during the 1979 adult Sogo bò theatre. Bamana peoples, Kirango, Mali. Photograph by Lynn Forsdale, 1979.

2.1. A young boy Aprolou Say tries on his first practice stilts. Dogon peoples, Tireli, Mali. Photograph by Walter van Beek, 1986.

2.2. Just before the funeral dance Atimè made a *kanaga* mask out of sorghum stalks. Dogon peoples, Tireli, Mali. Photograph by Walter van Beek, 1989.

2.3. The *sagiri* troupe enters a compound to dance. Dogon peoples, Tireli, Mali. Photograph by Walter van Beek, 1998.

2.4. A *kanaga* mask, drawn by Matiw Say, about 10 years of age. Dogon peoples, Tireli, Mali. Photograph by Walter van Beek.

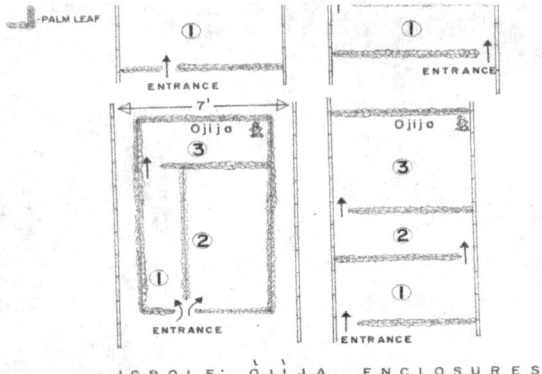

3.1. *Òjìjà* masquerader with girls accompanying him, Yoruba peoples, Ido, Nigeria. Photograph by John Ojo.

3.2. *Òjìjà* enclosures, Yoruba peoples, Igbole, Nigeria. Photograph by John Ojo.

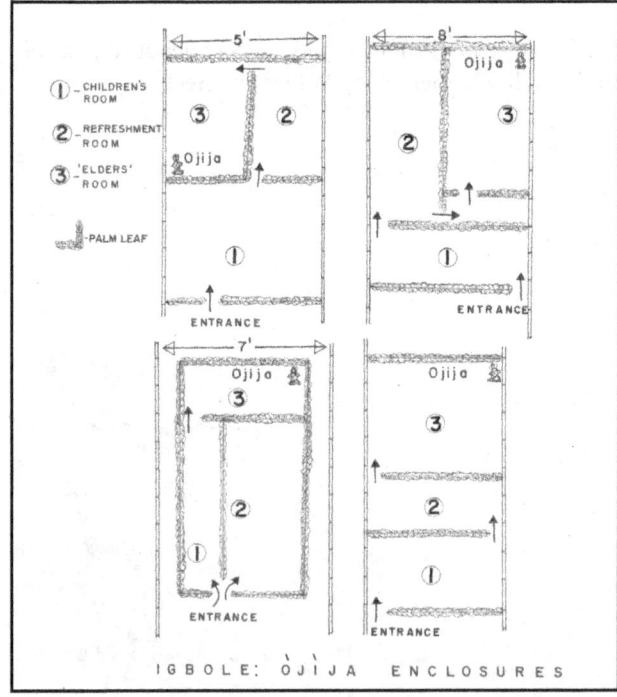

3.3. Girl preparing the *Ójija* carved wooden headdress for use, Yoruba peoples, Ido, Nigeria. Photograph by John Ojo.

3.4. Girl carrying wooden headpiece at girl's *Ójija* performance, Yoruba peoples, Ire, Nigeria. Photograph by John Ojo.

4.1. Boy with toy *Inuba* mask he made from a discarded gourd. Southern Kuba peoples, Democratic Republic of the Congo, Photograph by David A. Binkley and Patricia Darish, 1981.

4.2. *Kamakengu* mask (left) and *Kayeke* mask (right) dancing in the initiation camp. Northern Kete peoples, Democratic Republic of the Congo, Photograph by David A. Binkley, 1981.

4.3. *Inuba* mask surrounded by titleholders. Southern Kuba peoples, Democratic Republic of the Congo, Photograph by David A. Binkley and Patricia Darish, 1981.

4.4. *Bishuadi* masked figure surrounded by small boys. Southern Kuba peoples, Democratic Republic of the Congo, Photograph by David A. Binkley and Patricia Darish, 1981.

4.5. "Initiation dance" for small boys after the close of official initiation, Northern Kete peoples, Democratic Republic of the Congo. Photograph by David A. Binkley, 1981.

5.1. Boys' meeting house (right) and dressing shed, *ajaba* (left), on path to the farms outside of the village, Afikpo peoples, Mgbom, Nigeria. Photograph by Simon Ottenberg, 1959.

5.2. Boys' *mba* mask in the style of the adult form. Coconut tree bark fiber, coconut shell, European paint. Made for Simon Ottenberg in 1960 by Chukwu Okoro, Mgbom, Nigeria. Photograph by Jeffrey Smith.

5.3. Uninitiated boys' *Logholo*. They can speak, unlike initiated performers, except for the first time the latter perform. Afikpo peoples, Mgbom, Nigeria. Photograph by Simon Ottenberg, 1959.

5.4. Children's troupe at Christmas. The wood mask is in an Ibibio style, probably obtained at the Ekot Ekpene craft market. Afikpo peoples, Nigeria. Photograph by Simon Ottenberg, 1959.

6.1. Boy *Agaba* masquerader, Igbo people, Orlu, Imo State, Nigeria. Photograph by Robert W. Nicholls, 1976.

6.2. Boy *Agaba* masquerader wearing mask with long snout, Igbo people, Orlu, Imo State, Nigeria. Photograph by Robert W. Nicholls, 1976.

6.3. *Omepa* boys' masquerade. Igede peoples, Obohu, Benue State, Nigeria. Photograph by Robert W. Nicholls, 1978.

7.1. *Mgbula* form. Kalabari peoples, Bugama, Nigeria. Photograph by Anna Hlavácová.

7.2. Boy displaying his headpiece mask and costume. Kalabari peoples, Abonnema, Nigeria. Photograph by Anna Hlavácová.

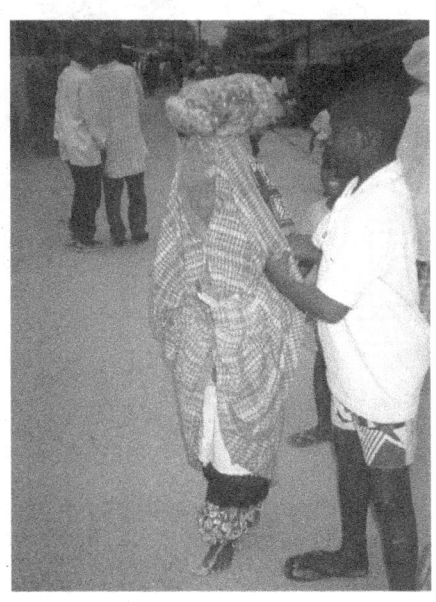

7.3. Boy with headpiece mask resembling a lizard. Kalabari peoples, Opobo, Nigeria. Photograph by Anna Hlavácová.

9.1. Jolly *devil* executing a handstand. Bo, Sierra Leone. Photograph by David Stafford, 1975.

9.2. Jolly devil *masquerader* with red ruffing on the hood, arms, legs, and a lace-like face. Bo, Sierra Leone. Photograph by David Stafford, 1975.

9.3. Deer Head Rainbow *devil* with a polychrome carving surmounted by a wire and wood frame from which hang veils. Bo, Sierra Leone. Photograph by David Stafford, 1975.

9.4. A dancing Talabi *devil* whose headdress sports three paper-mâché horns. Bo, Sierra Leone. Photograph by David Stafford, 1975.

10.1. Boys and young man working on a mask, Bissau, Guinea Bissau. Photograph by Harriet C. McGuire, 1995.

10.2. Bissau carnival masks. The mask on the right represents "Life and Death." Bissau, Guinea Bissau. Photograph by Harriet C. McGuire, 1995.

10.3. "Tchon-Tchon" Domingos Inacio da Silva Sa's prize winning Carnival masks drawing from the 1994 presidential election. The mask on the left represents the losing candidate Kumba Yalla and the mask on the right represents the winner President Nino Vieira. Bissau, Guinea Bissau. Photograph by Harriet C. McGuire, 1995.

10.4. Girls at Bissau Carnival. Bissau, Guinea Bissau. Photograph by Michelle Johnson, 1997.

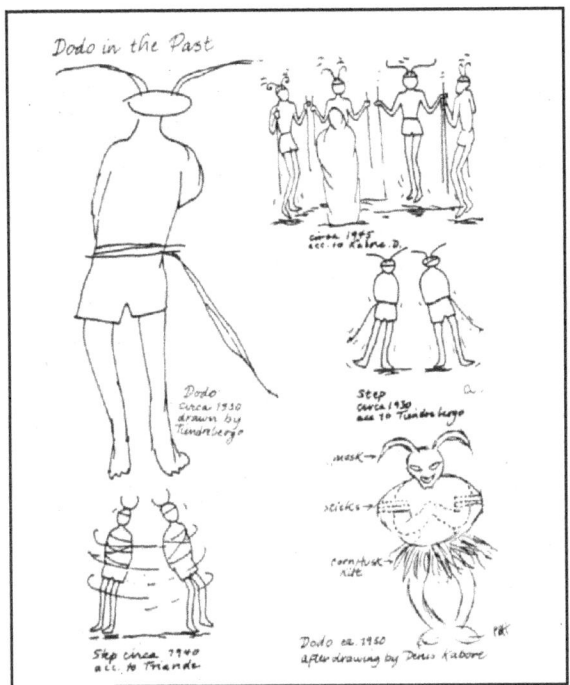

11.1. Dodo in the past, 1930-1950, drawn by informants for Priscilla Baird Hinckley, ca. 1983.

11.2. Newly painted Grand Dodo masks drying. Ouagadougou, Burkina Faso. Photograph by Priscilla Baird Hinckley, 1982.

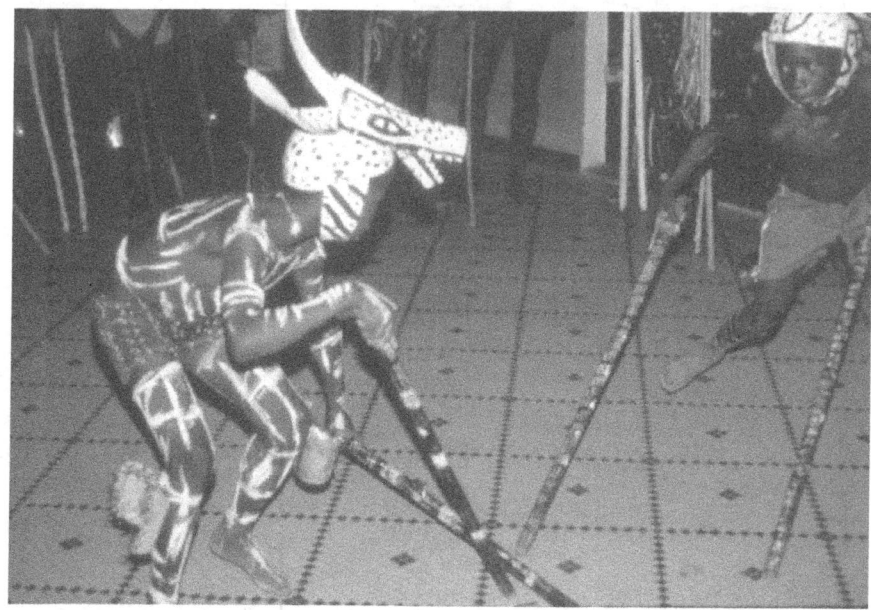

11.3. Poedogo neighborhood Dodo masked performers. Ouagadougou, Burkina Faso. Photograph by Priscilla Baird Hinckley, 1983.

11.4. Dassassgho Dodo troupe at national competition. Ouagadougou, Burkina Faso. Photograph by Priscilla Baird Hinckley 1982.

12.1. Nyau dancer. Chewa peoples, Kalungu village near Kaliza, Zambia. Photograph by Kenji Yoshida, 1985

12.2. Nyau yolemba. Chewa peoples, Lavu village near Kaliza, Zambia. Photograph by Kenji Yoshida, 1985

12.3. Chimdadada. Chewa peoples, Kaliza, Zambia. Photograph by Kenji Yoshida, 1985

12.4. Kachope. Chewa peoples, Kaliza, Zambia. Photograph by Kenji Yoshida, 1985

12.5. Ngombe. Chewa peoples, Kaliza, Zambia. Photograph by Kenji Yoshida, 1985

13.1. Two girls with play masquerade. Lunda peoples, Chitofu, Zambia, Photograph by Manuel Jordán, 1991.

13.2. Mupala *makishi*. Lunda peoples, Chitofu, Zambia, Photograph by Manuel Jordán, 1991.

13.3. Boy wearing play Chileya mask. Lunda peoples, Chitofu, Zambia, Photograph by Manuel Jordán, 1991.

13.4. Chileya *makishi*. Lunda peoples, Chitofu, Zambia Photograph by Elisabeth Cameron, 1992.

Part 3

Independent Masquerades

Part 1

Independent Measurands

9

The *Alikali* Devils of Sierra Leone: Play, Performance, and Social Commentary

Jeanne Cannizzo[1]

With the shout of "*Alikali cummot Kissi*," the boys of Bo, Sierra Leone, proclaim not only the beginning of a children's festival but also announce the arrival of the *devils*, or masqueraders, who embody many weeks of careful preparation, practice, and intense creativity.[2] On the major Muslim and Christian holidays, groups of school boys parade in formation down the public streets of town with their devils, stopping to perform before any adults who might appreciate their efforts sufficiently to offer a "dash" (a gift, usually monetary). When a likely group of spectators is spotted, the boys form a semicircle, facing the audience with the musicians behind the masker. A performance, lasting six to fifteen minutes, includes two or three dances by the devil, accompanied by a group of child musicians playing a variety of handcrafted instruments and a chorus singing songs drawn from the masking group's repertoire. During any one festival day, such a routine may be repeated twenty or thirty times, and a group can collect a considerable amount of money (the equivalent of an unskilled worker's wage for two or three days) and numerous followers.

These performances are sponsored by urban associations that are multiethnic, residentially based, and segregated by sex but not by religion or social status. Each group, composed of seven or eight boys age seven to twelve, maintains order, both political and performative, through a nonhierarchical structure made up of seven officers. The "owner" of the devil, who keeps the costume in his home and is responsible for its maintenance, is the founder of the group. Internal harmony is the responsibility of the "headman," who acts as spokesman in inter-group disputes. Often selecting both the festival route through town and the songs and dances for performance, he also collects the dashes. These he turns over to the "cashier," who safeguards membership fees and admirers' contributions and keeps a mental record of the accounts. The "controller" stations himself near the masker in readiness to re-arrange the costume should it become disturbed during dancing. If the group sports an aggressive devil, he also restrains the dancer, keeping him from going berserk. Although the possibility always exists in theory that maskers may run amok, usually the controller only has to manage smaller spectators who tend to close in on the devil in their eagerness to see the dance. This boy is also in charge of co-coordinating various elements in the performance, and if a group builds an enclosure in which to dress the masker, he selects the work detail for its construction. All members audition for the three performing positions, and by a process of elimination the group as a whole selects the head musician, who leads the dance music, the head singer, who supervises the chorus, and the dancer, who follows the musicians' lead and performs the Alikali dances particular to each of the four devil types.

The most common devil is *Jolly*, whose *dressing* or costume consists of three basic parts: the body of the dancer is covered in a long-sleeved, loosely fitting shirt, and a pair of full-length trousers; the head is hidden by a cloth hood with a circular inset of mesh or net over the face, through which the dancer can easily breath and see; the hands and feet are covered by pairs of socks, or sometimes by gloves, matching if possible (figs. 9.1, 9.2).[3] The Jolly wears no headdress, and there are no other prescribed accessories to his costume, which is usually made from solid-color cotton cloth, although the face covering, most often of white gauze, is separately inset. Heavily gathered ruffles, often in a contrasting color, outline this inset and the legs or arms of the costume; the use of unusual color combinations, the addition of decorative fringe belts, lace, and imitation fur contribute to the individual appearance of different Jolly devils.

The Jolly devil is said to be a jumper who turns about; his dance consists of a series of acrobatic stunts such as handstands, headstands, and somersaults (fig. 9.1). Most also run rapidly in circles with the body bent forward and inclined toward the earth. Individual varieties that I witnessed included a "woman" dance, which involved the shaking of nonexistent breasts and much *tumba* ("bottom") wiggling, and dances apparently influenced by the very popular kung fu movies shown in Bo, for they were punctuated with the sharp jabs and kicks typical of this form of self-defense.

The *Rainbow* devil is almost as common, and its basic costume is like that of the Jolly, although embellished by a *devil head* (headdress) of which there are two distinctive substyles differing in both subject matter and construction.[4] The rarer of the two is a carved and painted wooden deer head sewn to the cloth hood, on top of which is an elaborate wire and wood construction resembling a three-dimensional kite frame (fig. 9.3). Hanging from this frame are *veils* (long scarves or pieces of material) and various other kinds of finery, including balloons, fresh roses, feather plumes, yam strings, and pompons. The deer head Rainbow maskers also carry *whips*–wooden sticks topped with yarn or raffia that are similar to fly whisks.

Most Rainbows belong to the second substyle, in which headdresses are made from a wire and wood frame, covered with cloth and decorated with small mirrors, crepe paper, plastic flowers, and lace, in the shape of airplanes and birds. A feature peculiar to the Rainbow devil, although not in itself common, is the *ampa* (hamper), a cloth bag of transparent material filled with an assortment of expensive items that include plastic fruit (oranges, bananas, lemons), many pieces of *shine-shine* (Christmas tinsel) and tinfoil. These hampers are put on to make the devil beautiful and attract admiration, and are worn on the front of the dancer as well as the back.

The Rainbow dance is somewhat slower than that of the Jolly and does not include acrobatic stunts, as the headdress prevents the agility necessary for most jumps and turns. The dancer often starts by moving slowly about the dance area, allowing the spectators to admire his costume; he then begins the *shake-a shake-a* by placing himself in the middle of the cleared space with one foot firmly planted on the ground. With his other foot, the dancer propels his body around in a tight circle, keeping his movements in time with the music and taking two or three minutes to complete a full circle. The step is then repeated. He frequently raises his hands to the headdress, sometimes merely to adjust its weight or position but more often to call attention to the devil head itself, and thus he incorporates it into the dance.

The *Talabi* headdress is crowned by a collection of three or four cow horns (either real or made of wood or papier-mâché) attached to the head hood by a supporting structure such as a tin can or wooden platform.[5] These horns are the *devil's medicine* and imbue him with frightening power. Smaller boys and girls are supposed to flee from the Talabi for fear of his *medicine*, but group members cheerfully admit that in fact nothing would happen to a smaller child who did come into contact with it. Many of these boys are themselves afraid, of course, of the power of adult devils. One Talabi had large quantities of medicine, including snail shells, tomato paste cans, and a fur pelt, sewn onto the back of his costume; another had about twenty small red and blue cloth bags of medicine sewn onto the back of his costume. Talabis carry whips or sticks to beat people, further adding to their fierce demeanor.

In theory, the Talabi, because of his power, does not dance at all, but simply walks around the dance area displaying his aggressive capabilities. When I was in Bo, those maskers who carried whips made as if to flog smaller boys, and one Talabi brandished a plastic gun with which he menaced younger spectators. The most active Talabi tried to frighten girls by cornering them and also chased after bicycles, trying to leap on behind the cyclists.

In the *Kaka*[6] dance the masker throws himself to the ground, rolling in the dirt and dust of the street. He may also accompany himself by joining in the song chorus. Unlike his more elaborately costumed companions, the Kaka devil has no headdress, ampa, fly whisk or medicine, and while its *dressing* is basically the same as that described for the other three devil types, this costume *don poil* ("had spoiled"). The cloth is old rather than new and fine, holes and tears are obvious, and the costume itself is often dirty (fig. 9.4). Although the boys do not deliberately ruin good cloth to make this dressing, they do select cloth that is already spoiled, for the Kaka is the antithesis of the other three devil types.

The musicians are, of course, a very important part of each performance, as their playing determines the devil's dancing. Much of the music exhibits very sophisticated cross-rhythms, although some pieces have only a single rhythm, and all of it, coordinated by the head musician, is produced on a variety of percussive instruments.

The *bata* is a single-membrane, rectangular drum beaten with both hands, and the *keilei* is a slit-log drum beaten with one or two wooden sticks. A seated musician beats both fists upon a wooden crate, placed open side to the ground, know as the *box*. Other instruments include: the *agogos*, which are pieces of metal (automobile fenders or mufflers) struck with metal rods; tin cans of various sizes clanged together (the *tins*); enamel bowl and pans beaten with sticks (the *pans*); and the *shake-shake*, small tins filled with pebbles and shaken like rattles. It is unlikely that any of the instruments used by the young musicians for their masquerades were actually invented by children, but many of them are the result of a creative interpretation and modification of adult forms. The bata is, of course, a Yoruba drum, and although it is impossible to say exactly how it entered the musical inventory of Sierra Leone, it was most likely introduced through its use in the Egungun or Hunting societies or in the Shango cults, which were brought to the colony by freed Yoruba slaves in the nineteenth century. While in its Nigerian homeland the bata is a double-membrane drum of hourglass shape, the children have retained the basic attributes of the instrument–it is still a skin drum played with both hands, as part of a trio.

This process of musical abstraction, in which the physical form varies while the inherent nature of the instrument is refined or reduced to its essence, is also evident in the children's agogo. Its name indicates that this instrument again originated with, or at least through, the cultural mediation of the Yoruba, whose sacred iron bell or gong is called the agogo. Once more the children have stripped away a veneer to leave the irreducible elements of the instrument intact, for the agogo is quintessentially beaten iron, and their alternative name for the agogo is *irons*. Likewise, the instrument called the *shake-shake* by the boys is derived from the *shegbureh*, a women's instrument in Sierra Leone, made from a gourd enclosed in a string net to which shells or seeds have been attached. The boys make their shake-shake from tin cans filled with pebbles, and here again they have displayed the conservative nature of their innovations by preserving the immanent character of the instrument (the rattle motions) while radically varying its physical form.

But there is another avenue by which adult instruments enter the children's world, namely through miniaturization: the musical prototype is not altered in form but merely reduced in scale for the boy musicians. The slit-log drum used by many of the children's masking association and know by its Mende name *keilei* is an exact copy of the adult drum; it is played in the same fashion, although reduced in length from its usual 45-90 centimeters to only 30-50 centimeters.

It is clear that these various instruments form an orchestra. The most probable antecedent for this ensemble is the *mailo* band, developed during the 1960s by groups of adolescents and young men who belonged to mutual aid societies in Freetown, and which is itself the descendant of the older *Gumbe* band, which played traditional Creole music on different percussive instruments.[7]

It is apparent, then, that the children cull and glean artistic elements from several adult masquerading and music-making traditions, welding them into a new synthetic art form governed by a children's aesthetic. The term Alikali devils is currently reserved in Bo for children's masquerades. As such they have a distinctive identity, separate from that of the secret society masquerades in town, none of which were ever called by this name. It is unclear how the term came, at least in Bo, to refer only to children's masquerades, for originally it seems to have been associated with a society of teenaged males, many of whom appear to have been juvenile delinquents, according to Banton,[8] who suggests a Yoruba origin for the society, whose appearance in Freetown he dates to the 1940s.

The Yoruba influence on the Alikali masquerades is evidenced in part in the costuming, songs, and musical instruments, and also in the *devil slang* used by the boys, which is, in part, a recognizable, if confused, rendition of Yoruba words. The code that devils exchange on the streets when they meet is perhaps the most interesting example of this "secret" language. If the exchange is not correctly completed by either devil, the offender will be seized by the challenging group, who "make it their own" until a ransom of half the collected dashes is paid. If this payment is refused, a fight will ensue, as each side tries to prevent the monstrous humiliation of having its devil unmasked by rivals. However, as the boys readily admit, events rarely degenerate to this point, for most masking groups in Bo are familiar with the code; but presumably the possibility of a tumble adds to the excitement of street parading.

An explanation, however, greatly simplified, of the Yoruba influences on the children's devils must begin with the *Egungun*, the Yoruba ancestral and entertainment masquerade and society, which is known in Sierra Leone as *Ogugu*, or more commonly in Bo by the word for a local chapter of the society, *Oje*.[9] It was the most widespread secret society among the liberated Africans living in peninsular villages outside Freetown but within the boundaries of the nineteenth-century colony of Sierra Leone.[10] The society is still active, and masked figures very much like the "children of Egungun"[11] parade on the streets attended by lesser devils who, attired in costumes similar to those of the Jolly devil, later perform somersaults and acrobatic feats.

The Hunting society, at one time the chief rival of the Ogugu, emerged in the mid-nineteenth century and "developed into a Creole secret society which for many served as a more sophisticated replacement for Agugu.... By the twentieth century, the Hunters became a society about midway on the stratification ladder, between the extremes of the *Oje* at one end and the successfully revived

Masonic lodges of Freetown on the other."[12] The original Hunting society masquerade was a model, much embellished and modified, for the *Eri* devils of the young men's societies prominent in Freetown in the 1960s,[13] which, in turn, offer inspiration to the boys of Bo.

Lest it be thought that there is no connection between older, indigenous masking traditions and the Alikali devils, it might be pointed out that, while influenced by the Eri and Oje masquerades, the Talabi is also affected by the wider Sierra Leonean pattern of witch-finding or witch-hunting. In his red-suited, antlered headdress, he belongs to the West African artistic syndrome that Thompson has called "the horned embodiment of Power.[14] The most likely parallel for the Kaka as it now exists, with its emphasis on the violation of artistic canons, is that of the *Kongoli* and the *Gondi*, which make manifest similar anti-aesthetic sensibilities within the context of adult Poro (male) and Sande (female) masquerading.[15]

Superimposed on these patterns is a preference for a certain amount of artistic expression in the modern idiom and a positive emphasis on modernity. The effect of this empathy with the contemporary scene is evidenced in costuming, where it has prompted not only the use of Christmas garlands, plastic fruits, and toy guns but also the wearing of photographs of the masquerade (given by this researcher). This influence is also apparent in choreography and in song texts. Bars and stores constantly play records or cassette tapes of popular songs from the United States, the West Indies, or other African countries, and thus the boys are exposed to a wide variety of contemporary music, some of which provides the inspiration, and occasionally the words, for devil songs. Radio news, movies, and cinema posters offer useful information on non-African fads, tastes, and social customs, and many boys, under the influence of the movies, "kung fu" down the main streets of town singing the latest reggae hits.

The liberal eclecticism that characterizes the children's devil styles is, however, bounded, or more aptly, unified, by a set of artistic principles that give a certain coherence to the whole spectacle of the boys' masquerading. Each devil performance is an aesthetic whole. It is composed of separate, identifiable parts (costume, choreography, music, songs, festive atmosphere, and the human arena in which these activities are staged), but these components are seen as an indivisible unit, as a composite entity. It is also a creation of the group as a whole; as the manifestation of the collective creative and performing abilities of the boys, the devil has, of course, an extra-human dimension, and the dancer is merely an actor in the whole drama of animation.

To support this illusion, no part of the masker's body may be seen—hence the socks, gloves, long sleeves, face mask, and head hood to cover any human or identifying individual physical characteristics.[16] For the same reason, a devil has no voice. The attendant or headman is his mouthpiece, or he communicates thoughts and wishes to the musicians and singer through gestures and dance steps. This silent choreography is further testament to his supra-human nature.

The children who acted as informants on their masquerades were often both "appreciators," who identify art, and "critics," who not only identify but also evaluate works in accordance with a theory of excellence.[17] Some boys readily distinguished devils by type and then went beyond this to conceptualize quality in abstraction and to reconsider it in the concrete when judging particular performances.

The boys, in general, prefer the Rainbow masquerade, which because of its costly beauty is the epitome of devildom, while the Kaka is its very negation (figs. 9.3, 9.4). An examination of the Kaka's costume and choreography will reveal most clearly those standards it deliberately violates. The perversions of this devil are immediately apparent in its costume, for the cloth is old, dirty, smelly and torn, and these ensemble characteristics are selected for the signifying song of this masquerade: "*Kaka devil boss trousers*" (*boss* = burst). "*Ah de fall down*," the second line of this theme song, is a comment on another reversal of normal devil behavior—the dancer rolls over and over in the dust of the streets. The Kaka masker also sings in accompaniment to his own dance, which makes it clear that this devil is a human dressed up in a costume. The boys' most frequent comment about the Kaka was "*E no fine*" ("It isn't fine").

To be *fine*, a condition that the Kaka cannot achieve but a most desirable state for Rainbow, Jolly or Talabi, is to be three things: costly, *bright*, and new. The elements of expense, assessed by the number of *veils* hung from a headdress or the amount of plastic fruit in a hamper, was no small consideration when rendering a critical appraisal of a masquerade–the more money spent on a devil, the finer it was. These imported luxuries, representative of the actual and artistic wealth of the group, also contributed to the second component of fineness: *brightness*. To be bright is to be intense, clear, and luminous. The range of tonality and intensity (in the European sense of bright versus dull, light versus dark) of particular colors was sometimes included in the concept of brightness, but usually a color in and of itself was considered bright. Blue seems to be the most popular because of its brightness.[18] *Shine-shine* (Christmas tinsel and garlands in extravagant blue, pink, and silver) is the apotheosis of brightness, giving clarity as it outlines the contours of headdress and intense luminosity as it glitters in the midday, dry-season sun.

Brightness and expensiveness are worthless, and in fact unattainable, without newness—which here refers not to novelty but to a state of perfect condition, and it is this appreciation and expectation of the perfect that make the Kaka, in his spoiled costume, the anti-devil.[19]

A devil must also be *bluff*; it must have style in appearance, in motion and while striking a *stance* (the public pose at rest). The boy who dances with the devil must have the self-awareness and presence to display and present the devil, and children who are easily embarrassed do not become masqueraders.[20] The costume must be *tuff*, with a striking pattern and distinctive color combination. The stance must be bold, an aggressive assertion of virility.[21]

A devil must also approximate a model or ideal masquerade form. It must be distinctive and distinguishable from others of its type while being conceived and constructed within closely observed conventions. That a devil "must resemble a *devil*" is not a tautology but a statement of the principle that an art form, to be effective in any sphere, must conform to a known ideal, one that is neither so extreme in its conception as to be a lifeless copy nor so ingenious as to be an unrecognizable image. Each category of masquerade must wear, carry, or be accompanied by its own peculiar icons (as outlined above), and types should not be mixed; the boys were very critical of any devil whose appearance suggested more than one category. This sympathy for the unambiguous is paramount, and innovation per se is neither desired nor applauded.[22] Individual creativity is valued if it extends, but does not surpass, the limits imposed by stylistic boundaries.

Such basic conservatism stems not only from the appeal of the appropriate but also from an appreciation of perfect harmony and unity in performance. As noted earlier, the devil is a composite creation. The use of too many compellingly novel elements in a costume or the inclusion of a particularly idiosyncratic choreography does not enhance a performance but disrupts its internal balance by disproportionate attention to one aspect of the whole. This distorts the viewer's perception of the artistic entirety of the masquerade and lowers his appreciation of its totality. Unlimited or unstructured originality is disruptive and chaotic, and the creative act does not have to produce an original form. Rather, the child artists demonstrate their creativity in the selection and combination of forms available from the repertoire of Alikali masquerading. Performing artists all state that their ideas for their performances come from watching and imitating either their elders or their equals. Since no one group could or would exactly reproduce the whole performance of any other group, however, the copying of any particular element from a specific performance is irrelevant; it does not threaten the originality of the composition because a *fine devil* performance is not fortuitous coincidence but a patiently planned, carefully rehearsed and executed, fully orchestrated "happening."

These conventions do not restrict but rather define the masquerades as an exuberant celebration of juvenility. The desire for art in perfect condition is merely the preference for ephebism[23] on another plane, a preference that confirms the artistry of the boys as childish, not in the sense of being immature, but in its fuller meaning of being unblemished by time and struggle, of having the stronger power that comes from youth. The Alikali devils do not give rebirth to the ancestors, but they do incarnate the destiny of their creators as the children of contemporary black Africa.

* * *

These Alikali devils of Bo town may be compared to the masquerades made by the boys of Torwama, a Muslim Mende village of about one hundred people some seven miles from Bo. Here children's masking is an integral, if not central, part of adult festivals. There are no boys' masking associations in the village and any boy who wishes to make a devil does so by himself or with the help of his father. Musicians are recruited on the spot from the boys and girls in the village, and everyone, including adults, sings in Mende. The devil does not parade from house to house but dances near the *barri* (a centrally located meeting place where old men hang their hammocks, women gossip, and public announcements are made). Financial objectives do not prompt the performance, and indeed, monetary rewards from admirers are very rare, although words of encouragement and praise from both men and women reach the dancers from the circle of onlookers. The most popular masker was a small dancer of about six who wore a white cloth draped loosely over his head, with eyeholes cut into the fabric. Circlets of fresh green palm fronds were attached at the neck, wrists, and waist, thus leaving a large area of the body exposed, although the child was wearing a pair of shorts. He identified himself as a *Nafali*, a Mende devil that wears a cloth hood studded with cowry shells in a cross pattern and shaped like a bishop's mitre. A long-sleeved, striped shirt and trousers accentuated with a raffia shoulder mantle, skirt, and felt coverings make up the costume of the adult Nafali. The dance of the miniature Nafali also resembled that of the adult masquerader–both performances were characterized by very rapid hand trembling and foot shaking, punctuated by earth-touching sweeps, while the dancer was stationary.

This dancer appeared on December 2, the feast of Edi-ul-Ahda in the village and again on December 25 in conjunction with secular masquerades of the adult men's society, the Poro. He, along with the adult Torwama *Goboi* and *Falui*, came into the Teacher's College compound, about half a mile from the village, to honor the principal with a performance.[24] Although the boy dancer was accompanied by an age mate on the *keilei* (Mende log drum), most of the music for both his own performance and those of the society devils was furnished by the clapping and singing of village women with their *shake-shakes*, a young man playing a double-sided bass drum, which in a former life graced a North American high school football field, and another young man on a snare drum. One music specialist played only for the *Goboi* on a low-voiced muted horn whose tones exhorted the Goboi to more virtuoso displays. After the trio had performed for somewhat over two hours, the villagers returned en masse to Torwama.

The differences between the children's devils in Torwama and those created by the boys in Bo are very apparent. The physical setting of the town performances is very different for the boys do not parade their Alikalis while adult maskers are on the streets, nor do they perform together. In many cases, town children were in awe of, if not actually frightened by, the men's society masquerades. In Torwama, of course, the children were not only at ease in the presence of the adult performers, but even engaged in duets with them, appearing at the same time and in the same place.

The elaborate code words and competition between devils, the fighting mythology, and the dual Yoruba and modern idioms are of negligible influence in the village. The Torwama songs are in Mende, known to both adults and children as they are traditional tunes and verses, not the thematic variations based on popular hit tunes and sung in Krio so favored by the town boys. These differences stem from the actual nature of the two different styles of devils. The Bo Alikalis are ingenious improvisations inspired by the urban models of the Creole society devils, while the Torwama boys intend their masquerades to be, and successfully present them as, miniature versions of traditional Mende devils, which contribute to the continuity of the artistic traditions of which they are copies. The aesthetic considerations that shape these imitations of adult masquerades are childish attempts to implement the adult canons, rather than an original interpretation by the children themselves. Similarly, those aspects of cultural and social behavior that children acquire within the context of participation in an adult festival are not generated within the peer group, but occur under the aegis of the society. The Alikali devils, on the other hand, are independent creations, art forms that are produced by and for children.

Both of these masking traditions, however, offer numerous examples of what David Lancy has described as "how play trains children for four major cultural subsystems (namely): (1) social relations, (2) language, (3) technology, (4) ideology."[25] Both can be seen as lending some support to anthropological theories of play as fulfilling an enculturative function. In the case of the village, the children are, in Mackay's words,[26] assimilated culturally into the adult world while the boys of Bo are inducted into the culture of childhood by their peers.[27] But on another level, what thus appear to be the same sort of play is, in fact, a very different sort of "work."

The mask play in Torwama has what Sutton-Smith[28] has called an "integrative function," that is, it is part of "normative socializing" in which the boy is prepared through practice and imitation, to participate in Mende festivals which help define the divisions in rural society between male and female, chiefs and commoners, the initiated and the non-initiated.

The creation of the Alikali devils, on the other hand, provides a forum for socialization by innovation. "Play must socialize not simply by imparting behaviors that integrate the players into their cultural systems, but providing them with innovative alternatives that they may be able to use to change the culture system."[29] The world created by the boys in their masking associations is a meritocracy, a society characterized by an egalitarianism which runs counter to the hierarchies and boundaries that fracture adult life in Bo.[30]

Of course, this innovative style is equally integrative, but it is normative socialization within the culture of childhood. Sutton-Smith[31] has argued that:

> the ratio of these two, integrative-innovative, changes with the kind of cultural system. In a more authoritarian system, the children's play is more strictly imitative; in a rela-

tively open society like our own, the play is much more reversive and transformational as children feel free to attempt varying permutations of the possibilities before them.

While the unstated equation of authoritarian (closed, traditional) and non-authoritarian (open, modern) is perhaps too strongly implied, it is within this dichotomy of contemporary urban West Africa that children as children are beginning to appear. It is here that the growth of the nuclear family and the emerging importance of education have made the child synonymous with the schoolboy.[32] However, education most often separates the child from his parents. It has been suggested that the scientific revolution in knowledge further segregated the child from knowledge, for the

> ...differentiation of knowledge...meant reality was no longer the same for all men. There were various canons of truth. Men could no longer make judgments in confidence and in terms of immediate perceptual information. The affairs and understandings of adults became increasingly invisible to the children. As a result children were, in fact, increasingly innocent.[33]

In Sierra Leone where 75 to 80 percent of the adult population is illiterate (in English), the situation is, in a sense, reversed. The affairs and understandings of children become increasingly invisible to adults, for the boys' modern education ensures that there are currently at least two canons of truth, one mature and one immature in terms of age, if not in knowledge, or the modern world. The schoolboy is, however, increasingly dependent on his parents and family in a different way, for not only does his labor no longer make a significant contribution to the family income, but the family must provide his school fees and textbooks, as well as the annual tuition. As this dependency excludes the boys more and more from the world of men, they begin to create a children's world, where adults are excluded and where they themselves are interdependent.

Thus, while the Nafali masquerade is a celebration of creative and structural community, the Alikali devils mark artistic and social disjunction in a celebration of childhood itself.

Notes

1. This chapter is a reprint of my "Alikali Devils of Sierra Leone," *African Arts* 12:4 (1979): 64-70, 92, and a portion of my "Play, Performance and Social Commentary: The Alikali Devils of Sierra Leone," in Brian Sutton-Smith and Kelly-Byrne (eds.), *The Masks of Play*, 17-23. New York: Leisure Press, 1984.
2. Material for this article was collected in the course of fieldwork and research in 1976-1977, supported by a travel grant from the Anthropology Department of the University of Washington and a fellowship from the Graduate School of the same institution. While in Sierra Leone, an institutional affiliation was provided by the African Studies Programme of Fourah Bay College, the University of Sierra Leone. I also wish to thank the boys of Bo, who acted as informants, and J. Kebbie and R. Kabba, who worked as field assistants.
   (Editors' note: The civil war in Sierra Leone in recent years has almost completely obliterated any traces of the masquerades Cannizzo describes here. The boys are scattered, now as young men, some formerly with the rebel forces, others with

178   Playful Performers

        fighting units on the government side, or as refugees, and still others dead as a consequence of the conflict. The town of Bo, where the events described here occurred, is in ruins as a consequence of the fighting, is slowly recovering physically.

3. The name is probably derived from "Jolly Boys," a young men's entertainment and welfare society or *kompin* (see Dawson 1964). An alternative name sometimes used by Temne children for the Jolly was *Aguda*, a Yoruba word originally meaning "Christian," particularly a returnee from Brazil or Sierra Leone (John Picton, Museum of Mankind, personal communication, 1977).
4. Rainbow was the name of a particular Eri *devil* in Freetown but has become, for the boys in Bo, the generic term for a type of masquerade.
5. No informant could give a derivation or meaning for the word *Talabi* although it is a common Yoruba surname, originally the name assigned to a female baby born with fetal membranes still attached (John Picton: personal communication, 1977).
6. *Kaka* means "feces."
7. Steady 1973.
8. Banton 1957.
9. Peterson 1969.
10. Peterson 1969.
11. Thompson 1974.
12. Peterson 1969, 269.
13. Kreutzinger 1966.
14. Thompson 1974, 133.
15. Reinhardt 1972.
16. Note the similarity with Yoruba Egungun dancers. "To ensure perfect anonymity the masker must have no physical deformity or extraordinary characteristics such as limping by which he can be identified" (Olajuba and Ojo 1977, 26).
17. Thompson 1973.
18. Yoruba schoolboys also appear to be fond of blue. "A young Yoruba told Justine Cordwell that his favorite color was blue–"It is midway between red and black. It is not too conspicuous as red and it is not so dark as black. It is cool and bright to see" (Thompson 1968, 65).
19. Compare Crowley (1973, 24): "Chokwe artists and their public prefer the new to the old, comparing a new mask to a young man 'strong and fine looking' and an old mask to an old man 'sick and broken.'" See also Ojo (1966, 243) on the preference for perfection in masks in Yorubaland, where carvings are discarded and replaced as soon as blemishes (caused by the harmattan winds, the splitting of green wood, etc.) disfigure them.
20. Compare these comments by Yoruba performers: "One cannot be a masker and be shy. Only the eager ones may enter the costume" (Olajuba and Ojo 1977, 26).
21. This *stance* is very similar to the poses struck by young men lounging in bars, waiting in lorry parks or just resting on verandas. One shoulder is sloped or held lower than the other, the hands are hooked over belts or pockets, and the body is inclined forward with the pelvis leading (for a description of similar Afro-American male poses, see Cooke 1972).
22. Compare with Dillard's suggestion that "unlike most European tale-telling styles, the Afro-American stresses the familiarity of the tale rather than its originality; such emphasis frees the audience to concentrate on the skills of the teller rather than on the novelty of his material" (Dillard 1977, 138).
23. Thompson 1974.
24. *Goboi* is an important secular mask of the Poro society whose costume consists of a full raffia cape adorned with miniature prayer boards and crowned with a squat,

cylindrical headdress. *Falui* is another Mende mask which accompanies a baggy brown costume topped with a red cone and a feather tuft.

25. Schwartzman 1978, 110.
26. Mackay 1974.
27. This is not to say that certain aspects of peer group socialization—including the inculcation of sexual stereotypes, politico-judicial skills, and values such as courage and loyalty–are at variance with adult standards or that they are not acquired in other arenas under adult supervision.
28. Sutton-Smith, 1972.
29. Sutton-Smith 1979, 315.
30. Many adults in Bo operate both within an ascriptive system with a rural origin and a more achievement-oriented society generated in town. Whether achieved or ascribed, "traditional" or "modern," these status systems divide the adult world of Bo into many separate strata or spheres, be these segmented on the basis of birth into a chiefly family, or membership in an organization restricted to those of the same educational background and class. While it might be misleading to state that in their masking associations, the children resolve some of the conflicts that disturb the harmony of the parental generation, it can be suggested with some assurance that they dissolve some of the boundaries that confine adults to particular spheres. Whatever the conflicts within the Alikali groups, they are not generated by the same rivalries and prejudices that govern social relationships for men and women.
31. Sutton-Smith 1979, 315.
32. See Cannizzo 1978 for a fuller discussion of this process; the argument is similar to that first suggested by Philip Aries in *Centuries of Childhood* (1962).
33. Sutton-Smith 1972, 304.

Bibliography

Aries, Philippe. 1962. *Centuries of Childhood: A Social History of Family Life,* translated from the French by Robert Baldick. New York: Knopf.

Banton, M. 1957. *West African City.* London: Oxford University Press.

Cannizzo, J. 1978. "Alikali Devils: Children's Masquerading in a West African Town." Ph.D. Diss., University of Washington.

Cooke, B. 1972. "Nonverbal Communication among Afro-Americans: An Initial Classification." In T. Kochman (ed.), *"Rappin and Stylin" Out.* Urbana: University of Illinois Press.

Crowley, D. 1973. "Aesthetic Value and Professionalism in African Art: Three Cases from the Katanga Chokwe." In W. d'Azevedo (ed.), *The Traditional Artist in African Societies.* Bloomington: Indiana University Press.

Dawson, J. 1964. "Mental Health and Urbanization in a West African Country." In A. Kiev (ed.), *Magic, Faith and Healing.* Glencoe, IL: The Free Press.

Dillard, J. 1977. *Lexicon of Black English.* New York: The Seabury Press.

Fyle, C. 1962. *A History of Sierra Leone.* London: Oxford University Press.

Kreutzinger, H. 1966. "The Eri-Devil in Freetown, Sierra Leone." *Acta ethnologica et Lingustica* 9.

Lancy, D. F. 1975. "The Play Behavior of Kpelle Children during Rapid Cultural Change." In D. F. Lancy (ed.), *The Anthropological Study of Play: Problems and Prospects.* Cornwall, NY: Leisure Press.

Mackay, R. W. 1974. "Conceptions of Children and Models of Socialization." In Roy Turner (ed.), *Ethnomethodology.* New York: Penguin.

Ojo, G. 1966. *Yoruba Culture.* Ife: University of Ife and University of London Press.

Olajuba, O., and J. Ojo. 1977. "Some Aspects of Oyo Yoruba Masquerades." *Africa* 47:3, 253-275.

Peterson, J. 1969. *Province of Freedom.* Evanston, IL: Northwestern University Press.

Reinhardt, L. 1972. "Mende Secret Societies and their Costumed Spirits." Paper for the Ninth International Congress of Anthropological and Ethnological Sciences.

Schwartzman, H. 1978. *Transformations.* New York: Plenum Press.

Steady, F. 1973. "The Structure and Functions of Women's Voluntary Associations in an African City." Ph.D. diss., Oxford University.

Sutton-Smith, B. 1972. *The Folk Games of Children.* Austin: University of Texas Press.

_____. 1979. "Epilogue: Play as Performance." In B. Sutton-Smith (ed.), *Play and Performance.* New York: Gardner Press.

Thompson, R. 1968. "Esthetics in Traditional Africa." *Art News* 66:9, 44-45, 63-65.

_____. 1973. "Yoruba Artistic Criticism. In W. d'Azevedo (ed.), *The Traditional Artist in African Societies.* Bloomington: Indiana University Press.

_____. 1974. *African Art in Motion.* Los Angeles: University of California Press.

10

Masked Children in an Urban Scene: The Bissau Carnival

Based on the Writings of *Manuel Rambout Barçelos, Nicolau Fara Gomes, Felix Siga,* and *Harriet C. McGuire;* edited with additional comments by *Simon Ottenberg[1]*

Carnival in Bissau is an immense and magnificent event, which has developed its own unique style, and which has been associated with momentous times in Guinea-Bissau. Children play key roles in it as mask makers and masqueraders, and in dancing and singing groups. Without them it would be a dull affair.

History

In the 1950s, the indigenous Papel[2] were encouraged by Catholic Fathers, responsible for education in what was then a Portuguese colony, to join a pre-Lenten parade through the streets of Bissau.[3] European children wore imported cowboy hats, Zorro masks, and Indian headdresses: the Guineans made masks of cardboard. Priests, who directed the African primary schools, suggested that horned devil headpieces and masks were appropriate for the African children to wear. Thus, indigenous children of Guinea-Bissau children have been involved in carnival since its inception. Felix Siga states:[4] "It started out Christian, having been introduced by the priests to reach out to the pagans," but Nicolau Fara Gomes notes:[5] "During the colonial period carnival was a festival that scarcely touched the majority of the people."

In fashioning horned headpieces of cardboard, children developed their creative skills. The horns, set on top of a traditional cap, reminded the Africans not of devils' horns but of cows, much as they are found in traditional rituals and masquerades in Guinea-Bissau.[6] To make the masks, the children molded paper upon a clay form, using the pulp of the fruit of the baobab tree as glue. Their mothers squeezed the liquid out of this fruit, which conveniently ripened at the time of carnival. The clay was later scraped away when the paper was pulled off and dried (fig. 10.1), sometimes over an open fire. Various papers were employed, including used cement sacks. Papier-mâché made for light masks, which could be of considerable size, yet easily carried on the head or shoulders. Paint was added to make the African children's homemade masks as attractive as store-bought ones. "That was the only style we knew," said "Carlito" Carlos Alberto Teixeiro Barros, a child in the *Chao-de-Papel Varela* neighborhood in the 1950s. "Even today, children graduate from assisting other people's mask-making to producing their very own masks by starting with the *boca de baca* (cow's head) design."[7] Carlito assured McGuire that the technique of making carnival masks "developed in the backyards of the *bairro*, not at school."[8] The *bairros* most active in the festival all bordered on swampy rice fields with clay deposits, which children were familiar with and which were essential for making carnival masks. From these various mask forms gradually emerged, some worn by children, others by adults.

However, historian George E. Brooks cites a report by Augusto Dias de Carvalho,[9] who observed a carnival on the eve of All Souls' Day, November 1, 1898 in coastal Bolama, Guinea-Bissau, where: "Men and women with fantastic costumes, as if it were carnival, and swigging aguardente [brandy] and palm wine wander about for three entire nights in this manner until after daybreak, then they disperse, everyone returning to their dwellings, to come out again at night, and spending all day on the 2nd in singing and dancing." Bolama was largely composed of Luso-Guinean and Luso-Cape Verdean traders. Brooks argues that the coastal-riverine trading communities of Guinea-Bissau developed their own mixed culture. This drew on the remarkable similarity of West African customs to "pagan" Portuguese customs going back to medieval times. These were present in "the beliefs of the most illiterate or poorly-educated Portuguese mariners, traders, soldiers, and priests who ventured out to West Africa from the mid-fifteenth century onwards."[10] These were Portuguese men who married into Guinea Bissau families; thus the growth of a Luso-African culture along the coast. All Souls' Day appeared at about the end of the harvest season of indigenous rice, thus serving as a harvest festival. It was also a celebration of the time when traders annually set out from coastal communities into the interior for varying lengths of time. As a Christian celebration in honor of the dead, it was certainly congruent with African concerns for their ancestors, an event merging European and African religious beliefs, customs, and traditions. It is not impossible that some of this tradition carried over in the experience of Luso-Africans when Lenten carnival began in Bissau; thus an earlier origin of the idea of carnival in Guinea Bissau is possible. Whether the Bolama participants wore masks is not clear, but evidently both genders were involved, much in keeping with the later developments in Bissau carnival.

Manuel Rambout Barçelos states:[11] "The 1950s planted the seeds of carnival in Bissau, sparked by the opening of the first movie theater showing classic tales of the American West and Zorro's cloak and sword. These were the principal inspirations for the Carnival fantasies."[12] Barçelos[13] goes on to say, "For many participants, movie fiction and fantasy were simply transferred to carnival fantasy; for others the films were not seen as fiction, but rather as far away reality, hitherto unknown, which they could experience by entering the imaginary world through the long days of Carnival activity." The practice of children taking images from the outside to employ in carnival had begun.

Combining cut-out cardboard masks with the papier-mâché technique led to the prototypes for the monumental shoulder-supported masks that have become the signature pieces for the Bissau carnival. "Carlito" Carlos Alberto Teixeiro de Bollas, a mask maker, gives some credit to schoolteachers, saying they suggested copying the statues around town, such as monuments to the European discoverers of the area.[14] "Each *bairro* created its own carnival in the fifties,"[15] he reports. His own bairro always made carnival an important community event. A common site was chosen for the mask makers to work together; children helped the artists fetch clay and find paper and scrap materials, while women worked on other costume parts. Bairro and ward children were and are organized by age sets, always with a male or female guide. This arrangement undoubtedly has assisted their mask-making and performance activities.

Commentators agree that the traditional Papel bairro of Chao-de Papel Varela had the best carnival in the early part of the 1950s,[16] a tradition that has continued to this day.[17] Other bairros had more of a reputation for mischief. A young artist, "Tchon-Tchon" Domingos Inacio da Silva Sa, told McGuire that his father's memories of carnival in the 1950s were of young boys wearing masks running rampant through the Bandim market in Bissau, stealing items from women who had their wares on trays. Felix Siga, a man prominent in carnival over the years, suggests that at times pranks predominated in other areas of the city.

The only government role in carnival in the early days was announcing the dates. But by the end of the 1950s decade the authorities knew that security at the event was deteriorating and that mischief-making by children and adults could no longer be winked at. Carnival was confined to designated streets, subject to careful police control and restricted to daylight hours. At times, as anti-colonial sentiment grew, the Portuguese banned carnival entirely, as it had developed an anti-government tone. Barçelos writes[18] that "with the protective cover of mask fantasy, military and war themes grew more prominent and the masked figures could act out repressive gestures and actions." Havik[19] mentions an eyewitness at the end of the 1960s and in the early 1970s, who told him that when carnival was forbidden in the Bissau center, it moved out of town. It was then held at some distance away, one place being Joao Landim, some 20 kilometers north of Bissau. Horned masks were very common at the time. Havik believes it likely that holding the event away from the city contributed to the Africanization of its rituals and symbolism. He also thinks that this was accentuated by migration to the Bissau area in the second half of the 1960s and early 1970s as a consequence of the anti-colonial war, and again immediately after independence in 1974 until 1976.

With the displacement of rural peoples to Bissau in the 1960s as the liberation movement commenced military campaigns, the population of the city swelled, bringing in children and adults of a variety of cultural backgrounds. They put their rural cultural and new urban experiences to work in carnival, greatly varying and enriching it. But Havik writes of Bissau "that the process of Africanisation and the war [of 1963-1974] and the security measures contributed to a tensing of the atmosphere which obviously had its repercussions on the carnival celebrations;" and that toward the end of the war period the "great influx of 'animist' populations from literal areas, above all the Balanta...further strengthened the strong 'animist' character of the town."[20] Perhaps related to this, monster masks (also called devils and vampires) came to predominate the pre-independence era, which ended in 1974. Some were seen as subtle critiques of colonial repression,[21] others as inspirations of traditionally derived powerful rural deities still respected in the city, the *irans*. Carnival artists who were children in the 1960s told McGuire that they were inspired by comic books and movies,[22] always trying to improve on what had attracted notice. The use of the same masks for a second year was not frequent. In small towns in the rural areas built around the Catholic Church, its schools and colonial offices, pre-1974 carnival still existed in the earlier cowboys and Indians and face-paint stage. However, carnival was not popular in the predominantly Muslim third of the country, particularly among Fula elders.[23] Carnival was also celebrated in towns such as Bolama and Bafata. Siga writes:[24]

> [Processions] were, as a rule, quite orderly, except for the races between the masked participants. At that time masks could be imported, made of rubber, or homemade of painted papier-mâché. Older participants and small children either painted their faces or stuck on a false mustache or nose, or cross-dressed. Some children preferred, as they still do today, to wear costumes typical of the Manjaco, Papel, Bijago, Mandinga, Balanta, Felupe or other ethnic groups. It was enough to tie a feather with a string around your head to be an Indian. The teen-aged boys among the paraders...were costumed as cowboys, Arabs, or as Zorro. From time to time the Zorros and cowboys faced off, as small skirmishes were inevitable when parading with a warlike frame of mind. In those days the masked paraders scared the little kids and, in return, the boys and girls sprayed water on the masked ones whom they knew. There was a song in Crioulu [Creole]: *N'trudu medi iagu / n cololo' / n trudu n kunsi bu nomi*...The mask fears water because it was made of paper.[25]

The departure of the Portuguese in 1974 led to further changes in the event as the African Party for the Independence of Guinea and Cape Verde (PAIGC) took control of the country. Organizing the Bissau carnival was not a high government priority, though by 1978 the government revived carnival with strong central control. The government used it to create development messages for the country, for example, on the need for literacy and disease control. They awarded prizes for the best masks.[26] Development issues pushed by Guinea-Bissau's various national governments have been a feature of carnival ever since. As a propaganda medium, many individuals who had grown up making their own masks for spontaneous festivities felt it was no longer their festival. A Brazilian from Bahia organized the *Alegria do Povo* animation group, adding a samba rhythm to carnival. He imported the concept of a moving electrified flat-bed truck, from which popular music groups entertained the crowds along the parade route. A Cape Verdean artist, Domingos Ca-Mati, adapted the traditional papier-mâché technique to cover the entire body in articulated pieces. Several actors played as a lizard in 1979 and a dragon in 1980, images still remembered today. Carnival has gone through a variety of influences from post-PAIGC governments, which influenced the type of roles children played in it. While they have not been directly a part of the political process their carnival performances have been affected by it.

After the demise of the PAIGC government, carnival returned to its roots, reaching international fame beginning in 1981. Prizes were awarded for the best songs, dances, and masks, and the prize-winning 1981 mask was later sent to France for exhibition, representing Guinea-Bissau popular art. Children were sometimes involved in helping to produce prize-winning masks. Gigantic, original homemade masks appeared, presenting allegorical motifs responding to political and social themes of the day. Siga writes[27] of the 1981 carnival that "African and European artists, film-makers, journalists and photographers flocked in…a high number..." But despite the major role of children in carnival, they received little international recognition. In 1982, a Bissauan film-maker, Flora Gomes, commenced making a film on carnival.[28]

Violence and disruptions have occurred in some years in which children have played roles.[29] Barçelos writes:[30]

> In recent years carnival has acquired some violent overtones. At base this represents revolt against the difficult problems that affect young people in the cities, the worsening economic situation, deteriorating living conditions in the urban centers and increasing poverty.

Carnival continues to reflect the evolution of the country's society, even as some deplore the provocative character of contemporary satire and the impunity given by wearing costumes and masks in actions that otherwise would be punished. Nevertheless, one constant component through carnival's evolution in Guinea-Bissau has been masks with what might be called a traditional stamp; they are at the base of what makes this festival Guinean.

For children, carnival may be a release from parental authority, the gaining of the freedom of the streets, which some of them already enjoy in everyday life.[31] Yet neither Doran Ross nor Daniel Crowley, viewing carnival in 1987, mentioned violence or disorder.[32] But according to Siga, in 1991, the event in Bissau was restricted to those twenty years of age or older, and, in 1994, the police prevented any carnival violence, and there were no gross masks or obscene songs. In some years, the bairros have had a major say in carnival, in others the government has played the stronger role, in still others there has been a balance of forces. The struggle of the government in Bissau vis-à-vis the bairros' organizations and carnival producers, has determined children's activities in it, as well as, of course, that of adults. This is evident in the forms of the masquerades produced, how and where performances occur, and the general tone of carnival. Yet Eric Gable[33] suggests that many persons involved in carnival see it as a celebration of their country, the only Portuguese colony to defeat its colonial military forces. They are not against a government presence; it is their government after all. That carnival children develop attitudes of pride towards their country is a corollary of his remarks.

Mask Making and Masquerading

Four major forms of carnival masks are created and worn today, both by children and adults. The most impressive are the monster forms. On adults these shoulder-bearing masks are often huge, several feet high or more, and bulky. The masks worn by boys are less huge, and are often placed on the head rather than the shoulders.[34] Doran Ross, who viewed the 1987 carnival in Bissau with Crowley, indicates that the majority of monster mask makers and masqueraders were boys twelve to eighteen years of age.[35] Daniel Crowley describes[36] these forms in the 1987 Bissau carnival as follows:. "Goggle eyes, beetling eyebrows, tongues, sharp shark's teeth, horns protruding from foreheads and jaws, barbed tails, web like wings and ears, fish scales, beaks, and skull and crossbones were all featured in every possible permutation and combination and painted in shiny lurid enamels, sometimes with the use of spray guns." Some of these have specific meanings, such as "Vida e Morte" (Life and Death), others do not (fig. 10.2).

Since numerous children's hands are often involved in making monster masks, McGuire refers to this form as a collage. They are rarely skillfully produced, as groups of children still learning mask making are often involved. But since they are monster masks, this lack of children's expertise, whether guided by an adult or not, adds to their unusual appearance. Fierceness, grotesqueness, and imperfections are blended. McGuire suggests that monster masks may once have been political critiques of colonial government, but she does not clarify in what manner. Perhaps the masks suggest that government leaders were monstrous and grotesque, ugly and aggressive. Their assertive facial features mark the enthusiastic aggressive spirit of boys. Of course, the secular, nonreligious character of carnival makes for tendencies toward social criticism and political satire. Yet ostensibly secular, the monster images may possibly remind children of the power of traditional spiritual life. Monster masks, appealing to Bissau children, suggest the modern (and sometimes traditional) idea that big is good, as people view the bigness of buildings, cars, and the churches in the urban area, and in scenes in cinema, videos, and magazines. This is a common Western concept, not absent in post-colonial Africa. The masks and the sometimes wildly erratic movements of their wearers, contrast strikingly with the more symmetrical and synchronized dancing and singing of costumed girls and women, who move along the streets in orderly fashion. While there are some attractively dressed boys in unmasked dancing and singing troupes, the girls' presence is impressive. The contrast of the ugly and the beautiful in Africa, often linked to gender, has been called by scholars the "beauty and the beast" syndrome. It is frequently observed in traditional African masquerades.[37]

A second major type of carnival mask are forms based on human or animal faces. Bissau children's masks, among other images, emulate animals from comic strips or Disney characters.[38] Face masks of this type worn by adults may derive from traditional forms in the barrios or elsewhere, or depict known political figures, such as Guinea-Bissau's president, opposition leaders, or other persons (fig. 10.3).[39] A third mask form consists of those developed around the government theme of the year. These are created, perhaps, in the hope of winning government prizes, in the spirit of cooperation with the authorities, or simply to attempt something new. For the inoculation campaign theme of 1995, both children and adults created masks with one or more constructed needles on them, or the whole mask was composed of a syringe and needle. Children responded enthusiastically in their mask making and masquerading to the 1995 vaccination campaign.[40] Children appear to delight in imaginatively developing masks related to whatever the theme or themes of the year are. Lastly, there are the remarkable full or near-full-body articulated papier-mâché masks, representing animals—a lizard, dragon or chicken–or human-like figures. Sometimes two or three adults wear a single creation, while children may take part both in making and in wearing them.[41]

Boys, and sometimes girls, play key roles in mask creation, often, but not always, under the guidance of adult males in their twenties or older These small work groups each mold the clay on which the papier-mâché is glued. The clay mold is then destroyed, or the papier-mâché separated from it. Children also make their own masks individually and in groups, and they assist adults to make theirs. In turn, adults make their own masks and assist children to produce theirs. In time, boys grow into men and take on the other role. There is evidently companionship and interest in mask making.

Girls occasionally make and wear masks. The strict distinction by gender in masking in many African cultures, including parts of rural Guinea-Bissau, is absent from carnival. However, women seem never to mask at the Bissau events.[42] Girls without masks frequently form singing and dancing groups to accompany masqueraders, or act as separate performing groups. Female troupe members often dress alike, in raffia or manufactured raffia-like skirts and other costume elements from the Bijagos Islands. Or they wear cloth costumes of the Manjaco,[43] or appear in other dress identified with rural cultures (fig. 10.4).

At times, boy masqueraders parade in considerable numbers on the Sunday before Ash Wednesday, the first day of carnival, but they also take part on other days, as Daniel Crowley observed in 1987.[44] Padre Gino of Bula[45] noted in 1995: "In the old days...the very young could participate on the first day. On the last day you would see the most variety of costumes. Now it is different—everyone can participate." Philip J. Havik[46] states that Gino's remark "evokes the steady diffusion and expansion of carnival for the privileged few in the 1950s through to the broader cross-cultural spectacle of the 1980s and 1990s." Carnival became open to all children. They form an important part of carnival, in numbers, in creating masks, in developing new mask forms, and in innovative ideas.

At times, boys, and occasionally girls, perform masked as part of a larger group from their bairro. They may do so on Tuesday of the carnival period, or, perhaps for a little time on Wednesday, though this is a quiet period in the festival. The bairro performers are likely to appear on Thursday, when prizes for the best masks are awarded by government and private corporations. McGuire, Barçelos, and others mention periods when there is music and singing in carnival, including that by girls' groups, and there is Brazilian samba music, as we have noted. However, Daniel Crowley, in viewing the 1987 carnival, was surprised at the absence of music, an uncommon feature of African festivals.[47] However, this seems to be true only when the large monster masks appear. When traditional masqueraders from the bairros are present there is often music and song.

It is common to discard the non-traditional masks after the carnival season. Children, and sometimes adults, who take part look forward to selling their masks after the annual event, to the increasing number of NGO workers, tourists, scholars, gallery owners, and other foreigners. This is unusual in African children's masking, where receiving gifts for performances well done is more often the case. The need to produce new masks each year challenges the creativity of children and adults like, providing them with strong incentives to develop original mask forms.[48] This means considerable activity in the weeks before carnival commences. It represents a change from an older African masquerade tradition, where masks were often used until they were worn out, However, even tradition children's masks, often being fragile, are likely to be replaced with some frequency. Constant change in mask forms at the Bissau carnival are evidence of innovation and change, which characterizes post-colonial Africa. Bissau has succumbed to the current Western emphasis on the importance of the newness of its objects.

Unlike some traditional Guinea-Bissau masking there is little secrecy in Bissau carnival. Since the maskers do not represent spiritual or religious figures no secrecy is involved. A video by Gomes[49] portrays a man raising his large mask above his head for a length of time, doing so proudly. Yet there is some secrecy for children and adults alike, typical of many carnivals worldwide. This occurs when masquerade preparations go on in the bairros, so that mask and performance ideas will not be stolen and copied.

Daniel Crowley estimated[50] that in 1987 there were some "1,000 participants in the streets, 500 of them in elaborate masks and costumes, and the others in clown-like or traditional festival costumes." Philip J. Havik suggests[51] that if this were so, before the civil war that began in 1998, which drove many people from Bissau, there must have been thousands of performers as a result of the increase in the city's population. Boy carnival masqueraders are found elsewhere in the country. In 1995, McGuire encountered them with papier-mâché masks blocking the road at Bula in the country's interior, asking for small change to help support their carnival festivities.

Carnival is characterized by its processional quality, although there are also staged performances on the side, at arenas, theaters, and nightclubs. On the streets, the carnival audience sees each performing element in the parade only briefly, and there are many of them. However, the total experience is long in time, with a flow of boys, girls, adults, and floats and music. This leaves varied impressions, a plentiful visual and sound experience. Carnival differs from many traditional masquerades and rituals that are held in a village square, or some other central place. There one may observe the same performers over a quite a period of time, there are fewer of them, and they may reappear a number of times. However, processional performances do occur in traditional settings. The Asante of Ghana, for example, are well known for them,[52] though they do not involve masking. And they occur elsewhere on the African continent.[53] Carnival changes the quality of the streets for the event; ordinary activities, traffic, and business cease. A temporary inversion occurs. What Victor Turner has called the "subjunctive mood" develops, in contrast to an everyday "indicative mood."[54] Children appear to delight in this, as well as adults.

Some performers, including children, create their masks and masquerades in their rural areas before coming to Bissau for carnival. At times, children from rural areas arrive for carnival bringing pigs, palm oil, woven mats, and chickens to sell to pay for their return trip home. In turn, Bissau performers sometimes tour the interior. Some traditional Bijago Islands masquerades at home now employ papier-mâché masks rather than wood ones for the less important masquerades. These features indicate active Bissau-rural links with carnival, sometimes involving children.

Childhood and the Experiences of Mask Makers

McGuire interviewed a number of male masquerade artists in 1995 who had taken part in mask making and masquerading as children for the carnival.[55] Her interviews suggest that some of them continue to play carnival roles into middle age, sometimes working with children at mask producing and in performances. One way to become a successful adult masquerade artist is to begin as a child. Some artists McGuire talked with were born upcountry and some were from Bissau. Some were Western educated as children, but still continue with carnival. However, a portion of Bissau's Westernized elites go to the beaches during carnival to get away from its bustle and crowds and the potential violence. One male adult McGuire talked with, who was very much involved in the masquerades, had no Western education at all.

"Carlito" Carlos Alberto Teixeiro de Barros,[56] born in 1947 in Bissau and of Papel ancestry, was already making masks in 1952. Attending secondary school in Portugal and studying architecture in the USSR, he returned in 1984 to Bissau and became involved in both the PAIGC and carnival, helping to evolve the monster mask form and experimenting with the use of imported paints on masks. He unsuccessfully tried substitutes for baobab fruit pulp paste in the construction of papier-mâché masks, which turned out to become very smelly from the body heat of the masqueraders. He led prize-winning Chao-de Papel Varela groups, retiring from carnival in 1983, but returning to take part in 1992 when the French were making a carnival film. He clearly has been an inspiration and a model for children and others in carnival.

Tony "Mbake" da Silva,[57] born in 1965 of mixed Papel-Cape Verdean ancestry, learned mask making through assisting Carlito; he made his first cow's head mask in 1981. He later formed his own masquerade troupe. In 1994 and 1995, he became the reigning mask maker in Bissau, capturing top prizes. Some smaller masks made by him alone are technically more skilled than larger masks made by a number of hands, including those made with the assistance of children.

"Tchon Tchon" Domingos Inacio da Silva Sa[58] was born upcountry in 1961, of a Papel father and a mother of mixed heritage from Balanta in the interior and from the Cape Verde islands. He made his first Bissau carnival mask at the age of ten, after assisting a brother for several years. In 1975, his family transferred to the Bijagos Islands where Tchon-Tchon learned a great deal about the traditional arts of the island, which he later brought to carnival. In the 1980s, he was an active leader in his bairro carnival activities, making a two-person tiger in 1981, and a pot-bellied cartoon figure the next year, which he considers to be his trademark. In 1995, he was still involved with carnival, directing mask making (fig. 10.3), costuming, dancing, writing songs and selecting his carnival group's candidate for the queen contest. Formerly employed at a now-defunct ceramic workshop, he works independently. He adopts papier-mâché techniques and forms to create miniature masks, portrait caricatures, and hand puppets. The international community in the 1990s was more interested in buying these than the larger masks. He is a professional artist whose skills developed out of his childhood mask making experience.

Unlike the three carnival artists just discussed, the Mendonca brothers—Epifanio, born in 1971, and Bendito in 1974—are from the Mankanya culture (a subgroup of the Papel), and yet grew up in a Bissau bairro. McGuire thinks that they may be typical of the generation of mask makers born after independence. They are barely able to speak Portuguese and without prospect of salaried employment in Bissau's commercial sector. By the age of five each was assisting neighborhood mask makers, and by about ten years of age they were producing their own masks. They began making carnival masks for others on contract in the early 1990s. They are not stars among mask makers. Some youngsters order masks from them, in 1995 paying about four U.S. dollars for each one. They assisted the Cape Verdean carnival artist, "Ca-Mati," whom we have mentioned, to create a very large lizard in 1979 and a substantial dragon in 1980. The brothers continued to work with him until he returned home. They can still describe with pleasure these large pieces that they created, which covered the performers' hands, feet, and legs in detail. However, they have never had sufficient financial backing to consider production of a mask of this size on their own. While children take part in mask building, or may purchase a mask of their own, it is adult mask producers who bear the main financial burden, and must frequently seek finances to produce large mask forms. In recent years, the real money to be made is in producing carnival extravaganzas in nightclubs and hotels, not in the streets of Bissau, something the brothers lack resources or contacts to do.[59] They are strong advocates of monster masks, but do not see themselves as artists, as those discussed above do, only making masks because children in the neighborhood ask them to. They feel that their designs are trite and stale, but lack a patron to accomplish anything better.

Influences

Carnival in Bissau exists in a multicultural city and presents a multicultural face. It came to the city through Portuguese Catholic missionaries as a secular pre-Lenten Christian carnival. Daniel Crowley indicates that carnival "has its roots in the classical Mediterranean and took shape in early medieval times."[60] In Bissau, its religious aspects did not last long, overcome by urbanization, secularization, the PAIGC, and later governments. The idea of masquerading has been common in rural Guinea-Bissau,[61] and with the Papel indigenes in the city. Carnival shows the influence of many Guinea-Bissau cultural groups, some of whose members now reside in the city. These rural influences on it occur in mask forms, costumes, songs, and performance styles, for example, in the Bijagó, cow horn masks. Philip J. Havik writes[62] "that we are dealing with loaned images from age groups preceding initiation, i.e., adolescents and young men/women, which run from 10 years of age..."

Both children and adults in Bissau view films and videos, and read articles on the Brazilian carnivals and even those originating from the former Portuguese colony of Macau near Hong Kong. There is the influence of musical forms from Brazil, and of individuals who formerly resided in Bahia. Ideas have come from a popular character in a newspaper comic strip published in Bissau.[63] Other qualities of carnival come through American movies and comics.[64] Philip J. Havik[65] suggests that beginning in the 1990s, television, especially Brazilian "telenovelas," projected "characters and stories which immediately appealed to the Bissau population.... Face form masks therefore began to include figures from these 'telenovelas' at the time." Although carnival exists in Angola it does not appear to have had any influence on Bissau carnival.[66] Few influences have come from other African countries, except nearby Cape Verde,

Senegal, and Guinea. Then there have been the efforts of various Guinea-Bissau governments, colonial and post-colonial, to control the creativity of carnival and to develop primary and even secondary themes for it, while allowing local and bairro ideas to emerge.

There has been impact on Bissau carnival from the former Portuguese colony of Cape Verde, some distance off the coast of Bissau, whose people have ties of marriage, commerce, and politics with Guinea-Bissau. Persons from these islands form the basis of the Crioulu population in Bissau, and in the past held many government positions in it. Perhaps 4 percent of Guinea-Bissau's residents are Crioulu (Creole), mostly residing in Bissau. Nominally Catholic, a good many of them are of mixed European and Cape Verdean ancestry. Carnival also occurs on the Cape Verde islands.[67] And some children and adult carnival performers in Bissau have Cape Verdean heritage in their background.[68] But in recent years other cultural forces appear to be swallowing up influences from Cape Verde. Phillip J. Havik[69] believes that Cape Verdean influences should not be overstated, for after the 1980 coup in Guinea-Bissau, there was an increasing influx of Guinean traditions into the increasingly multicultural Bissau scene.

Mask forms have come from the Bijagos Islands off of Bissau. They also came in the past from the Nalu of southern Guinea-Bissau, who formerly produced Nimba masks, but who have ceased masquerading, as they are now Muslims.[70] Michelle Johnson indicates that members of different ethnic groups wear their traditional ethnic dress during carnival. "For those who don't belong to a single ethnic group but want to dress 'traditionally,' they dress like the Bijugos...known for being the most 'traditional' and the most 'exotic' ethnic group in Guinea-Bissau."[71] Rural children who come to live in numbers in Bissau with their families or without them, carry memories of rural masquerades which may or may not be carried out in the city. In any case, carnival for them is a new and more secular world. Barçelos writes:[72] "Perhaps only through Carnival and the act of costuming could the city kids show that they still had links to traditional ethnic life without facing ridicule from urban society with so many nationalities and other ways of comportment."

Masks of foreign origin occasionally appear at carnival.[73] Portuguese Catholic religious activity in carnival has virtually disappeared, and there is only a little influence from *irans* and other traditional Guinea-Bissau spiritual forces. During PAIGC's political reign, artists from Guinea-Bissau were trained in Cuba and eastern Europe. They brought some of their experiences back to Bissau, possibly including ideas from Cuba's carnival.[74]

In the increasingly multicultural atmosphere of Bissau, children have a good deal of freedom to create, despite the uneasy political atmosphere in the country. They experiment, drawing ideas and inspiration from a variety of sources, and they fantasize–so important in the maturation of children. They accept suggestions from men who guide them, and sometimes assist them to produce masks. These are men who themselves are drawing from a variety of masquerading influences, including from their own childhood. Carnival exhibits a high degree both of individual and group agency, as well as strong colonial and post-colonial hybridity.

Carnival and the Larger World

Carnival draws both on tradition and on the modern world, while outwardly representing the face of modernity in Guinea-Bissau. "It is rather defined by its occupation of the zone between these two poles," that of tradition and the modern, as Barber[75] writes of other African situations. It is a mélange, a collage of popular culture.[76] Consider the masquerader that is second from the left in figure 10.2. The mask was created employing indigenous clay as a mold, using pulp from the fruit of a local baobab tree, but the paper was probably imported, as was the idea of papier-mâché. The paint is probably European. The concept of masking is indigenous to the country, but it is also European, Caribbean, Brazilian, and American. The cloths appear to be of European origin, and not African made, although the style of the costume derives from Manjaco culture. Yet the mask wearer is not necessarily of that group. The outfit is typical of present-day carnival; it forms a synthesized entity with multiple meanings. The whole, drawn from disparate parts, exemplifies popular culture in Africa today. Carnival *is* popular culture. Because it is not elite performance art or "high art," and since it involves a substantial number of children, it might be assumed that it is not complex. This is not so. Carnival has multiple orientations by age and gender, considerable ambiguity, as in the meanings of the monster masks, fluidity in performance, and the ability to change over time. It is as complex and difficult to read as a Chinua Achebe novel, a drama by Wole Soyinka, or a poem by Christopher Okigbo, though it can be enjoyed without deep analysis.

Various influences on children and adults have arisen during the rapid population growth of Bissau, now somewhat over fifty years old. As in many other African cities, there has been little city planning and there are marked contrasts in riches and poverty, in housing and in lifestyle. It has had mobile populations, including its children, who have moved in and out of the city as the political climate has changed. The city has gone from colonialism, through the long fight with Portugal for independence, through various post-independence governments, and through the 1998-1999 civil war to the present; Guinea-Bissau has been a country of fragile governments, though with a people of high ideals. During this time, there have been many new settlers to the city of Bissau, whether refugees, or persons who have deliberately moved there. They have wrestled with the chaos left by Portuguese colonialism and the fight for freedom. Carnival has been one way of dealing with these problems, and children have contributed to issues of unity in it, although fights sometimes break out between youthful participants. Given the country's history, is it not surprising that there has been a tendency to violence in Bissau's carnival, as noted by Siga and Barçelos as well as others? Problems of control in Carnival mirror problems of control in the country. The ritualized aggression of carnival has a tendency to become genuine aggression.[77] This has been particularly so at carnival during times when there has been little strong government control, in the absence of modern religious controls, and with the weakening influence of traditional elders in the bairros. When children see adults in disorder it may encourage them to do likewise. The tendency of both children and adults to violence in carnival is a release from the pent-up frustrations of everyday life and its unfulfilled visions.

At times, the government of Guinea-Bissau has encouraged carnival to develop, in the hope that its multiethnic origins and its involvement of a wide range of individuals and groups would act as a unifying force in a small country, made up of numerous cultures and religions.[78] But carnival, by itself, cannot unify a country; it is too brief an experience. If Bissau carnival creates only a temporary and ephemeral sense of unity among its performers and witnesses, it undoubtedly increases the sense of unity within the bairros. Their members come home to take part in carnival, or are already there. Preparations for the event within the bairro are intense over a period of time. The bairros compete to produce the most interesting and spectacular troupes. All of this helps to create a sense of unity within each bairro. Birmingham's[79] comment on the 1987 Luanda carnival, that "rivalry between competing groups was probably... more important than the outward message to the world," is probably also true of the Bissau carnival. Children involved in Bissau carnival have the opportunity to get to know bairro members with whom they would otherwise seldom have contact, and the competition in mask presentation and in performance provides them with a strong sense of bairro identity.[80] In fact, several identities exist for the children: with the bairro, the city of Bissau, the country, and at the global level. These contain some contradictory elements, but they are the stuff of present-day life in Bissau.[81] Carnival exposes children to the world of Disney and Brazil, and to national issues and politics. It intensifies relationships within the bairro, and has links to the indigenous cultures in Bissau and its countryside. With the new government in place after the emptying of Bissau during the recent civil war of 1997-1998, and the subsequent reoccupation of the city, changes in carnival are undoubtedly occurring that affect children as well as adults. Philip J. Havik informed me that carnival began again in 2000, with the return of security in the country. It has continued in various forms to this day despite continued political problems in the country.

Children in an Urban Masquerade

Carnival masquerade is quite a different form of experience for children than rural masquerades, such as those described in this volume. Yet similar underlying experiences occur. Children learn how to make and to wear masks, and how to cooperate in performances in a group of other boys. They develop their bodily abilities, and they progress from simple to more complex skills. Carnival allows children to choose roles that fit their particular talents and interests, and thus develop skills as mask makers, costume makers or designers, masqueraders, singers or dancers. Children can carry on with carnival masquerading when they grow up, and as men they assist boys in the preparation of masks and in performances. If carnival children go through traditional initiation rites in Bissau or in the countryside, they bring to these a wealth of carnival masquerade experience, though differing in kind. The masks are not the same, as a rule, nor is the music. In carnival, boys mask side-by-side with men and sometimes with girls, whereas in their indigenous initiations they are not likely to do so.

Masquerading helps children who have moved to Bissau to go from a sacred to a secular environment, from control by village elders to the authority of the city of Bissau, and the bairros, and to its elders, who sometimes critique carnival masks and performances. The carnival moves rural children with a background in a single culture into an urban center of mixed cultures, where children participate with other youths of various cultural backgrounds and mixed ancestry. While schooling in Bissau, in so far as it exists, tends to separate children from fathers and other relatives with learning by direct methods, Bissau carnival lets boys have close contact with older males on an informal basis, in mask making and in the organizing of performance troupes. The latter is in marked contrast to school learning. And carnival children surely delight in seeing adults play as children, as adults delight in seeing the children play, all involved in a mass playfulness not ordinarily occurring in Bissau. This creates cross-generational links differing from the age-boundedness sometimes found in traditional African settings. Bissau carnival allows children a chance to participate in the changing world, to play a creative and positive role in it, as Gable has suggested is occurring even among youths of somewhat older ages among rural Manjaco in Guinea-Bissau.[82] Carnival, Philip J. Havik points out,[83] provides opportunities for children to meet youths from other bairros as well as their own. Children's involvement in the carnival forms part of a larger pattern of an increasing emphasis on persons of younger ages in the country, and a greater attention to children as performers, whether at school or in masks. Carnival is part of a movement of children toward a distinct culture of childhood.[84]

Carnival in Bissau reflects the struggle of single individuals and groups to control and direct their activities in terms of government efforts to direct them to specific themes and to police carnival. This issue, certainly the concern of adults, also influences what kinds of masks children prepare for themselves and others and how they perform. No one in Carnival, including the children, is free of political issues. These matters are also common in other carnivals and large public displays, whether children are involved or not—in Trinidad, London, Toronto, and Brazil, and also in Freetown, Ouagadougou, and in the annual masquerades festivals of southern Nigeria.[85] The issue of who controls these large events is inevitably connected to issues of order and disorder, and to the interests of governments in controlling the performances for their own political purposes. Linked to issues of the politics of control of carnival are the political expressions through carnival performance of the mask makers and players, sometimes critiquing or satirizing government or its leaders, as in the Bissau carnival, in which children sometimes taken part. The extent of the performers' expressions of political sentiments that are allowed, of course, depends upon the degree of government control. This is really not too different from what occurs in rural regions of Guinea-Bissau, or elsewhere in rural Africa. Political authorities, be they elders, priests, secret society leaders, or others, control and regulate how, when, and where children perform.

At carnival there are masses of people on the streets for a number of days, from children and adults of the poor and the ordinary, to art specialists and those skilled in producing music. Judges, who are likely to be of the elite, are stationed at various points on the route. There are the well-off sitting in the grandstands while most people stand or sit at the sides of the streets. All of this is the politics of the people, of the mass. It is an expression of popular will, in which children are heavily involved. The forward movement of great numbers of children and adults, over time for a number of days, can be seen as a metaphor of a wish for the country and its people to move forward, to progress in a society which has had difficulties in doing so. Carnival is a particular form of expression of popular will. Aesthetics and politics are inextricably mixed. This annual event of only a few days duration creates the illusion for youths of some change in the social order, of youths being in control, rather than the everyday authorities. Children's masquerades and adults' roles in carnival add to the people's sense of being urbanites (or, if they come from the countryside, some of them hope to become so), and of motion towards a different world, both inside and outside of the country.

In addition to several carnivals in Africa, there have been other large post-colonial art festivals, such as the art biennales in Dakar and in Johannesburg, several World Black and African Festivals of Arts and Culture, for example, the 1977 FESTAC[86] in Nigeria. While not all of these include masquerades, they are new forms of African artistic activity in post-colonial Africa, characteristically multicultural and multicountry, and often urban oriented. The annual village or town festival of past times, with many participants and visitors from neighboring communities, has become the state or urban festival, larger in size, involving many cultures, foreign and country-based, with visitors from various nations. Bissau carnival, as these other large-scale events, fits into the conception of a country's identity since colonialism. Its carnival states that it has something worthwhile to display and the ability to do so. Bissau children are drawn into this conception, whether they are conscious of it or not. Such mass events temporarily offset a country's internal political and economic troubles, exhibiting a positive African face to its members, to other African countries, and to the world. While Bissau children play a part in this, their own interests probably focus more on play and on developing their performance skills.

What is unusual about Bissau in contrast to most large African festivals and carnivals is the considerable involvement of children. Another example is the annual government-sponsored children's masquerade at Ouagadougou, discussed in Priscilla Hinckley's chapter in the volume. Why children should be involved in masquerades is not fully clear, though in both these cases they have been from the beginning. In Bissau, the carnival's origin in Portuguese colonial days established a tradition of children's participation. This was followed by the post-independent PAIGC government's desire to be inclusive of persons of all ages and gender in carnival, a policy continued by some later governments. In Ouagadougou, the government of Burkina Faso, appropriated boys' masquerades in the city's quarters, turning them into a national festival in a stadium, and enveloping children into government interests through awarding prizes and providing prestige for the winners. Perhaps it is better to have some government control over children and their masquerades, than to have them free to carry guns and kill, pillage and rape, as they have in a number of African countries—Liberia, Sierra Leone, Somalia, the former Zaire, Rwanda, Burundi, Angola, and elsewhere—grotesque forms of entertainment.

Bissau carnival is a secular ritual, fitting well into Moore and Myerhoff's[87] general discussion of this ritual form, although carnival's tendency to change performance styles and procedures over time does not follow their scheme. But carnival's secular quality does not mean that either the more traditional, or the Christian and Muslim religions are dead in the country. However, Barçelos writes:[88] "The shapes used for Carnival have moved way past the dictates of traditional religion. Urban youth live in a different world and they want to represent and act out other realities."

Finally, Barçelos[89] writes: "We can see in the masks reflections of the evolutionary phases in the life of the nation and of the cultural influences which have affected urban society along the way....I believe Guinean Carnival will continue to evolve parallel with development in the urban centers, taking on new forms influenced by awareness of foreign cultures, while keeping a base in the tradition of mask-making from its ethnic cultures." In this process children will continue to play important roles.

Notes

1. Editors note: Harriet C. McGuire, wife of Roger McGuire, former Ambassador to Guinea-Bissau, wrote a very useful survey of the carnival and gathered the papers of three Guinea-Bissau authors for this editor. She has also, through various letters, provided me with further information, and interesting photographs. She also obtained a copy of a video of the carnival, *A Màscara*, directed by Flora Gomes, which has been of considerable assistance to me. In addition, as editor, I have made use of unpublished and published sources, which are included in the bibliography and I have added comments here and there. Much of the conclusion represents my own interpretation of the carnival, which I have not myself viewed. This paper, then, is a compilation of sometimes contradictory views, both African and European. I also

198   Playful Performers

wish to thank Luis Goncalves, Harriet C. McGuire, Michelle Johnson, Eric Gable, Nicolas Argenti, Philip J. Havik, George E. Brooks, and members of the 15th Satterthwaite Colloquium on African Ritual and Religion, April 18-21, 1999, for comments on this chapter, Frances Harding for general discussions on carnival and performance. In Portuguese, the national language of Guinea-Bissau, carnival is spelled *carnaval*.

2. Harriet C. McGuire and Felix Siga in this chapter, and E. Crowley (1990) spell it Papal. Bernatzik (1933) and Michelle Johnson (personal communication) use Pepel. Murdock (1959, 265), in his listing of African cultural groups, lists both spellings.
3. Bissau was then a small community, not yet the capital of what was then Portuguese Guinea, but is now Guinea-Bissau.
4. Siga 1994, 1.
5. Fara Gomes 1995, 1.
6. See Bernatzik 1933, vol. 2, plates 23, 30, 181-183, 202, 216-218; Bernatzik 1960, photographs opposite pp. 49, 64, and 128. Philip J. Havik (personal communication) informs me of the link of these cow horn masks to wooden forms of the Bijagó, living west of Bissau (also called Bidjogo in Criolu). Also see Wallace and Williams 1985. Bijagó women wear ceremonial cow horn headdresses, but not masks (Duquette 1979, 93). Horned masks worn by males are common in the nearby Casamance area of Senegal. See Mark 1992.
7. McGuire 1995, 4.
8. Ibid.
9. Brooks 1984, 1, and fn 2; Dias de Carvalho 1944, 74-75.
10. Brooks 1984, 12.
11. Barçelos 1995, 2.
12. However Philip J. Havik (personal communication) informs me that this movie theater, which still survives today, was quite Portuguese-oriented. It was restricted to Africans who were either in the Portuguese designated class of "civilisado" and "asimilado," that is, for privileged Africans. But Ottenberg suggests that ideas derived from this cinema probably diffused from elite Africans to other Africans.
13. Barçelos 1995, 2-3.
14. Philip J. Havik (personal communication) states that from the colonial viewpoint "installing 'Portuguese values' in Guinean kids from the bairro was naturally a noble initiative at the time."
15. McGuire 1995, 5. On "Carlito" see p. 190 in this chapter.
16. In 1997, this *bairro* won the contest for the best masks.
17. Guinea-Bissau's former president, prime minister, and a significant portion of the former reigning political leadership of the African Party for Independence of Guinea and Cape Verde first worked together in mask-making projects in this bairro as 5 to 12 year olds. Philip J. Havik (personal communication) comments that the Christian community in Bissau, or *kriston,* Kriol for the Guineans of this faith, had strong kin links with the Pepel. This was especially in the female line. In contrast, the *Crioulu* generally had Cape Verdean links, especially in the male line.
18. Barçelos 1995, 3.
19. Philip J. Havik, personal communication.
20. Ibid.
21. Philip J. Havik (personal communication) doubts this interpretation, arguing for the view that in "the tense political situation...in which symbolism would take recourse to a kind of expurgation or exorcism of the 'feitiço,' the (bad) spell, put on society by the war."
22. However, Philip J. Havik informs me that when the UDIB Theatre opened in Bissau in the 1950s, "still by the way, the biggest cinema in the country, its impact

upon popular iconography was only partially valid; 'non-civilized' or 'assimilated' children could not attend. I presume a lot of imagery was conveyed to African kids by means of posters. The influence of television in the late 80s cannot be underestimated of course, Brazilian 'telenovelas' were significant in sculpting popular culture, above all in the capital Bissau."

23. Nevertheless, according to Michelle Johnson, who carried out research among the Mandinga of Guinea-Bissau, the Muslim *kankaran* boys' initiation masquerade of the Fula, Mandinga, and other Islamic groups is more prominent in the country than the cow-horn masquerade.
24. Siga 1994, 2.
25. Another interpretation provided to Michelle Johnson by Gina Barbosa, an elder Guinean woman living in Lisbon, is: "The mask is afraid of water, the mask knows your name," e.g., the mask fears water in part because it is made of paper, and if the mask knows your name it will come to get you, and you had better run!" "*N'trudu*," according to this woman, is an older term for masks of a form no longer made today for carnival, which now show Brazilian influence and are called *maskaras*. *N'trudu* masqueraders used to run through the city stealing from shops and scaring people. Philip J. Havik informs me (personal communication) that the term *N'trudu* "is of Portuguese origin: '*entrudo*' literally means beginning entrance into new year, but also refers to the fun and games associated with this festivity."
26. Philip J. Havik observes (personal communication) that "successive bad harvests and a failing market system greatly heightened the tension at carnival (above all in 1979). The abolishment of the civilisado/assimilado/indigena distinction in 1961 also increased the African pulse of the event."
27. Siga 1994, 3.
28. "Flora Gomes," 1993.
29. This is not unique; it is a frequent occurrence elsewhere, as in London (Cohen 1993; Alleyne-Dettmers 1998), Trinidad and Tobago (Cowley 1996; Koningsbruggen 1997; Liverpool 1993), Rio de Janeiro (Da Matta 1977, 1991; Turner 1987), northeastern Brazil (Linger 1992), and Cuba (Bettelheim 1991). It reflects the presence of large crowds difficult to control, the release of personal and economic frustrations, a sense of freedom and antagonism toward governing authorities.
30. Barçelos 1995, 4.
31. Philip J. Havik (personal communication) points out that the economic stabilization program, which began in 1983 and the Structural Adjustment Program (SAP) from 1987 onwards, led to an increased poverty gap and heightened tensions in Bissau, undoubtedly affecting carnival. Michelle Johnson comments (personal communication): "Unfortunately, many adults are now forbidding their children from participation in Carnival because of the violent nature of the event. Parents told us that although they used to let their kids mask and run in the streets for days, now they prefer to have their kids watch Carnival on TV. Despite these concerns, I think you can still call carnival a children's event."
32. D. Crowley 1987; Ross 1993. Eric Gable suggests that the increasingly difficult conditions that the Structural Adjustment Program created after Crowley's visit led to violence at carnival. Yet, as indicated above, there are accounts of earlier violence as well. Philip J. Havik (personal communication) confirms the frequency of disruptions, deaths, and alcoholism in carnival from 1982 onwards.
33. Eric Gable, personal communication.
34. See "Carnaval Bissau," 1993, p. 61, second photograph down the left side.
35. Ross 1993, 64. See his fig. 9 for an example of a monster mask.

36. D. Crowley 1987, 76.
37. For example, see Blier 1976.
38. Ross 1993, fig. 9, depicts some of these children's' forms.
39. Ross 1993, fig. 6, shows three face masks modeled on Chinese construction workers who were building a hospital in Bissau.
40. Ross 1993, figs. 1, 5, and 8. D. Crowley 1987, 78, indicates that in 1987 at least fifteen groups chose to portray this theme. He writes (pp. 78-79): "Several groups came out as doctors and nurses in white smocks, starched capes, mirrored headgear, suitcases marked with Red Cross symbols, and of course large papier-mâché needles, some of which (built around bicycle pumps) shot streams of bright red liquid).... A few maskers also became animated syringes or injection needles, and one group was inspired to represent the various diseases to be cured by the vaccination campaign..." However, Philip J. Havik (personal communication) feels that masks and dress "based on government inspired themes, mostly refer to the 'official' procession, and much less to what the kids themselves present..."
41. Ross 1993, fig. 8, pictures a full-body hypodermic needle, and in fig. 3, two six-foot-high papier-mâché chickens were developed to promote poultry raising.
42. As for the rural areas not far from Bissau, Michelle Johnson (personal communication) knows of one Mandinga traditional female masquerade, called "Ulo," and that women "own" "Nyrin-Nyrin," a female masquerade figure, which, however, is performed by males. Philip J. Havik (personal communication) that "among the Bijagó, not far from Bissau: uninitiated girls (10-20), the 'kampune,' also wear masks, but usually smaller in size depicting cows and other animals, such as crocodiles (the toothed jaws sticking upwards) and certain species of fish."
43. A style that Eric Gable informs me, Manjaco girls wear at boys' initiations and at funerals.
44. D. Crowley 1987, 78.
45. Padre Gino of Bula, 1995, 1.
46. Philip J. Havik, personal communication.
47. D. Crowley, 1997, 82, writes that the papier-mâché groups at that year's carnival "do no dancing or singing whatsoever, but merely shuffle, bent forward, through the streets without any pretense of ordered formation or any kind of pattern. There were no musical instruments in evidence, much less any musical or rhythmic effects. Imagine an African festival with no music or dance! Evidently, the relatively recent introduction of the monster theme has not yet generated music or dance forms."
48. D. Crowley 1987, 78, estimated that some 90 percent of the monster masks in 1987 were either new or repainted, "so that very few showed the signs of wear inevitable in so fragile a material as papier-mâché–cracked paint, disintegrating material, or loose or broken parts." In the record of one monster mask which he owned, and which belongs to his estate he suggests that "Faces of many of the Bissau carnival masks resemble old horror film monsters. 'The Creature from the Black Lagoon' was the inspiration for many of the earliest Bissau Carnival masks."
49. Gomes c. 1993.
50. D. Crowley 1987, 80.
51. Philip J. Havik, personal communication.
52. See Cole 1975.
53. For an Igbo example of a masked parade, see Ottenberg 1975, 147-170., and Ottenberg 1979.
54. Turner 1987, 76, refers to the subjunctive mood in terms of "its mood of feeling, willing, and desiring, its mood of fantasizing, its playful mood; not its indicative mood where it tries to apply reason to human action and systematize the relation-

ships between ends and means in industry and bureaucracy." Though I generally agree with this comment with reference to Bissau carnival there is exaggeration to it, as much "reason to human action" and "ends and means" occurs in the preparation and carrying out of carnival.

55. McGuire 1995, 10-18.
56. Ibid., 11-13.
57. Ibid., 15-17.
58. Ibid., 13-15.
59. These seem rarely to involve children. Philip J. Havik (personal communication) comments that the "fast growth of nightlife, including bars and discotheques, dates from the second half of the 1980s, emerging as a result of the SAP [Structural Adjustment Program]. They hold their own carnival celebrations and organize lots of parallel events."
60. D. Crowley 1987, 74. Masquerades and carnivals continue to exist in Europe today. For example, see Blum 1998; Gilmore 1998; Poppi 1998; Kertzer 1988, 144-150; Cohen 1993.
61. See Bernatzik 1933, vol. 2, plates 21, 23, 30, 49, 148, 150, 151, 201-202, 216-218, 226-227.
62. Philip J. Havik, personal communication.
63. D. Crowley 1978, 78 writes: "This was Nturi Palan, a black boy with large ears, a protruding abdomen with [an] umbilical hernia, and large feet—the cartoon character invented by 28-year old twin brothers Fernando and Manel Julio (their school name, their African 'title' being Nnati).... *Nturi* means "deceiver" in the local Balanta language, and *Palan*, from Portuguese *'Planear'* or English 'plan,' implies plotting, so that this likeable underdog is the local manifestation of the classic Trickster known throughout world folklore." He further describes this mask form on this page. Also see Ross 1993, fig. 8. Philip J. Havik, personal communication, states that this comic strip "was extremely popular among children and adolescents in Bissau and for the first time catapulted their own Kriol—note that the language used was Kriol and not Portuguese—and some irreverence onto the public stage."
64. The carnival of the Cape Coloured peoples in South Africa, which has some masking, has also been influenced over many years by American culture. See Martin 1999.
65. Philip J. Havik, personal communication.
66. Birmingham 1988, 97, writes of carnival in Luanda, the capital of the former Portuguese colony of Angola, that it began as early as 1620. It involves "pagan rituals from the Mediterranean pantheons, Christian rituals from the Iberian church, and...Mbundu and Kongo rituals, designed to foster fertility and prosperity, and to overcome the disasters of colonial conquest." Like Bissau carnival, it has been influenced by carnival in Brazil and Cuba.
67. *CVS Newsletter 1996;* Sharfstein 1996. I wish to thank Richard Lobban for calling these two references to my attention. Philip J. Havik (personal communication) comments that the "Cape Verdean carnival has of course a lot more in common with syncretic but Catholic traditions as found in Brazil, than the one in Bissau...the influence of the samba in Bissau is therefore limited." According to Michelle Johnson (personal communication), a form of Bissau carnival without masking also occurs in Lisbon among "animist" or "Christians" though not among Muslims. There is much partying, and the decorating of the streets, as the Portuguese do during carnival and Saint Day celebrations. She was told by Guineans in Portugal, "*karnival li ka sabi*," meaning "Carnival in Portugal isn't sweet" like it is in Guinea-Bissau. Since there is considerable contact between Guineans in Portugal and Guinea Bissau it is likely that influences on carnival have gone both ways.

202   Playful Performers

68. Since substantial numbers of Cape Verdeans now live in southern New England in the United States, and have close contacts with their home islands, influences on Bissau carnival may have come from there by way of Cape Verde. See Lobban 1995, 58-59, 63-64, 65.
69. Philip J. Havik, personal communication.
70. Nimba masks are better known from Baga of the former French colony of Guinea, south of Guinea-Bissau. See Lamp 1996.
71. Johnson also cites the case of *bairro* Sintra-Nema in the 1997 carnival, which chose the theme: "Sintra-Nema: Unity Through Diversity." The members of the bairro all dressed in their respective ethnic costumes, playing music and singing songs in their various languages, a case of multicultural unity within a single bairro.
72. Barçelos 1995, 4.
73. Ross 1993, fig. 11, depicts a plastic Bugs Bunny Halloween mask and a red-painted wooden one from Guatemala.
74. Bettelheim 1991; Nunley and Bettelheim 1988.
75. Barber 1997, 1.
76. On popular culture, see Barber 1997, 35; Fabian 1997, 18-19.
77. Linger 1992, chap. 3, has a good discussion of these two forms of aggression in his work on carnival in Sao Luis in northeastern Brazil.
78. D. Crowley 1987, 85, has suggested that "this carnival could become the centerpiece of Bissauan nationalism and a unifying force badly needed in so divided a country." The recent fighting in Guinea-Bissau suggests that it has not succeeded. Philip J. Havik (personal communication) is skeptical of Crowley's suggestion. He writes: "The idea of carnival as a unifying force...is a serious error of judgment. Not only for [carnival] being essentially a 'foreign' and Bissau-based festival, with all the overtones that that has for Guinea-Bissau, but also in view of the serious incidents that have accompanied it over the years. And, of course, frowned upon by elders, an important power base." And, of course, the more rural Muslim population is hardly involved in Carnival, as Havik mentions elsewhere.
79. Birmingham 1988, 98.
80. See Bettelheim 1991, 68, for a similar argument in the case of carnival in Cuba.
81. For example, see Poppi 1997.
82. Gable 1995, 1999.
83. Philip J. Havik, personal communication.
84. Aries 1962.
85. See Nunley 1987 on Freetown lantern parades and other masquerades; Hinckley, 1985, 1986, and this volume on the Ouagadougou masquerade, and Reed 1996 on the Enugu Igbo masquerade festival in southeastern Nigeria.
86. *FESTAC '77*, 1977.
87. Moore and Myerhoff 1977.
88. Barçelos 1995, 2.
89. Ibid., 5.

Bibliography

Alleyne-Dettmers, Patricia Tamara. 1998. "Ancestral Voices: *Thriven*—A Case Study of Meta-masking in the Notting Hill Carnival. *Journal of Material Culture* 3:2, 201-221.

Argenti, Nicolas. 1998. "Air Youth: Performance, Violence and the State in Cameroon." *Journal of the Royal Anthropological Institute*, n.s. 4:4, 753-781.

Aries, Philippe. 1962. *Centuries of Childhood: A Social History of Family Life*, translated from the French by Robert Baldick. New York: Knopf.

Barber, Karen (ed.). 1997. *Readings in African Popular Culture*. Bloomington and Oxford: Indiana University Press and James Curley.

Barçelos, Manuel Rambout. 1995. Untitled, 5 typescript pages, translated and edited by Harriet C. McGuire.

Bernatzik, Hugo Adolf. 1933. *Äthiopen des Westens: Forschungsreisen in Portugiesisch-Guinea.* 2 vols. Vienna: L. W. Seidel & Sohn,

_____. 1960. *Im Reich der Bidjogo: Geheimnisvolle Inseln in Westafrika.* Berlin: Verlag Ullstein.

Bettelheim, Judith. 1991. "Negotiations of Power in Carnaval Culture in Santiago de Cuba." *African Arts* 24:2, 66-75, 91-92.

Birmingham, David. 1988. "Carnival at Luanda." *Journal of African History* 9:1, 93-103.

Blier, Suzanne Preston. 1976. *Beauty and the Beast: A Study in Contrasts.* New York: Tribal Arts Gallery.

Blum, Dieter. 1998. *Basler Fasnacht: Menschen Hunter Masken.* Basel: Museum der Kulturen.

Brooks, George E. 1984. "The Observance of All Souls' Day in the Guinea-Bissau Region: A Christian Holy Day, an African Harvest Festival, an African New Year's Celebration, or All of the Above?" *History in Africa* 11, 1-34.

"Carnaval Bissau," 1993. *Revue Noire* 8, 58-62.

Cohen, Abner. 1993. *Masquerade Politics: Explorations in the Structure of Urban Cultural Movements.* Berkeley: University of California Press.

Cole, Herbert M. 1975. "The Art of Festival in Ghana." *African Arts* 8:3, 12-23, 60-62, 90.

Cowley, John. 1996. *Carnival, Canboulay and Calypso: Traditions in the Making.* Cambridge: Cambridge University Press.

Crowley, Daniel J. 1987. "The Carnival of Guinea Bissau." *The Drama Review (TDR)* 33:2, 74-86.

Crowley, Eve Lakshmi. 1990. "Contracts with the Spirits: Religion, Asylum and Ethnic Identity in the Cacheu Region of Guinea-Bissau." Ph.D. diss., Yale University.

CVS Newletter, 1984, June. "A Tabannca de Ilha de Santiago de Cabo Verde." Cape Verde, 3.

Da Matta, Roberto. 1977. "Constraint and License: A Preliminary Study of Two Brazilian National Rituals." In Sally F. Moore and Barbara G. Myerhoff (eds.), *Secular Ritual.* Amsterdam: Van Gorcum, 244-264.

———. 1991. *Carnivals, Rogues and Heroes: an interpretation of the Brazilian Dilemma.* Notre Dame: University of Notre Dame Press.
Dias de Carvalho, Henrique Augusto. 1944. *Guiné: Apontamentos inéditos.* Lisboa: Divisão de Pubicações e Biblioteca, Agêncie Geral das Colónias.
Duquette, Danielle Gallois. 1979. "Women Power and Initiation in the Bissagos Islands." *African Arts* 13:2, 31-35, 93.
———. 1983. *Dynamique de l'Art Bidjogo (Guinée-Bissau). Contribution à une anthropologie de l'art des sociétés africaines.* Lisbon: Institute de Investigação Científica Tropical.
Fabian, Johannes. 1997. "Popular Culture in Africa; Findings and Conjectures." In Karen Barber (ed.), *Readings in African Popular Culture.* Bloomington and London: Indiana University Press and James Curley, 18-28.
Fara Gomes, Nicolau. 1995. Untitled. 4 typescript pages. Translated and edited by Harriet C. McGuire.
FESTAC '77. 1977. London: Africa Journal Limited and the International Festival Committee.
"Flora Gomes: Cineasta—Film-maker—Cinéaste." 1993. *Revue Noire* 8, 56-57.
Gable, Eric. 1995. "The Decolonization of Consciousness: Local Skeptics and the 'Will to be Modern' in a West African Village." *American Ethnologist* 22:2, 242-257.
———. 1999. "Beyond Belief? Play, Skepticism, and Religion in a West African Village." Unpublished paper, presented at the 15th Satterthwaite Colloquium on African Ritual and Religion, April 18-21, 1999.
Gilmore, David D. 1998. *Carnival and Culture: Sex, Symbol and Status in Spain.* New Haven: Yale University Press.
Gomes, Flora (director), Manuel Rambout Barçelos (text). c. 1993. *A Màscara.* A video of Guinea-Bissau carnival. Paris: La Huit Distribution.
Harding, Frances. n.d. "African Aspects of Carnival." Unpublished working paper.
Hill, Errol. 1972. *The Trinidad Carnival: Mandate for a National Theatre.* Austin: University of Texas Press.
Hinckley, Priscilla B. 1985. "'Let Them Dance Before You.' The Educative Role of Performance in a West African Children's Masquerade." Ph.D. diss., Boston University.
———. 1986. "The Dodo Masquerade of Burkina Faso." *African Arts* 19:2, 74-77, 91.
Johnson, Michelle. 1998. Letter to Simon Ottenberg, June 15, with enclosed photos.
Kertzer, David L. 1988. *Ritual, Politics and Power.* New Haven: Yale University Press.
Koningsbruggen, Petrus Hendriks van. 1997. *Trinidad Carnival: A Question of National Identity.* London: Caribbean, Warwick University Caribbean Studies.
Linger, Daniel Touro. 1992. *Dangerous Encounters: Meanings of Violence in a Brazilian City.* Stanford: Stanford University Press.

Liverpool, Hollis. 1993. "Rituals of Power and Rebellion: The Carnival Tradition in Trinidad and Tobago." Ph.D. diss., University of Michigan.

Lobban, Richard. 1995. *Cape Verde: Crioulo Colony to Independent Nation.* Boulder, CO: Westview Press.

Mark, Peter. 1992. *The Wild Bull and the Sacred Forest: Form, Meaning and Change in Senegambian Initiation Masks.* Cambridge: Cambridge University Press.

Martin, Denis-Constant. 1999. *Coon Carnival: New Year in Cape Town, Past and Present.* Cape Town: David Phillip Publishers.

McGuire, Harriet C. 1995. "Introduction." [to Bissau carnival]. 18 typescript pages.

Moore, Sally F., and Barbara G. Myerhoff (eds.). 1977. *Secular Ritual.* Assen/Amsterdam: Van Gorcum.

Nunley, John W. 1987. *Moving with the Face of the Devil: Art and Politics in Urban West Africa.* Urbana: University of Illinois Press.

Nunley, John W. and Judith Bettelheim. 1988. *Caribbean Festival Arts: Each and Every Bit of Difference.* St. Louis and Seattle: St. Louis Art Museum in Association with the University of Washington Press.

Ottenberg, Simon. 1975. *The Masked Rituals of Afikpo: The Content of an African Art.* Seattle: University of Washington Press.

―――. 1979. "Analysis of an African Masked Parade." In Justine Cordwell and Ronald A. Schwarz (eds.), *The Fabrics of Culture: The Anthropology of Clothing and Adornment.* The Hague: Mouton, 177-187.

Padre Gino of Bula, Guinea-Bissau. 1995. Untitled. 1 page typescript statement, based on an interview in Italian 6/6/95 by Ms. Alda Gambian. Translated into Portuguese by Dina Adao, and into English by Harriet C. McGuire.

Poppi, Cesare. 1997. "Wider Horizons with Larger Details: Subjectivity, Ethnicity, and Globalization." In Alan Scott (ed.), *The Limits of Globalization: Cases and Arguments.* London: Routledge, 284-305.

―――. 1998. "Was Frazer Right?" Cultural Ecology, Knowledge and Masks in West African and Alpine Cross-cultural Perspective." *SM Annali de San Michele* 11, 231-246.

Reed, D. Bess. 1996. "Engendered Spirits: Politics and Performance in a Nigerian Masquerade Festival." Ph.D. diss., University of California, Santa Barbara.

Ross, Doran H. 1993. "Carnaval Masquerades in Guinea-Bissau." *African Arts* 26:3, 64-71.

Sharfstein, Daniel J. 1996. "On Cape Verde, Carnival is Down to Earth." *New York Times*, Sunday, February 4, sec. 5, p. 8.

Siga, Felix. 1994. "Carnival: The Greatest Public Celebration of Guinea-Bissau." 7 typescript pages. Translated and edited by Harriet C. McGuire. To be published in *Tcholona* magazine, Bissau.

Turner, Victor. 1987. "Carnival, Ritual and Play in Rio de Janeiro." In Alessandro Falassi, *Time Out of Time: Essays on the Festival.* Albuquerque: University of New Mexico Press, 74-90.

Wallace, Gail, and Jeri B. Williams. 1985. "Bidjogo." In Herbert M. Cole (ed.), *I Am Not Myself: The Art of African Masquerade.* Los Angeles: University of California, Museum of Cultural History, Monograph Series, No. 26, pp.40-44.

11

The Dodo Masquerade of Ouagadougou

Priscilla Baird Hinckley[1]

Although research has begun to study the innovative activities of children, such as making toys and masquerades,[2] there has been little suggestion that these have important meaning for the rest of the community. Yet Victor Turner,[3] noticing how liminal components of rituals resembled play, speculated that play provides a society with new behaviors needed to resolve conflicts to survive.[4] In Ouagadougou, the capital of Burkina Faso, the children's play activity known as the Dodo masquerade has become a means by which youths express their new sense of being powerful, up-to-date Africans. In doing so, they have opened a dialogue between the generations and helped to affirm a traditional culture beset by the problems of modern urban life.

History of the Dodo Masquerade

The present form of Dodo has undergone significant changes from the traditional Ramadan children's entertainment. Informants in Ouagadougou recount that Hausa traders introduced the masquerade in the mid-nineteenth century. During the full moon of the Muslim lenten month, older boys would secretly wrap themselves in white cloth with a hump on their backs and a rope tail, whiten their bodies with kaolin, and don a calabash headpiece sprouting two horns. They would go from compound to compound performing a slow dance, accompanied by clapping and singing in Hausa, in return for gifts of food. One elder reported that the Dodos of Ouagadougou in the nineteenth century had a close relationship with the Mogho Naba, the leader of the Mossi people, who resided in the area and acted as a sponsor for the dancers, even though he was not a Muslim at that time.[5]

This form of Dodo, with many incidental variations, gradually spread through the urbanizing area that was later to become Ouagadougou. Charles Beart, principal of the Lycée William Ponty in Dakar and later a colonial *inspecteur de l'enseignement*, seems to provide the only information in the literature on the Dodo before World War II. In 1934, he visited the city and described groups of such performers, composed of Christian and animist children—but no Muslims—singing in Hausa (fig. 11.1). He claimed that varieties of the Dodo mask existed from "Niamey and the north of all the neighboring territories, at far as Liberia. In Muslim country, these masks are worn during Ramadan when the Dodos pass the hat to collect for the feast at the end of the month."[6] Ramadan being the last month of the year, the feast was, in effect, a New Year's celebration.

An elder told me in 1982 that the origin of the masquerade could be traced to a Hausa story. A hunter had promised his good friend, the Emir, not to kill anything on the Muslim holy day, Friday. One day, responding to a plea for help from some shepherd boys whose cattle were being threatened by a monster, the hunter fired his gun without thinking. He killed the monster and was immediately transformed into a creature half-man and half-beast. In his shame, he ran off into the bush. The Emir, mourning his friend, sent an army to find him, and they subsequently returned with the "beast." The chief was happy to have his friend restored, and when the village children asked if the creature could dance with them in their Ramadan celebrations, he consented. This pleased everyone, and many years later, when the beast died, the chief suggested to the children that they make animal masks in memory of the hunter who had saved the boys. The calabash headpiece with horns made of the borassus palm had become the symbol of Dodo.

According to informants, about the time of World War II, Dodo changed dramatically. The masquerade began to reflect local Mossi culture. Instead of singing in Hausa, the boys sang in More, the local language. Drums and tin cans replaced hand clapping. Mossi dance steps were incorporated, and the movements were more varied and dynamic. Each dancer began carrying long sticks, permitting more sweeping movement patterns. Rhythms quickened. Pantomimed animals emerged from local folklore to delight and frighten viewers. In addition, young boys between the ages of seven and twelve began to form their own groups, called Petit Dodo, which paralleled the Grand Dodo of the boys aged twelve to about sixteen. By the mid-1950s little boys were dancing Dodo in many Mossi villages and towns around Ouagadougou and as far north as the city of Ouahigouya. It continued to be a secret affair whose preparations were hidden from girls and women.[7]

Dodo Masquerades in the *Quartiers* of Ouagadougou

Today Dodo remains a child-initiated, child-guided play activity. As the Ramadan season approaches, boys form groups in their neighborhood, or *quartier*, consisting of a principal singer and a chorus, five or more dancers, a drummer, sometimes a few costumed wild animals, and a leader who tells the group when and where to perform and who bargains for gratuities. He may be dressed in military style with a Sam Browne belt. Informally, boys make a drum and decide on roles and dance steps, usually elaborating on a dozen commonly accepted patterns. Each dancer decorates two sticks, about a meter in length, by peeling away the bark in stripes or other patterns or by applying paint or kaolin. Knee bells are created out of can tops with metal rings around the edges. All the members of the group help to make the masks and costumes, scrounging much of the materials. Fathers and older brothers contribute to the purchase of supplies if they are able, but to their pride, the boys organize the rest themselves.

On the night of the full moon during Ramadan, wearing masks they have made and with bodies decorated, the troupe goes from compound to compound, singing and dancing in return for gifts of money.[8] The performance lasts about fifteen minutes and is composed of five parts: the greetings and entrance; vigorous dancing in a circle; the pairs competition known as the "two by two"; the entrance of animal masquerades, such as a lion, monkey, or elephant, sometimes accompanied by a hunter; and the exit.

Standing outside the compound gate, the chorus sings the greeting to the head of the house, asking to perform for everyone. One neighborhood Dodo troupe's song was recorded as follows: "We greet the Naba [chief] Saaga./ We greet the Naba Kugri, a rock we can depend on which will be difficult to ever remove./ Peace be with you./ Is the owner of the house in?/ If he is away, God protect him. Our grandfather Adam will give him health./ Our grandmother Eve will give him health./ Peace be with you./ Is the head of the house sleeping?/ We want to bring you good news. Brother! Don't you hear?/ Bring out your twenty-five francs./ And give it to the Ouidi [a *quartier*] boys./ Give it to the Larlé boys./ Peace be with you./ Our ancestor Adam will give you health./ Our ancestor Eve will give you health./ God will give you health." After the head comes to the gate and gives some money, the spokesman turns and shouts the amount to the hiding masked Dodo, thereby communicating how long and how complex the performance should be. The singers and drummers enter, usually followed by a collection of neighborhood children.

Suddenly the beat of the Dodo drum becomes very loud and assertive. Out of the black night into the courtyard leaps a line of maskers. They jump up and down in unison, pounding the earth with the flat of their feet and sawing the air vigorously with two sticks clutched together in both hands. Younger boys may wear headdresses of metal stripping bent into simple representations of animals, the Muslim stars and moon, or fanciful shapes like spirals. More popular are the traditional black-and-white painted calabash face masks with long horns made of borassus palm (fig. 11.2). The Dodos dance into a circle and perform a series of coordinated, intricate steps, their knee bells emphasizing the beat. They are accompanied by a song like the following that I recorded: "Who has called for the beautiful Dodo?/ Hurrah for the Dodo!/ The young boys really know how to dance!/ They learned to dance when very small. The Dodo boys really know how to dance!/ Hurrah for the beautiful Dodo!/ The hare is stubborn. Unless you burn the thicket, it will not come out.[9]/ Let's review the troops for Saye Zerbo.[10]/ We greet you, great Naba!/ When the Ouidi Naba passes by,/ Respect God and provide him with water.[11] / It is painful to be thirsty./ When the

Dapoya [a *quartier*] Naba passes by,/ Respect God and provide him with water./ It is painful to be thirsty./ When the Ouagadougou Naba passes by,/ Respect God and provide him with water./ It is so painful to be thirsty."

Now the exhausted troupe retires and pairs of boys come forward to challenge each other in fast footwork; this is the "two-by-two." The drummer speeds up the rhythm and the principal singer follows, giving a litany of Mossi chiefs. The boys' explosion of energy subsides, and a new pair comes forward until all have danced.

Next come the pantomimed animals, portrayed mainly by boys wearing cardboard masks (fig. 11.3). Petit Dodo has fewer of these, generally at least the lion or the monkey. The lion charges around, terrifying young children among the spectators. The monkey romps about doing acrobatics and makes people laugh.

Then the group is ready to leave. Dropped rattles and broken sticks are picked up. The dancers reassemble in a line and dance out as the principal singer expresses thanks and gives good wishes for the coming year. In one performance I witnessed, the chorus sang: "Lent is almost over./ May God enable us to see another year./ Here you see children./ Children of Ouidi having fun,/ And now the children of Ouidi are leaving."

Grand Dodo is a more elaborate and finished performance than Petit Dodo. The boys may paint their bodies with kaolin in stripes and dots, carrying out the animal theme, or create other designs on their bodies, like butterflies; even words are used. I've seen: "Fanta" for the popular drink, and "Bobo" for Bob Marley, the Caribbean singer of liberation songs, a hero to the young. The masks of cardboard, traditionally representing wild animals, more and more often express young people's interests. Frequently, they incorporate contemporary symbols of power—motorcycles, airplanes, and clocks. Some have batteries and light bulbs that flash on and off. Many are simply individual fantasy constructions.

Government Inspired Dodo Performances

In Ouagadougou today, a competitive Dodo performance in front of a paying audience has developed out of the traditional performance in the compounds of the quartier. In the early 1970s, the director of the Cultural Affairs Office, looking for an indigenous dance to promote, remembered fondly his own boyhood experience with Dodo. In 1972, he organized a Dodo competition in the city auditorium and was amazed by its success. Each year the audience grew. The enthusiastic response, lack of citywide coordination and riotous behavior over prizes led the government in 1975 to turn over sponsorship of the competition to the city's Youth Center. Each of the estimated forty-four quartiers has a Youth Center which functions according to local needs and resources. Each neighborhood was encouraged to form a troupe of its best dancers to enter the annual competition. As residents began to mobilize behind their boys, a measure of stability and continuity to Dodo troupes emerged.

The Dodo competition performance differs greatly from its neighborhood origins, being performed at the Ouagadougou auditorium, La Maison du Peuple. Each quartier trains a troupe of about thirty performers that competes over several nights in front of about 3,000 spectators who pack the city auditorium, ready to try to influence the judges by their loud support of their neighborhood's entry. A government representative welcomes the eager, restless audience and introduces the first troupe. A costume chorus and musicians start the music with "*Salaam aleikum*" (Peace be with you), greeting the audience and dignitaries. The drum beat picks up, the singing becomes louder, and suddenly twelve to fifteen boys enter the stage, dancing vigorously. The singing still recounts the Mossi rulers' genealogy, but adds contemporary ideas. For example, in 1982, one group sang: "Our brothers abroad, may they come together again for the country's development. We invite them to return because their nation is getting going." Another sang to encourage the nation's farmers, telling them that the young people of the town have not forgotten them. Songs may refer to the local scene–to soccer matches as well as political events.

The greatest changes, however, have been visual. A new representationalism is the goal. Some people even say children are learning natural science by making the animal masquerades that accompany the Dodo dancers–the giraffes, elephants, ostriches, buffalo, snakes, and zebras that pound circus-like around the stage (fig. 11.4). Some of these animals are 2.5-3.0 meters tall; the four-legged creatures are made from sheets of flexible foam plastic and must be worn by two boys, one maneuvering the front half, the other the back. The dancers no longer perform in a circle but in a straight line, their movements synchronized . Increasingly, members of the chorus are wearing costumes and dancers are covering their heads with naturalistic painted masks made of foam plastic. The tradition of the calabash face mask and painted body seems to be waning. References to the modern world abound. In 1983, national colors appeared everywhere. To send a message of national unity, one chorus was costumed as the Pope, an *imam*, a soldier, a woman, and a farmer. A masker called Apollo appeared the year a man walked on the moon. Humor is much appreciated; clowns satirize the military, an ostrich lays an egg.

Since 1972 the public performances have become polished, more varied, and, of course, more expensive. Materials tend to be purchased rather than scrounged. Shortage of money for costumes led to the present plan whereby gate receipts from the three nights of performances provide cash prizes for winners and also subsidize participating troupes and help to fund youth activities with the quartiers. In 1983, more than 10,000 people went to the event, producing over three million francs in receipts. Attending the competition is considered to be an appropriate way to celebrate the end of Ramadan, or at least a national holiday.

The Role of Girls in Dodo

Girls participate in the Muslim holy month children's activities in five ways, two of them traditional, and three of them representing a recent departure. They have several kinds of musical performances which they perform alone; they participate in Petit Dodo groups by singing and hand clapping; they sometimes dance in Grand Dodo performances; and less often, they take part in the public competition.

When the moon is waxing in the early part of Ramadan, I would see groups of little girls scurrying around the streets of Ouagadougou, some in costume. Although I am not sure what all of them were doing, I can say that, from the vantage point of my own quartier, the groups of pre-adolescent girls did go from courtyard to courtyard, doing a little song in return for a gift of money.

The first female performance I saw was the '*Wale Wale.*" The group of maybe five or seven in number comes to the gate and sings, or sometimes just stands and waits until they are noticed. When invited in, they group around one or two girls who, kneeling on the ground, are producing music by hammering with spoon-sized calabashes on the back of a large calabash, overturned in a basin of water. The group accompanies with clapping, and they all sing a short song in light, frail voices. The words are in Dyula, indicating an origin west of Ouagadougou (M. Triande suggests a Malian origin). The groups I saw wore no special clothing, but a man I spoke with who came from Koudougou, west of Ouagadougou, claimed that the girls there dressed up for the occasion and were much more beautiful than the Wale Wale girls in Ouagadougou. When I asked women for translations to the songs, I was usually met with giggles and embarrassment and polite refusals. Finally, I found a Muslim woman who works as secretary for an international agency, who gave me the words and translations. It took her several days to do so, she said, because, "We sing them when we are very little, but it is forbidden to sing them after Carême, so you forget them:"

> *Wale Wale Wale*
> *Ile wale sira*
> *Wale Wale Wale*
> *Mahamadou demba nouma*
> *Tari soro soumou*
> *Et soumou kadi*
> *Soumou douma aike*
> *Et aike tito*
> *Sougalo lora lomi*
> *A lora demba lou begnana*
> *Djakouma ni kalo*
> *Dja soughalo be ti keleye*

> Thus is it done
> Thus did it happen
> It happened in the presence of all the good mothers who are
> descendants of Mohamed
> I found a wonderful fruit tree
> With delicious fruits.
> Good fruit doesn't grow on an evil tree.
> The first day of Carême
> When the moon was sighted,
> All the good mothers were present
> And it appeared like a cat
> Remember! Carême is penance for only this year's sins.

This is frequently followed by another short song:

> *Laila delimamou, laila delimamou*
> *Saya nana lomi*
> *Mouri saya nana lomi*
> *Ali kabrou kafisa ni dunoumane*
>
> The day when death came into the world
> The Muslims discovered
> That the tomb is worth more than terrestrial life.

When the girls finish singing, they stand there, looking shy and embarrassed. They are given some money–usually 100 francs–and they run out of the gate.

The other kind of performance the girls give is called by many "The Pregnant Woman." Again, it is a small group of pre-adolescent girls, sometimes with faces and hands whitened. One of the group is costumed like a pregnant, older woman. She carries a stout stick which she leans on while doing a series of pelvic thrusts to mark the music's rhythm, placing herself about a meter in front of the group, which stands behind her, singing and clapping. The song, as translated by my neighbor, sung in More, follows:

> *La Femme en Grossesse*
> *Que le dodo vient*
> *Dans la journée elle n'est pa enceinte*
> *La nuit maintenant elle est*
>   *est enceinte*
> *Elle n'a qu'a dancer*
> *On va voir*
>
> The Pregnant Woman
> Let the Dodo come
> In the day she is not pregnant
> Now at night she is pregnant
> We shall see.

The Wale Wale in Ouagadougou is sung in Dyula, but the similarities of the two accounts reveal that the girls' performance with gifts, at the same time as the boys perform Dodo, has existed in the Muslim areas west of Ouagadougou for some years.[12]

Girls also appear in the Petit Dodo and Grand Dodo groups in the quartiers. If they want to join the musicians, they are welcome. Out of eleven Dodo groups I questioned, ten reported that girls did come with them on their rounds; two said to clap, one said to clang tin cans together, and seven reported that they came to sing.

It is much more unusual for the girls to actually dance with the boys. M. Triande assured me that it was not forbidden for girls to do this. He said that in the Ivory Coast girls did wear masks, but Dodo had always been considered (by men at least) too rough and vigorous. One woman suggested that perhaps Dodo developed as a boys' activity because it used to be forbidden for the girls to play with boys in the village. Some others say hunting is a men's activity traditionally, and since Dodo is the tale of a hunter, girls were never thought to be interested.

However, a young artisan reported to me that about six years ago in his quartier of Moinbin, girls did dance with the Grand Dodo, and they were very good. I heard of one other district that experienced the same situation, so I went to talk with the organizer, Zakaria Traore, about it. He explained,

> It was a few years ago...I was looking to recruit some really athletic boys as Dodo dancers. I looked among the basketball players, and there were some girls who played very well so I asked them if they'd like to try dancing....They danced very well! [He smiles broadly, remembering]...but the year after the person in charge stole all our money, so we didn't have Dodo the next year..We had to reorganize....Then the girls were married.

One of the young men, who since has become a leader in the group, commented: "They [the girls] were very good. I think the boys danced better because the girls were there. Most of the time they just follow the boys."

An older man from Dapoya II quartier, B. Parfait, an artist, commented, referring evidently to how men treat women in later life: "Girls can do it but Dodo is a boy's thing. It wouldn't bother me if the girls danced...some girls are very athletic....It will probably happen in the future...a good thing, too. If boys get to know girls when they were young, they will take better care of them when they are older." But, in general a more conservative attitude prevails, as a Dassassgho quartier Dodo official said in a radio interview in 1982: "Why don't we have any girls? Like most Dodo groups, we don't undervalue women but we believe certain masculine activities aren't appropriate to women...The presence of women is frequently a cause of misunderstanding among the men. We hear it said that women are the equal of men but traditional Mossi custom is not yet convinced!"

Conclusions

Adults are proud of the boys and responded enthusiastically to my questions about Dodo.[13] Although it reflects new concerns and interests, most saw it as validating traditional African culture. They believe the Dodo is an important educational activity in which youth learn not only artistic skills but also the traditional values of self-discipline, cooperation and group solidarity, and respect for elders. One youth said: "I've been dancing for seven years. We all grew up in Ouga. You know, Dodo is a group sport, where everyone develops his individual abilities while learning to get along in a group. Some of us older boys hope to get in the competition this year. I think the competition enables those who have worked hard to be appreciated. Of course it also allows a part of Voltaic culture to be seen publicly. Even foreign tourists come to see it." When asked why they dance, little boys tend to reply, "Because my friends do" or "Because it's fun." Some boys are proud to continue a tradition bequeathed to them by fathers and older brothers.

In general, the number of boys interested in Dodo increases every year. Though Muslims no doubt feel validated as the source of the tradition, thus restoring a balance in their competition with Christians, many people claim it is no longer a Muslim dance but a national culture event. In Dodo, Muslims, Christians, and traditional believers get along.[14] It is an ideal example of community.

The satisfaction that this publicly performed Dodo provides must be seen against a troubled social and economic context. The population of Ouagadougou has been growing 10 percent a year as immigrants from the countryside stream into the city. Many of these new residents retain rural values and beliefs, and are in conflict culturally. The society has only recently become monetized, and they must grapple with an unfamiliar cash economy that demands urban job skills. Tremendous pressures exist in all services. Rivalry exists between ethnic groups and between Christians and Muslims, and there are shortages in jobs and housing. Over half the citizens of Burkina Faso are under the age of fifteen, and Ouagadougou is also predominantly young. The generation gap has appeared in Africa; sons are breaking with traditional dependency on their fathers, getting jobs, and marrying women of their choice. Many of the young have been to school, if only for a few years, and have developed a knowledge of the modern world unimagined by their elders. Added to these problems and discontinuities is the sense of powerless and dependency that is the legacy of colonialism.

Dodo affirms the old, but also makes a new synthesis. A young artist told me: "Dodo is a serious art form. When they sing '*Ana mbool Dodo...sara...sara...*' it's as if spirits are coming from some other place. I feel it. When the dancers enter the people become quiet. Dodo is theater, a circus, everything together. We mustn't allow ourselves to be so influenced by Occidental culture. We have something very fine here." Through Dodo people experience how it feels to be both African and up-to-date. New immigrants supporting Dodo troupes learn the meaning of quartier membership and become acculturated into urban life. The youths who have grown up in the city show their parents some of the strategies of modern living within a well-loved medium that affirms traditional values. The naturalistic representation of animals encourages adults to see elements of the natural world objectively rather than as sacred manifestations of oneness. On a social level, the boys are letting their elders know they are ready to take on more responsibilities. The hunter pantomime and the straight-line dancing similar to traditional warrior dance formations may elicit comparisons between the individualistic hunter economy–in which one must be persistent, strong, skillful, swift, and fearless–and the modern world. One anthropologist of African dance says: "The use of relatively large space and angular lines of the men's warrior dance suggests a metaphor for engagement in the wider, dangerous and unstable world."[15] Although the boys may be unaware of much of what they are projecting, it is clear that they are expressing the exhilaration of newfound powers, their sense that they are a vital vigorous force in the nation.

Because Dodo was imported, it can change and develop in a way not allowed many traditional events. Indeed, only if the boys are allowed freedom of expression will the art form live. People have come to expect innovations in the competition performances each year: one might even say the audience goes to be educated. We can assume that the attendance figures for this latest development in the Dodo masquerade tradition will continue to reflect adults' enjoyment of these messages from the young.

Notes

1. Reprinted from Priscilla Baird Hinckley, "The Dodo Masquerade of Burkina Faso,"*African Arts* 19:2 (1986): 74-77, 91, and excerpts of a section on girls and Dodo from her Doctor of Education dissertation at the School of Education, Boston University, "'Let Me Dance Before You:' The Educative Role of Performance in a West African Children's Masquerade," 1985. Fieldwork was conducted in Ouagadougou during the 1981, 1982, and 1983 Ramadan seasons. I have in my collection sketches of the Dodo masqueraders that can be photocopied. For information, please write to Priscilla Hinckley, 69 Pine Grove, Amherst, MA 01002.
2. Davison 1983; Cannizzo 1979.
3. Turner 1979.
4. The investigation of children's play as a source of societal regeneration is recent. Brian Sutton-Smith (1971, 1976) also suggested that the ability to adapt is tested in play, and Edward Norbeck (1973, 1-2) proposed that play, which includes "games and sports, theatrical performances and other forms of mimicry, painting, music, dance and the entire range of arts" is important to survival of the human species.
5. The story of early Dodo was reconstructed by Karim Dakambari, an elder in Ouagadougou, as reported in the local newspaper, *Dunia* (no. 4, August 27, 1979.
6. Beart 1955, 580-581.
7. There is evidence that Ramadan is still marked by a variety of children's entertainments in other Muslim areas of the world. Toumani Triande saw an example in Libya (personal communication, June 1982).

8. Before the moon is full, boys dance under the city street lights, but this is a recent addition to the traditional courtyard performance, as boys try to capitalize on Dodo's money-making potential.
9. A local proverb meaning good things don't happen without danger and excitement.
10. The name of the head of the government in 1982.
11. Words from a traditional song sung on joyous occasions.
12. A reference with some resemblances to these two songs is found in Beart 1955, 581.
13. This aspect of my study is largely based on questionnaires completed by seventy-two people from ten *quartiers*, and on ten focused interviews.
14. However, some Christian children don't participate, as their parents still understand Dodo to be a strictly Muslim affair. A few respondents forbade their sons to join because they felt the urban troupes were unruly gangs.
15. Hanna 1977, 94.

Bibliography

Béart, C. 1955. *Jeux et jouets de l'ouest Africain.* Dakar: Institut Francais d'Afrique Noire, *Memoire* 42.

Cannizzo, J. 1979. "Alikali Devils of Sierra Leone." *African Arts* 12:4, 66-70, 90, and reprinted in this volume.

Davison, P. 1983. "Wireworks from Southern Africa." *African Arts* 16:3, 50-52.

Hanna, J. 1977. *To Dance is Human.* Austin: University of Texas Press.

Norbeck, E. 1973. "The Anthropological Study of Human Play." *Rice University Studies* 60, 1-8.

Sutton-Smith, B. 1971. "A Syntax for Play and Games." In R. F. Herron and B. Sutton-Smith, (eds.), *Child's Play.* New York: Wiley & Sons.

———. 1976. "Play as Adaptive Potentiation." In P. Stevens (ed.), *The Anthropology of Play.* New York: Leisure Press.

Turner, V. 1979. *Process, Performance and Pilgrimage.* New Delhi: Concept Publishing Co.

Part 4

Girls' Masquerading

12

Kalumbu and Chisudzo: Boys' and Girls' Masquerades among the Chewa

Kenji Yoshida

In the field of African arts, Chewa people are known for the masked initiation association called *nyau*. Nyau is composed of men and boys that have reached the age of at least twelve or thirteen years. There is also female initiation among the Chewa called *chinamwali*. Chewa men and women are considered adults only when they join the nyau or the chinamwali societies. Almost all literature on Chewa performing arts, including my own, refers only to the adult activities of these societies. Little interest has been paid to children's activities (Birch 1988, 1996; Kubik 1987; Schoffeleers 1976, 1992; Yoshida 1992, 1993). However, in reality, Chewa boys and girls actively perform masked dances throughout the year.

The neglect of children's masquerades may derive from the notion of authenticity. It is commonly held that masks made by adults, who are believed to have sufficient knowledge and technical experience in masking, are authentic, while masks made by children who have little such knowledge are mere imitations of adult forms. As will be shown in this chapter, however, the knowledge of nyau characters is in fact widely shared by both initiated individuals and noninitiates alike. This chapter suggests a reconsideration of the stereotypic distinction between adults and children, or the authentic and the inauthentic.

The chapter discusses the relationship between children and adult forms of masquerade as well as gender differences in children's masquerade. In the first half, boys' and men's activities will be described, and in the second half, girls' and women's activities. In discussing these, following the process of Chewa knowledge acquisition, I will first present public or "outsider" knowledge of nyau masks or chinamwali, the women's initiation ceremony, and then proceed to describe boys' and girls' masquerades. I will conclude with an account of their relation to adult nyau and chinamwali ritual activities. The following description is based on observations made between 1984 and 1994 in and around Kaliza village, which is located in Chadiza District in the Eastern Province of the Republic of Zambia. The population of the village was about 150 in 1984, and 180 in 1994.

The Chewa Setting

Chewa peoples who refer to themselves as Chewa (pl. Achewa) live in the area where Zambia, Malawi, and Mozambique meet. The Chewa are farmers, growing mainly maize, with some livestock. Hunting continues to be conducted sporadically by only a limited number of men. No account of labor among the Chewa would be complete without referring to the migration of men from Chewa villages to work for wages. At least one or two members of each generation of an extended family stay in "towns," namely Lusaka, Chipata, or in towns in the Copperbelt.

The basis of the Chewa social system is matrilineal lineages. Normally, residence is uxorilocal. However, in more recent years many newly married couples settle in the

> husband's home village. This is because of intermarriage with the Ngoni, who trace patrilineal descent and practice virilocal residence, as well as because of government policies. Husbands and wives retain their lineage affiliations; children are affiliated with the group of their mother and mother's brothers, in accordance with the principles of matrilineal inheritance and descent.

Public Knowledge of the Nyau

Among the Chewa, almost all boys between the ages of twelve and fifteen are initiated into the nyau association. Each village has its own association, but membership achieved at one village holds good at any other Chewa community. The association and its dancers are called nyau. The major function of the association is to perform dances at funerary rituals, especially at the rite called *bona* that marks the end of the mourning period.

It is said that, in principle, nyau dancers should participate in all funerals for adults. But, in reality, they appear only at funerals for initiated members of the nyau association. They never attend funerals for Christians. However, Chewa people consider that a bona for a certain man can also function as bona for all recently deceased members of his family. In this respect, the nyau plays an indispensable part in Chewa views of life and death.

There are two types of nyau. One retains the form of a human being though the head is usually covered with a feathered net mask or wooden mask (fig. 12.1). This type of nyau may be simply called nyau, though they may be further divided into more than fifty characters, each of which has its own name, songs, and styles of dance. Each nyau dance is a combination of several basic movements, such as rotation (*uzungulira*), skating (*uyenda*), stamping (*uponda*), kicking to right and left (*upalasula*), and backwards and forwards movement of the waist (*utopola*). Specific combinations of these movements characterize the dances of respective nyau.

The other type of nyau is a large zoomorphic structure. Because many of these structures dance by turning round and round, they are collectively called *nyau yolemba*, "nyau which draw (circles)" (fig. 12.2). There is a variety of nyau yolemba forms, most of which are in the shape of wild animals, such as an antelope, a lion, and a hyena.

The men of the nyau association are said to be friends of nyau. Children and women, who are not members of the association, are taught by men that nyau are dead persons (*munthu wakufa*) who have been revived, and that nyau yolemba are real wild animals (*nyama yam'chire*). Even when they ask men what the nyau is, men will give a simple answer, "nyau ni nyama" (the nyau is an animal). Children and women are not supposed to know anything more about nyau. As might be expected, however, there are always some children who bluntly say that nyau are men in disguise. When this infraction is discovered, the children are whipped by nyau called *kang'wing'wi* when they perform at a funeral.

During the funeral period, women joke with some nyau called *kasinja* while brewing beer; women also sing songs for various nyau as they dance. Children may join in singing songs for nyau. On other occasions, women and children avoid nyau dancers. Whenever nyau appear in the community, women and children immediately rush into their houses. A single nyau excites the entire community. Through direct contact and avoidance, concealment and revelation, fearfulness and joyfulness, the nyau performance at a funeral constitutes a major amusement for Chewa people—men and women, adults and children—both the living and the dead.

The Boys' Masked Society, *Kalumbu*

In many Zambian Chewa villages, the uninitiated form a group called *kalumbu*, whose main purpose is to perform masked dances. The masked dancers are also called kalumbu. There were ten active members of the kalumbu at Kaliza in July 1984, and twelve in September 1993. Although it is not a requirement for all boys who enter nyau to have been members of the kalumbu, almost all boys voluntarily join the group when they reach the age of five to seven years. Those who want to join kalumbu pay an initiation fee: at Kaliza village, 50 ngwe (0.5 kwacha) was charged the novices in 1984 and 1985, and 2 kwacha in 1993. Some boys obtain the money by hunting and selling small birds and field mice. Others are given the initiation fee by their parents or grandparents who want them to join.

Having paid the initiation fee to the leader (*lumbwe*) of the group, the novices, who are called *namwali*, are taken to the bush outside the village. There is no special designated meeting place for kalumbu boys. In the bush, novices are required to keep their heads down. Elder members of the kalumbu beat novices with switches made of branches. When the whipping is over, novices are taught secret riddles and terminology, which are shared by the members of the kalumbu.

They are also taught not to reveal the fact that kalumbu are boys in disguise when they perform.

One of the riddles taught in the initiation at Kaliza in 1984 was "*Kalumbu ni ciani? Kalumbu ni citsa cowaula*" (What is kalumbu? Kalumbu is a burnt shrub). In 1993, there was a slightly different riddle, "*Make wa kalumbu ni ciani? citsa cowaula*" (What is the mother of kalumbu? It is a burnt shrub). Though no boy could give a reason why kalumbu (or mother of kalumbu) is a burnt shrub, it may be that kalumbu masks are often made from the fresh leaves of new shoots on burnt shrubs.

Some examples of kalumbu terminology are shown on table 12.1. This terminology is quite different from that of the nyau association. In kalumbu, a part of the human body is often called by a special term that is formed by adding the *ma* prefix to the duplicated infinitive form of a verb relevant to the bodily part. Although there are minor differences between the terms collected in 1984 and those in 1993, the terminology as a whole is more or less the same.

Table 12.1
Secret Terminology of the Kalumbu, in 1984 and 1993

usual Chewa terms	kalumbu terms in 1985	kalumbu terms in 1993
maso (eyes) (upenya = to see)	mapenyapenya	mapenyapenya
mutu (head) (ugunda = to knock)	magundagunda	magundagunda
pakamwa (mouth) (uidya = to eat)	aidyaidya (udyela = to feed)	madyeladyela
mphuno (nose) (uima = to blow)	maminamina	maminamina
zanja (hands) (ugwila = to grasp)	magwilagwila	-
msana (back) (usana = to stretch)	masanasana (grass mat)	mpasa
minyendo (legs) (uyenda = to walk)	mayendayenda (uponda = to step on)	mapondaponda
phazi (foot) (uponda = to step on)	mapondaponda	
mimba (stomach) (granary)	nkhokwe	nkhokwe
matako (buttocks) (ukhala = to stay)	makhalakhala	makhalakhala
mbolo (penis) (ukwata = to copulate)		makwatakwata

As soon as the instruction is finished, boys begin to mask their faces. Every novice may wear a mask. However, at least two or three boys remain unmasked and serve as escorts for other masked dancers or as drummers for the dancers in the village. Kalumbu boys make their own drums of broken mortars, plates or plastic tanks. Ideally, the kalumbu dance requires five drums, the same as the nyau dance, though boys may make do with three or four drums. Songs that accompany kalumbu dancers are sung by girls of approximately the same age as kalumbu members. Kalumbu dancers first summon girls by shouting in falsetto before they begin dancing.

There are only two types of kalumbu dancers: kalumbu and *chimdadada*. Kalumbu wear masks and skirts made of bunches of leaves (see Introduction, fig. I.8). Some kalumbu cover their faces with their own shirts instead of leaves. Songs that accompany kalumbu performances are unique to them. There are no similar songs among the nyau. On the other hand, like the nyau dance, each dance of kalumbu is a combination of several basic movements, such as rotation, skating, stamping, kicking to right and left, and backward and forward movement of the waist. Though there is no differentiation by name among kalumbu dancers, each kalumbu dancer attempts to imitate a certain nyau character. The most common form is the one imitating *kasinja* that is characterized by frequent use of rotation and kicking to right and left. The following are examples of the songs that are performed for this type of kalumbu dance.

(Song 1) Kalumbu ni msoka masamba — Kalumbu is the one who weaves leaves
Kalumbu ni msoka masamba — Kalumbu is the one who weaves leaves
anatenga malaya — he took his shirt
anaika kumutu — and put it on his head
kuti aziti ni kalumbu — saying that he is a kalumbu

(Song 2) Kalumbu wathaya mkaka — Kalumbu has spilt milk
Kalumbu wathaya mkaka — Kalumbu has spilt milk
ng'mobe zayamwa — A cow drank it

Another common type of kalumbu imitates a nyau called *katoitoi* that thrusts out the waist backwards and forwards. The movement is a blunt imitation of sexual intercourse. One of the accompanying songs is:

(Song 3) Gwedu, gwedulila nkumba — Open, open the pig's (kraal)
kuno, kuli akapado — Here are male pigs

Chimdadada is a coneshaped structure covered with leaves that envelops the entire body of the dancer (fig. 12.3). This type of kalumbu mask was created by a boy called Josef Phiri in 1984. He explained to me that he made this new type of kalumbu imitating a nyau yolemba called *kacala*. During performance, it rotates in the same way as kacala does. Its name chimdadada is derived from the sound it makes when it runs on the ground. The following song was also composed by Josef Phiri himself.

(Song 4) Chimdadada　　　Chimdadada
　　　　　njila ya galimoto　The road for motor cars
　　　　　dadada　　　　　dadada

When the dance is completed, the chimdadada is broken to pieces. Even though, in 1993, boys could not make chimdadada in the same manner as Josef Phiri did, chimdadada was still the most popular character of all kalumbu. When all the kalumbu dances for the day are over, novices are taken back to their parents. The parents or grandparents of each novice will say to their child, "Today, you have grown up. You should not cry any more." The first line is the same as that given to the novices of nyau and chinamwali when they are taken back to their parents.

While kalumbu initiation ceremonies are held only sporadically, the kalumbu may dance at any time throughout the year except at funerals, where nyau perform their masquerade. Unlike the nyau, activities of the kalumbu have no ritual importance. When kalumbu appear, however, not only children but also adults attend the dances and cheer the dancers on. The kalumbu is clearly considered by nyau members to be a form of training for nyau masquerade.

Boy's Initiation into the Nyau

When boys have reached the age of twelve to fifteen years, they are initiated into the nyau association. In principle, the initiation must be performed along with a funerary rite, especially the rite of bona that marks the end of the mourning period. Bona is performed along with beer brewing. The beer is said to be for the people attending the rite, and also for the spirits of the dead embodied by nyau. On the evening before beer brewing is to begin, several groups of nyau dance on an open ground near the outskirts of the community to announce the commencement of the ritual. While nyau are dancing, the novices (*namwali*), led by an instructor, leave the village and head for the *liunde*, a place deep in the bush, where men have disguised themselves as the nyau.

When the group reaches liunde, nyau members, some of them masked and others not, attack the novices and beat them with whips made of torn branches. After the whipping, the novices are gathered in one place. Nyau members stand in front of them and admonish each by recounting their past wrong doings and whipping them. When Joseph Phiri, who created chimdadada imitating a nyau yolemba called kacala, was initiated, the leader of the nyau said:

> Today you have seen us at the place of nyau. What is the nyau? The nyau is a human. From now on, stop being childish. Never again step inside the bedroom of your mother and father. Never touch cooking pots used by women. Stop your childish behavior. Never play kalumbu. You made a kalumbu in the same manner as we make kacala. It

was a great offence. Never get near to kalumbu boys again. Otherwise, you will die and relieve your bowels.

The heart of the secret adamantly kept by the members of the nyau is the fact that "the nyau is a human in disguise." They have devised various means of keeping this secret: by using falsetto and nasalized voices for nyau; by making the masks, including nyau yolemba, in the bush distant from the village; and by giving special names of materials and tools used to make the masks. Finally, members use riddles to determine whether a newcomer is really a member of the association. The first riddle taught in the initiation is always the one mentioned in the leader's admonishment, that is "What is the nyau? The nyau is a human."

It should be noted here that novices of the nyau are already familiar with these methods to keep secrets because they are, in principle, identical to those of the kalumbu. Even the fact that the nyau is a man in disguise is already known to them. What *is* new to the novices is the content of the secret terminology and riddles, and the method of making masks including nyau yolemba. The novices gain knowledge of these things from a tutor (*phungu*) with whom they lodge, and in the daytime from the men who stay in the bush preparing for the funeral.

It is customary for every member of the association to make his own feathered or wooden mask and to wear it on appropriate ritual occasions as long as it lasts. Nyau yolemba, on the other hand, are collectively made by members of the nyau every time there is a bona. The method of making nyau yolemba is as follows. First, the perimeter of the bottom of the structure is drawn on the ground, and the branches are planted along the outline at equal intervals. By tying crosspieces to the branches, a sort of basket is made to serve as a frame. The men then cover the frame with grass, attaching it by passing strings crosswise and lengthwise. Finally, husks of corn are placed between the strings to cover the entire structure. It takes at least three days to make a single nyau yolemba.

On the night before the last day of brewing, all the available nyau and nyau yolemba in the form of various wild animals appear in the village and dance one after another. At dawn, all nyau yolemba return to the bush, where they are immediately burnt. According to the Chewa, the spirit of the deceased (*ciwanda*) remains on the earth after the burial to roam in and around the community. In contrast, the Chewa say that ancestral spirits (*mudzimu*), which are to be reincarnated in the bodies of their descendants, are freely moving around the world like the wind. Nyau yolemba, especially those in the form of antelopes, are said to capture the lingering spirit of the deceased. When they are finally burnt and the smoke disappears into the wind, it is said that the spirits of the deceased also disappear into the wind and become ancestral spirits.

The novices of the nyau eat the ashes of nyau yolemba as medicine to make them immune to the "hotness" of the deceased's spirits. This is the reason why initiation into the nyau is normally held along with funerary rituals. After the ashes are administered, the novices are taken back to their parents, which also marks the end of the bona rite.

In 1992, ten years after his initiation into the nyau, Joseph Phiri, the inventor of a new type of kalumbu called chimdadada, made a nyau yolemba in the form of a helicopter for a bona of the late village headman of Kaliza. As far as I know, this was the first nyau yolemba of a helicopter in Chewa history. Joseph saw a helicopter of the Zambian army at the school grounds of a primary school. It was sent to make a counterattack on the RENAMO guerrillas who raided the region in 1990. It was his intention to refresh people's memory of the event.

Though nyau yolemba are said to portray wild animals, they include representations of cattle, motor cars, and so on. Association members themselves say that cattle and cars are things that originally did not exist in Chewa communities. Indeed, cattle were not introduced until the end of the nineteenth century, when the Chewa were conquered by the pastoralist Ngoni. Therefore, cattle and cars are seen as being not of the community, but rather of the bush, and thus, belong to the same category as wild animals. This is true for the helicopter as well. People were excited by the appearance of Joseph's helicopter. In 1994, Joseph introduced another new nyau yolemba in the form of a python, which was also well received. Joseph's personal history of invention of masquerades demonstrates the continuity between kalumbu and nyau in terms of artistic creativity as well as of customary practices.

Public Knowledge of the Women's Initiation Ceremony, *Chinamwali*

There is also a women's puberty ceremony among the Chewa called chinamwali. Just as knowledge presented to male initiates about nyau mask is kept secret from women, so the teachings presented in chinamwali are kept secret from men. Although masks are not employed in chinamwali, a brief description of what children know about chinamwali will help to understand Chewa boys' and girls' masquerades.

Chinamwali is a ceremony in which a girl, who has had her first menstruation, is secluded in a house for a period of time and is taught the manners and accomplishments necessary for an adult woman. The girl to be initiated is called *namwali*, the same term used for novices of the nyau and the kalumbu. Other participants in the rite are limited to women who are already members of the association.[1] Men and children can attend the ceremony only when a namwali returns to her home after the seclusion period. Upon nearing her home, the namwali is carried on the shoulder or the back of her tutor (phungu), and cheered with a song by other women. The body of the namwali is decorated with black, white, and red dots. It is the most conspicuous moment in the life of a Chewa woman.

(Song 5)	Dzaone nanga dzaone	Look, hey look!
	Namwali dzaone	It's the girl who has grown up, look!
	Ukaone cili kumbuyo	Look at the one on the back
	Cati mwanga	She has the colors and pattern
	ngati nsato	of the python
	Dzaone nanga dzaone	Look, hey look!

Having arrived home, the namwali performs the dances she has learned to the accompaniment of a drum played by two women. Then, the tutor and another woman perform a skit employing women's cooking paraphernalia, including mortars, pestles, pots, and ladles, to teach the proper behavior required of a mature woman. Often, the skit will employ a plot in which an insolent girl is scolded by her mother for her misbehavior. It is now common in the skits to also refer to preventive measures against AIDS. After the skit, the head of the namwali is shaved. While the namwali is being shaved, each of her relatives stands up in turn and admonishes her:

"Respect your parents"
"Respect the elders"
"Say 'yes' and do immediately what you are asked to do."

The namwali is then bathed in water, dressed in new clothes, and taken home. This marks the end of the ceremony.

The Girls' Masked Society, *Chisudzo*

In Zambian Chewa villages where boys form the kalumbu association, girls often have a masked association of their own corresponding to kalumbu. The girls' association and its masked dancers are called *chisudzo* (pl. *visudzo*).[2]

The chisudzo association is a voluntary association, being composed of young girls who have not yet gone through the puberty ceremony, chinamwali. To join the chisudzo, girls are also required to undergo an initiation ceremony. In July 1984, my wife, Mariko Yoshida, was initiated into the chisudzo. The following description is based on her observation.[3]

When my wife joined, the chisudzo association at Kaliza was composed of seven girls. She paid altogether 56 ngwe (0.56 kwacha) to the leader of the group, who shared the money with group members. Four other girls also joined at the same time, each of which was charged 2 ngwe. The novices, who are also called namwali, were taken to a location outside the village; there is no special place for chisudzo girls. In the bush, namwali were urged to keep their heads down and to obey what the elders said. When they failed to follow the instructions, elder members struck them on the face with the palm of the hand, but not with switches. First, the novices were taught secret terminology shared by chisudzo members.

Table 12.2 shows the terms they learned on this occasion. It is surprising that chisudzo secret terminology is, in fact, identical to that of the kalumbu. Needless to say, neither chisudzo nor kalumbu members are aware of this fact.[4] Just as knowledge about kalumbu is kept secret from girls, so the teachings given in chisudzo are kept secret from boys.

Table 12.2
Secret Terminology of the Chisudzo (1984)

usual Chewa terms	chisudzo terms
maso (eyes) (upenya = to see)	mapenyapenya
mutu (head) (ugunda = to knock)	magundagunda
pakamwa (mouth) (uidya = to eat)	maidyaidya
mphuno (nose) (uima = to blow)	maminamina
zanja (hands) (ugwila = to grasp)	magwilagwila
msana (back) (usana = to stretch)	masanasana
minyendo (legs) (uyenda = to walk)	mayendayenda

Chisudzo girls also disguise themselves in the bush. Unlike kalumbu, however, a chisudzo girl masks her face with a loincloth (*chitenge*) that is usually worn around the waist over her skirt. Each masked character has its own name, songs, style of mask and dance. The songs are only sung by chisudzo girls. Some unmasked girls escorted masked dancers to the village and sang songs for the dancers.

Most dances and songs are unique to the chisudzo, though there are several that emulate those of the chinamwali. The following are examples of chisudzo dances and songs.

Kachope is a dancer who holds a stick on top of her head; both her head and the stick are covered with chitenge clothes (fig. 12.4). The dancer rhythmically tilts the stick back and forth, right and left, to the accompaniment of this song:

(Song 6) Kachope wamukulu ni kachope   Big kachope is kachope
          Chope   Chope

Because only this song mentions the term *wamukulu* (great), kachope is said to be the mother of all chisudzo. On the other hand, no chisudzo member was able to explain what kachope meant. However, the term seems to be associated with the verb "uchopa" meaning "to strike (of a snake)." If this is correct, we may interpret the movement of the kachope dancer as resembling the head of a snake.

Chikangwala is a chisudzo whose hands are horizontally stretched with a long stick. The hands as well as the head of the dancer are covered with chitenge clothes. The dancer turns round and round while running. It is said to portray a crow called khangwala (*Corvus albicollis*).

(Song 7) Chikangwala   A big crow
          choluka   flies

Another figure called Chimimba has a big belly stuffed with chitenge clothes. The face of the dancer is also covered with chitenge. The dancer swings her belly to and fro, and right and left.

(Song 8) Abwele achimimba   A woman with a big belly has come
         uja umati agona njala   She is the one who used to say that she
                                         goes to bed with an empty belly

The chimimba dancer portrays a pregnant woman. Not only the dance but also the song is rich in sexual implications. The chisudzo called *ngombe* (cow) is composed of a chain of dancers. Each dancer bends down and holds the waist of another dancer in front of herself; the dancers are then covered with chitenge clothes (fig. 12.5). They meander accompanied by the following song:

(Song 9) Ching'ombe deede   Big cow, deede
         Ching'mbe   Big cow

Some chisudzo were clearly remembered as having been introduced by newly arrived residents. Among them is a chisudzo called *chigwangwaila*. This type of chisudzo was brought by a girl named Sesutina Phiri from Sakwi village, which is located about 10 km from Kaliza. The dancer of chigwangwaila lies on the ground with her legs in an upright position. Both her head and feet are wrapped in chitenge clothes: her head on the ground is considered to be the "feet" of chigwangwaila, and her feet held upright to be its "head." The dancer has an escort, who sings and asks the dancer questions. Chigwangwaila answers the questions by either nodding or shaking its "head."

(Song 10) Zamve Zamve Zamve   Zamve Zamve Zamve
        Zamve Zamve Zamve   Zamve Zamve Zamve
        Ndani anachiona   Who saw the Chigwangwaila
        Chigwangwaila Chigwangwaila   Chigwangwaila
        ee aa ee   ee aa ee
(The escort questions)
            Amako nda?   Who is your mother?
            Ambuye wako nda?   Who is your grandmother?
            Amuna wako nda?   Who is your husband?
            Amunawako ni Aselemani? Is Mr. Selemani your husband?
            na Zulu?   or Mr. Zulu?
            na Ambewe?   or Mr. Mbewe?
            na Phiri?   or Mr. Phiri?
            na Zeleguze?   or Mr. Zeleguze?
(The song continues)

There are also some chisudzo that are directly connected with the female puberty ceremony chinamwali. A chisudzo called *kanamwali*, who just covers her face with a cloth, dances exactly as a namwali, that is, as a novice of the chinamwali does.

(Song 11) Kanamwali ee   The small novice
        Kanamwali ee   The small novice
        Kabwela lero Kanamwali ee   The small novice came today
        Kabwela ni mwana   She came with a baby
        Kanamwali ee   The small novice

In 1985, I witnessed a dancer who performed to Song 9 and also performed another dance to the following song:

(Song 12) Nsato yalemba ambuye,   A python glides, grandmother
        yalemba   it glides

The dancer knelt down with her knees touching and made her shins and waist move backward and forward. This dance is, as will be mentioned below, a dance that was previously performed at the most secret stage of the chinamwali puberty ceremony.

   At the end of the day, following the initiation of girls into the chisudzo, elder members of the group take the girls (namwali) back to their parents. In front of her parents, each novice, without covering her face but with a cloth around the waist, dances in a squatting position to this song:

(Song 13)   Pamsana pali kaingo   On the back there is a leopard

Pamsana pali kaingo	On the back there is a leopard
Mai dona	Mother, Mrs. Dona
aiya ee oo lile aiya ee	aiya ee oo lile aiya ee
Pamsana pali kaingo	On the back there is a leopard

This song resembles a song sung when the novices of the chinamwali are taken back to their parents (Song 5). In the song, it is mentioned that the girl on the back (of a lady) has the colors and pattern of the python. In this chisudzo song, the python is replaced with the leopard. When this song is sung, novices of the chisudzo make their waist move backward and forward, which is also an imitation of the dance of novices of the chinamwali ceremony.

Chinamwali, the Women's Initiation Ceremony

When a girl has her first menstruation, the girl's grandmother is immediately informed. The grandmother at once takes possession of one of the houses in the village and secludes the girl there. At the same time, she selects from among the adult women in the village someone to serve as tutor (*phungu*) for the girl. The tutor educates and takes care of the girl throughout the ceremony. From this first day on, the girl, now called namwali, stays inside the house provided. During this period, she is taught the various responsibilities of a mature woman.

The content of the teachings given during the ceremony, presented mostly through songs and dancing, can be classified into two types: instruction in womanly manners and practical instruction in sex and childbearing. The namwali is now forbidden to dance chisudzo.

In the past, the namwali were taken to the bush for the last stage of the ceremony. There, small clay figures (*vilengo*) in the form of a python, a crocodile, and a tortoise, etc. were made by the tutor, and the namwali were taught to dance around these figures. Every figure was decorated with red, white, and black dots, in imitation of the spotted pattern of the python. Informants mentioned that Song 12, recorded above, was originally sung when the namwali were taught to dance around the python figure.

Clay figures are no longer produced during chinamwali, which has adopted many elements of another women's initiation ceremony called *chisungu*, which is practiced by the neighboring Nsenga people. However, when the namwali returns to her parents, her naked body is painted with red, white, and black dots. Informants noted that the dots on the body of the namwali imitate the pattern found on the body of the python. Among the Chewa, the python is considered a messenger (*wamthenga*) of God (Mlengi or Chauta) who brings rainfall and ensures the fertility of the land and human beings. Women possessed by the python spirit become spirit mediums with the power of raincalling. Moreover, it is said that they used to be in charge of the women's initiation ceremony chinamwali. Although no mediums of the python spirit appear in the chinamwali today, there are many elements in the ceremony that suggest its connection with the python or the python spirit. Needless to say, this does not mean that the girls metaphorically become the spirit mediums. What is important is that the girls who have acquired powers of reproduction are initiated into a condition connected with the python that is thought to be in control of the fertility of the land and human beings.

Kalumbu and Chisudzo as "Models" of Nyau and Chinamwali

It is clear that the major concern of chinamwali is reproduction. This is in sharp contrast to the men's nyau association, which is in charge of funerary ritual. The men of the nyau actually say, "Because women make a secret of birth, we make a secret of death." Chewa men are excluded from witnessing births and are never told openly how a child is born. That information belongs only to the women who have completed chinamwali. On the other hand, that men "make a secret of death" means that funerary rituals are controlled by the men of the nyau association and that the process of transforming the spirit of the deceased into an ancestral spirit is concealed from women.

The nyau and the chinamwali are also in marked contrast to each other in several other respects. While men wear masks when they dance on the occasion of funerals, women dance naked during the chinamwali ceremony. As for the use of space, the initiation into the nyau is performed in the bush. By contrast, the women's initiation ceremony, chinamwali, is held in the village.

Similar contrasts can also be seen between boys' and girls' masquerades. While kalumbu boys mask their faces with tree leaves collected in the bush, chisudzo girls cover their heads and bodies with chitenge clothes which they usually wear. On the other hand, these methods of "metamorphosis" adopted by children contrast with those used by adults. Chisudzo girls who cover their heads and bodies with clothes are in sharp contrast to the nakedness of namwali on the occasions of chinamwali. Kalumbu's masks made of fresh leaves are differentiated from nyau masks made through carving or wickerwork.

The world of male and female, adults and children, are thus clearly differentiated. As we have seen, however, the overall pattern of initiation and the method of keeping secrets is practically common to all of the four "secret associations." Even the exegesis of rituals, especially those of the nyau masked rituals, are widely shared among people regardless of age and sex.

In the nyau association, there is no official teaching of what each nyau character portrays and what it is performing. The member of the nyau can only infer these from the name of the nyau, the songs sung when the nyau dances, and from the general notion, "nyau are dead persons who have been revived; nyau yolemba are wild animals." which they were already told before becoming members. The form of the mask a nyau wears is not always helpful in identifying the character, because, though some nyau are said to have wooden masks of specific form, dancers are quite free to replace them with feathered masks. The information available to men in interpreting nyau characters and performances, that is, the names, the associated songs, and the general notion of nyau, is in fact common knowledge to women and children. It may safely be said that the knowledge about nyau characters and performances is, in effect, widely shared among both men and women, adults and children in Chewa society. Skill in dancing nyau is also widely shared. In most cases, there is no need to train novices in dancing because they have already mastered the skill while they were in kalumbu. What is interesting in this respect is a riddle that is shared by nyau members. The riddle states:

> "Nyau ni kalumbu, chachikulu ni chiani?"
> "Kalumbu, cifukwa akuluakulu anayamba uvina kalumbu."
> "Which is bigger, nyau or kalumbu?"
> "Kalumbu, because even elders started up in masquerade with dancing kalumbu."

Children's masked dance is not a mere imitation of adult masquerade. Although we do not know the historical process of the formation of the nyau nor the kalumbu, it is at least certain that Chewa men acquire the skill of dancing through the activities of kalumbu and then further develop it by participating in nyau performances. In this sense, we may as well say that the kalumbu is a model of the nyau as say that the nyau is a model of the kalumbu.

Among the Chewa, the kalumbu group is not considered the lowest grade of the nyau association. The kalumbu is an independent association run by boys themselves. However, masquerading as a kalumbu constitutes a part of, or more precisely the basis of, nyau men's experience. This is also the case with the relationship between the chisudzo and the chinamwali. Dancing as a chisudzo is the basis of chinamwali women's experience.

I have said that skill in dancing and the exegesis of performances are widely shared among people regardless of age and sex. However, it does not follow that the content of the secrets declared during the initiation is unimportant. Contributors to a recent publication entitled *Secrecy: African Art that Conceals and Reveals* have noted that the substance of secrets is "less important than the social delineation resulting from their acquisition, ownership and controlled revelation" (Nooter 1993: 20). Although it holds true of Chewa "secret associations" that the existence of secrecy creates a group of "insiders" and "outsiders," the actual content of secrets still has vital importance because it is the very content of the secrets that forms one's experience as a member of a certain secret association. And it is through an active process of contrast and assimilation between the nyau masquerade and chinamwali ceremony, the kalumbu masquerade and chisudzo dance, the nyau masquerade and kalumbu dance, the chinamwali ceremony and chisudzo dance, that the experience of manhood and womanhood, of childhood and adulthood, is realized.

Notes

1. For this reason the data on the chinamwali was mostly collected by my wife Mariko Yoshida.
2. According to Rangeley (1949, 42), in Malawian Chewa chisudzo (pl. visudzo) is the generic term for all types of nyau excluding zoomorphic structures that are called nyau yolemba in Zambia. In Zambia, the term chisudzo is never used in the context of nyau.
3. When I revisited the Chewa region in 1992, 1993, and 1994, chisudzo dances were actively performed by young girls. Since I was not accompanied by my wife, however, I could not collect detailed information about chisudzo during my stay.
4. I would sincerely request that readers of this chapter not reveal this fact to Chewa boys or girls until they graduate from chisudzo or kalumbu.

Bibliography

Birch Faulkner, Laurel. "Basketry Masks of the Chewa." *African Arts* 2, 3 (1988): 2831, 86.

Birch de Aguilar, Laurel. 1996. *Inscribing the Mask: Interpretation of Nyau Masks and Ritual Performance among the Chewa of Central Malawi*. Sankt Augustin: AnthroposInstitut.

Kubik, Gerhard. 1987. *Nyau: Maskenb nde im s dlichen Malawi* (Ver ffentlichungen der Ethnologischen Kommission NR.4). Wien: Verlag der sterreichischen Akademie der Wissenschaften.

Nooter, Marry H. (ed.). 1993. *Secrecy: African Art that Conceals and Reveals*. New York: The Museum of African Art.

Rangeley, W.H.J. "Nyau in Kotakota District." *The Nyasaland Journal* 2: 2 (1949): 3549.

Schoffeleers, J. Matthew. "The Nyau Societies: Our Present Understanding." *Society of Malawi Journal* 29: 1 (1976): 5968.

_____. 1992. *River of Blood: The Genesis of a Martyr Cult in Southern Malawi, c.A.D.1600*. Madison: University of Wisconsin Press.

Yoshida, Kenji. "Masks and Transformation among the Chewa of Eastern Zambia."
Senri Ethnological Studies 31 (1992): 203273.

_____. "Masks and Secrecy among the Chewa." *African Arts* 26, 2 (1993): 3445, 92.

13

Playing with the Future: Children and Rituals in North-Western Province, Zambia

Elisabeth L. Cameron and *Manuel A. Jordán*

The children of Chitofu village, North-Western Province, Zambia, organized a play *mukanda*,[1] complete with camp and *makishi* (masquerades).[2] Based on the makishi characters that had appeared in the adult masquerades, girls and uninitiated boys devised imitation masks by recycling the framework of baskets originally used to hold and transport fish. These structures, made from bent branches tied together, resembled the head superstructure of aggressive makishi types (figs. 13.1, 13.2). Girls placed these on their heads to impersonate three types of ancestral masks which they called by their names: "Utenu," the angry ancestor; "Mupala," the lord of the initiation camp; and "Mwendumba," the lion. The girls disguised a boy who was younger than most of the other children as Chileya, the spirit of an old and sometimes foolish ancestor. They covered his face with cloth and placed tufts of white cotton on his head, imitating the cotton-covered head of Chileya[3] (figs. 13.3, 13.4). He then danced, imitating Chileya performances he had seen.[4]

The next year in Chitofu village, after attending a nearby women's initiation (*mwadi*), the children reconstructed a play mwadi. They chose a girl to play the initiate and a smaller boy to be her attendant (*kasonswelu*). Older girls raided their mother's cooking fires and used ashes to paint designs on their bodies. They stripped branches from small trees to create grass dance bustles, which are the dress of either the close female relatives of the initiate or the women performing men's masquerades at the women's ceremony.[5] Throughout the play initiation, the children sought the advice of Flora, a young woman who had been one of these girls' playmates only a few years before and had recently undergone the ceremony herself. Laughing, Flora commented on the performance while the children danced in a circle around the initiates.

At another family *mwadi* in a nearby village, while adult women sang and danced around the prone initiate, several recently initiated men escorted a young boy dressed to resemble Mupala, a *likishi* that only appears in the context of men's ceremonies. The play masquerader came to the edge of the family compound where he was completely ignored by all the participants in the "real" ritual. After a few minutes of frustration, he left.

In North-Western Zambia, children create their own ceremonies in the periphery of the adult definition of what is socially appropriate or acceptable. Children's rituals do not often officially exist and so these improvised performances occur "under the guise" of play. Children, through play, react to, experiment with, and re-define the adult world. To understand the significance of children's rituals, it is essential to consider a few of the roles and meaningful ramifications of the adult versions of these ceremonies.

Adult Initiation Ceremonies

Chokwe, Lunda, Luvale, and related peoples of northwestern Zambia perform both men's and women's initiations in which a liminal period between childhood and adulthood is deliberately and dramatically created through this ritual process. During this liminality, the community may experiment with the definitions and constraints of its social life, which its members may take for granted in more usual circumstances (Turner 1982: 105).

The basic sequence of events for men's and women's initiations are the same. The first day, adults take the girl or boys to *ifwila*, the dying place, then seclude them in a specially constructed, temporary structure. The men's initiation camp, located in the bush, is *mukanda*. In *mwadi*, the temporary building in the village is called *nkunka*, while a second enclosure built away from the village is referred to as *mukanda*. Initiates, whether male or female, undergo food, bathing, and movement restrictions. After a period of training, when adults decide the initiates are ready, they are presented to the gathered community where they display dancing skills they have learned during seclusion. Then the novices are dressed in new clothing and brought back into the village. The newly made adults sit on a mat where the community greets them and gives them gifts of money. In the past, men's initiations lasted around a year; currently the time varies from several weeks to occasionally a year. Women's initiation has also been shortened to between two days and several months. Length of either initiation depends on family interest, resources, and other demands on the child's time such as school. Many boys can be initiated at one time with the involvement of a large segment of the initiated male population. In contrast to the men's initiations, girls are usually initiated singly. Although most of the women in the community participate, there are only three people necessary for a successful female initiation: the initiate, her attendant, and the teacher.

During mukanda, adult men create and perform masquerades with the goal of presenting, affirming, and manipulating essential social, historical, political, religious, and moral principles through public performances.[6] Over one hundred types of masked ancestral characters with different physical and behavioral attributes and characteristics exist and a selection comes to life during the initiation. Among these characters, a male chief, Chihongo, educates the community about chiefly manners and composure; a female character, Pwo or Pwevo, portrays female beauty and comments on the essential role of women as providers of life; a pig mask, Ngulu, and an "idiot," Ndondo,[7] behave irrationally to present negative role models *not* to be emulated by the spectators. One category of aggressive masks, with exaggerated facial features and large head superstructures, is designed to control audiences, protect male initiation camps, and illustrate the more ambiguous behavioral qualities of ancestors in front of public audiences. Aggressive masks include Mupala, Utenu, and Mwendumba makishi, the same characters created by the girls from Chitofu village.

For girls, mwadi begins when the gathered adult women place the initiate at the base of the *muudi* tree. The initiate's position is the same as for a burial of an unweaned child: nude, lying on her side, facing the east and the muudi tree. From sun up to sun down of that day, the women dance in a circle around the initiate and sing special songs designed to instruct her. While no masquerades appear, women do take the same roles as makishi in men's initiations, entertaining the community and protecting the initiate.

The knowledge about initiation belongs to the initiated. Men swear never to reveal the secrets of mukanda to the uninitiated and their claims to secret and privileged knowledge are made public through mask performances. Although essentially a male institution, mukanda requires the cooperation of all members of society; women and uninitiated children follow set rules when interacting with makishi or when discussing these in public.[8] An inappropriate comment about a mask, in some instances, may result in punishment for a child and a legal case or monetary fine for a woman. Without women's and children's reciprocity, the social statement made by men's claim to privileged information would be irrelevant. Women and children take part in the overall organization of the camp's procedures and provide an interactive "other-half" that renders performances complete. Women's initiations welcome any women who have passed puberty. Just as masquerades reinforce and advertise men's secrets, women also advertise their activities. The initiate's enclosure is often in the village itself where men can overhear the proceedings and often songs are designed to alert the community to events inside the enclosure.[9]

The social dramas involved with initiations, whether the makishi of the men or the presentation of a young woman, provide a basis for the negotiation of gender tensions and the definition of social roles. Through time, for example, makishi have been reinvented and modified to represent new aspects of a cosmology (or related cosmologies) and to address pressing social and political issues. The paradoxical nature of makishi masquerades "plays" upon the dilemmas of life itself, aiding people by requiring them to actively confront the forces that inevitably affect them.

The drama of adult masquerade performances and women's ceremonies is in itself a ritualized version of play. Women claim that a major purpose of the masquerade figure's village appearance is to *play* with the initiates' mothers, to honor them, and make them happy. In return, the mothers must enthusiastically and appropriately respond by dancing, singing, and clapping with the masquerades, or taunting, screaming, and running from them. The entire community criticizes any initiate's mother who does not participate. When the masquerade comes to "play" with the women, the word used is *kuhema*, the same word used for children's play. Or the masquerades are said to "*kuhemesha*" the women or "play with" them, a word that also is used for something that is not to be taken seriously.

Both play and ritual take thoughts and ideas and put them into action. In the play world, the child's idea that he or she will one day be a part of initiation ceremonies is put into action in play rituals. The appearance of masquerades in the village brings to life the communities' belief in the power of the ancestors. This is both the "ritual" and the "play" world brought to life. Both play and ritual worlds have strict rules. For these masquerades, women know that they may approach, speak to, dance with, and flee from the masquerader. But they must not touch him or they suffer dire consequences. If pregnant, they will miscarry. If not, they will menstruate without stopping. To become well, the women must go to a male healer and obtain special medicines for a fee. Rules in the play world revolve around acceptance of its existence. Although there are rules, a masquerade performance does not follow a set pattern. Each one is unique depending on the performer and the enthusiasm of the women. This characteristic of spontaneity is usually classified with play rather than ritual.

The enemy of both the ritual and play world is the spoilsport. For the child, the spoilsport is one who will not acknowledge that his or her play ritual is to be respected and therefore collapses the play world. In the ritual world, the spoilsport is likewise someone who forces the mundane into that which is set apart, who does not follow the rules of the ritual and expects no consequence for his or her actions. An example of a ritual spoilsport is Chitofu's daughter Maria who, during a masquerade performance grabbed the arm of the likishi. Because she was post-menopausal, she knew she could touch him without physical harm. To reinstate the ritual rules, the men later levied a large fine against her.

Play, Initiations, and Community Involvement

As in the case of play masquerades and rituals, children often engage in the re-creation of adult roles and activities. Chokwe, Lunda, and Luvale girls may make play dolls from mud, wood, and other materials (Cameron 1996: 16). The presentation and handling of these dolls often re-enacts the moment when a young mother brings a baby to the village for the first time. The relatives of the newborn gather and apply white clay or powder to their faces to symbolize the positive transition that has occurred.[10] The mother will hand the baby to her parents and then to her siblings, each of whom will pay cash as a gift for the honor of holding the baby. Young girls may follow the same conventions when playing with dolls by applying white powder (often cassava flour stolen from their mothers) to their faces and that of the doll. This game prepares them for the future role they will fulfill in society as mothers and providers of continuity in their communities.

Among other leisurely games, children's sand drawings recall ritualized drawing performances documented among Chokwe and related peoples in Angola and Zambia (Fontinha 1983). In the adult practice, an artist or ritual-specialist draws images on the sand, in front of an audience, to represent visually and explain verbally (through proverbs and story-telling) different cosmological principles held by the peoples in the area. Boys and girls similarly draw images on the sand but in their case they aim at representing the material things they wish to have as adults. Large and beautifully decorated houses are often the subject of children's sand drawings. Other images created by both girls and boys include drawings of the children's favorite makishi characters. This suggests that children recognize the relevance of masquerades in their lives.

Although male mukanda and female mwadi formally introduce children to adult life, by the time they reach the age to be initiated, children have a good idea about what initiation and adult life entails. Children are physically present (and often underfoot) at the center of most public events whether these are sponsored by male (mukanda) or female (mwadi) adult institutions. Children are, nevertheless, rarely mentioned when masquerades and other ritual and ceremonial performances are discussed in the literature, although one purpose of the public components of (essential secretive) initiation events is to educate and prepare children for their own initiations.

From an early age, children participate in ceremonies while wrapped in baby carriers around the backs of their mothers. During initiation ceremonies, boys, and occasionally girls, will play drums whenever these are left unattended by adults. They will also dance, play music with sticks, and sing the songs of initiation as part of the community chorus in public performances. The play masquerades and rituals initiated and performed by children may occur concurrently with mukanda and mwadi ceremonies (normally during the dry season), when children re-enact the adult mask performances and other rituals they have recently observed and participated in. Performances may also happen during the off (rainy) season, as children sing, dance, and play music by beating on stool-drums, imitating rituals they witnessed earlier during past ceremonial seasons. Children's masquerades do not always require the actual use of a face mask or costume by the mask impersonator. A child dances like a particular likishi or acts like the adult masquerader does when he is in that character. The other children play along, treating the performer as a mask character. Mbuya, the headman's great-grandson, for example, often danced pretending to be the mask that represents a female ancestor, Pwo or Pwevo. Mbuya did this by wrapping some clothes around his waist in imitation of a women's dance bustle worn by Pwevo performers to emphasize dance movements and then dancing with

Pwo's characteristic hip motions. More elaborate play masks and costumes may also be created by children. Adult makishi are thought of as ancestral presences with personality, distinctive voices,[11] particular movements, and stylized dances specific to the character. The adult use of the mask is merely an aide in transforming the dancer into the likishi character. Children's makishi do not need actual face masks because, in the play world, children use their imaginations to complete the characterization.

The children of Chitofu village regularly recreated and reenacted adult life. A favorite playtime was the creation, a short distance from the village, of a "play" village, complete with small houses, hearths, and fields. The boys and girls paired off in husband/wife pairs and a headman was selected. Life in this village reflected what the children saw as their future life. Both traditional and innovative ways of doing things were tried out as the children explored their gender roles, work relationships, and leadership roles. Adults encouraged this parallel play world as a form of training for future community leaders. Play masquerades, although nominally discouraged because of their sacred nature, alerted the adults that the children were considering roles of masked dancers for their own future. In an area where fewer and fewer *mukanda wa makishi* (men's initiations with masks) are being performed, the children's play indicated to the adults that they were interested in future participation. Adults, therefore, turned a blind eye to the performances or laughed and played along.

Just as children appropriate elements of adult life to serve their social needs, there are aspects of adult initiation performance that may, in turn, draw from children's performances and play. Many of the songs that accompany makishi performances, for example, relate current stories and events that may have originated in the context of children's play and performances. Among these songs, one praising Argentinean soccer player Maradona, and a song about love that declares, "today is like second-hand clothes," are very popular in adult rituals. These most probably originated from children listening to the sports news on the radio, and overhearing gossip in the town's market. Children, in addition, often influence mask performances by beginning to sing a particular song (in choir form). If the children are united and persistent, the other participants will follow their lead and the song will be sung.

Playing with Fear

To an uninitiated child—boy or girl—a likishi represents a "spirit from the grave," something to be feared. If a child misbehaves, a parent may say that makishi are going to come from the graves to take away the child. Some makishi may actually "steal" a young child from the mother's arms, pretending to run away with him or her as part of the masquerade performance. The child and the mother usually become hysterical until a male relative rescues the child from the arms of the likishi. During community performance, children, nevertheless, play with their fear of masks, approaching and taunting them, then screaming and running away when chased by the makishi. Although this is part of the social drama of initiation, a daring uninitiated boy may risk great punishment by venturing into an initiation camp uninvited. The family of the young intruder may be penalized with a fine and the child risks being "whipped" by makishi or the camp attendants.[12]

During the first day in a 1992 Lunda mukanda in North-Western Province, Zambia, at the time of the actual circumcision of initiates, Mbuya walked towards the initiation camp. The camp attendants saw him coming and yelled for him to go back to the village or be grabbed by the makishi ancestral spirits. In his own mind, Mbuya was ready for initiation,[13] and so he proceeded to the camp where he was "captured" by men and finally added to the initiation. Mbuya had not been part of the original initiation plans because men thought he was too young or that "he did not have the right mind yet." Mbuya, nevertheless, had decided it was time and he graduated from the mukanda and with great honor.[14] Mbuya had approached the camp with fear, but he was more worried about being left behind than having to deal with the punitive makishi.

Like adults, children have a need to negotiate their own fears and to "put to the test" the constraints of their social realities to find prospects for their own aspirations. Masquerade performances allow them to deal directly with a fear instilled throughout their childhood. A more concrete way of dealing with the fear is to actually create and perform masquerades, to be the ones who decide what the masquerade does, how it moves, and who it may grab or chase.

Playing with Gender

Through these playful rituals, children are able to appropriate the adult institution to experiment with social and cultural elements not normally accessible to them. Gender roles are a special target of exploration. Although the children knew that mwadi was a woman's ceremony and the participants should be female, a boy played the role of a female initiate's attendant. The girls knew that only men could perform or even touch masks, yet girls actively performed the masks. This exploration of male and female initiates agrees in principle with adult attitudes that all initiates are genderless. Both male and female initiates can be called *tundanji* and informants stressed that this signified their ambiguous nature. Adults watched the children's gender experimentation, laughed, and turned a blind eye.

When play attempted to challenge too many boundaries, it was a failure. The boy who dressed as a play likishi and then tried to perform at a real mwadi attempted to play with gender roles and the intersection of play and ritual in an uncomfortable and unacceptable way. While playing rituals in a quiet village is tolerated by adults, it is not accepted in the context of an actual ritual. Play and ritual worlds do overlap, but this play masquerade was rebuffed at a "real" ritual because the play world it offered interfered with reality.

Not only did it bring play and ritual into conflict, it also brought men's and women's ceremonies together in uncomfortable ways. Women say that if a likishi from a man's ceremony saw a female initiate, he would beat her and she would never bear children. The adults and other children attending the mwadi who also saw the play likishi ignored it or made comments about the boy's childishness. Even a play likishi proved to be too much of a threat to be accepted in the same area as the female initiate. The people attending the mwadi commented that the boy was being childish, in contrast to the joking manner of the adults watching play ceremonies in their quiet village.

Conclusion

For Chokwe, Lunda, Luvale, and related peoples of Angola, Democratic Republic of the Congo, and Zambia, masquerades are paradoxical devices employed strategically to allow for the transmission of crucial ideological information, as well as the negotiation of relevant issues affecting communities. In a playfully reinvented form of liminality, children employ similar strategies to explore aspects of culture that are not normally controlled by them. Through their "forbidden" masquerades, children are able to mediate the ambiguous constraints of their own place in society, "getting away" with the improbable and "playing" with the possibilities of fulfillment for their own hopes and aspirations.

In Chitofu village, by the time the adults noticed the "alternative" rituals, the children were pretty much done. Perhaps recognizing that play rituals prepared the children for future successful completion of adult ceremonies, the grownups laughed and played along with the masquerades. Soon after the adults noticed them, the children stopped playing. Children organized the masquerade from the beginning to a wisely timed end.

Notes

1. Men's circumcision and initiation camp.
2. Manuel Jordán wishes to thank the Project for the Advanced Study of Art and Life in Africa, the University of Iowa, for generously funding twenty-six months of field research in Zambia. Thanks are also extended to the Kotze family in Lusaka, Henry Kaumba, Geoffrey Kaweza, and Bernard Mukuta Samukinji for their help, and to Christopher Roy and Allen Roberts for their support throughout his studies. Elisabeth Cameron wishes to acknowledge an IIE Fulbright for funding fourteen months of field research in Zambia. She would also like to thank the Brooks family for their hospitality and Herbert Cole and Doran Ross for encouraging "play" with ideas. Both Manuel and Elisabeth would like to thank the Chitofu family near the town of Kabompo for their assistance and friendship, and Mrs. Ilse Mwansa of the Institute of African Studies at the University of Zambia for her support. Despite the generosity of these agencies and individuals, we alone take responsibility for the contents of this article.
3. The cotton on the Chileya's head represents the white hair of an elderly person. The cotton is usually taken from an old European pillow or a cotton-stuffed mattress.

4. All of these *makishi* represent male characters. All are categorized as "masks that chase," except for Chileya, which is a dancing mask. A performance of masks that chase resembles a game of tag, with the masked person chasing the uninitiated boys, all girls, and women around the village. It is perhaps the lively character of these aggressive masks that makes it attractive for children's play.
5. For a discussion of women's masquerades in *mwadi*, see Cameron 1995, 1998.
6. See Bastin 1961, 1984 for information about Chokwe mask types and their meaning.
7. Ndondo is short, wears a tattered costume, and has a bloated stomach.
8. Lunda women explained that a woman may know that her husband is disguised as a mask character but will pretend not to know it. Addressing the mask as her husband is a socially inadmissible form of behavior. A man will similarly pretend not to know details of female initiation. Married men and women may exchange "secrets" of initiation they swore they would not share with members of the opposite sex (Cameron 1995).
9. One such song details what the women are doing with the initiate and includes verses such as "We are now combing her hair," "We are now bathing her," and "We are now dressing her."
10. The color symbolism of the Lunda is explored by Victor Turner (1967). He explains that white is a color associated with life-giving. The women's ceremonies center around the *muudi* tree that has white sap like mother's milk. White then is assigned to positive and successful transitions during life, including birth, initiations, and marriage (Turner 1967: 60-61).
11. Some of the *makishi*, especially those that dance, talk to the gathered community. Usually aggressive masks that chase the women and children do not speak.
12. Except for times of special teaching that usually occur at night, uninitiated girls are welcome in the *mwadi* enclosure. Boys often try, usually successfully, to peek through the fence of the mwadi enclosure. As a result, they tend to be fairly well informed about mwadi proceedings. We never heard of a boy actually attempting to enter the enclosure or of a girl attempting to enter men's *mukanda*.
13. As explained to Manuel Jordán by Mbuya's uncle who was in charge of the mukanda.
14. Ironically, Mbuya was the only initiate to finish that mukanda. The father of the other two participants took them from the village camp, back to Lusaka, after having serious quarrels with one of his own father's wives.

Bibliography

Bastin, Marie-Louise. 1961. *Art Decoratif Tshokwe*. 2 vols. Lisbon: Companhia de Diamantes de Angola, Publiações culturais, no. 55.

———. "Ritual Masks of the Chokwe." *African Arts* 17:4 (1984): 40-45, 92-93, 95.

Cameron, Elisabeth L. 1995. "Negotiating Gender: Initiation Arts of *Mwadi* and *Mukanda* among the Lunda and Luvale, Kabompo District, North-Western Province, Zambia." Ph.D. diss., University of California, Los Angeles.

———. 1996. *Isn't S/He a Doll? Play and Ritual in African Sculpture*. Los Angeles: UCLA Fowler Museum of Cultural History.

———. Women=Masks: Initiation Arts in North-Western Province, Zambia." *African Arts* 31, 2 (1998): 50-61.

Fontinha, Mário. 1983. *Desenhos na areia dos Quiocos do nordeste de Angola*. Lisbon: Instituto de Investigação Cientifica Tropical.

Turner, Victor. 1967. *The Forest of Symbols*. Ithaca, NY: Cornell University Press.
Turner, Victor (ed.). 1982. *Celebration, Studies in Festivals and Ritual*. Washington, D.C.: Smithsonian Institution Press.

Contributors

Mary Jo Arnoldi is curator of African ethnology and arts in the Department of Anthropology, National Museum of Natural History, Smithsonian Institution, Washington, D.C. She has carried out extensive research in Mali on arts and performance. Her recent books include *Playing with Time: Art and Performance in Central Mali* (1995), and she has co-edited *African Material Culture* (1996) with Christraud Geary and Kris Hardin. She has curated numerous exhibitions of African art and was lead curator on the permanent exhibition, "African Voices," which opened in December 1999 at her museum.

Manuel Rambout Barçelos, born of a mother of Belgian and Cape Verdean background and a Portuguese father, and of a Bissau Creole stratum, came to Bissau as a ten-year-old in 1956, and is a Guinean citizen. He obtained a secondary school education in Bissau and a university education in Portugal. He returned to independent Guinea-Bissau in 1976, taking numerous government positions, including Minister of National Education in 1989-1991. He wrote the screenplay for Flora Gomes' 1992 film about Carnival in Bissau, *Le Masque*, produced only in incomplete form by the French Cultural Center in Bissau. He has been associated in politics with an opposition political party PRD (Party for Renewal and Development), and with the government Institute for Adult Education (INAFOR) in Bissau.

David A. Binkley was Chief Curator and Senior Curator for Research and Interpretation at the National Museum of African Art, Smithsonian Institution where he developed and supervised the development of a number of tradition-based and contemporary art exhibitions. He was also Curator for the Arts of Africa-Oceania and the Americas at The Nelson-Atkins Museum of Art and Research Associate Professor at the University of Missouri-Kansas City. He has published a number of articles on Kuba and Northern Kete arts associated with funeral and initiation rites. His research interests include colonial and post colonial discourse on Central African artistic traditions and their interpretation in Western scientific and popular thought. Current projects include the development of the exhibition "Kuba: Art of a Central African Kingdom."

Elisabeth L .Cameron currently teaches in the History of Art and Visual Culture Department at the University of California, Santa Cruz. She has published a number of articles on initiation arts in Zambia and the Sala Mpasu peoples of the Democratic Republic of the Congo. She has also curated the exhibitions "Ancestors: Art and the Afterlife" and "Music for the Eyes: The Fine Art of African Musical Instruments" at the Los Angeles County Museum of Art and "Isn't S/He a Doll? Play and Ritual in African Sculpture" at the Fowler Museum of Cultural History, University of California, Los Angeles.

Jeanne Cannizzo teaches the anthropology of the material world at the Department of Social Anthropology, University of Edinburgh. She has conducted extensive research on children's masquerades among the Mende. In 1999, she curated an exhibition concerning cultural production and construction, "O Caledonia! Sir Walter Scott and the Creation of Scotland."

Nicolau Fara Gomes, a Guinean with rural roots, was born in Canchungo and is of the Manjaco cultural group. He first came to Bissau in 1974 at age fifteen to enter high school and has never travelled or studied abroad. Living in Tchado Bairro in Bissau, a neighborhood not dominated by the Papel, the local Bissau cultural group, he produced the legendary three-man dragon mask in 1980 under the direction of an artist from Cape Verde. He has worked for Radio Nacional for at least five years, developing programs oriented toward rural areas. He has been concerned that rural youth have been left out of opportunities to develop their creativity at carnival, being more intent to come to Bissau to watch it. He wishes to encourage the youth to make their own carnival in their hometowns.

Priscilla Baird Hinckley is trained as an artist and art educator. The adventure of living with her family and teaching in Ghana in the 1960s led to a lifetime interest in Africa. While working with Kofi Antubam, the Ghanaian artist, she was introduced to African culture and art. Later, she taught in Tanzania, and then did Peace Corps service in Burkina Faso. The latter activity enabled her to study children and art there and resulted in her doctoral research at Boston University. In 1989, she co-produced an award-winning video called "Chantal's Choice," created with Burkina Faso secondary school students. She has also done African outreach in schools and she has been active in the curating and educational components of African art exhibitions in the United States. For several years, she taught African art at Tufts University. She is now retired.

Anna A. Hlaváčová trained at the Academia Istropolitana in Bratislava, Slovakia, and specializes in theater anthropology and in directing. She studied in Moscow and Paris with Anatoli Vasiliev and Ariane Mnouchkine. She then took part in Eckhard Breitinger's research project at the African Studies Center, Bayreuth University, Germany, and has written a monograph, *Pre-Modern Images and Imagery*, based on materials collected in her field research in southeastern Nigeria, where she mostly worked with Amatu Braide of the University of Port Harcourt. She later wrote a monograph on the film director Andrei

Tarkovski and the Russian anthropologist Pavel Florenski's influence on him. Her interest in the phenomena of masks is strong and she has studied Nô on a Japan Foundation scholarship in that country. Her interests have shifted from art phenomenology to problems such as the relationships between icon and mask and the origin of masked performances. Living in Bratislava, she works as a lecturer and theater director.

Manuel A. Jordán is curator of African art at the Cantor Arts Center, Stanford University. He obtained his Ph.D. in African art history at the University of Iowa. He has conducted extensive fieldwork in North-Western Province, Zambia among Chokwe, Lunda, Luvale, and related peoples. He organized the traveling exhibition "CHOKWE! Art and Initiation Among the Chokwe and Related Peoples," and he has contributed to a number of publications on the theme of Chokwe-related art and culture.

Harriet C. McGuire has specialized in African arts, education, and political developments since her undergraduate study at Smith College. Her knowledge of African art was enhanced by docent training and subsequent volunteer work at the privately owned Museum of African Art in Washington, D.C. (now the National Museum of African Art, Smithsonian Institution). Her first trip to Africa was with Operation Crossroads Africa in 1968. She subsequently lived and worked in Botswana, Zambia, Namibia, Mozambique, and Guinea-Bissau, as well as on four other continents, while she and her husband pursued tandem careers as U.S. Foreign Service officers with the Department of State and the United States Information Agency. Research for the Guinea-Bissau article was done while she was a Research Associate of INEP, the National Institute for Research and Studies in Guinea-Bissau (1992-1995), while accompanying her husband's tour of duty as U.S. Ambassador to Guinea-Bissau. She was public affairs officer at the American Embassy in Maputo, Mozambique.

Robert W. Nicholls, professor at the University of the Virgin Islands, has conducted research on the music and dance of the Igede of Nigeria for the Institute of Education, Ahmadu Bello University, Nigeria. He has also studied masking in the U.S. Virgin Islands for the University Islands and the Virgin Island Humanities Council. He is the author of *Old-Time Masquerading in the U.S. Virgin Islands* (Virgin Islands Humanities Council, 1998).

John R. O. Ojo taught for many years in the Department of Fine Arts, Obafemi Awolowo University, Ile-Ife, Nigeria. He is now attached to the Institute of Cultural Studies at the same university. He has written extensively on Yoruba culture, art, and life. He studied in Britain and Nigeria both in the fields of art, especially painting, and in social anthropology, and his art has appeared in a number of exhibitions in Nigeria.

Chika O. Okeke completed his Ph.D. in art history at Emory University in 2004 on the topic of "Nigerian Art in the Independence Decade 1957-1958." His dissertation is concerned with the first generation of post-independence Nigerian artists and their art. Of Nigerian background, he has published numerous articles on contemporary Nigerian art, a topic that he has been deeply involved in as an artist, art historian, art critic, and curator. Currently, he is an assistant professor in the Department of Art History at Pennsylvania State University.

Simon Ottenberg, emeritus professor of anthropology, University of Washington, has carried out extensive field research among the Igbo of Nigeria and the Limba of Sierra Leone. He has published in a number of anthropological fields, including those of kinship, micropolitics, childhood maturation, and art. He is best known for his *Masked Rituals of Afikpo: The Content of an African Art* (1975). Among his other publications are *Boyhood Rituals in an African Society* and *Seeing with Music: The Lives of Three Blind African Musicians* (1996). In 1997, he curated an exhibition at the National Museum of African Art, Smithsonian Institution, "The Poetics of Lines: Seven Artists of the Nsukka Group," with an accompanying book, *New Traditions from Nigeria: Seven Artists of the Nsukka Group* (1997), and an edited volume, *The Nsukka Artists and Nigerian Contemporary Art* (2002), based on a symposium held prior to the exhibition opening.

Felix Siga was born of the Balanta cultural group in upcountry Bissora, Guinea Bissau in 1954. He came to live in Bissau in 1969 after completing primary school, working as a carpenter's assistant and later at the port. He went to work in 1974 for the youth organization of the government's ruling party, the PAIGC, in his hometown, spending the next decade in party youth activities in the interior of the country. In 1985-1986, he studied in Berlin at the Karl Marx Institute. A self-taught poet, writing in Portuguese, Crioulu, and the Balanta languages, his first works were published in 1986 and he is included in two anthologies of Guinean poetry. He has lived in Bissau since 1987, working in government administrative positions. As director of culture, beginning in 1995, he supervised the 1995 Carnival.

Walter E. A. van Beek teaches cultural anthropology at Utrecht University in the Netherlands. His first research was in Cameroon, among the Kapsik/Higi on the Cameroon/Nigerian border in the Mandara Mountains. Since the 1980s, the Dogon of Central Mali have been the subject of his research, part of an ongoing project on livelihood and religion in the West African Sahel. He is co-author of *Dogon: Africa's Peoples of the Cliffs* (2002). His main interests are religion and ecology. He is part of the directorate of the CERES research organization, a graduate school that unites most of the development-oriented research in the Netherlands.

Kenji Yoshida is associate professor in the Department of Museum Anthropology, National Museum of Ethnology, Osaka, Japan, and teaches museum anthropology at the Graduate University for Advanced Studies at the same museum. He has specialized in the study of expressive culture in Africa and published widely on the masks and spirit possession of the Chewa of Zambia. He has also edited, with John Mack, the exhibition catalogue *Images of Other Cultures*.

Index

Abiodun, Rowland, 16
Adams, Sarah, 21
Adult initiation (Igbo), 120-121, 123
Adult initiation (Zambia)
  event sequences, 238
  masquerading goals, 238-239
  play benefits from, 240
  ritual benefits of, 240
  as secret, 239
  social drama in, 239-240
  women's rituals, 239
Adult masquerading (Igede)
  men's masquerading ensembles, 136-137
  mixed-gender ensembles, 139-140
  women's ensembles, 137-138
Adult masquerading (Ijo)
  ceremony description, 151-153
  purpose of, 152-153
Adulthood
  boy's masquerading importance, 17
  children associating with, 17-18
Afikpo masquerading
  disappearing of, 19
  troupe organization, 19-20
  vs adult masquerading, 20
Africa
  artistic activities in, 196-197
  boy's masquerading experiences, 22
  boy's socializing process, 106
  childhood meaning in, 132
  girl's pre-initiation masquerading, 32-35
  girl's socializing process, 105-106
  Ijo masquerading views, 151-156
  Kalumbu masquerading, 29-30
  mask traditions, 25, 129
  masquerading outcomes, 244
  rite of passage structures, 105
  secular independent masquerading, 31
  self-directed learning in, 140
  social mask attitudes, 156
  spiritual architecture of, 155
  Western influences on, 2
African pedagogy
  adult masquerading as, 141
  dance imitating as, 140
  methods for, 140
  Onyeweh uniqueness, 141
Alikali Devils
  aesthetic concepts of, 26
  boy's dance preferences, 173
  children copying, 171
  city characteristics and, 25
  disappearing of, 25
  eclecticism characteristics, 172
  emulating nature of, 25
  harmony from, 174
  holiday performing of, 167
  Jolly dance of, 168
  Kaka dance, 169
  locations of, 26
  modernity emphasis, 172
  musicians and, 170-171
  performance quality, 173-174
  play as training, 176
  Rainbow devil, 168-169
  socializing from, 176-177
  Talabi dance of, 169
  urban associations sponsoring, 167-168
  vs rural masquerading, 25-26
  vs Torwama masquerading, 174-176
  Yoruba influences on, 171-172
Argenti, Nicolas, 28
Aries, Philippe, 25
Arnoldi, Mary Jo, 12, 49

Baba, dance characters of, 59
Bamana boy's masquerading
  benefits to, 63-64

253

characteristics of, 49
gender social customs, 49-50
knowledge linked to, 50
pre-adolescent masquerading, 49
ritual masquerading, 50-55
Sogo bò mask play, 55-64
Bamana girls
gender learning, 58
miniature Sogo bò, 60-62
Bamana of Mali. *See* Bamana Ndòmò masquerading
Bamana Ndòmò masquerading
characteristics of, 11
focus of, 11
masquerading categories, 12
vs boy's fighting, 11-12
Bandiagara Cliffs of Mali. *See* Dogon masquerading
Barber, Karen, 193
Barçelos, Manuel Rambout, 181-182, 185, 188, 197
Barros, Carlos Alberto Teixeiro, 182-183, 190
Beart, Charles, 207
Beier, Ulli, 17
Bissau Carnival
characteristics of, 189
childhood and, 185-186, 189-191
girl's roles in, 27
government role, 183, 184-185, 194
headpiece wearing, 181-182
history of, 181-186
influence of, 191-193
mask making, 26-27, 186-189, 192
origins of, 181-183
population growth and, 193-194
roots returning to, 185
rural culture in, 184
as secular ritual, 197
shoulder-supported masks, 183
society evolving and, 26-27, 185
tradition and modern world in, 193
urban masquerading, 187, 194-197
violence and, 185
vs other carnivals, 193-194
Bissau Carnival influences
Cape Verde, 192
Catholic support, 191
mask forms, 192
media, 191-192
multicultural atmosphere as, 192-193

Bissau Carnival masquerading
forms of, 186-188
mask discarding, 188
making of, 186-189, 267
participant quantity, 188-189
rural area participating, 189
secrecy of, 188
Bobo boys' masquerading
cult origins for, 14
leaf costumes of, 13
zymology of, 17
Boston, John, 21
Boy's emulating masquerading
Afikpo masquerading, 19-20
boy's learning experiences, 22
Chewa boys and, 223-228
Kalabari masquerading, 20-21
Kuba boys, 18-19
learning from, 22-24
Mende boys, 21
Omepa masquerading, 20
Onyeweh masquerading, 20
Southern Nigeria masquerading, 21
Boy's integrated masquerading
adult world incorporating, 17-18
Bamana Ndòmò, 11-12
Bobo, 13-14
Dogon, 12-13
Yoruba, 14-17
Boy's masquerading (Igede)
ages in, 134
dances by, 134
Onyeweh ensemble of, 134
Boy's pre-initiation masquerading
girl's role in, 7
preponderance of, 6-7
Bravmann, René, 30
Birmingham, David, 194
Binkley, David A., 1, 18-19, 105
Brooks, George E., 182
Burkina Faso. *See* Bobo masquerading

Ca-Mati, Domingos, 185
Cameron, Elisabeth L., 19, 32, 237
Cannizzo, Jeanne, 25
de Carvalho, Augusto Dias, 182
Chewa masquerading
boy's initiation into, 226-228
boy's society for, 223-226
children's masquerading neglecting, 221
gender society models, 233-235

Index

girl's society for, 229-233
locations of, 222
as Nyau, 221
public knowledge of, 222-223
settings for, 222
women's initiation into, 228-229, 233-234
Children (Ijo)
  adult masquerading ceremony, 151-153
  age system for, 153-154
  generational tensions, 154
  Kalabari masquerading, 153-154
  Opobo masquerading, 154-155
  societal attitude factors, 156
  vs riverine societies, 153-154
  Western influences, 154
Children masquerading
  adolescent initiating and, 3
  adult mask making from, 189-191
  boy's emulating with, 18-24
  boy's independent, 24-32
  boy's initiations and, 11-18
  cultural changes and, 2-3
  gender and, 6-7
  girl's pre-initiation, 32-35
  history of, 1-3
  learning from, 3-5
  limits of, 6
  origins of, 1-2
  play as, 7-8
  pre-initiation classifications, 8-11
  research on, 1
  researcher's difficulties, 2
  troupe social relationships, 8
  Western influences on, 2
Children's music and dance (Igede)
  adult world and, 131-132
  as recreational, 133
  sacred and secular, 131
  society's role of, 132-133
Chinamwali initiation
  body painting, 233-234
  clay figures uses, 233
  initiation process, 228-229
  process for, 233
  secrecy of, 228, 235
  song examples, 229
  vs Nyau, 234
Chisudzo masquerading
  characteristics of, 229
  dance and song examples, 230-233

girl's association, 229
ritual process, 229-230
song origins, 231
terminology examples, 229-230
Christianity
  Bissau Carnival support, 191
  boy's masquerading and, 28, 122
  buro rituals and, 78
  Christmas masquerading, 29, 160
  Dodo support, 28, 215
  ensembles influenced by, 139
  Imwo society demise, 138
  vs Muslims, 215
  vs Nyau dances, 222
  See also Islamism
Circumcision
  frequency of, 81-82
  ritual of, 82-83
  sagiri participating, 81
  symbolism of, 83
Cole, Herbert, 105
Crowley, Daniel, 185-188, 191

Dancing
  Adiya and, 132-133
  Baba's Segou dance, 59
  Chisudzo examples, 230-233
  dance queens, 135
  Èmna interpretations, 75
  funeral mask dance, 71
  Igede and, 131-135
  Jolly dance, 168
  Kaka dance, 169
  Kalumbu and, 225-226
  Owu dance, 21
  Talabi dance, 169
  tree dances, 72
d'Azevedo, Warren, 29
Democratic Republic of the Congo. *See* Kuba masquerades
Dodo masquerading
  adults supporting, 215
  as art form, 215-216
  changeability of, 216
  Christian interest in, 28, 215
  conclusions on, 214-216
  girl's roles in, 35, 211-241
  government and, 27-28, 210-211
  as Hausa story, 208
  history of, 207-208
  independent masquerades and, 28
  Islam and, 27

mask designing, 27
origins of, 207
population increase problems, 215
post-World War II, 208
Quartiers location of, 208-210
urban spreading, 207-208
Dodo paid performances
government sponsoring, 210
money uses, 211
vs neighborhood origins, 211
Dodo Quartiers masquerading
as child-initiated, 208
description of, 208-210
grand vs petit in, 210
Dogon fox funerals
as masked dance, 70
reasons for, 67
traditions of, 67
Dogon masks
adult activities integrating, 83-84
childhood culture as, 86
circumcision importance, 81-83
conclusions on, 83-86
Emna masks, 70-76
fox funerals, 67-70
initiation into, 85
learning from, 85
Sagiri masks, 76-81
vs death-mask complex, 84
women severity from, 85-86
Dogon masquerades
adulthood initiation, 13
as art specialists, 12
interest in, 13
masks as rites, 13
symbology of, 17
Drama performance
boy's passage as, 72
importance of, 72
mask making, 72-73
tree dances, 72
women and, 74
young performers in, 73-74
Drewal, Henry, 16
Drewal, Margaret, 16

Ekine masks, 20-21
Ekpo masquerades, 21
Èmna masks
boy's "bush-like," 75-76
drama performance, 72-74
dance interpreting, 75

descriptions of, 74-75
fox funerals and, 70
funeral masked dance, 71
male superiority from, 74
performances using, 70-71
Emulating masquerades
characteristics of, 10
tensions in, 23-24
Euba, Akin, 130

Fear, children addressing, 242-243
Feminization
meaning of, 145-146
reincarnation beliefs, 146
vs youthization, 146
Foss, Perkins, 21
Frankel, Andrew, 16
Funeral mask dance
boy's role in, 71
description of, 71
village reactions to, 71
Funeral masks (Kuba)
creativity in, 112
hierarchy of, 111
mask making activities, 111

Gable, Eric, 186
Gbini masquerading, 29
Gelede festival, 15
Gender
boy's pre-initiation masquerading, 6-7
children masquerading and, 6-7
genderless initiation, 243
learning of, 58
mask making and, 32
masquerading as differentiating, 19
role exploring, 243
social customs and, 49-50
vs ritual performing, 243-244
Girls
African socialization process, 105-106
Bissau Carnival and, 27
boy's circumcision ritual and, 82
boy's masquerading roles, 7
Chisudzo associations for, 229
emulating masquerading by, 34
excising of, 81
Igbo masquerading, 91, 120-121
Kalumbu masquerading, 30
Liberia and, 32-35

masking role of, 32-33
Öjija performance roles, 91, 93
pre-initiation masquerading, 32-35
Sagiri mask and, 80-81
vs boys, 32-33
See also Women
Girl's masquerading (Chewa), as Chisudzo, 229-233
Girl's masquerading (Dodo)
  boy's reactions to, 214
  mixed gender performances, 214
  The Pregnant Woman performances, 213
  types of, 212
  Wale performances, 212-213
Girl's masquerading (Igede)
  Adiya dance, 132-133
  Adiya ensemble demise, 134
  adult music and, 135
  dance queens, 135
  gender groups, 133
  head beads, 134
  masquerading company of, 131
  Ogbete songs and, 135
Girl's pre-initiation masquerading
  as adult forms, 33-34
  Bissau carnival and, 32
  as emulating masquerading, 34
  gender roles in, 32-33
  Guinea examples, 34-35
  as independent masquerading, 32
  Ougadougou masquerading and, 35
  research lacking, 6, 32
  roles in boys masquerading, 7
  vs boy's performances, 33
Glaze, Anita, 105
Gomes, Flora, 185, 188
Gomes, Nicolau Fara, 181
Grosz-Ngate, Maria, 53
Guinea
  Christmas costumes, 29
  girl's masquerading, 34-35
  rural boy's masquerading, 29
Gusunkenes Kulturgut, 84

Hardin, Kris, 50
Havik, Phillip J., 183-184, 188-189, 191, 194-195
Heat-Moon, William Least, 114
Hinckley, Baird, 27
Hinckley, Priscella, 27, 35
Hlaváčová, Anna A., 20, 151

Hoejbjerg, Christian K., 29, 34
Horton, Robin, 21, 152

Idikwu, John Eriba, 135
Igbo masquerading
  adult masquerading emulating in, 120-121
  adult vs boy's masquerading, 123
  benefits from, 124
  as boy's activities, 120
  boy's society initiating, 118
  boy's society levels, 118
  Christian communities and, 122
  community characteristics, 117
  dying out of, 117
  enjoyment in, 122
  gender role distinctions, 117
  girl's reactions to, 120-121
  learning from, 125-126
  male emulation and, 123-124
  models for, 123
  mother bond breaking, 118-119
  origins of, 124-125
  physical strength in, 123
  second level characteristics, 119-120
Igbole Ojija performance
  animal characters, 92-93
  enclosures building, 91
  girl's roles in, 91
  performers in, 91
  preparations for, 91
  songs in, 92
  starting of, 91-92
Igbole town
  children's performance in, 90
  Ëlëfon festival, 91
  Öjija performances in, 91-93
Igede masquerading
  adult music and dances, 136-140
  benefits of, 129-130
  boy's ensembles, 134
  characteristics of, 130
  dance visual art, 131
  girl's ensembles, 134-135
  mask traditions, 129
  men's associations, 130
  music and dance feminizing, 145-146
  music and dance of, 131-133
  pedagogy of, 140-141
  song texts of, 141-145
Ijo masquerading
  children and adult, 151-153

258   Playful Performers

Kalabari masquerading, 153-154
   masquerade playing, 153-156
   Opobo masquerading, 154-155
Independent masquerades
   Africa uses in, 25
   Alikali Devils and, 25-26
   Bissau Carnival and, 26-27
   conditions for, 30
   Dodo masquerades and, 27-28
   Ghana and, 30-31
   growth of, 31-32
   influences on, 31-32
   rural boys and, 28-30
   rural and urban with, 31
   vs adult masquerading, 10, 24
   without adult masking, 30-31
Initiation masks (Kuba)
   boys observing, 109
   characteristics of, 109
   Kamakengu figures, 109-110
   other figures, 110-111
Initiation to adulthood, childhood preparations, 3
Integrated masquerading, characteristics of, 9
Ira Öjija performances
   controversial issues in, 94
   figure's role in, 94
   frequency of, 93-94
   girl's vs boy's actors, 93
   Öjija figures, 93
   performance sequences, 94-97
   social events and, 97-98
   song elements, 94
   song themes in, 97
Islamism
   buro rituals and, 78
   Dodo masquerades and, 27
   Dodo masquerading and, 207, 209
   Sogo bò theatre and, 55
   vs Christianity, 215
   See also Christianity

Jones, G. I., 21
Jordán, Manuel A., 19, 32, 237

Kalabari masquerading, 153-154
   adults imitating of, 21
   Ekine masks and, 153
   emotional responses in, 20
   Fiasiri dancing clubs, 154
   masks sources for, 20-21

Kalumbu masquerading
   Chewa initiation process, 223-224
   dance types of, 225-226
   girl's masquerading, 30
   importance lacking for, 226
   as model, 30
   terminology examples, 224
   uninitiated and, 223
   vs men's masquerading, 30
Kasfir, Sidney, 131, 133
Kuba boy's masquerading
   emulating men by, 18
   gender differentiation from, 19
   individual basis for, 18
Kuba masks
   funeral masks, 111-112
   initiation masks, 109-111
   performances using, 108
Kuba masquerading
   behavior modeling, 108-112
   boy's abilities and, 114
   boy's initiation and, 113-114
   conclusions on, 113-114
   girl's vs boy's socialization, 105-106
   masks fabricating interest, 106-107
   play organizing for, 107-108
   rite of passage and, 105
   secrecy in, 112-113
Kuba play activities, village councils and, 107-108
Kuranko, masquerading benefits, 53

Lamp, Frederick, 29
Lancy, David, 176
Le Moal, Guy, 13-14
Learning
   childhood masquerading and, 3-4, 22-24, 125-126
   masquerading concepts and, 4
   masquerading purposes, 22-23
   non-verbal communication, 5
   performance payments, 4-5
   "prestigious imitation" as, 58
   rules of culture, 5-6
   self-directing, 140
   See also African pedagogy
Liberia, girl's masquerading, 32, 35

McGuire, Harriet C., 181, 183-184, 186, 188-189
Mackay, R.W., 176
Marley, Bob, 210

Mask making, gender roles in, 32
Mask secrecy (Kuba)
    Inuba preparations and, 112-113
    uninitiated boys and, 112
    vs socialization, 113
Mead, Margaret, 91
Mende boy's masquerading
    adult emulating, 21
    initiation ceremonies, 90
    mask description, 18
Mendonca, Bendito, 190
Mendonca, Epifanio, 190
Mgbula, 20
Mixed gender masquerading, 139-140
Moore, Sally F., 197
Mukanda masquerading, initiation ceremonies, 90
Myerhoff, Barbara G., 197

Nafali masquerading, 29
Ndòmò ritual masquerading
    boy's benefits from, 53-54
    cultural power from, 54-55
    gender identity process, 50-51
    mask uniqueness, 51-52
    masquerading association for, 50-51
    organization chapters, 52-53
    organizations importance, 54
    symbolism complexity, 53
Nicholls, Robert W., 20, 129
Nigeria masquerades, children controlling, 21
Nyau initiation
    age for, 226
    animal portraying, 228
    mask making, 227
    reincarnation beliefs, 227-228
    ritual process, 226-227
    secrecy of, 227
Nyau masquerading
    boy's initiation into, 222
    children masquerading, 235
    funeral dance focus, 222
    as men's experience, 235
    as secret, 235
    types of, 222-223
    vs Chinamwali, 234
    vs teaching in, 234-235
    women's roles in, 223

Oguntuyi, A., 97
Öjija children
    ceremonial activities role, 89
    Igbole town and, 90-93
    Ire town and, 93-98
    performance differences of, 98-100
    performance etymology of, 90
    performance skills categories, 89-90
    performing by, 90
    researchers ignoring of, 89
Öjija performances
    adult performance linking, 98-99
    boy's vs girl's in, 98
    ceremony future, 100
    other ceremony linking, 98
    song contrasting, 99
    town accessibility, 99
Ojo, John R. O., 15, 33, 89
Okeke, Chika O., 159
Okigbo, Christopher, 193
Oku masquerading
    location of, 28
    origin of, 29
    pre-colonial period, 28-29
    themes in, 28
Okumkpa, description of, 19
Omepa masquerading
    adult masquerading as, 20
    dance ensemble, 134
Onyeweh masquerading, 20
    ensembles for, 134
    as money earning, 20
Opobo masquerading
    adult's assistance for, 155
    costumes for, 155
    traditions in, 154-155
Osunin, Erin, 16
Ottenberg, Simon, 1, 19, 26, 29, 105, 108, 117, 181
Ougadougou. *See* Dodo masquerading

Parfait, B., 214
Phillips, Ruth, 18, 29
Phiri, Joseph, 225-226, 228
Pipim, Peter, 31
Playing
    adult initiation and, 242
    adult reactions to, 153
    adult recreation, 242
    imitating masquerading roles, 240-241
    initiation expectations from, 241-242
    Kuba organization for, 107-108
    masquerading as, 7-8

non-society masquerading, 153
sand drawings, 241
Sogo masks as, 56-57, 59-60, 62-63
as training, 176
village councils and, 107-108
Pre-initiation masquerading
adult classifications, 9
adult masking linking, 8-9
emulation masquerading, 10
independent masquerading, 10-11
integrated masquerading, 9

Ranung, Bjorn, 130, 139, 144-145
Reinhardt, Loretta, 21
Religion's influences. *See* Christianity; Islamism
Richards, Audrey, 89
Ross, Doran, 185-186
Rural masquerading
Chewa and, 29-30
Guinea and, 29
Nafali and, 29
Oku and, 28-29

Sagiri masks
agriculture associating, 78
buro ritual and, 78-80
descriptions of, 76
fertility associating, 78
girls and, 80-81
masks succession, 77
proceeding of, 77
rain and, 80
rituals and, 76
rituals vs dance, 77
vs Èmna masks, 76
Sierra Leone
girl's masquerading, 32, 35
See also Alikali Devils; Mende masquerading
Siga, Felix, 181, 183-185, 193
da Silva, Domingos Inacio, 183, 190
da Silva, Tony, 190
Social relationships
Alikali Devils and, 176-177
masquerading troupes and, 8
social skills for, 8, 97-98, 105-106
Sogo mask play
adolescent performers, 63
animal masks in, 55-56
children copying, 60-62
dance as self-mastery, 59

gender learning, 58
mastery requirements, 63
performance skill learning, 57-58
performer praising, 60
play observations, 56-57, 59-60, 62-63
"prestigious imitation" learning, 58
puppet masquerading, 56
social values and, 56
youth associations and, 55
Song texts (Igede)
characteristics of, 141-142
examples of, 142-145
sarcasm in, 142-143
women's association's examples, 143-145
Soyinka, Wole, 193
Sutton-Smith, B., 176

Toure, Younoussa, 59
Traore, Zakaria, 214
Turner, Victor, 189, 207

Umuahia children's masks
as complex, 162-163
costume preparations, 162
vs Umuoji culture, 161-162
Umuoji children's masks
Christmas masquerading, 160
festival season for, 160-161
location of, 159
vs Umuoji culture, 161-163
war and, 159-160
Urban masquerading
aesthetics and politics, 196
children's benefits, 195
control struggles in, 195-196
vs rural masquerading, 194-195

van Beek, Walter E., 12, 14, 19, 29

Weil, Peter, 33
Women
Bamana dance qualities, 59-60
Bamana performer praising, 60
buro ritual and, 78-79
drama performances and, 74
forms of, 33-34
initiation ceremony (Chewa), 233-234
masking rules for, 32-33
masks afraid of, 71, 74
masquerading (Igede), 137-138

masquerading under-reporting, 32
Nyau masquerading, 223
pregnant women performances, 213
ritual severity to, 85
rituals (Zambia), 239
song text of, 143-145
See also Feminization; Girls; Mixed gender masquerading
Women (Igede)
dance of, 131
death meaning, 132

Yoruba boy's masquerading
Alikali Devils influences, 171-172
characteristics of, 15
Egungun society and, 16
Gelede festival, 15-16
as performance training, 14-15
videos of, 16-17
vs girl's ceremonies, 15
Yoshida, Kenji, 29-30, 221

Zahan, Dominque, 50-51, 54-55
Zambian rituals
adult initiation ceremonies, 238-240
children ritual playing, 237-238
community involving, 240-242
conclusions on, 244
fear and, 242-243
gender and, 243-244